BAD MOON RISING

D1555357

BAD
MOON
RISING

How the Weather Underground Beat
the FBI and Lost the Revolution

ARTHUR M. ECKSTEIN

Yale

UNIVERSITY PRESS

New Haven and London

Published with assistance from the Louis Stern Memorial Fund.

Yale University Press books may be purchased in quantity for
educational, business, or promotional use.For information,
please e-mail sales.press@yale.edu (U.S. office) or sales@yaleup.co.uk
(U.K. office).
Designed by

Set in   type by
Printed in the United States of America.

Library of Congress Control Number: 2016933043
ISBN 978-0-300-22118-3 (hardcover: alk. paper)

A catalogue record for this book is available from the British Library.

This paper meets the requirements of ANSI/NISO Z39.48-1992
(Permanence of Paper).

10 9 8 7 6 5 4 3 2 1

Contents

BAD MOON RISING

Introduction

WRITING THIS BOOK WAS a journey back into my own younger days, and into old feelings. I am part of the Sixties Generation; born in 1946, I was at UCLA between 1964 and 1968: years of transformation in politics, society, and culture. Then I went off to graduate school at Berkeley, arriving in the autumn of 1968. While I am now a professional historian, and in *Bad Moon Rising* I have sought to write objectively about the facts as I see them in a professional way, no one who was politically involved as a young person in the sixties can write about those years without emotion. I was politically involved. I deeply supported the civil rights movement, generally supported the Black Panthers, was involved in antiwar demonstrations, witnessed some street violence (and even participated in it). This puts me in the 15 percent of my generation who were active politically on the Left—only 15 percent, but people who would come to have a large influence in culture and society (and especially in the university world).[1] I was, however, ultimately more a hippie than a campus radical, and in the summer of 1969—right when the Weatherman faction was taking over Students for a Democratic Society—I gave up on politics altogether. By contrast, my dear friend Susan Reverby, who has been a constant source of advice and support as I worked my way through the historical problems associated with Weather, was a real campus radical, an active member of SDS at Cornell in the sixties who remained highly political far into the 1970s, whereas I attended a total of one SDS meeting in Berkeley, in winter 1968–1969, and after May 1969 I recall participating in only one other antiwar demonstration.[2]

I well remember my first antiwar demonstration on June 27, 1967—a march of about twenty thousand people at the Century Plaza Hotel in Los Angeles, where President Lyndon B. Johnson was staying. The march turned into a confrontation with the Los Angeles Police Department, whose officers attacked the crowd. I was angered by the police violence, and saw many innocent people clubbed and beaten. But the attack wasn't altogether a surprise. Friends in SDS had told me before the march that the leaders planned to stop the crowd in front of the Century Plaza, in violation of the city march permit they had been issued, in hopes of provoking exactly the sort of police riot that occurred. I was simultaneously radicalized by the event and left with a cynicism about how SDS leaders had manipulated the thousands who had gathered to peacefully protest the war.

In Berkeley in autumn 1968 I witnessed from the outskirts of the crowd the demonstrations over Eldridge Cleaver, whose appointment to teach a class had angered Governor Ronald Reagan and other conservatives. That winter the demand for the creation of "Third World Studies" at Cal resulted in further confrontations: seeing police pelted with rocks by students on the roof of the Student Union, I thought, "They won't allow this to happen to them again." In the spring of 1969 I participated in the demonstrations over People's Park. I was in the march to the park that led to another terrible police riot, and two days later I threw rocks at the cops in a confrontation in downtown Berkeley, along Shattuck Avenue. Decades later, I came to realize just how dangerous it was to do these things, but I didn't see it at the time (even though James Rector had been killed by police shotguns on the first day of demonstrations, and another bystander blinded); I guess I was just too young.[3] Like a lot of people on campus, I was later hit with pepper gas sprayed indiscriminately from a National Guard helicopter. But I was never arrested.

Nevertheless, the violent events of 1968–1969 were emotionally draining, and I left Berkeley and didn't come back until the autumn of 1971, when I returned to do graduate work in Roman history, my first love. It is fair to say that in the early 1970s I was not upset about Weatherman bombings, though not approving either; I was thus part of that segment of vaguely sympathetic leftists that Jonah Raskin, an aboveground Weatherman sympathizer and ally, once described as spectators and spectators only.[4] I received my Ph.D. under a series of inspiring advisers and mentors in spring 1978, having spent three years teaching independent courses (including one on "Freedom and Authority") in the Division of Interdisciplinary and General Studies—another Berkeley experiment from the sixties that was eventually discarded.

My political trajectory bent in an anticommunist arc over the next decades. In part this was as a result of reading Solzhenitsyn's *Gulag Archipelago* in 1976. In part it was a result of my minor involvement in the trade union movement Solidarity in its struggles with the Polish Communist government in 1980–1981. This involvement also led my wife and me to a friendship with the novelist Jerzy Kosinski. Because of his support of Solidarity, Kosinski was defamed as a CIA agent by the Polish Secret Police—defamations that were eagerly picked up and spread by some writers for the *Village Voice* in New York, where Kosinski then lived. I found this naïve and vituperative character assassination appalling. This sort of denialism tainted other issues as well, such as the bitter and steadfast refusal in some diehard corners of the American Left to believe that Julius and Ethel Rosenberg were Soviet spies and allies when the evidence against Julius was overwhelming. I grew steadily suspicious of my own political milieu even as I still held to my youthful ideals, which as a budding historian included allegiance to the truth, however politically uncomfortable. This led me to write essays which looked, for instance, harshly at the whitewashing of the Hollywood Ten (all of whom were devoted apologists for Stalinism) by modern supporters who really had no idea the extent to which belonging to an orthodox communist party meant toeing a party line at the expense of intellectual honesty. But my critical reevaluation of one element of leftist dogma didn't signal a lurch to the cultural Right. The core of my sixties activism—human rights—remained just as sacred in the nineties, when I played a leading role in securing equal rights for gay people on my own campus at the University of Maryland, and received recognition from the LBGT community and from minority organizations for my efforts in protecting minority faculty members against a system that tried to undermine or prevent their success.

The response to the 9/11 attacks by some on what was left of the far Left—essentially blaming the United States for the terrorism inflicted on it, while excusing or turning a blind eye to the religious fanaticism prompting the attacks (as long as such fanaticism was associated with Islam, even in its most extreme form; fundamentalist Christianity did not get such a pardon)—deepened my disillusion. But the manipulative and dishonest official rationale for the Iraq War took me aback, and by 2008 my wife and I were donating to Barack Obama's campaign for president. Thus by 2010 I found myself more or less back on the moderate Left, where I remain.

My scholarly work had been on the nature of imperial expansion in antiquity, with an emphasis on the integration of modern political science theory with ancient events; but in the autumn of 2012 I was unexpectedly asked by William Roger Louis at the Woodrow Wilson Center—a fellow scholar of imperialism who knew I had been something of a hippie in my youth—to deliver a paper on the differences between the counterculture and the New Left. I was intrigued by the idea of such a talk. As I prepared my lecture, I became interested in the memoirs and essays by Weatherman veterans that had been published in the previous ten years. I quickly saw that there was a major discrepancy, seemingly intended, between what Weatherman leader Bill Ayers had written in *Fugitive Days* (the first memoir to appear, in 2001), and what other Weather veterans had written since: Cathy Wilkerson, Jonathan Lerner, Howard Machtinger, Mark Rudd, David Barber, and Mark Naison, unlike Ayers, presented a darker version of Weatherman. I was intrigued by the conflict of memory among Weatherman veterans. Jeffrey Herf, a friend and colleague—himself a veteran sixties radical whose politics had changed—urged me to go see what was available on Weatherman in the National Archives, a good part of which were located on the Maryland campus where I taught. I was reluctant to get involved in such a large project, so Jeff went himself, and discovered that thousands of pages of previously unavailable FBI files on Weatherman had been released to the public in June 2011. He brought me to the National Archives, and the archivists brought out two hand trucks with boxes and boxes of material. The archivists even provided a "table of contents" for the boxes, in which they had underlined the boxes they thought would be of special interest, and which they thought I should examine first. In September 2013, when another large tranche of FBI documents on Weatherman was released, the archivists immediately informed me and gave me access to them.[5]

Curiously, no one had bothered to look at the entirety of this vast trove, not even so determined a reporter as Bryan Burrough of *Vanity Fair*, who was then embarked on a book that he would publish in 2015 about Weatherman, among other groups bent on violent revolution; the second tranche of released FBI documents (September 2013) apparently came out too late for him.[6] I set to work on the mass of documents. I began to contact and interview some of the Weatherman veterans. Meeting personally with them brought me up short. They turned out to be serious, self-reflective, self-critical, and highly principled people. I liked them, in part because they were generous to me with their time and information, but mostly because of the type of people they were. From Weatherman's reputation as a callous group of radical zealots, I had not expected this. My response to meeting three-dimensional people—not political cardboard cutouts—no doubt colored somewhat how I would come to view the group and its actions. It certainly led me to consider the human story of Weatherman, while mindful of the specter (and reality) of violence that the group represented, especially in the early months of 1970. In the end, for those of us who were even peripherally involved in the general sixties tumult, it must be conceded that the Weathermen were and are "our people," with many of the same virtues and vices—even though they were the most extreme among us—and it should be remembered that they and we were all very young.

But I should also stress that the people I talked to, and who were willing to talk to me, were uniformly the "rebels" against the version of Weatherman history that has been the "party line" put out by some members of the old Weatherman central committee (the Weather Bureau) ever since December 1970, and for which Bill Ayers remains the most articulate and devoted tribune. This did not mean that the ex-Weather people I spoke to had renounced the essential precepts of the Left, but they evinced an admirable allegiance to telling uncomfortable truths. Their dissent from the central committee version of Weather's violent arc should, in fact, now be seen as an important part of the history of the Weatherman organization. My attempts to contact former members of the Weather central committee to get their side of the story were frustrated, except for one reply that reminded me how rigidly dogmatic and stern many of the Weather people could be back in the day.

Unfortunately, I was unable to contact any of the FBI agents involved in the effort to defeat the Weatherman. The reason is simple: the Weather people are themselves now in their early seventies, but the FBI agents who hunted them between 1969 and the late 1970s were a full generation older; they were mostly World War II veterans (often decorated ones). None is alive today.[7] The Weatherman war was a true conflict of generations, with each side incomprehensible to the other, and now only the people of my generation remain.

In what follows, I have depended in great part (though not totally) on FBI files on the Weatherman underground movement. These were collected for the trial of FBI officials Mark Felt and Edward Miller in District of Columbia Federal Court in the autumn of 1980; they were released to the public in 2011 and 2013. All FBI documents referred to can be found in the National Archives under Record Group 60, Department of Justice File 177-160-33. The story these documents tell is of FBI concern over a national threat that officials believed Weatherman bombing and other acts of violence posed, especially in 1970. By late 1971, worry that the FBI failure against Weatherman was becoming a political football was palpable—along with the humiliation of not being able to catch them.[8]

These documents should be believed. They circulated in the FBI in a period before the passage of the 1974 version of the Freedom of Information Act provided ordinary citizens with relatively easy access to such documents. That is: the writers of these memos and reports had every reason to expect them to be secret, and to remain secret. They believed they were discussing real problems with other law enforcement professionals. As an FBI official wrote in protest of the 1974 FOIA rules, "In the preparation of these various documents, the writers [wrote] with full expectation that their material would always remain privileged, set forth not only statements of fact, but also candid assessments of various situations then existing."[9] Anyone who reads these documents will see that enormous investigative efforts against Weatherman went into the production of the information in them; in addition, careers in the Bureau depended on these reports being as accurate as possible, because otherwise cases were not going to be solved.

Two examples of this element in FBI culture: in February 1970 the FBI informed the White House that there was no evidence of foreign funding of the American far Left—a message that incurred the anger of Richard Nixon. Similarly, in July 1972 Edward Miller, the head of the FBI Domestic Intelligence Division—the most important investigative division—informed FBI Acting Director L. Patrick Gray that Weatherman had no significant ties to foreign hostile countries; this information was highly unwelcome to Gray, who wanted to use the alleged foreign connections of Weatherman as a legal reason to permit burglary and trespass in the Weatherman cases.[10]

In addition, recent memoirs of Weatherman veterans tend to be surprisingly congruent with what is described in FBI memos. For instance, the FBI believed that the accidental Greenwich Village townhouse explosion of March 1970 was related to a Weatherman program of intended lethal violence. Weatherman leader Bill Ayers still denies this, but both Cathy Wilkerson's memoir and Mark Rudd's either imply or bluntly state that the bombing planned in the townhouse was widely known and approved of within the leadership of the Weatherman organization. Other Weatherman veterans with whom I talked confirm this.[11]

Two general caveats: This book is not—nor can it be—an authoritative history of Weatherman; and it is not—nor can it be—a complete history of the FBI battle against the organization. A complete history of Weatherman is not possible. Jonah Raskin, who was close to the group, has explained why. To begin with, a complete history of Weatherman would have to include information on (a) who made each of the Weatherman bombs, (b) who planted them, and (c) who decided on what targets.[12] This information is known only to a few Weather veterans (and mostly *not* known to the FBI). For instance, we know now that Howard Machtinger led a dynamite pipe-bomb attack on the Berkeley, California, Police Department on February 12, 1970; the pipe bombs—set off with no warning—injured several officers. And Ron Fliegelman has now said he made and helped place the Weatherman bomb that damaged New York Police Headquarters on June 9, 1970.[13] But it remains unclear who ordered the attacks and who ordered, made, or placed any of the other Weatherman bombs, including the U.S. Capitol bomb in March 1971 or the Pentagon bomb in June 1972.

Moreover, an authoritative history of Weatherman would have to explain in detail how the Weather Bureau (the central committee) functioned, provide a list of its (changing and secret) membership, and describe the meetings where strategy was hammered out (including who said what). We would also want to know how the complex sexual histories in Weather were entangled in its politics, for changing personal relationships occasionally played a role in how things developed; but some of this is politically secret, some of it probably too intimate to be revealed by the surviving participants. In addition, aside from official communiqués—which were propaganda—no internal Weatherman documents from the 1969–1973 period are available to the public. Nonetheless, the broad outlines of the group's origins and evolution, fleshed out with many details that have now come to light, can be convincingly and reasonably drawn.[14]

Thousands of pages of FBI documents on Weatherman have recently become available to the public, and these change our understanding of events, but they still make up only part of the FBI dossier on the Weather Underground. Almost all the Weatherman material has now been declassified (that is, issues of national security no longer apply to them), but thousands of documents remain restricted because of concern for the privacy of individual citizens. Archivists at the National Archives must review these documents for privacy issues before the documents are released. For instance, there are thousands of still-restricted pages concerning the FBI investigation of the March 6, 1970, New York explosion. But the process of reviewing and lifting restrictions is excruciatingly slow, and there are not enough people available at the National Archives to do it faster. Also requiring review before release are hundreds of FBI reports both on all known Weathermen and on all known aboveground Weatherman supporters. These run to thousands of pages. A *complete* history of the FBI hunt for Weatherman would have to await this material becoming public. That will take years.

What follows, then, is a new exploration, based on important new information, but with no claim to being a final picture. The picture I draw is not going to make everyone happy. Some ex-Weather people (but not all) want to forget how "armed struggle" can brutalize those who engage in it. And many people on the Right and in the center like to imagine that you can count on a high level of professionalism from those engaged in law enforcement—and they are going to be disappointed. The depiction here is of a messy reality. What emerges most clearly is that the government elite (not least the president of the United States) panicked over the extreme rhetoric and extreme behavior of some radicals in the late sixties and early seventies, that the FBI was ineffective in its effort to capture and defeat the Weathermen, and that those engaged in fierce rebellion (some even embracing lethal tactics) were often themselves way over their heads, had no idea what they were really doing, and did not create the revolution they wanted—or any revolution at all.[15]

CHAPTER ONE

"Angels of Destruction and Disorder"

ROUND 11:55 ON the morning of Friday, March 6, 1970, a series of massive explosions wrecked a three-story townhouse at 18 West 11th Street, in a fashionable neighborhood of Greenwich Village in New York City. As all three floors of the elegant residence, owned by wealthy Connecticut businessman James Wilkerson, collapsed, windows shattered up to the sixth floor on the building across the street. After firemen finally put out the fires that consumed the townhouse, parts of three bodies were found in the wreckage. At first the explosion was thought to have been the result of a gas leak, but it was soon clear to the New York City police, from the dynamite and from pamphlets found in the ruins, that the townhouse had been a bomb factory of the radical Left organization called Weatherman.[1]

Fires burned in the townhouse for the next eight hours. In the wreckage, firemen and police first found two dismembered bodies: a headless female, consisting of the back, one arm, and one leg (all that was left of Diana Oughton), and a headless male, armless but with legs (all that was left of Terry Robbins). They found the relatively intact corpse of Ted Gold the next day. Only good luck had prevented bystanders, too, from being killed. The explosion blew a huge hole in the wall of the building next door, but it had only one occupant at the time, a maid, and she happened to be standing in a spot in the living room where she was not killed when the brick fireplace blasted outward from the explosion. A woman and her three-year-old son would have been right in front of the townhouse at the moment of the explosion, or going upstairs into the building next door, and thus would have been obliterated—except that the little boy was late getting out of nursery school. Buildings on the south side of West 11th, on both sides of the townhouse, were structurally weakened by the explosion: the entire chimney suddenly collapsed in one of them twelve hours later. The city of New York condemned them as unfit for human habitation, and repairs took months.[2] But at least two people escaped from the townhouse as it collapsed: Cathy Wilkerson (whose father owned the building) and Kathy Boudin. Boudin was the daughter of Leonard Boudin, a prominent attorney who had for decades represented clients on the Left, and his wife Jean, the sister of the iconoclast muckraker I. F. Stone.[3]

Eventually, the police also found in the townhouse fifty-seven sticks of unexploded dynamite in four cartons; another carton with five more pounds of dynamite; four large lead pipes a foot in diameter packed with dynamite and with wires leading from them; and three packages of eight sticks of dynamite each, bound together with tape studded with roofing nails. A munitions expert declared that had all these explosives detonated, it would have leveled everything on both sides along that block of Eleventh Street.[4] It eventually emerged that what became known as the Townhouse Collective had been planning an attack on March 6 against a noncommissioned officers' dance at the army base of Fort Dix, New Jersey, and that the dynamite bombs with roofing nails were being fashioned into antipersonnel weapons. It is likely that dozens of people would have been killed if the plan had succeeded.[5]

When the mother of the Weatherman leader Howard Machtinger learned of the explosion, she was beside herself; Yetta Machtinger knew what her son was involved in. She called her sister, Ruth to find out whether she had heard anything, but Ruth knew nothing either, and told Yetta to call the mother of Kathy Boudin to find out more. Yetta did, and Jean Boudin evidently contacted Howard, for later in the day he called his mother and told her he was okay. It was not Howard Machtinger who was dead, but Ruth son, Ted Gold. He was Howard's cousin.[6] The father of Terry Robbins refused to believe that his beloved son was dead; the remnants of Robbins's body were never claimed from the NYPD morgue. Two months later, in early May, the corpse remained unidentified.[7]

Out in California Thomas (Tim) Ayers, Jr., a film editor at KPIX-TV in San Francisco, reacted to the news of the explosion with alarm. He immediately associated his brother Bill Ayers with the townhouse, and feared that Bill—a Weatherman leader—was one of the still-unidentified townhouse dead. He quickly got in touch with Roger Rappaport, a writer with ties to Weatherman, and urged him to use his Weatherman connections to find out whether Bill was all right. Rappaport eventually reported back: his sources told him that Bill was safe; he had not been in the townhouse at the time of the explosion.[8]

The mystery of the third townhouse corpse was not resolved until May 21, when Bernardine Dohrn, speaking for the Weatherman Underground, listed Terry Robbins with Ted Gold and Diana Oughton as the martyred townhouse dead. This was part of Weatherman's official declaration of war against the United States.[9]

The townhouse explosion was the most spectacular event in the career of Weatherman, and has always occupied a special place in the history of the group. The explosion was devastating; the dead had all been founders of the Weatherman faction within Students for a Democratic Society (SDS). They had then become leaders of the effort to actually wage war on the American imperium, calling themselves by the spring of 1970 the Weatherman Underground.[10]

What part did the townhouse explosion play in shaping the subsequent history of the Weatherman?

For decades, the narrative of the townhouse tragedy has been controlled by a handful of former Weather leaders. According to them, the Townhouse Collective's lethal plan against Fort Dix was essentially a rogue operation, neither known to nor approved by other collectives nor by the Weather Bureau (as the Weatherman's central committee was called within the group). The situation supposedly epitomized the decentralized nature of Weatherman in early

1970. When the nature of the target (a dance) and the weapon prepared (antipersonnel dynamite bombs wrapped with roofing nails)
became known to the leadership and the other collectives, the
reaction was repulsion—and the emergence of second thoughts
about methods in the escalating campaign of violence that was
Weatherman's declared purpose. These second thoughts domi-
nated a meeting of the Weather Bureau near Mendocino in north-
ern California in May 1970 that led to a decision to abandon lethal
bombing. The leading advocate of pursuing a purely military road,
John Jacobs, the New York regional leader, was expelled from both
the Weather Bureau and the Weatherman organization. Although
over the next seven years Weatherman would detonate two dozen
bombs, including spectacular attacks on the Pentagon, the State
Department, and the Capitol building itself, Weathermen took
care always to telephone warnings once the bombs had been set, in
order to allow people to escape the buildings before the explosions.
No one was ever killed or even injured by those bombs—and no
major Weatherman was ever caught by the police or FBI. A legend
was born.

This version of events was first set out in "New Morning/
Changing Weather," a communiqué released by the Weather
Underground on December 6, 1970—nine months to the day after
the townhouse explosion. Bernardine Dohrn, with the undisclosed
help of aboveground Weatherman supporter Jonah Raskin, wrote
the communiqué.[11]

The argument in "New Morning" was straightforward. Faced
with intractable U.S. racism at home and U.S. imperialism abroad
(especially in Vietnam), Weatherman abandoned demonstrations as
useless, in favor of an underground resistance network. This network would form the basis for a guerrilla war against the U.S. government. The militant and violent nature of Weatherman, and its
revolutionary goal, is thus clear from the start in the communiqué.
But after a brief statement indicating that "we had been wrong
with our direction," the authors shift focus from "we" to "they"—
to the Townhouse Collective. "Diana, Teddy and Terry: their collective began to define armed struggle as the only legitimate form
of revolutionary action." In late February 1970, the Collective had
firebombed the house of the judge in a New York trial involving

Black Panthers. "To many people this was a very good action," wrote the communiqué's authors. But "within the group"—that is, the Collective in contrast to everyone else—the feeling was that the attack on the judge had not been a large enough blow against the empire. "So within two weeks' time, this group had moved from fire-bombing to anti-personnel bombs" and planned "a large-scale almost random bombing offensive." But in their zeal to act quickly, technological safety was ignored—and, in the event, they blew themselves up.[12]

"This tendency to consider only bombing and the gun as revolutionary, with the glorification of the heavier the better, we've called the military error." Confronted with the townhouse explosion, "we called off all armed actions." The leaders decided to adopt an alternative direction that some collectives favored: to turn away from lethal bombing to bombing property.

Note "we" here—as opposed to "they," the Townhouse Collective, the crazy ones. For decades not much was added to this account by any Weatherman source, or by historians. Most of the key figures were hiding underground throughout the seventies, and once they surfaced into U.S. society again, it took a long time before any of them began to write about their experiences. Bill Ayers, currently the most visible and loquacious ex-Weather leader, was the first to publish his memoir, *Fugitive Days*, in 2001; he hewed to the "New Morning" line. According to Ayers, after the Days of Rage riots in Chicago in October 1969, Weatherman split into three parts, based on geography and ideological outlook. While all believed in a clandestine fighting force, the New York leaders—Terry Robbins and John Jacobs—favored pure guerrilla war. Bernadine Dohrn and Jeff Jones, on the West Coast, were against a sole focus on guerrilla war and championed an underground resistance that would work in combination with aboveground mass organizing. Ayers, geographically in the middle as the midwestern leader in Detroit, identified himself as ideologically in the middle, too; he also resented that his girlfriend Diana Oughton had been drawn away to New York by Terry Robbins. In 2003 he said that he thought Robbins was insane.[13]

Ayers has repeatedly asserted in the years since *Fugitive Days* was published that—except for the Townhouse Collective—the

Weathermen were not intent on lethal harm, and were guilty merely of vandalism. They attacked, he insisted, only property and took pains never intentionally to injure or kill anyone.

His view is echoed in the documentary film *Weather Underground*, by Sam Green and Bill Siegel. The film was nominated for an Academy Award as best documentary of 2003, and it was probably seen by more people than will ever read a book about the Weather organization. According to the film, "the organization in early 1970 had been *unable* [voice emphasis] to resolve the issue of how far to go in terms of violence"; meanwhile, the Fort Dix plan originated with "a small *autonomous* [voice emphasis] collective" in New York. Bill Ayers is interviewed and says, "Terry [Robbins], more than anyone else, represented the view that it was too late for any kind of conciliation, and the best we could do was bring about a catastrophic series of actions." To be sure, a vague and general Weatherman moral responsibility is briefly accepted for the townhouse. Ayers says that after the Mendocino meeting, "We were very careful not to hurt anybody, and we never did hurt anybody," a statement then supported by David Gilbert—who, the filmmakers have not yet revealed, is serving a seventy-five-year sentence for complicity in the killing of a bank guard and two policemen during a botched Nyack, New York, bank robbery in 1981. *Weather Underground* is essentially a filmed version of the "New Morning" communiqué.

The first serious academic book on Weather came out in 2004: Jeremy Varon's *Bringing the War Home*, a careful comparative study of Weatherman violence with that of the Red Army Faction, also known as the Baader-Meinhof Gang, in Germany. But for Weatherman history, Varon took "New Morning" as a reliable explication of the townhouse events: the Townhouse Collective had been off on its own, driven by John Jacobs and Terry Robbins. Varon's interviews with Bill Ayers and the Weather soldier Robin Palmer reinforced this impression. Ayers said that Terry Robbins had been his best friend, and then described him this way: "I don't want to demonize Terry ... but I used to say that if there hadn't been a movement [he'd] be the guy up in the Texas Tower"—that is, Charles Whitman, the deranged sniper who opened fire on university students in 1966, killing more than a dozen people. Ayers quickly qualified his judgment: "It wasn't just Terry. Terry's extremism was an impulse in all of us." But if Robbins was not alone in the temptation to hyperviolence, he was, according to Ayers, the only one who truly succumbed to it. Robin Palmer gave Varon a similar evaluation of Robbins: meeting Robbins in early March 1970, he thought him a frightening figure and his plans for Fort Dix "crazy." Palmer backed away.[14]

According to *Bringing the War Home*, then, it was the Townhouse Collective that had gone off the rails. A Detroit project is mentioned but dismissed in two sentences as having produced crude bombs that failed to detonate. Varon also accepts Bill Ayers's story from *Fugitive Days* that on March 6 he was in the countryside, nowhere near Detroit.[15]

Thai Jones, writing in 2004 with the authority deriving from his unique access to information as the son of Weather leaders Jeff Jones and Eleanor Raskin, also characterized the Townhouse Collective and its leaders in harsh terms. In his dual biography of his parents, he wrote that while Jeff Jones in California was creating a network of safe houses, an autonomous collective in Manhattan had developed "a different agenda." Motivated by a desire to prove themselves the most revolutionary and "heaviest" of the collectives, they planned a huge bombing of the officers' dance at Fort Dix. Thai Jones stresses that dozens of young military couples might have been maimed and killed. Jones accepts the view that the Collective acted on its own, motivated by fanaticism and even by a sort of competitiveness.[16]

Dan Berger's *Outlaws of America* (2006)—a work generally sympathetic to Weatherman violence (it is dedicated to David Gilbert)—gives much space to the townhouse explosion. But Berger barely mentions Terry Robbins; he focuses instead on the ultramilitant New York regional leader John Jacobs. Berger devotes only two sentences to Detroit, where he has one bomb, placed outside a police station (as we will see, this confuses two different planned attacks). He admits that this "crude bomb" could have caused casualties or even deaths, but stresses that the bomb "was built in part by an FBI infiltrator," implying that the bomb was somehow the FBI's fault.[17]

Tom Hayden was a founder and president of SDS in the early 1960s, later a defendant in the Chicago Eight trial for his role in organizing the protests at the 1968 Democratic Convention, and then for many years elected repeatedly to the California legislature. Hayden was never a Weatherman but remained friendly with many of its leaders. He was sympathetic to many of the ideals that drove them, while distancing himself from the desperation that underpinned much of their politics. In his memoir-cum-history entitled *The Long Sixties* (2009), Hayden, too, follows the "New Morning" line regarding the Townhouse. In Hayden's version of events, Terry Robbins and John Jacobs—without the knowledge of others in leadership—secretly plotted an action beyond anyone's imagination, namely, deliberate politically motivated killing. Hayden's focus is mostly on Terry Robbins, whom he describes as "a fanatic dreamer . . . [who] knew very little about dynamite." It was Robbins who controlled the Townhouse Collective through fearsome psychological manipulation—and so the plan for the massacre went forward despite any doubts.[18]

Yet this narrative, in which the Fort Dix attack was essentially a rogue operation, has always prompted dissent in the ranks of the Weathermen and people close to them. When Jeremy Varon and Thai Jones published their books, the counternarrative was rarely voiced in public, but it has since become more common. The first hint of a darker story came in 1997 from Ron Jacobs. Jacobs asserted in his book that Weatherman in early 1970 did not consist of completely autonomous collectives. Rather, each cell committed to armed action would assemble a list of targets, which was transmitted through couriers up to the Weather Bureau. Bureau leaders would discuss the advantages and disadvantages of each target, and approve or disapprove. Difficulties in creating secure communications meant that some collectives might not know what others were doing, but the Weather Bureau, Jacobs indicated, knew what everyone was doing. Jacobs still holds this view: "My understanding was that the Weather Bureau knew what targets were being considered, and approved or disapproved them."

This understanding of Weatherman targeting-procedure has obvious implications regarding the Fort Dix project. But how did Ron Jacobs know about the hierarchical structure of early Weatherman bombing procedure? Jacobs says that his source was in fact John Jacobs (no relation)—the head of the New York collectives in early 1970 who was expelled from Weatherman in May

1970 as the leading advocate of "the military solution." If John Jacobs was telling the truth, it is reasonable to conclude that the Townhouse Collective was not in any meaningful sense acting autonomously.[19]

But the implications in Ron Jacobs's book passed unnoticed. The first dissent from "New Morning" by a participant in the Weatherman movement itself appears to be an unpublished May 2001 interview with the late Alan Berkman, a radical physician who helped Weather in 1970–1976. He objected to the ongoing attempt to portray the townhouse group as "renegades" acting on their own, and to the assertion that the Weatherman leadership at that time had a different idea; he doubted that this was true.[20] But it was Cathy Wilkerson, herself a survivor of the townhouse explosion, who—breaking ranks—raised the first public dissent from the dominant "New Morning" line. Bill Ayers's relatively sunny view of early Weatherman and his assertion that Terry Robbins was a madman drew a bitter response from Wilkerson in a review of *Fugitive Days* in the online magazine *Z* in December 2001.

The fact was, Wilkerson wrote, that many people in Weather had decided to embrace lethal tactics: "Everyone in [the] Weather leadership argued very convincingly for far more drastic steps than symbolic attacks." The leadership, she insisted, wanted a fighting force that could do real material damage. She continued:

> Most importantly, I think it is dangerous that a young person today could read this book and never realize that Ayers was one of the architects of much of the insanity he blames on others. ... He joined the leadership of the Weather Underground. During that time he developed a language of confrontational militancy that became more and more extreme over time. Yet he never mentions these speeches.

Wilkerson stresses that most people who heard Ayers's fiery rhetoric in that period—including herself—took it seriously. If debate was occurring among the leaders behind the scenes, she says, it was not visible to ordinary cadre, nor even to those (like herself) with direct access to the leadership. What the leadership showed its followers was a united front committed to maximum violence.[21]

For Wilkerson, then, the Townhouse Collective's project was the result not of Terry Robbins's personal demons but of the Weatherman leadership's own reckless rhetoric and policies. Indeed, Wilkerson ends her review of *Fugitive Days* by defending Terry Robbins from Ayers: Robbins was an intense, difficult, and even dangerous person, she writes, but that did not make him unique among Weatherman leaders; moreover, as the ideas and policies of Weatherman became more extreme, Robbins and Bill Ayers were "inseparable."[22]

"Inseparable": that was the view, too, of Bill Ayers's older brother Thomas (Tim), when—thirty years earlier—he had been interviewed by the FBI (April 30, 1970). Asked whether he knew where Terry Robbins was (this was before Weatherman revealed that the dismembered second body in the townhouse was Robbins's), Ayers said: "Find Bill and you will find Terry. . . . Terry follows Bill around like a puppy."[23]

Wilkerson repeated her point about the leadership in an interview with Dan Berger in 2005. The townhouse explosion, she said, derived from the ultraviolent politics that the Weather Bureau had been pushing for months. The Weather soldier Jonathan Lerner, in another early response to *Fugitive Days*, agreed, underlining that in this early period there was much "glib discussion about the possibility of injuring innocent people."[24]

Wilkerson offered more specific information in her 2007 autobiography. She said that a couple of days before March 6, Diana Oughton joined the leadership group of the townhouse: Oughton came from Detroit, where Bill Ayers was the leader; and she arrived (a) fully aware of the Fort Dix plan, and (b) fully determined to carry it out.[25] Though Wilkerson is not explicit about the implications of what she is saying, her account of Oughton means—startlingly—that well before March 6 the attack on the Fort Dix dance was probably known and approved by some Weather leaders outside of New York. And Diana Oughton was not only in the collective headed by Bill Ayers, she was Ayers's girlfriend—and Ayers, in turn, was the best friend of the townhouse group's leader, Terry Robbins. If Diana knew about the Fort Dix plan before she came to New York, then in all probability so did Ayers.[26] Wilkerson's impression was, further, that Oughton was extremely militant, and that the

Detroit Collective was every bit as fanatical as the Townhouse. When the FBI in 1973 interviewed Nancy Ann Rudd, a veteran of the Detroit Collective, she agreed on the fanaticism in Detroit and said that Diana Oughton was a leader in it.[27]

Wilkerson in her memoir again defended Terry Robbins: he was passionate for justice as he understood it, intense, and committed to violence, but also inwardly doubting and fearful, and capable of intimate friendship; he was no madman. This was also the view of the late Carl Oglesby, an older and moderate SDS leader who was a friend of Robbins's and considered him a person sensitive to the concerns and problems of others.[28] Nor, Wilkerson says, was Robbins the only leader who kept the members of the Townhouse Collective in line about the murderous Fort Dix plan; the other Townhouse leaders were doing the same.[29]

In 2008, another scholarly study of Weatherman appeared: David Barber's *A Hard Rain Fell*. Barber was in the unique position of being both an ex-Weatherman and a trained academic historian. He accepted that the Townhouse Collective's lethal plan was unique in Weatherman, and driven by the personality of Terry Robbins. Yet he also stressed that the violent ideology behind the plan was widely shared in Weatherman, and that Fort Dix was an expression of a broader, more lethal attitude pushed by the leaders. Barber argued that this ideology of violence led to Weatherman contemptuously rejecting Black Panther advice to focus on peaceful mass organizing of white people to protest oppression in the ghetto; instead they foresaw embarking on what, if successful, would amount to an urban guerrilla war. Barber found this to be odd conduct for a group that prided itself on its antiracism stance and support of the Panthers. He also speculated that the Weather leadership wanted to provoke new ghetto riots via bombings of police. Barber's book was not widely reviewed and had little impact on the standard narrative.[30]

In 2009, the Weather veteran Howard Machtinger also responded to Ayers's memoir. He asserted on the one hand that if one defined terrorism as the intentional attack on civilians for political purposes, then he agreed with Ayers that the Weathermen had not been terrorists. But Ayers, he said, was also "disingenuous" to claim that Weatherman was merely part of the antiwar movement: Weatherman had not been antiwar, it had been *pro*-war—

revolutionary war. And it was wrong to pretend that the townhouse bomb was not the logical outcome of the ideology of deliberate violence pushed by the leaders—though they had never admitted it. So it was no accident, argued Machtinger, that remnants of Weatherman later participated with the Black Liberation Army in the Nyack bank robbery of October 1981, in which three people were killed. For Machtinger, the townhouse at the beginning stood with Nyack at the end as revealing an essential and terrible part of Weatherman ideology that had never been sufficiently confronted.[31]

The memoir of early Weatherman leader Mark Rudd, also published in 2009, joined the growing chorus of ex-Weather leaders who sought to distance themselves from Ayers's version of events. Rudd was in New York City in early March 1970 and says that the Fort Dix plan was known to and approved of by the other two New York City Weatherman collectives, including Rudd's, which was headed by John Jacobs. Rudd also says that he personally knew about and approved of the Fort Dix action beforehand, and even knew the date when it was to occur: that is why he provided himself with an alibi for the evening of March 6, by preparing to go with a friend to see Antonioni's movie *Zabriskie Point.*[32]

Rudd's view is supported by ex-Weatherman Ron Fliegelman, an important operative in 1970, who knew all the people involved. Fliegelman says about the townhouse: "Terry [Robbins] and JJ [John Jacobs] didn't go off and do something on their own. Things didn't happen on an individual basis. Nothing happened that the Weather Bureau didn't know about. All the main leaders knew what was going on with the townhouse."[33]

Rudd also had startling things to say about the May 1970 expulsion of John Jacobs in Mendocino, the momentous meeting where the Weather Bureau renounced lethal violence against people in favor of attacks on property, over the strenuous objection of Jacobs.

Rudd says that on the night of Jacobs's expulsion the two went to a bar in nearby Fort Bragg, and he records the following conversation:

> JJ: I'm accepting my expulsion for the good of the organization. Someone has to take the blame. Bernadine, Billy and Jeff are right about the military error.

RUDD: "But everyone knew what was being planned. We were all together in New York with Terry the week before the action, and nobody raised any objections.

JJ: It doesn't matter. We have to create the fiction that they were always right so that they can lead the organization.

According to Rudd, Jacobs went on to compare himself to Rubashov in Arthur Koestler's novel *Darkness at Noon*. Like Rubashov, Jacobs would perform one last service to the party: permitting himself to be used as a scapegoat.[34]

Rudd adds his own commentary to this scene:

JJ seemed to me like a victim of one of Stalin's old purges ready to falsely confess for the good of the party. . . . For the new leadership, JJ's expulsion was a brilliant maneuver that successfully rewrote history. Suddenly no one remembered how universally accepted the old "Fight the people, all white people are guilty" line was. The new regime regarded that as JJ and Terry's error, and no one else's.

Weather's history had been conveniently cleansed.

According to Rudd, "Everyone knew what was planned." If that is so, then the subsequent characterization of the townhouse plan as an essentially rogue operation was false. Rudd condemned this whitewash.

Ron Jacobs agrees with Rudd that John Jacobs was made to take the rap. "JJ was a soldier. He took one for the team. He sacrificed himself for the revolution." Jacobs eventually settled in Vancouver, British Columbia, and become a Buddhist; he died of cancer at age fifty.[35] At his request, his ashes were buried at Che Guevara's memorial in Cuba.

Jonathan Lerner, a midlevel Weatherman—editor of the SDS newspaper *New Left Notes* and then the Weatherman newspaper *Fire!*—vividly remembers the mood of Weatherman in winter 1969–1970: "My image of what we were going to be was undiluted terrorist action. I remember talking about putting a bomb on the [Chicago commuter railroad] tracks at rush hour, to blow up people coming home from work. That's what I was looking forward to."[36]

Of these competing views of events that occurred nearly a half-century ago, which is the most accurate? Fifty years is a long time; memories fade, are notoriously flawed, become confused. In 2013, ex-Weatherman Mike Spiegel asserted that the deadly plans of early 1970 were merely the product of the handful of people in the townhouse who blew themselves up, while the rest of Weatherman "never thought about hurting anyone."[37] Other ex-Weather people disagree. Howard Machtinger was blunt in a 2011 interview: "The myth, and this is always Bill Ayers's line, is that Weather never set out to kill people, and that's not true—we did. You know, policemen were fair game."[38]

Machtinger knew what he was talking about. And there is evidence outside Weatherman memories themselves that show where the weight of likelihood falls, and how much of the disobliging truth was being deliberately concealed in the "New Morning" communiqué.

To start, there is the testimony of a controversial and arguably untrustworthy source: Larry Grathwohl. He was the principal police and then FBI informant inside Weatherman in early 1970.

Although actual FBI agents were never able to penetrate the New Left after 1965 because of J. Edgar Hoover's insistence that they wear conservative business suits, which made them instantly recognizable, local police and the FBI had considerable success in using civilian informants within Students for a Democratic Society, and even in the Weatherman group when it was still merely an aboveground faction of SDS. In early 1969, the FBI had about 120 informants in the New Left, mostly in SDS; so Clyde Tolson, second in command in the FBI, informed Hoover in February.[39] And there were still FBI informants in the national office of SDS in late summer 1969, when Weatherman controlled it and was still aboveground.[40] But when Weatherman went underground, forming itself into small and clandestine collectives of deeply committed activists who had known one another personally for a long time, informant penetration of Weatherman became close to impossible. The FBI complained continually about this problem.

Preventing informers had been one of the purposes behind
Weatherman's creation of these small groups; Weather leaders understood that they had been successful.[41] As far as is known, Larry
Grathwohl was one of only two informants reporting to the FBI
during the early period of the Weatherman Underground. He was
then twenty-two years old, and was with Weatherman and witnessed its birth pangs during the crucial seven months from
September 1969 to April 1970.[42]

In autumn 1969, Weatherman had been interested in recruiting tough white street kids who already knew how to fight cops,
rather than the university students who had been the bedrock of
Students for a Democratic Society. Larry Grathwohl was the sort
of person Weatherman was looking for: a tough working-class kid
and Vietnam veteran (101st Airborne Division). He was hanging
around the "hippie area" of Cincinnati, his hometown, and found
himself being recruited by Weatherman, and eventually invited to
join a collective. At first curious, then appalled, Grathwohl, at the
urging of his father-in-law, soon became an informant for the
Cincinnati police, then for the FBI. The Weatherman leadership
acknowledged in the summer of 1970 that Grathwohl had indeed
joined Weatherman in autumn 1969, and was a member of various
Weatherman collectives: first in Cincinnati (late 1969–January
1970), then in Detroit (February 1970), then with a bombing
group in Madison, Wisconsin (March), and finally in the Buffalo,
New York, collective in April.[43]

In 1976 Grathwohl published a book about his experiences.
The book, however, was heavily redacted from the original manuscript, and rewritten first by a professional writer and then by the
publisher—so it is somewhat problematic.[44] But apart from this
work, we have other Grathwohl evidence: (a) the information he
gave the FBI in September 1970 concerning his understanding of
how Weatherman had functioned that spring, and (b) his testimony
in October 1980 at the Felt-Miller trial. In September 1970,
Grathwohl's information was fresh in his mind. In October 1980,
Grathwohl was, to be sure, testifying on behalf of Felt and Miller,
so there is a bias in the FBI's favor. But he was testifying under
oath, and in his own words (in contrast to the doctored text of his
book). Thus in the book Grathwohl often used pseudonyms for

people in Weatherman, but on the witness stand and under oath, he gave the true names of people, so we never have to guess (as we do in the book) who he is talking about. Furthermore, he was subject to cross-examination by the prosecutors, and it was not gentle. Their position at the trial was that Weatherman was a small and "wacky" group that did not pose much of a threat to national security—making FBI actions against relatives and friends of Weatherman more reprehensible to the jury. In fact, the prosecutors tried to prevent Grathwohl from testifying at all, fearing he could damage the benign view of Weatherman they wanted; but Judge William Bryant eventually ruled against them.[45]

In his September 1970 FBI interview in San Francisco, Grathwohl was asked how much control the leadership, called here the Central Committee, maintained over the local collectives— called *focos* in the interview (the term was popularized by Regis Debray in his influential tract, *Revolution within the Revolution*, based on the Cuban revolutionary experience). Grathwohl said that a *foco* could generally do as it pleased, but the Central Committee designated the region where a foco would operate. He added: "It also decides what targets are to be hit and how." When asked whether the collectives could move around without central approval, his answer was that this was true as far as housing and theft, but that, again, "all bombings are subject to approval of the Central Committee." Then Grathwohl was asked directly who made the decision on bombing targets. His answer: "All bombing targets are decided on by the Central Committee."[46]

If Grathwohl was being truthful, his testimony would undermine the assertions that the townhouse plan was a rogue operation. According to Grathwohl, there were no rogue bombings. His 1970 account of the Weatherman command structure confirms what John Jacobs told the historian Ron Jacobs in 1997, and what Ron Fliegelman said in 2014: the local collectives passed possible targets up to the Weather Bureau for approval and to give the go-ahead. In a 1977 interview with the FBI, ex-Weatherman Karen Latimer, too, stressed that the Weather Bureau preapproved all bombing projects.[47]

At the Felt-Miller trial, Grathwohl was not asked about Weatherman command structure. He did testify, however, that the

Weatherman collective in Detroit in which he lived in February 1970 was focused on lethal bombing. Everyone knew, he said, that innocents were at risk of being killed. The leader of the Detroit Collective was Bill Ayers. Grathwohl said that in late February 1970 the Detroit collective began planning a double bombing attack, intending to inflict significant casualties, against two institutions linked to the Detroit Police Department. One target was the Detroit Police Officers' Association Building (a single-family brownstone house that had been converted into offices); the other was the headquarters building of the Detroit 13th Precinct. Grathwohl said he was ordered to scout the DPOA Building in order to "determine when the greatest number of police officers would be in the building so that we could detonate the device at that time." He added that Diana Oughton was present during all lethal planning in Detroit. He himself participated in making one of the two bombs.[48]

The two Detroit police targets, Grathwohl said, were picked because both had connections to black discontent in the city in the aftermath of the great Detroit riot of July 1967, in which almost fifty people had been killed. During the chaos of July 1967, three policemen shot to death several alleged black rioters at the Algiers Motel, an event which John Hersey later made famous in *The Algiers Motel Incident*. In late February 1970, an all-white jury in Flint, Michigan, acquitted these policemen of murder. The Detroit collective chose the two targets to destroy, claimed Grathwohl, because the Detroit Police Officers' Association had been a source of defense funds for the accused officers, while the precinct headquarters was the one from which the accused Algiers Motel policemen had operated during the riots. The Weather collective believed that the destruction of these two buildings would have great propaganda value within the Detroit ghetto.[49]

Grathwohl claimed that he became alarmed that a powerful bomb was going to be placed in the narrow alley between the DPOA and the Red Barn restaurant, which would endanger innocent diners who might well be killed. He said he warned Bill Ayers:

> A. I told Bill that if the bomb was left there . . . the people in the Red Barn restaurant were in jeopardy. I felt that a good number of them would be killed.

Q. Did he heed your advice?

A. He replied that sometimes the innocent people have to die in order to attain your ultimate goal.

According to Grathwohl's testimony, there was apparently no plan for a phone call to be made ahead of time to warn anybody that these bombs were going to go off.[50]

Grathwohl says he managed to warn the FBI about the targets before Ayers sent him and three comrades to Madison to carry out an action there. The FBI and the Detroit police found the bombs and defused them. Meanwhile, according to Grathwohl, in Madison he contacted FBI Special Agent Thomas Madden, whom the FBI had sent to Madison in early 1970 to look into a spate of bombings there.[51]

Is Grathwohl's account credible? Or might he have been an agent provocateur and planted the bombs himself?

Curiously, unlike their numerous other bombings for which they were eager to take credit, Weatherman never claimed responsibility for the Detroit bombs. Moreover, Grathwohl in his 1976 book, and later under oath in 1980, claimed that Ayers in Buffalo in early April 1970 possessed suspiciously detailed knowledge of another bombing—the fatal bombing at the Golden Gate Park police station in San Francisco two months earlier (February 16). Ayers has explicitly denied this, and has called Grathwohl—who began earning a monthly stipend from the FBI in January 1970—"a paid dishonest person."[52]

The Park Police Station bomb was a powerful dynamite device, wrapped with nails, that killed one police officer (Sergeant Brian McDonnell), blinded another (Officer Robert Fogarty), and injured a dozen more. The culprits have never been named or captured, although a grand jury was investigating a Weatherman connection as late as 2009. The investigation was not based on anything from Grathwohl; it started from allegations made by ex-Weatherman Karen Latimer. The FBI interviewed her at length in January 1975 and again in April 1977. She had excellent Weatherman credentials: she was one of the Motor City Nine, whose raid on a community college outside Detroit in July 1969 first brought Weatherman to national attention. She said she was in a Weatherman collective in Berkeley in February 1970, claimed to have witnessed the planning of the bombing, and fingered those she alleged made and placed the bomb. The names are redacted in the FBI report later made public, but at the trial in 1980, FBI Special Agent James Vermeersch testified that he had read the un-redacted file and said Latimer named Howard Machtinger as the builder of the bomb. Latimer also claimed that she did reconnais-sance of Park Police Station for the collective, that the bombing was approved by the Weather Bureau in a meeting in Marin county two weeks earlier (she gave the exact address), and that the death of McDonnell and the other injuries caused "no remorse or panic" in the collective afterward.[53]

There is no doubt that Latimer was a member of the Berkeley Weatherman collective in February 1970. The collective was stay-ing at the house of Bay Area radical leader Leibel Bergman, and FBI surveillance of the Bergman house often records her there. She was arrested by Berkeley police on March 4, 1970, for illegal possession of a weapon. She also correctly identified Bernardine Dohrn's doctor in Berkeley.[54] Leibel Bergman, for his part, thought the Weatherman collective camping at his house in Berkeley had done the Park Station bombing, and he suspected that his son Lincoln had been involved; he started staying away from the house because he feared everyone there would be arrested. This is known from FBI electronic surveillance of his home.[55]

There also is the alleged physical evidence. Special Agent William Regan testified at the Felt-Miller trial that the dynamite used at the Park Police Station was identified by FBI explosives ex-perts as coming from the same batch as that found in late March 1970 in a Weatherman safe house in Chicago. And as with the townhouse bombs, the Park Station bomb was constructed as a group of dynamite sticks laced with staples.[56]

Given the preponderance of at least circumstantial evidence, why was there never a Park Station indictment of Weatherman lead-ers? It appears that the prosecutors in San Francisco did not trust Karen Latimer. Given what she said was her own role in the recon-naissance of Park Station, if she was telling the truth she was an accomplice, and would have to be given immunity if she was to tes-tify in court. But while the FBI considered Latimer's information valuable, at the time she was interviewed (in 1975 and 1977), she had converted to an evangelical Christian sect and made it clear to the interviewers that her testimony of personal involvement in past radical actions was motivated by religious fervor. How credible a witness was she?[57] And despite her conversion, the prosecutors feared that she remained secretly loyal to her Weather comrades, and that once given immunity she would take the entire blame for the Park Station bomb on herself, thereby making any future prosecution of Weatherman leaders impossible.[58] Moreover, in September 1971 a Black Liberation Army stalwart, Anthony Bottom, had confessed to the Park Station bombing, claiming white people had provided the bomb he had used. Bottom was already facing an indictment for the San Francisco death of Sergeant John Young at the Ingleside Police Station in August 1971.[59]

Nothing has emerged over the years sufficient to indict anyone for Park Station. Bottom's confession would have given Weatherman defense attorneys a field day in court. Leibel Bergman's opinion in late February that the bombing was the work of the Weatherman collective staying at his house, interesting as it is when combined with Karen Latimer's testimony, was only his opinion, and it was inadmissible in court anyway, because it was obtained through FBI electronic surveillance that was done without a search warrant or court order. Further, if the Weather collective at Bergman's house had carried out Park Station, how was it that they were not overheard discussing it by the FBI? (Neither after 1976, nor certainly after 1980, was there reason any longer to keep such FBI eavesdropping secret; by then, everyone knew it had been going on.) The alleged similarities between the San Francisco and the Chicago dynamite are only allegations. Karen Latimer died several years ago. Maybe she confused Park Station with the Berkeley bombings four days earlier, which Weatherman took credit for and had carried out; or maybe Ayers was confused—or boasting—in Buffalo in April. Regarding Grathwohl's veracity, the San Francisco bombing issue is thus unclear.[60]

Detroit is another matter. The Detroit Police Officers' Association bomb (nine sticks of dynamite) was real, and was discovered by the Detroit police and the FBI in the narrow alley between the DPOA and the Red Barn Restaurant early on the morning of March 6, 1970. The much larger 13th Precinct bomb (thirty-five sticks of dynamite) was also real, and was discovered by the Detroit police and the FBI in the midmorning of March 6 (just about the time the townhouse blew up in New York). Both Detroit bombs were found by the police and the FBI exactly where Grathwohl had told them the bombs would be planted by the Detroit Weatherman collective; both were defused before they went off—the DPOA bomb just in time. On March 6, Grathwohl himself had been gone from Detroit for two days, sent on a Weatherman bombing mission to Madison, Wisconsin, so he was hundreds of miles away—as the FBI knew from Special Agent Thomas Madden in Madison. And the second bomb was found in a women's bathroom. Grathwohl did not plant those bombs.[61]

The discovery of the bombs demonstrates the veracity of Grathwohl's claim about the intentions of the Detroit collective. We now also know that the Detroit collective contained a rather mysterious second police informant (whose name has never been disclosed); whatever that person said did not contradict Grathwohl. Finally, the lethal nature of these bombs is not in dispute: the DPOA bomb would have caused many casualties; the 13th Precinct bomb, three times as large, would probably have destroyed the precinct headquarters and everyone in it.[62]

In fact, it was the Detroit bombs in *combination* with the New York townhouse, not the townhouse explosion alone, that convinced the FBI leadership in Washington that Weatherman posed a significant threat on a national scale.

The news from Detroit went right to J. Edgar Hoover. Hoover responded on March 12 with an emergency memo sent out to the FBI field offices in the cities where Weatherman had been most active. In it, Hoover gave the name of one of the suspected bombers he was most worried about: Bill Ayers. Hoover demanded that the field offices try harder to penetrate the Weatherman collectives: it was imperative, because the Bureau now had information that the Weathermen were preparing dynamite attacks against police and military installations. Hoover then gave an example of the threat as he saw it: "A Weatherman group led by Bill Ayers recently made plans to dynamite the Detroit Police Association building."[63]

A week later, on March 19, Hoover ordered all FBI field offices to try to locate thirty-three prominent Weathermen. Though they had not yet been indicted for any federal crimes, the two large dynamite bombs discovered in Detroit police installations, Hoover said, proved how dangerous the Weathermen were[64] On April 9, Hoover underlined the nature of Weatherman threat in a memo to Attorney General John Mitchell. He recounted the townhouse explosion of March 6, then added:

> In late February, 1970, William Ayers was the leader of a group of Weathermen in Detroit which made plans to bomb the Detroit Police Officers Association Building. On March 6, 1970, bombs consisting of ten sticks of dynamite and thirty-four sticks of dynamite were located in an unexploded condition at this building, and at the 13th Precinct of the Detroit Police Department, respectively.

Hoover noted that fifty-nine sticks of dynamite had just been found in a Weatherman apartment in Chicago (March 30). This was especially sinister to Hoover because one of the people in the Chicago apartment before it was raided was the Weatherman Naomi Jaffe, and, Hoover told Mitchell, "she ... was in contact with Ayers shortly prior to March 6, 1970, when the dynamite was found in the Detroit police installations."[65]

Similarly, when on April 10 Assistant Attorney General Will Wilson of the Criminal Division requested Hoover to begin an immediate investigation of the Weathermen on grounds of possible multiple violations of federal bombing statutes, Wilson mentioned not only the two Detroit antipolice bombs but Bill Ayers specifically. Wilson was a conservative Texas Democrat turned Goldwater Republican who hated the New Left and the anti-Vietnam protestors.[66] Wilson himself continued to take great personal interest in the investigation of the Detroit bombs in the months that followed; but he was forced to leave the government in 1971 because of his association with a real estate scandal in Texas.[67]

In the three months after the March 6 events, as Weathermen fled underground and the FBI intensified their pursuit, the Detroit bombing appears at least fifteen more times in FBI memos. The townhouse, of course, was a more dramatic event, since the bombs had detonated and three people had died. But in FBI memos from March through June of 1970, the townhouse explosion appears only once without being paired with the Detroit bombs. The discovery of a large Weatherman "bomb-factory" in Chicago on March 30 sealed the conclusion that the FBI faced a nationwide radical conspiracy of lethal intent. Hoover and his agents were sure there was a link between the townhouse and Detroit, and the dynamite found in Chicago in turn matched the dynamite of the Weatherman bombs found in the Detroit (both batches came from the same company in Colorado). Not surprisingly, an FBI report in June—"Special Study: Bombings and Arsons in the United States"—noted that the Detroit bomb plot and the townhouse explosion had occurred on the same day.[68]

Nevertheless, during March, Hoover was reluctant to allocate the men and resources to investigate possible Weatherman bombings. The concern was that the Bureau would end up dealing with a large number of local bombings of uncertain origin and not with those by Weatherman. The FBI simply did not have enough manpower to handle a large number of local bombing investigations while also looking for Weatherman communes. The policy changed after March 26, however, when Assistant Attorney General J. Walter Yeagley of the Internal Security Division formally requested the FBI to investigate Weatherman bombings:

Since the February implementation of terroristic tactics by the Weatherman, we now have the clear intent to engage in such tactics coupled with known overt acts by them in Detroit and New York City. We are no longer dealing with isolated unknown subject bombings. We are confronted with a conspiracy to use terroristic tactics in furtherance of a Marxist-Leninist revolution.

On those grounds, the memo urged that the FBI determine the manpower and financial costs of instituting a nationwide investigation. Hoover knew that behind Yeagley stood Attorney General John Mitchell and President Nixon.[69]

Two weeks later, Assistant Director William Sullivan reported the results of an emergency assistant directors' conference to Cartha DeLoach, the FBI third in command. Sullivan reiterated that based on the townhouse explosion and the Detroit antipolice bombs, as well as evidence from Chicago that Weatherman was continuing to stockpile firearms and explosives, the group now had to be seen as "a menace of national proportions." Sullivan estimated the cost of shifting men and resources to combat the threat at more than $14 million, and possibly much more.[70]

References to the Detroit bomb plot continued to appear repeatedly in FBI memos, summaries, and retrospectives from spring 1970 onward: in a special report to government officials in May;[71] in the June special report already referred to;[72] in interrogations of Weathermen in jail on riot charges in June;[73] in memos in September;[74] in a special report sent to all FBI special agents in charge in April 1971, which was also distributed to fifty local police chiefs in September 1971;[75] in a different report distributed to local police officers at a special conference in November 1971;[76] in "FBI Special Report: The Urban Guerrilla in the United States," distributed within the Bureau in February 1972;[77] and in the special agent training program "New Left Terrorist Groups" in November 1972.[78] When Special Agent Jack Kearney became the head of "the Weatherman Squad" in the New York field office—the main FBI group in the field hunting the Weatherman fugitives—his notes show him well aware of the Detroit bombs.[79] The summary of the Weatherman national threat prepared by a committee of intelligence agency heads for the White House in June 1970 listed the pair of Detroit bombs as one of the three main actions of radicals, black and white, that, taken together, seemed to pose a national threat.[80]

These intelligence memos and reports were secret; they all took place before the Freedom of Information Act was passed in 1974. Thus the FBI and Justice Department officials and agents were not writing with the idea of making propaganda for a broader public— trying to exaggerate the threat in order to boost their budgets, perhaps. On the contrary, they did not think this material would ever *become* public. They were discussing a real law-enforcement problem among themselves.

Yet the Detroit attacks of March 6, 1970, were not reported at the time in either the *New York Times* or the *Washington Post*. Nor did Detroit appear in the major article "Terrorism on the Left," in the March 23 edition of *Newsweek*. After all, no bombs had actually exploded in Detroit. But Weatherman's alleged attack on police in Detroit was certainly a story of major interest to midwestern newspapers.[81] Similarly, at the July 23, 1970, press conference held to announce federal bombing indictments against the Weatherman leaders, Assistant Attorney General Wilson said that investigators had so far found only one actual incident of planting of bombs— the Detroit bombs of March 6. The thirteen Weatherman leaders indicted on bombing charges were Bill Ayers, Kathy Boudin, Robert Burlingham, Bernardine Dohrn, Dianne Donghi, Linda Evans, Ronald Fliegelman, Naomi Jaffe, Russell Neufeld, Mark Rudd, Jane Spielman, Cathy Wilkerson, and Larry Grathwohl (the latter's inclusion was an attempt to preserve Grathwohl's cover in Weatherman; it would ultimately fail).[82]

By July, the government also had in its hands what appeared to be a startling new piece of evidence about the Detroit plot and its leader. In late June, agents from the FBI field office in Detroit interviewed two Michigan state troopers (their names are blacked out in the report, which came to light only with the release in 2013 of previously unavailable FBI documents). According to the interview notes, these men, in civilian clothes, had been part of the stakeout of the DPOA Building established after Grathwohl warned the police and FBI that the DPOA was a target for a Weatherman dynamite bomb. According to the notes, around 6:30 A.M. on March 5, 1970, the troopers spotted a young man inspecting the building, walking around it several times, including through the narrow walkway between the building and the Red Barn restaurant. He then left, trailed by one of the Michigan troopers. The surveillance lasted two hours, during which, the trooper said, the subject was seen boarding on a bus, having breakfast at a diner, and finally entering a house a couple of miles from the DPOA. The trooper noted the license plate of an automobile parked nearby, which the report said later turned out to be owned by a member of the Ayers family. On June 25, the FBI agents showed photographs of possible suspects to the Michigan trooper who had followed the subject. The trooper picked out one photo: it was of Bill Ayers. This identification, if true, makes Ayers not merely the likely general organizer of the antipolice bombings in Detroit (which was what Grathwohl had alleged), but very possibly a direct and active participant.[83]

Thirty years later, in his memoir, *Fugitive Days*, Bill Ayers actually admitted to leading a bomb plot that targeted a police station around the time of the townhouse explosion—and the details he set out are largely congruent with what we know of the planned Detroit attacks. Ayers writes that after recovering from the shock of the townhouse explosion and Diana Oughton's death, he and his group decided to respond with a bomb attack that was planned to take place in Cleveland. Detroit is unmentioned. "A squad of cops in Cleveland had dragged Black men from a motel and shot them down in cold blood, and now we would, I thought, even the score." His group had scouted "the precinct house" target, and had found a likely hiding place for the bomb—a package of dynamite with a cigarette fuse, which would be shoved into a vent. "How inevitable it seemed then. . . . The device never went off—out of oxygen, it exhausted itself a millimeter short of an imagined modern-day Harper's Ferry."[84]

Ayers places his bomb attack on a precinct house in Cleveland four days after the death of the H. Rap Brown supporters Ralph Featherstone and Che Payne when their automobile blew up in Maryland. That explosion occurred on March 9, 1970, which in turn puts Ayers's attack on the police station on March 13, not on the sixth, the day of the townhouse. But no bomb was found in any precinct house in Cleveland in March 1970. And the choice of this precinct house as the target because a squad of cops from this precinct had dragged black men from a motel and killed them seems very similar to the Algiers Motel incident in Detroit, not to any event in Cleveland; it certainly sounds like he is describing, with a thin geographical and chronological disguise, the Weatherman attack on Detroit's 13th Precinct, home precinct of the cops who killed the men at the Algiers Motel. Even the detail about the cigarette fuse fits with Detroit, for one of the Detroit Collective's dynamite bombs found on March 6 had a cigarette fuse.[85]

Reading only slightly between the lines of Ayers's own memoir suggests that Larry Grathwohl told the truth, both in his 1976 book and in his 1980 testimony. While Ayers's account in his memoir is distorted, it is not so distorted that, with our knowledge from other sources, we cannot now tease out the disobliging truth which Ayers is reluctant to admit—for that truth would make a hash of his effort to depict Weather as having never been intent on lethal violence. Perhaps, of course, the distortions and omissions here arise from what Ayers claims is his untrustworthy memory.[86]

Ayers's remark about Harper's Ferry is also revealing. The Weatherman leaders had looked to John Brown's October 1859 raid on Harper's Ferry, Virginia, as an exemplary instance of moral solidarity and exceptional courage on the part an enlightened white man and his sympathizers, both black and white, willing to employ deadly violence in an effort to inspire a general slave rebellion in the American South.[87] In Weatherman thinking, the black ghettos of the United States were the equivalent of oppressed third-world people living in dictatorial white-ruled colonies. This view was central to the Weatherman's founding manifesto, "You Don't Need a Weatherman to Know Which the Way the Wind Blows." Terry Robbins told Jonah Raskin in late 1969 that "the civil war between blacks and whites *has* begun."[88] Moreover, Detroit in early March 1970, after the February 26 acquittal of the Algiers Motel cops, was a particular tinderbox. A favorite Weatherman slogan was "John Brown—Live Like Him!"[89]

That this was a Weatherman goal was stressed by four Weathermen who dropped out in early 1970 and in June wrote an essay criticizing Weatherman politics. They said that the Weatherman leaders believed that most whites would never help black people in the United States to carry out a revolutionary war; the black "colony" would thus have to carry out the war of liberation on its own, with aid from only a few enlightened white revolutionaries, specifically the Weathermen. It was the John Brown model. In their article, the ex-Weathermen also asserted that to bring the revolutionary war about, the Weatherman leaders thought it necessary for white revolutionaries to carry out actions in black communities that would encourage blacks to take armed struggle themselves "to a higher level." The plans for Detroit appear to have been of a piece with this objective. Moreover, it seems likely that the New York Townhouse Collective's March 6 plan against Fort Dix was connected with, and coordinated with, the double March 6 action in Detroit, in which an alleged central role—if the Michigan State troopers and Larry Grathwohl are correct—would be played by Bill Ayers; it would have occurred on the same day and would have been quite as deadly as Fort Dix. The revolution was intended to start off with a bang.

It wasn't only dynamite. Beginning in December 1969, some Weatherman collectives—enraged at the Chicago police assassination of Black Panther leaders Fred Hampton and Matt Clark—started to firebomb Chicago police cars. In 1974 the Weather Underground publicly admitted these Chicago firebombings.[90] It seems that the police cars were empty when the bombs were set, but Weatherman Laura Whitehorn, who set one such bomb, remembered hoping it would be lethal. Jonathan Lerner remembered testing a gasoline bomb at the front door of a derelict New York building in which he knew people were sleeping: "That's how much we cared about people. Thank God it didn't blow up." According to Karen Latimer, in January 1970 in Detroit she and Diana Oughton placed a large gasoline bomb with a cigarette and cherry-bomb fuse at a commercial building in Detroit; it didn't go off.[91] At the 1980 Felt-Miller trial, where FBI burglaries of the parents of Judy Cohen Flatley were at issue, the prosecution and defense agreed that Cohen, as head of the Milwaukee Weatherman collective in January 1970, led it in the firebombing of the ROTC building at the University of Wisconsin at Milwaukee. The firebomb did thousands of dollars of damage, and could have been lethal. And both the prosecution and defense stipulated that Cohen in January 1970 also led the Milwaukee collective in firebombing the National Guard Armory in White Fish Bay, Wisconsin; a suburb of Milwaukee, this was the hometown of Bernardine Dohrn.[92] Meanwhile, also in January, two members of the Weatherman collective in Seattle, Silas and Judith Bissell, placed a large firebomb beneath the entrance stairs to the ROTC building at the University of Washington; it was discovered before it exploded, and the Bissells disappeared underground.[93]

Thanks to Bryan Burrough's reporting in his 2015 book *Days of Rage*, we now also know a great deal of what happened in Berkeley, California, on the night of February 12, 1970, when a Weatherman commando led by Howard Machtinger set two dynamite-filled pipe bombs beside Berkeley police cars in the parking lot of the city's police headquarters. No warning was given: "We wanted to do it at a shift change, frankly, to maximize deaths," said one participant. When the bombs detonated, dozens of plate-glass windows were shattered in the municipal building next door, one policeman, Paul Morgan, ended up with his left arm mangled, and other cops had their eardrums broken. "Basically, it was seen as a successful action. But others were angry that a policeman didn't die. There was no one who was anti-that. That was what we were trying to do."[94]

Nine days later, on February 21, 1970, the Townhouse Collective exploded three firebombs at the home of Judge John J. Murtaugh, the judge in a trial in New York City involving twenty-one Black Panther defendants accused of conspiring to bomb targets in New York City. Two of the firebombs did serious damage to the front of the Murtaugh house. A third firebomb was detonated under the gas tank of the Murtaugh automobile, parked in a narrow driveway beside the house; if it had set off the gasoline in the car's tank, the explosion could have been lethal. But a neighbor, alerted by the first two explosions—big enough to shake the Murtaugh house—came running, saw the firebomb under the automobile, and extinguished the bomb with snow. For the next eighteen months, Judge Murtaugh's wife and son went everywhere accompanied by police bodyguards.[95]

Since Murtaugh was the judge in the "Panther 21" trial, suspicion naturally fell not on Weatherman but on the Black Panther Party. Thus a few days later, the Panther 21 defendants were in the embarrassing position of having to declare to Judge Murtaugh in open court that their organization was not responsible for bombing his house.[96] The radical columnist Andrew Kopkind, who was sympathetic to Weatherman and counted a number of them among his friends, understood that the bombing of Judge Murtaugh's house was prejudicial to the Panthers' case. "If whites did that act," he wrote, "they should have made it their own responsibility—and they should have set its political meaning straight." But the Townhouse Collective did not. Only in the "New Morning" communiqué, ten months later, did the Weather Bureau admit that the Murtaugh bombing had been one of theirs and that moreover many in the organization had thought it "a good action."[97]

The Townhouse Collective was busy that night, throwing fire-bombs at a police car and two armed forces recruiting stations, and setting one off on the steps of the Columbia University Law Library. The targets were the legal system and the military.[98]

And then, there was Cleveland, on March 2.

In September 1972 a young man claiming to be a former member of the Weatherman collective in Cleveland came to the FBI with a story about the group's firebombing of the home of a Cleveland policeman on March 2, 1970. The informant's name and his wife's are redacted in the documents, released in 2013, but it appears that in 1969 he was a high school student in Milwaukee, and he claims to have become involved with the local Weatherman collective. In January 1970 he was sent from Milwaukee to Cleveland. At first he stayed with Weatherman Howard Emmer, at the Emmer family house at 3133 Sycamore Street in Cleveland. In the Cleveland Weatherman collective he claimed he was told that the current goal was to start the revolution by provoking incidents between the black community and the police, by targeting police-men and police installations. There had been insurrections in the black areas of Cleveland in July 1966 and in July 1968; the Cleveland collective was beginning a bombing campaign whose purpose was to reignite those insurrections. The informant said that the leader of the collective was John Fuerst. The informant was taught how to construct pipe bombs—to provoke "armed struggle" in the city—by Weatherman Leonard Handelsman.[99]

Shortly after February 20, 1970, an individual whom the informant later identified from a photo array as Bill Ayers visited the collective and met with John Fuerst. According to the informant, after Ayers had gone, Fuerst told the collective that Ayers, a member of the Weather Bureau, had instructed them to concentrate on police targets related to the case of Ahmed (Fred) Evans, a black leader who had been convicted of killing three Cleveland policemen.[100]

The informant said that he was then sent with Joanna Zilsel to buy tacks and staples, which were to be included in bombs; a lit cigarette would act as a timer for the fuse. On March 2, 1970, he participated in the attempted firebombing of the home of a Cleveland policeman.[101] The informant then left Cleveland to transport arms and ammunition between other Weatherman collectives. In summer 1971, he said, he went with Weather leader Judy Cohen to New York to meet with City College of New York professor Bernard Lefkowitz, who was working on a book on the New Left; they wanted assurances from Lefkowitz that he would not say anything that could be dangerous to underground fugitives.[102]

Circumstantial evidence indicates that the informant was telling the truth. A second unnamed informant gave the FBI a list of the Weather collective in Milwaukee in autumn 1969; it corresponded with the list given by the main informant. Again, the people in the Weather collective in Cleveland described by the main informant were all connected to the Weatherman collective there—John Fuerst, Howard Emmer, Leonard Handelsman, Joanna Zilsel.[103] The bomb laced with large staples was typical of Weatherman in early 1970; the lit cigarette fuse was used on the alleged the Weatherman bomb at the Detroit Police Officer's Association on March 6. The Emmer family did live at 3133 Sycamore Street, which was indeed a center of Weatherman activity in Cleveland. Thus when an FBI agent interviewed the mother of Cleveland Weatherman Bobbi Smith, the mother said she had a phone number by which she could reach her daughter; when the FBI checked, the phone number was registered at the Emmers' house, 3133 Sycamore. Similarly, when the father of leader John Fuerst wanted to phone his son, he too called a phone number that was registered at 3133 Sycamore. The home of Cleveland police detective Frank Schaeffer was firebombed on March 2. The informant said he brought weapons from Milwaukee to Chicago, and gave them there to Bernardine Dohrn. When the police raided the Weatherman Chicago apartment on March 30, 1970, weapons were found that had been purchased in Milwaukee, and Dohrn had lived there. Finally, Bernard Lefkowitz was indeed a professor at City College of New York, and told the FBI that in summer 1971 he was indeed writing a book about radicals, and was visited by Judy Cohen, along with two other individuals whom he knew only as "Dennis" and "Mary Lou." "Dennis" must be the informant.[104]

The informant said that the Cleveland Collective was focused on the case of Ahmad Evans. A centerpiece of the aboveground Weatherman conference in Cleveland on August 29–September 1, 1969, was, in fact, a "Free Ahmed Evans" demonstration. And in the September 12, 1969, edition of Weatherman's newspaper *New Left Notes*, the case of Ahmed Evans was again singled out, and the police were accused of framing him for murder in order to destroy a radical black leader. Ahmed Evans also appears as an important political prisoner in the Weatherman Underground's communiqué of July 25, 1970—paired with H. Rap Brown. All this both explains and lends credibility to the informant's statements about the Cleveland Collective's intense interest in Evans, who by 1972, when the informant came to the FBI, was an obscure figure.[105]

In detonating firebombs against Judge Murtaugh, then, the Townhouse Collective did not go beyond what other collectives were doing. But, the "New Morning" communiqué says, the Townhouse leaders now went for something unique: dynamite. Fort Dix was the largest army base in the Northeast. A large-scale dynamite attack would strike a material blow against the military establishment pursuing the Vietnam War. Fort Dix was also infamous to radicals in New York City—including the Weathermen—for its military prison. It thus shared "police" characteristics with the Detroit Police Officers' Association, Detroit Police Precinct 13, Judge Murtaugh, the Cleveland operation, the Berkeley operation, and numerous other Weatherman targets. The "stockade" on the base was notorious for its inhumane conditions: hideous overcrowding, barracks that were de facto racially segregated, brutal discipline. On June 5, 1969, there had been a major riot, put down by hundreds of military police. The ringleaders were savagely beaten, and the army brought court-martial charges against thirty-eight men. The potential sentence for the five facing the most serious charges—mutiny and conspiracy to mutiny—was fifty years in prison. These men were quickly dubbed the Fort Dix 38.[106]

The radical community in New York City was incensed. Fort Dix had been a focus for demonstrations as early as November 1968 (demonstrators were teargassed), and a plan to disrupt the graduation ceremony of trainees in February 1969 had been foiled only by a massive show of military police. After the June 1969 riot, radicals played up the racial angle: in a newsletter titled *Ft. Dix 38 Speak–Out*, the lead article was headlined, "Brothers—We'll Never Be Slaves Again!" An enormous demonstration in support of the Fort Dix 38 took place at the base on October 12; the agenda for the final organizing meeting on October 6 featured a movie entitled *No Vietnamese Ever Called Me Nigger*, which focused on black antiwar soldiers discussing their experiences, as well as coverage of a large antiwar demonstration held in Harlem in 1967.[107]

The Weatherman group in New York City was in fact heavily involved in planning for the Fort Dix demonstration that autumn. For them, "the Fort Dix 38" equated with "the Panther 21." In planning the demonstration with soldiers and civilians of the "Ft. Dix Coffee House" group in September 1969, the Weathermen advocated a violent assault on the installation, bursting through military police lines and into the stockade itself. Moreover, while other radical organizations each sent a few people to this planning session, the New York Weathermen came en masse—an attempt to "pack" the meeting that alienated the other radicals. The Weathermen listed the targets they wanted to attack: "the stockades, the court-martial halls, the MP's, the station where the coffins with dead GI's from Vietnam arrive"; three of these four targets were police targets. Weatherman Shin'ya Ono said in December that the Weathermen accepted that during such a mass attack on the stockade, "a few of us" might get killed.[108]

The Fort Dix coffeehouse people and the GI leaders were appalled. They wanted to propagandize the MPs about the war, not physically assault them. They opposed the carrying of Vietcong flags in the vanguard of the demonstration—an act the Weathermen viewed as ideologically essential—because of the sensitivities of the soldiers.[109] The Weathermen ascribed this negative reaction to false consciousness. The next day the Weathermen unexpectedly agreed not to carry the Vietcong flags—perhaps a reflection of the demonstration's importance, and evidence that even Weather ideologues were prepared to curtail their more extremist inclinations under certain circumstances.[110] But Weatherman's hardball tactics at the planning meeting, and the violent and even suicidal nature of their plans, created great distrust. The GI and Ft.

Dix Coffee House leaders now canceled the demonstration as originally planned for September 28 and rescheduled it for October
12—when the New York Weathermen would be on the road returning from their Days of Rage demonstration in Chicago, and
thus be unable to participate. And in fact they did not: although
some Weathermen who had remained in New York urged at the
last minute that they be included, they were refused.[111]

The October 12, 1969, demonstration turned out to be the
largest held at a military base in the Northeast during the Vietnam
War, and was radical in its own way, including a helmeted "wom-
en's brigade" in front—not unlike the "women's action" on the second day of the Weatherman Days of Rage in Chicago. The
demonstrators did march onto the base and toward the stockade.
But in the end, although there was some tear gas, the October 12
demonstration went off relatively peacefully. Then, on February
14, 1970, someone threw a hand grenade into the Ft. Dix Coffee
House, causing several injuries. The coffeehouse had been harassed
for months by the army, local town officials, and right-wing vigi-
lantes. The February 14 attack caused its permanent closing, and
this was major and upsetting news among radicals in New York.[112]

Thus when two weeks later, at the end of February 1970, the
Townhouse Collective turned to doing violence at Fort Dix, it was
not a new Weatherman idea. The target had connections to the police (especially the military police)—as Shin'ya Ono makes clear—
as did numerous other Weatherman bombing targets in early 1970.
To be sure, civilians would be at the Fort Dix dance—but there
would have been plenty of civilians in the Red Barn Restaurant
in Detroit, next to the DPOA Building, if not in the DPOA itself,
and plenty of civilians inside Detroit's 13th Precinct, too. What
stood out was the size and number of the bombs the Townhouse
intended to detonate at Fort Dix. Yet even here, the 13th Precinct
bomb in Detroit was itself larger than any of the unexploded
bombs found in the townhouse.

"In times of revolution, just wars, and wars of liberation, I love the
angels of destruction and disorder." This was how the Black
Panther leader Eldridge Cleaver, the party's minister of information, spoke of his support for Weatherman in early November

1969, from his exile in Algeria. Unlike other white groups that sat around talking, these young people, Cleaver wrote, were unafraid "to pick up the gun," as the old Panther slogan had it. That they were prepared to kill for the revolution only increased his respect.[113] Despite later denials by some ex-Weather leaders, the evidence is clear that significant actors in the unfolding drama of Weatherman were ready, even eager, in early 1970 to kill policemen or military police—and to countenance the death of civilian bystanders too, if that were necessary, as so-called collateral damage—in order to upend the American imperium and to drive a stake through its racist heart.

CHAPTER TWO

"We Sentence the Government to Death"

OW HAD IT COME to this? Why were educated young people in New York and Detroit making dynamite bombs? How was it that they were prepared to kill— and kill on a large scale—in the name of revolution?

The Weathermen were graduates of the country's most prominent independent left-wing student organization, the Students for a Democratic Society, founded in 1962. Numerous explanations have been offered for their emergence out of SDS, mostly focusing (rightly) on issues of American politics and American culture. Jeremy Varon's list of explanations for, Weatherman's emergence, for instance, includes anger and despair over the failure of even huge demonstrations to bring about an end to the Vietnam War; the apparent failure of legislative reforms to end institutional racism and root out racial prejudice; some white university students' wish to fight on the side of the oppressed, both in America (with African Americans, especially the Black Panthers) and internationally (especially with the Vietnamese); the desire, in a culture that produced floods of shoddy and "plastic" commodities, to be *authentic* in one's life (that is, to be authentic revolutionaries) and to demonstrate this authenticity in the most militant fashion (first by street-fighting, then by bombing); the desire for "instant gratification" typical of American society—that is, Weatherman's refusal to wait for antiwar demonstrations to have an impact—which reflected, ironically, the American "ideology of consumer culture"; and finally "a characteristically American preference for action over critical reflection."[1]

Perhaps, too, the Weathermen had simply embraced, with typical American susceptibility to publicity, their own overblown image in the media, and thus saw themselves as a truly revolutionary force. Or perhaps the Weatherman impulse to violent action was at heart religious—they were "moral apocalyptists," as Peter Marin called them. For social theorist Christopher Lasch, the Weathermen acted on "an ideal of personal heroism, not from an analysis of the sources of tension in American society." On the other hand, feminist radicals Jane Alpert and Robin Morgan argued that terrorist groups such as Weatherman were at heart an expression of patriarchal and toxic masculinity. (Alpert was the lover of Sam Melville, responsible for some of the earliest radical dynamite bombings, for which he was caught in 1969 and sentenced to Attica prison, where he died in the uprising of 1971.) Cathy Wilkerson also partly takes this view: "That was the real problem: all these macho guys with their macho posturing." And then there is the view first set out by the Weather Underground's "New Morning" communiqué, in which the Townhouse Collective's intended bombing was essentially a product of the damaged psychology of leaders Terry Robbins and John Jacobs.[2]

The unkindest hypothesis came early: the Weathermen were merely spoiled children. So wrote James Glassman in the *Atlantic* in December 1969, describing their Days of Rage riot in Chicago in October. The account of the Days of Rage in *Time* magazine was similar: children throwing a temper tantrum. Fifteen years later, Rothman and Lichter's study of the New Left dismissed Weatherman as young people "play-acting" at militance in an essentially permissive society.[3] Nicholas von Hoffman, then a columnist for the *Washington Post*, attributed the violence of the townhouse to the willfulness of the young and rich who resided there. The alleged elevated social status of the members of the

Townhouse Collective was also stressed by Mel Gussow in the *New York Times Magazine*, quoting a neighborhood graffito: "Too Much Money, Not Enough Brains." Thomas Powers's biography of Diana Oughton echoed the sentiment and called the Weathermen "children of the rich ... it was their class which ruled the country."[4] In 1979, Milton Viorst agreed, characterizing them as "the children of the upper classes"; in 2006, Matthew Carr, in his history of terrorism, claimed that the leaders mostly came "from well-connected white families"; in 2013 the political scientist Luca Falciola described them as mostly "affluent"; in 2015 the historian Harvey Klehr described them as "children of privilege."[5] A high point of sorts here was reached when the *Seattle Times* inaccurately identified Weatherman leader Jim Mellen as Jim Mellon, heir to the Mellon banking fortune.[6]

Many find this view of Weatherman comforting. Those on the Right use it to dismiss Weatherman's politics as merely the actions of spoiled children; those on the Left use it to avoid grappling with the extreme Marxist-Leninist politics that was the driving force behind Weatherman's worldview.[7]

But the "rich kids at play" analysis—or "rich kids throwing a tantrum"—is mostly wrong. For one thing, detonating large-scale dynamite bombs can hardly be called "play-acting." But more important are the financial demographics. It is true that some Weatherman came from wealthy families, but this wasn't typical. Bill Ayers's family was wealthy; the families of Diana Oughton, Cathy Wilkerson, and Kathy Boudin had significant money (though not on Ayers's scale), as did the family of John Jacobs.[8] The townhouse itself was an elegant home filled with antiques, in a fashionable New York City neighborhood. But it was not large, and Wilkerson and her comrades were there only temporarily. It belonged to her father, from whom she was estranged (her parents were divorced), and he was reluctantly letting her use it for a few days only, and only on condition that she not bring her scruffy friends. That is, the townhouse as the site of the explosion was accidental, not typical; Weathermen usually lived in poverty-stricken neighborhoods. Neither Terry Robbins nor Ted Gold, who died with Diana Oughton in the townhouse, came from wealth: Gold was middle class; Robbins's father worked in a garment factory.[9]

Other major Weatherman figures were at best only middle class in origin. Jim Mellen's father was an alcoholic who abandoned the family; his mother worked as a soda-fountain clerk. Jeff Jones grew up in a modest tract house in Sylmar, a downscale part of the San Fernando Valley. Naomi Jaffe grew up on a communist chicken farm in the Catskills.[10] Howard Machtinger came from modest circumstances; Mike Justesen was raised in poverty by a single mother; Judy Clark's father was blacklisted and unemployed for many years.[11] Judy Cohen's father described himself as "a hard-hat working man"; her parents lived in a tiny apartment in New Jersey. Russell Neufeld's family was middle class and had to mortgage its home to pay his legal expenses when he was indicted on federal charges. Bernardine Dohrn's father owned an appliance store in White Fish Bay, Wisconsin.[12] Many other examples of middle-class origins could be cited. With Weatherman we are not dealing with the spoiled children of the rich.[13]

Citing the alleged upper-class origins of many Weathermen dodges the need to take their politics seriously. Ideology is not the whole story, but Weatherman's violence is not the whole story either. Former Weathermen such as Mark Rudd and Jonathan Lerner rightly stress the malign and growing influence of Marxist-Leninist theory—and of the alleged historical successes of that theory of revolution—on the Weather people groping for a more systematic strategy to advance their cause. That is: the history of Weatherman is not merely part of the history of terrorism; it is also part of the history of ideas. It is part of the history of left-wing ideology and the theory of the vanguard party.

It's important to recognize that the New Left, the seedbed of Weatherman, was begun in recognition of the exhaustion and enfeeblement of the Old Left orthodoxies, including Marxism-Leninism. By the early 1960s, it was increasingly obvious, as made clear in the Port Huron Statement—the founding document of SDS—that the world was adrift on a sea of social, economic, and cultural changes. The old contest of classes—oppressed industrial workers versus capitalist exploiters—that had captured Marx's imagination in the nineteenth century no longer served fully to explain the upheavals of the twentieth. Modern industrial society had created institutions and forms of mass politics and culture—and, equally important, vastly increased levels of consumer production —that called for fresh thinking. Traditional strategies of reform were obsolete. For the young authors of Port Huron in 1962, the archaic doctrines of past radicalism, including Marxism-Leninism, helped neither to interpret the world nor to change it. As for the USSR, it was just another stodgy, oppressive, and bureaucratic state structure, not the dream of socialism. Yet in the late 1960s, SDS and its Weatherman outgrowth did become part of a worldwide movement among young people seeking a vehicle for change in a fundamentally socialist direction; this was why the example of Castro's revolution seemed so promising. Castro, after all, had been denounced by the traditional Cuban communist party as a reckless "adventurer," a petty bourgeois "putschist." Mao Tse-tung, for his part, had sided with the peasantry and then, during the Cultural Revolution that began in 1966, seemed to regard young students as the spear of perpetual revolution, capable of unseating authority and unmasking corruption. Students (and young people more gen-erally) appeared to embody a kind of revolutionary zeal and ideal-ism that seemed synonymous with their very youth.

Perhaps a new kind of Marxist-Leninism could be invented. After all, the traditional working class, hostage now to relatively well-paying factory jobs, seemed hopelessly addicted to consumer-ism and, at least in the United States, irredeemably racist as well. Regis Debray, a young French intellectual who had befriended Fidel Castro in the early 1960s, became one of the leading propo-nents of a new kind of Marxist-Leninist analysis. His book *Revolution in the Revolution?*, translated into English in 1967, tried to tease out general lessons from the Cuban example, where a small group of militarized and daring revolutionaries had over-turned the system via direct attacks on the police and the army, without strenuous politicking with the working class. Debray's ideas proved to be enormously influential among aspiring revolu-tionaries all over the world, including Weatherman. They took in-spiration from Debray's tale of successful exemplary violence enacted by a handful of committed revolutionaries, and the idea that oppression was, at heart, psychological, and thus could be overturned by sheer revolutionary action and will. Frantz Fanon, the Caribbean psychologist, was influential with young leftists as well: he ennobled violence as a necessary purgative required for the oppressed to rid themselves of the impotence and *psychological* suffocation imposed by their oppressors. As Mao had put it in another context, under certain conditions only a spark was needed to set off a prairie fire.[14]

To the SDS leader Carl Oglesby, writing in 1969, the seriousness of Weatherman's version of Marxism-Leninism was clear, and he feared where that seriousness would take things. Much later, a former Weather leader would also stress the power of ideas within the group: "We were intellectuals ... people who lived on ideas." When someone who had been in the Washington, D.C., office of SDS with Cathy Wilkerson in 1968–1969 was asked what Wilkerson was like at that time, he answered, "Oh—she was a total Marxist-Leninist. Mike Spiegel too. That was the language they spoke."[15]

SDS began in 1962 as a youth wing of the League for Industrial Democracy. The LID was founded at the beginning of the twentieth century by such luminaries as Jack London and Upton Sinclair; it was socialist but (by the 1920s) anticommunist.[16] SDS originally had a commitment to nonviolent socialist reform, as well as to what the Port Huron Statement called "participatory democracy"—an ideal its members sought to realize in marathon meetings where wide consensus was sought before any action was taken.

The Port Huron Statement forbade the participation of anyone believing in a totalitarian creed—that is, anyone who was a member of the Communist Party U.S.A. But the anticommunist plank had been approved only after a fierce battle led by Michael Harrington against younger SDS figures. Later, the younger leaders prevailed when the prohibition against antidemocrats (communists) was abolished by a vote at the national convention in spring 1965. That autumn, SDS also broke with the LID, which had provided much of its funding, primarily over LID's support of the Vietnam War. Many in SDS, seeking the widest alliance against the war, saw no reason to spurn outright communists in that effort. Their willingness to countenance such cooperation was a major element in the break with their old patron.[17]

SDS in its early years, despite a fuzzy democratic socialist inclination, possessed no systematic ideology. Important in only a few universities, it reached out from campus to the poor and especially to black people. This was not just compassion: to reform society in a socialist direction, SDS knew it needed a larger and more powerful social lever than students. Thus SDS founded the Economic Research and Action Project (ERAP) to organize the poor in various cities, including Newark and Cleveland. SDS also always had a special interest in working-class youth.[18]

While individual SDS members had participated in the civil rights struggles in the South in 1962–1964, the organization as such was not much involved. And ERAP, despite much hard work, would fail either to alleviate conditions in urban neighborhoods or to create a large wave of support among the poor for the students. It was the Vietnam War that propelled SDS's spectacular growth in membership and influence between 1965 and 1968. The organization had always opposed what it viewed as imperial Cold War American foreign policies (for instance, against Castro's Cuba); now Vietnam became its focus, and SDS led countless teach-ins, antiwar demonstrations and antidraft efforts across the country. By the autumn of 1968 it had three hundred campus chapters nationwide and at least eighty thousand members.[19]

The stunning growth in the size and influence of SDS coincided with the rise of an increasingly fierce critique of capitalism. The group's leaders especially sought to locate the Cold War policies of the United States in an economic imperative for which a traditional Marxist analysis was congenial. The idea spread that the ills of American society—intractable racism, the deepening war in Vietnam, the 1965 invasion of the Dominican Republic—were expressions of a single social-economic structure and that structure had a name: capitalism. The continuation of the Vietnam War despite mounting casualties, ever more massive but nonviolent demonstrations, increased international isolation, and, after the shock of the Tet offensive in February 1968, a realization that military victory was impossible—all this, it was widely felt, could not be merely the result of pride or of governmental blunder or incompetence or of bureaucratic rivalry among establishment apparatchiks. No, the war in Indochina, like the persistent stain of racism, had to be the product of larger forces, the consequence of a system whose rapacious behavior had to be rooted in some more compelling if elusive logic.[20] By 1967, many leaders were declaring overtly that the problem was U.S. capitalism and imperialism. Many people had begun to turn for insight to such independent Marxist journals as Paul Sweezy's and Paul Baran's *Monthly Review*, or their book, *Monopoly Capital*—where, according to Jeffrey Herf, "a world of hidden motives stood revealed."[21] In this view, Vietnam was the logical result of U.S. capitalism's need to exploit the resources of the third world. And the cause of black poverty and white racism also lay in the capitalist exploitation of labor; blacks were an American "internal colony" from which capitalism extracted wealth—employing a racist ideology to justify it. Social evil flowed from economic facts. And if black Americans were inhabitants of an unacknowledged internal colony, then perhaps their liberation would depend, like the anticolonial struggles of their brothers and sisters in the third world, on a movement, perhaps a war, of national liberation.[22]

The growing agony over the Vietnam War increasingly gave those in SDS who advocated militant action an opportunity to urge others to move from protest to resistance. The moral high ground seemed to be legitimately occupied by those who asked others for greater sacrifices and a willingness to contemplate ever more radical steps in a movement aiming at ever more profound change. SDS President Greg Calvert also pointed for inspiration to the insurrections in the black ghettos in summer 1967, especially Newark and Detroit. The idea took hold among a number of disenchanted and increasingly impatient leaders that the powers that be, embedded in a logically coherent system of avarice and inequity, rooted in racism and an unjust international economic order, were simply not susceptible to partial or peaceful change.[23] Autumn 1967 saw the first largely white-radical street-fighting against police, especially during the "Stop the Draft Week" in Oakland in October, and in New York City to protest Secretary of State Dean Rusk in November. While SDS was not a major organizer or participant in the Oakland protest, the demonstration having been mounted by other longtime Bay Area radicals, the organization was deeply involved in the New York protest. Later, the first issue of the Weatherman newspaper *Fire!* in November 1969 commemorated the Oakland action, citing it as an inspiring precursor to Weatherman's October 1969 Days of Rage demonstrations.[24]

Another factor in SDS's radicalization was the arrival of a younger generation of leaders, many from the Midwest. SDS had originally intended to fight poverty, but soon most members found themselves consumed by the escalating war in Vietnam. The violence of the war, the pressure of the draft on young men, the seemingly immovability of the government, all produced in "the Prairie Power" generation—including some of the people who would lead Weatherman—a conviction that ever-more militant action might be the only effective approach to an otherwise obdurate government.[25]

Finally, a critical factor in SDS's gradual radicalization was the role played by the Progressive Labor Party. PL believed in world revolution and had broken with the Communist Party U.S.A. because it lacked revolutionary zeal and supported the Soviet Union instead of China, which PL regarded as the embodiment of a genuinely revolutionary state. PL members began to infiltrate SDS in the mid-1960s, aiming to take it over. PL showed the power of a disciplined cadre to act as a unified phalanx capable of successfully battling for control over local chapters. Their disorganized opponents, by contrast, were often unable to resist PL's tactics, even though they were often in the majority. The advantages of centralized and highly disciplined organization seemed to trump "participatory democracy." Perhaps the old Bolsheviks had had it right after all, both with respect to their general Marxist outlook and to their devotion to notions of a vanguard party—what would be called Leninism. Revolution could be brought about by the concerted action of a disciplined elite, a vanguard party of intellectuals. The first quotation from Lenin appeared in the SDS newspaper *New Left Notes* in May 1967.[26]

PL provoked an intense debate within SDS over who would make the revolution. Students alone, however enlightened, didn't seem sufficient. Could the white working class be won over? Could an alliance be fashioned with African Americans? Could a strategy of what PL termed "long-term base-building" among the working class be pursued instead of the immediate revolutionary action (whatever that meant) advocated by others eager to hasten change?

PL pushed a traditional Marxism, focused on industrial workers as the engine of revolution, and they viewed blacks merely as an intensely exploited part of the working class. But Lenin in *Imperialism* (1920) had already expressed suspicion that industrial workers might be "bought off" by the material benefits of capitalist empire. A pessimistic view of the working class was also expressed in C. Wright Mill's 1961 essay "Letter to the New Left," and in Herbert Marcuse's influential *One Dimensional Man* (1964)—works widely read within SDS. Besides, everyone knew that despite years of effort, PL had failed to gain many working-class recruits.[27] All the old assumptions seemed up for grabs even as militants groped for a strategy of organizing and tactics of change that might be up to the challenge of upending the old order.

The debates intensified in the latter half of 1967; distinctions were sliced and diced, old texts were dusted off, quotations from this authority and that authority were hurled at each other, dialogue was hostage to rhetoric, nuance leached out of the conversation, and the language became ever more strident and shrill. Invective became a hallmark of radical intensity. The stakes seemed ever higher and people found themselves "gut-checked" (asked to go farther and farther) at every turn. The Tet offensive in February 1968 led to President Johnson announcing in March that he would not stand for reelection, and suggested that the imperial power of the United States could be defeated.[28] On the other hand, the assassinations of Dr. Martin Luther King in April and of Robert F. Kennedy in June, and the nomination of Johnson's pro-war Vice President Hubert Humphrey at the Democratic National Convention in Chicago in August—while thousands of protestors were brutalized by police outside the convention hall—appeared simultaneously to show that pathways to peaceful change in the United States were being blocked. Yet at the same time, some in the more radical wing of SDS were thrilled at the massive riots in the ghettos, including the one in Chicago that followed Dr. King's assassination; these uprisings suggested a revolution in the United States was really possible.[29]

SDS had at first disdained going to the Chicago Democratic Convention as a waste of time, but the leadership changed its mind and, in the event, many SDS activists did go. They were prominent

in the demonstrations that week—and were both angered at the escalating police violence and increasingly enthralled at the possibility of responding in kind. Bill Ayers, a Chicagoan by birth, was
naturally there in the demonstrations, as were his girlfriend Diana
Oughton and his best friend Terry Robbins—who, Ayers says,
already wanted to unleash violence against the police who were
protecting a corrupt system. Jeff Jones was there, and so was Cathy
Wilkerson. John Jacobs was there, as was Susan Stern, the later
Weatherman memoirist. If Chicago in August 1968 seemed to
prove that America's establishment would not be reformed, indeed
would resist change tooth and nail—if the movement had reached
the outer limits of what young people could politically accomplish
relatively peacefully—then by autumn 1968 the answer for some
had to be—and could be—all-out revolution. That was Bernardine
Dohrn's view.[30] Her view was shared by others. By late 1968 a vanguard party—or, if not exactly a traditional party of the Left, then a
militarized, unsentimental and highly disciplined group (on the
model of Regis Debray's version of the Castro revolution)—
was now seen by a minority of leaders in SDS as the only type of
organization that could threaten the powers that be while simultaneously aiding and abetting efforts elsewhere in the world to
challenge and defeat the American imperium. In short—revolution.

The only question was who, exactly, would constitute the vanguard party. Would it be PL or some other group? The presence of
charismatic personalities—Dohrn, Ayers, Mark Rudd—would
count strongly in creating the Weatherman group in the circles in
SDS that disliked PL.[31] But beyond charisma, the ideological clash
with Progressive Labor over where the impetus for revolution
might be found was a crucial factor in the theoretical clash that
would divide SDS. From this remove, decades later, the debate
may strike some as delusionary; but at the time it was argued with
zeal and the utmost seriousness. The stakes struck all parties to the
dispute as enormously high.

Three groups of SDS radicals eventually came together in winter
1968–1969 to form the main opposition to Progressive Labor. One
was based in Chicago; one originated in New York; and one was
centered at the University of Michigan.

The Chicago group included Noel Ignatin (real name Ignatiev), who would later earn a Ph.D. in history from Harvard, and Howard Machtinger, then an M.A. student in sociology at the University of Chicago. In influential articles in *New Left Notes* in 1968, Ignatin and Michael Klonsky argued that the white working class would never be the agent of major social change in the United States because it had been bought off by the capitalists, and because of its acceptance of what they called (a new term then) "white skin privilege." Since students were insufficient to bring about a revolution, and since the traditional industrial working class was hopeless, Klonsky in particular suggested that support might come from the working-class young, who he assumed were not yet corrupted by the economic and moral compromises of their elders. Hence the title of his essay: "Towards a Revolutionary Youth Movement."[32] This wasn't a new idea. It can already be found in the urban ERAP projects of 1963–1965. SDS leader Rennie Davis had observed in 1965 that the high school dropouts he knew "are a potential revolutionary force. . . . The force that is least afraid of the police."[33]

The New York group was led by Mark Rudd and John Jacobs. Their commitment to action was not in doubt, as their takeover of buildings at Columbia University in 1968 had shown. But both Rudd and Jacobs were keen to yoke practice to theory, and Rudd acknowledges the growing influence of Marxist-Leninist thought. Jacobs, too, was searching for a way to provide "a powerful anti-imperialist theoretical framework." Also influential was David Gilbert, who was a member of the Columbia group. In 1967, he had cowritten a theoretical essay, "The Port Authority Statement" which had urged SDS to seek the mass necessary for revolution not in the (hopeless) industrial working class but rather in "the new working class," which in the conditions of advanced industrial society was made up of white-collar, technology, and intellectual workers.[34] This view, although rooted in a materialist analysis, had little in common with traditional Marxism, which insisted on the primacy of blue-collar workers. The sentiments had more to do with Marcuse's insights than with Marx's prescriptions. It was the suffocating complacency of the "one-dimensional" society that cried out to be disrupted. It seemed clear that Marx's "proletariat" wasn't up to the job. A new engine of change was needed. But where was it?

The Michigan group was notorious for its extreme conduct. Led by Bill Ayers and Terry Robbins, the group has been accused of being "actionists" and anarchists, not Marxist-Leninists.[35] Ayers was boyishly handsome and charismatic, and he certainly favored action: he had led one of the first antidraft sit-ins, in 1965. Robbins was by any measure a zealot, and so was Ayers's girlfriend Diana Oughton.[36] But the third leader was Jim Mellen, at age thirty-one older than the others, and well versed in Marxist theory. Mellen had spent two years in Tanzania in the mid-1960s, and his experience there with African revolutionaries had led him to conclude that the world revolution would begin with the third-world peasantry, as in China and Vietnam. He had a doctorate in political science from the University of Iowa, his dissertation had become a book published by University of Iowa Press, and he had taught at Drew University.[37] In April 1969, Mellen and Ayers cowrote an essay in *New Left Notes* explaining how the required revolutionary mass necessary to topple the American empire might come from a combination of black people, youthful proletarians, and the international peasantry.

Bernardine Dohrn soon joined this group. She was a graduate of the University of Chicago Law School and a veteran antiwar activist whose first article for SDS was one of the first feminist articles to appear in *New Left Notes* (March 1968). While Dohrn certainly favored action as opposed to "base-building," she was by no means allergic to theory, and soon she cowrote an essay that followed the David Gilbert line, urging SDS to focus on "the new working class" as the best agent of social change.[38] She has been described as magnetic, sexually provocative, and a spellbinding speaker.[39] But she was also a trained lawyer and could hold her own in long political debates with Carl Oglesby, who was almost ten years older than she and a past president of SDS.[40] At the June 1968 SDS National Convention her blunt declaration "I consider myself a revolutionary communist" catapulted her to election as interorganizational secretary. This post was one of three positions that now ran the SDS National Office (the presidency having been abolished). Mike Klonsky was elected national secretary. Together, they would form the nucleus of "the National Office" faction.[41]

In the December 1968 SDS quarterly meeting, with Nixon having been elected president, Klonsky successfully pushed the views in "Towards a Revolutionary Youth Movement" as formal SDS policy, despite fierce Progressive Labor opposition. He had the support of Mellen, Oughton, Ayers, and Robbins. The National Office faction now began to call themselves the Revolutionary Youth Movement. By this time they had embraced—as had PL— the essential precepts of Leninism as the best form of vanguard leadership needed to provoke revolution. Thus the leaders would lay down the "correct line" after discussion among themselves, and others were to follow it. "Participatory democracy" was to be re- placed by the Bolshevik notion of "democratic centralism," as a necessary requirement to maintain discipline among the rank and file, a feature thought to be crucial to making a revolution.[42]

All sides to the sectarian struggle that gripped SDS that winter felt that it was dreadfully important to get the theoretical analysis right. Since the non-PL groups believed that the U.S. working class was hopeless, they had to find another social lever; otherwise revolution was *theoretically* impossible, a conclusion few wanted to face. If the situation was truly that dire, then for many radicals the only option was total withdrawal from American society, a fleeing to rural hippie communes. In 1968–1969, this flooding into the countryside and communes was in fact beginning to happen.[43]

On the eve of SDS's national convention, to be held in Chicago in June 1969, the Revolutionary Youth Movement issued a ten thou- sand–word manifesto, "You Don't Need a Weatherman to Know Which Way the Wind Blows." Dense with Marxist jargon, it ran six full pages in small type in the SDS newspaper *New Left Notes*—the longest article the newspaper had ever run. The document had eleven authors, including Ayers, Dohrn, Jacobs, Jones, Machtinger, Mellen, Robbins, and Rudd.[44] But the title came from a Bob Dylan song, "Subterranean Homesick Blues," and implied an acceptance of the countercultural ideas which, like Marxism, were sweeping through SDS—long hair, rock 'n' roll (replacing folk music), freewheeling sex and the recreational use of drugs such as marijuana. The title of the manifesto was thus another slap at the straitlaced cadre of Progressive Labor, which believed that countercultural behavior alienated the working class. PL favored short hair and conservative dress.[45]

The argument of the Weatherman Manifesto came in several parts. (a) A worldwide revolution was under way against capitalist imperialism, led especially by the Vietnamese peasants: this was the way the wind was blowing. Anything American radicals did would thus be part of this worldwide rebellion, so they did not need immediate mass support inside the United States to start a revolution. (b) Within the United States, the black national liberation struggle was pointing toward a massive uprising, and white radicals had a moral obligation to support it—with deeds, and not just words. (c) Working-class white youth would also have a special role and could be radicalized because they had not yet succumbed to the racist blandishments of the prevailing order, as had their parents, but (d) the white working class in general was hopeless, bought off by a combination of materialism and racism. (e) The task was to open an American front in an anti-imperial war: this meant armed struggle, a Red Army; (f) to lead this new Red Army, a vanguard group was needed—clandestine, centrally controlled, and trained in military tactics—as opposed to the current loose and aboveground organization of SDS.[46]

The showdown between the National Office or Revolutionary Youth Movement and Progressive Labor came at the SDS convention held in the Chicago Coliseum on June 16–18, 1969. Weatherman had allies in Mike Klonsky's "Revolutionary Youth Movement II," which differed slightly from the RYM in ideology, but which was also bitterly opposed to PL.[47] The convention quickly disintegrated: claques began shouting at each other, chanting competing rhythmic slogans of "Ho-Ho-Ho-Chi-Minh" (from the group that would become Weatherman) versus "Mao-Mao-Mao-Tse-tung" (from PL); meanwhile, a number of Black Panthers appeared, and their misogynist remarks from the podium caused pandemonium. Yet amid all this chaos, the theory of revolution in the Weatherman Manifesto was vigorously debated. Howard Machtinger, at the racism panel, laid out the reasons why the black nationalist movement should be seen not as antiworker (as PL did see it) but as a crucial part of the revolution.[48]

On the second evening, Bernardine Dohrn led a walkout of supporters from the hall, while the PL stalwarts shouted at them to stay and argue. Dohrn and her faction then met separately and declared themselves the real SDS. That night they seized the national offices, including the bank accounts and the expensive printing press, and the next day they announced the expulsion of PL from SDS. Then they elected new national officers: Bernardine Dohrn, Jeff Jones, and Bill Ayers.[49]

But there is another part of story, which until now was unknown. Dohrn's faction was backed by the FBI.

In the 1960s, the FBI's secret counterintelligence program (COINTELPRO) targeted both far right and far left extremists and sought to create or exacerbate rivalries and divisions in these groups. The program was large-scale: in 1978 the intelligence services claimed that one out of six participants in the Chicago Democratic Convention demonstrations in August 1968 had been an informant.[50] The FBI had engaged in surveillance of SDS from early on, and as SDS grew in numbers and became more radical, government surveillance intensified. By early 1969 there were FBI wiretaps and hidden microphones in SDS headquarters in Chicago; further, in February, William Sullivan, the head of the FBI Domestic Intelligence Division, told his superiors that the FBI had about 120 informants within SDS and other New Left groups.[51]

According to a retrospective in August 1969 from the special agent in charge in Cleveland, FBI headquarters that spring told all fifty-nine field offices to order their local SDS informants to attend the Chicago SDS convention in June—not merely to observe but, as delegates, to vote. And they were ordered to support one group, and one group alone: "All informants were instructed to support the National Office faction during convention proceedings." The reasoning behind this move was explicitly given: "Bureau informants [should] support the National Office faction in SDS against the PLP faction on grounds that PLP control of SDS would transform a shapeless and fractionalized group into a militant and disciplined organization." It appears that the FBI was worried that if Progressive Labor gained control of SDS, the result would be a mirror of PL itself, disciplined and militant—a transformed organization that would prove a more dangerous threat to national stability than SDS already was in its current configuration. The lesser evil, therefore, was to support PL's major opponents, as a way both of dividing SDS and isolating its most dangerous elements (that is, PL). Thus the FBI ordered its informants to support the National Office group at the convention—in other words, to support the group which was emerging as Weatherman.[52]

We do not know exactly how many FBI informants turned up in the crowd in Chicago as supporters of the National Office in June (the number is blacked out in the August memo), but the FBI's detailed knowledge of what then happened suggests that many did. Nor do we know precisely how many FBI informants were among the six or seven hundred attendees who followed Bernardine Dohrn out of the convention hall on June 17 to form "the real SDS." It is reasonable, however, to assume that dozens, acting under their FBI orders, did.[53]

On August 1, 1969, the FBI assessed the impact of their skullduggery:

> The precise effect of support rendered by these sources to the NO [National Office] cause cannot, of course, be determined. As the Bureau is well aware, however, the convention did result in a split of the SDS with the result that PLP was required to form its own "rump" organization; the SDS as the mainstay of the New Left Movement is now seriously divided and, to this extent, weakened; and the National Office faction is gradually being forced into a position of militant extremism which hopefully will isolate it from other elements.[54]

The FBI here takes significant credit for helping to break apart SDS—and for a situation now "forcing" the National Office faction (Weatherman) towards extremism—and hence, possibly, isolation. There is an obvious element of boasting in the memo, and we should not take it to mean either that the FBI created Weatherman, or that the FBI operation at Chicago was essential to the splitting of SDS. The Weatherman faction was being pushed toward increased militancy by the logic of its own ideology, as well as by other radicals,[55] and SDS also had been severely split between PL and the anti-PL factions for at least year and a half. A major clash at Chicago was bound to occur. Nevertheless, the FBI, to the extent that it could, attempted to steer SDS toward Weatherman—which the FBI saw, initially, as less dangerous than PL. This was the first FBI misjudgment of Weatherman; it would not be the last.[56]

After the June convention, Weatherman as SDS continued to proclaim a Marxist revolutionary message. *New Left Notes*—which they now controlled—published articles on typical Marxist topics, written in turgid Marxist language. It is simply not true that theorizing disappeared, replaced completely by "fascination with force and violence."[57]

To be sure, the Weathermen pushed the virtue of immediate action.[58] The Weathermen believed that just as the Vietnamese were winning their war against American imperialism—as Nixon's plans for American withdrawal showed—so too were oppressed people all over the world successfully rising up against the American empire. The imperialist system was crumbling. Thus the Left should not give in to "defeatism" on the question of revolution. American capitalist society and institutions might well seem on the surface to be unalterably strong, but radicals should not worry.[59] And if capitalist-imperialist America was already essentially defeated, then all it would take was a good sharp shove to push over the entire tottering edifice and send it crashing to the ground. It is not the case, as some critics have claimed, that the Weathermen knew that attempting revolution was suicidal but—moved by despair—they did not care. As Bernardine Dohrn said in August 1969, "The collapse of the United States government is upon us."[60]

Outsiders mistakenly thought this was action at the expense of theory. Special Agent Robert Glendon of the Chicago FBI field office wrote in November 1969 that Weatherman disdained discussion of theory and believed that action by guerrilla bands would be enough to bring the masses over to their side. He concluded that for Weatherman, "ideology is not important."[61]

Weathermen certainly did not want to spend all their time discussing Marxist-Leninist dialectics. But this does not mean they acted without an ideological framework. This was provided especially by Regis Debray—pupil of the Marxist philosopher Louis Althusser and friend of Che Guevara—in his book *Revolution in the*

Revolution? According to Debray, the Cuban revolution showed that you did not need the backing of a mass party to make a revolution. Under the right conditions, dramatic actions by small bands of committed revolutionaries could precipitate the revolution, bringing over the otherwise immobile masses. Debray's theory of revolution helped Weatherman believe revolution was possible— and led to a commitment to violence. There was no need to wait for the right conditions to present themselves; in fact, it was counterrevolutionary to wait.[62] After all, hadn't Che Guevara himself proclaimed that "the duty of every revolutionary is to make the revolution"? Debray's extreme vanguard-partyism was the basis of the pamphlet handed out at the last meeting of Weatherman as SDS—at the Flint, Michigan, "War Council" in December 1969: worldwide revolutionary war was under way, the authors insisted, and it was reactionary to wait while trying to educate the masses; making war on the state would in itself raise revolutionary consciousness and in itself create proper revolutionary conditions.[63]

"I feel like part of a vanguard," wrote Diana Oughton. Jim Mellen said: "We [Weathermen] figured ourselves a small leadership group of a mass movement which could have a critical role in the development of the history of imperialism: that is very heavy stuff." At the meeting in September 1969 to plan the demonstration at Fort Dix, Weatherman had claimed the right, as the vanguard formation of the revolution, to run the demonstration. The same vanguard-party claim was made in Chicago in October 1969, during Weatherman's Days of Rage riots.

As one Weatherman leader later said: "I want it to be on record that we at least had a theory, or believed we had a theory."[64] In fact, in December 1969 Weatherman leaders explicitly *attacked* the sort of "actionist" attitude that their critics have often ascribed to them; they criticized radical people who found "getting into nonstrategic terrorist activity . . . a way of *doing something*." Weatherman did *not* believe in just "doing something." They were intellectuals. They stressed that you had to have a theory. Debray provided it.[65]

And they believed they had the historical precedents to back up the theory. First there was the example of the insurrection at Columbia University in spring 1968. There the "Action Faction" of SDS (comprising only twenty or thirty people), in conjunction with black student radicals, had managed to mobilize hundreds of students to seize and hold half the university for a week, over issues of racism and the Vietnam War. Other student leaders (including some in SDS) had wished to negotiate with the Columbia administration, but the militants seized buildings anyway and held them, red flags flying. When the administration finally struck back and police attacked the occupiers—resulting in dozens of injuries and hundreds of arrests—the brutal conduct of the police in turn radicalized a great part of the Columbia student body.[66]

The Action Faction counted it a great success: not because of the reforms offered afterward by a chastened university administration, but because it showed how few activists were needed to embolden a mass of students. Thus did a theory of the revolutionary potential of a vanguard party take root. And because Columbia was located in New York City, the media capital of the world, the boldness of the Action Faction had brought SDS huge publicity: revolution by theater.[67] If this could be replicated on a much larger stage, one might jump-start a real revolution. Later Weatherman leaders Mark Rudd, John Jacobs, Ted Gold, and David Gilbert had all been leaders in the Columbia events.[68]

An even more crucial historical example, precisely because of its larger scale, was the Cuban revolution as Debray had depicted it. He emphasized the ideological power of action itself. Fidel Castro had started with only a handful of men. Victory had been won not through mass organization or demonstrations but via a small band of military revolutionaries who launched physical attacks upon the agents of the Batista regime, undermining the prestige of soldiers and policemen—on which the regime's power ultimately depended. According to Debray, "This prestige constitutes the principal form of oppression. . . . It immobilizes the discontented." Debray argued that dramatic action against the state was the key to mobilizing popular support: "The public execution of a police torturer is more effective propaganda than a hundred speeches. . . . During two years of warfare, Fidel did not hold a single political rally." The population's assumption that the police and the army were unassailable could be undermined only by killing soldiers and policemen: "Strike one—educate a hundred." Thus a small clandestine and ruthless military force—originally separate from the populace—could ultimately win: Castro had shown the way. This was the so-called *foco* theory. The Spanish *foco* means "nucleus": a small guerrilla band, if committed enough, could—through violence against the state ("the propaganda of the deed")—eventually become the nucleus of a large people's army.[69] Ultimately, after just two years of guerrilla warfare, the Batista regime collapsed. Castro's rebel army of three thousand armed men had defeated a government that fielded a vastly superior military force of eighty thousand troops. What Debray failed to mention were the years of resistance and political organizing that had taken place in Cuba's cities. He ignored the significant role played by the urban resistance, composed mostly of middle-class moderates. Instead, he swallowed hook, line, and sinker Castro's view of his own path to success, which tended not to recognize the diversity and contribution of other actors in the effort to overthrow Batista.[70]

Debrayism was in fact an old idea, at least as old as Danton's call for "Audacity, more audacity, always audacity." The radical notion of the "propaganda of the deed" marked the nineteenth century, and Joseph Conrad had made it a centerpiece of *The Secret Agent*, his novel about the secret world of revolutionary terrorism. Lenin had well understood the necessity of exemplary action when leading his Bolsheviks. Mao, too, had echoed it in his slogan "Dare to struggle, dare to win." Notions of bending history to one's will, of never underestimating the subjective factor over so-called objective conditions, were now given the dignity of theory. Other leftists besides Weatherman found this new "third world" type of Marxism-Leninism attractive. In fact, even the FBI directorate fell under its spell, believing in this period that small groups of radicals could mobilize large numbers of people via catalytic action, and—like Weatherman—they too thought that the Columbia seizure showed this. (Of course, to the FBI it was a warning, not an inspiration.) In 1971 FBI Assistant Director Edward Miller, attending an FBI-sponsored conference in Washington, presented a scenario of Weatherman revolution that began with attacks on police by small groups; this strategy, he said, came from third-world revolutionaries and their theorists. He meant Debray. Debrayist ideas even found their way into the Nixon White House. Tom Charles Huston, who was personally close to Nixon and an important

White House aide, was convinced that small groups of highly dedicated radicals could mobilize mass support via dramatic and violent actions: "That was the way governments have historically been overthrown in the 20th century."[71]

Another example of a successful ideology of action came from the Tupamaros in Uruguay. Castro's army had been based on the peasantry; but the Tupamaros were urban guerrillas; they showed what could be done in modern cities—cities like American cities. Their daring operations (including kidnappings and bank robberies) gained them fame in the radical Left. The October 2, 1969, edition of *New Left Notes* was devoted mostly to them—and included a long section from Debray's book. The Tupamaros' theory of action was extolled in the headline: "Live Like Them" The important lesson to be learned was that carrying out violence that violated "bourgeois legality" would in itself create revolutionary consciousness and then the proper conditions for the revolution itself.[72]

Weatherman found such ideas congenial. They were tired of protest. They wanted to prepare for war. And so they took the authorities by surprise when they conducted their Days of Rage in Chicago, October 8–11, 1969. The authorities thought the action was going to be simply another protest demonstration. Not so: Days of Rage was not a protest. It was intended as the opening salvo in a war—a war that had a basis in a theory.[73]

The editors of *New Left Notes* on August 23 declared that Weatherman was coming to Chicago for action, not "to register a complaint." The point was to show "the existence of a fighting force that's out—not primarily to make specific demands." It was thought that toughness, and violence against the authorities, were the ways to expand Weatherman's base of support—specifically by attracting working-class youth as a new mass base.[74]

While Weatherman saw no hope of immediate support from the white working class, its leaders thought this might eventually happen if, once a guerrilla war was set in motion, the American social and economic situation degenerated. The question, then, was how to instigate a crisis. They sought the soldiers they needed in working-class street youth: if their anger, alienation, and hostility to cops could be politicized, they would form a ready-made revolutionary army. Local white youth gangs had, perhaps surprisingly, been a presence in the demonstrations organized to protest the Vietnam War at the Democratic National Convention in Chicago in August 1968. It is important to realize that the Weathermen were not alone in their belief in the revolutionary potential of the disaffected proletarian young. It was shared, for instance, by many in the student movement in 1968–1969 in France.[75] (Modern-day jihadists too have found alienated working-class youth to constitute a significant pool of recruits.)

With these hopes, the Weathermen decided on a major "National Action" in October. Tireless attempts to recruit young working-class toughs went forward during the summer and early autumn of 1969. Weatherman staged events they hoped would attract street youth. For example, they carried Vietcong flags onto a beach in Detroit where lower-class youth gathered; this led to fistfights, but the Weathermen felt that by fighting they gained respect. Developing a *personal* willingness to fight in the streets also was a way for the middle-class students who largely made up Weatherman to show—to themselves first of all—that they were becoming hardened revolutionaries. Weathermen also invaded community colleges and high schools, disrupting classes and urging students to abandon study and join the revolution. These "jailbreak" actions garnered Weatherman as a group its first national headlines—but few recruits.[76]

In Chicago on September 24, at the start of the trial of the "Chicago Eight," the Weatherman group began its new level of struggle. When police tried to block their protest march, Weathermen attacked them. They did the same on September 27 in Detroit (one of the leaders was Diana Oughton). The police reacted savagely. Russell Neufeld recalled that on September 24 he saw Weatherman Danny Cohen beaten to a pulp in the basement of a police station—while a cop held a gun in Neufeld's mouth. There was a feeling that the war had already begun.[77]

Yet Weatherman's plans for Days of Rage violence were also opposed by many; representatives of the Vietnamese and Cubans advised the Weather leaders not to engage in violent actions. They were ignored. In July 1969 Weatherman leaders went to Havana to talk to representatives of the Cuban government and the

Provisional Revolutionary Government of South Vietnam (the Vietcong). The Havana meetings had been arranged by both sides, and—based on information from informants—the FBI alleged that the project even had a code name: "Operation Harry." The eventual public position of the Weatherman leaders was that the Cubans and the Vietnamese advocated violence and even guerrilla war, and this has recently been reasserted in Bryan Burrough's book.[78]

But the Cubans and Vietnamese had urged no such thing, as we now know from recently released FBI documents. Instead, they counseled the Weatherman leaders to do everything they could to reproduce the massive and aboveground antiwar demonstrations that had shaken the American administration in 1967. Bernardine Dohrn's own notes taken in Havana were seized by the FBI in a police raid on a Weatherman safe house in Chicago on April 14, 1970, and are now available to the public at the National Archives. They show that the Vietnamese urged massive aboveground demonstrations. Dohrn confirmed this in a 2006 interview with David Barber, and others who were there—Carl Davidson, Robert Burlingame, and Eleanor Raskin—say the same. So does Mark Rudd, who had other contacts with the Cubans, and regrets not having protested what was being said about the Cubans' position. Russell Neufeld, too, knew the truth; he had his own ties to the Vietnamese.[79]

Yet after John Jacobs and Bill Ayers met the returnees from Havana in Nova Scotia in late July, the story changed. It turned out that the Vietnamese and the Cubans urged Weatherman to violence against the American state. In *Fugitive Days*, Ayers blamed John Jacobs for the distortion, while he himself was an innocent bystander. But Eleanor Raskin blames both Jacobs and Ayers, and Ayers in "A Strategy to Win" in *New Left Notes*, September 12, 1969, depicts himself as haranguing the returnees from Havana on the necessity of the attack in Chicago.[80]

Those favoring violence apparently seized on the fact that Bernardine Dohrn admitted, under pressure from Ayers and Jacobs in Nova Scotia, that the Vietnamese at one point said: "When you go into a city, look for the person who fights the hardest against the cops. That's the person to talk to all night. ... Look for the one who fights." The phrase "Look for the one who fights" was end-lessly repeated that autumn by Weatherman leaders, as if it were a Vietnamese call to general violence. This was a distortion: the statement merely had to do with local tactics and recruitment. But Weather leaders chose to regard it as a clarion call to promote a vio-lent escalation not only of tactics but of strategy too. The title of the September 12 *New Left Notes* essay on Havana was "Bringing the War Home." The main message brought back from Havana was "*Kick ass.*" "Building a real fighting force" would both help to end the war in Vietnam and create a revolutionary movement in the United States.[81]

Given the public statements of the Weatherman leadership, it was natural for the *New York Times* to report that the Days of Rage came from Cuban and Vietnamese advice; and this, in turn, served to confirm Nixon's Chief of Staff H. R. Haldeman's belief in "for-eign control" of Weatherman. Some in the FBI itself believed this as well.[82] The truth lay elsewhere. In September, Weatherman leaders met with a Cuban diplomat in Riverside Park in New York City, a meeting arranged by Martin Kenner. The Cuban made it clear that Havana firmly disagreed with the plans for attacks on po-lice. Bernardine Dohrn denounced him as a counterrevolutionary.[83]

The FBI had an eavesdropping device inside the Cuban mis-sion to the United Nations, which was housed in a turn-of-the-century mansion off Fifth Avenue. According to an FBI report that has now become available, the Bureau learned that

> On August 20, 1969, Orlando Pereira, First Secretary, Cuban Mission to the UN, made the following comments:
> He and Jose Viera, Counselor, CMUN, had met with Mark Rudd and Jeff Jones the previous week in New York City. They encouraged Rudd and Jones to have SDS change the slogan for the fall demonstrations in Chicago from "Bring the War Home" to something more under-standable and acceptable, such as "US Take Occupation Troops Out of Vietnam." Pereira thought that Rudd and Jones were stunned by the criticism; however, they were receptive. Pereira believed they had probably gotten too caught up in their own rhetoric and in "Third World" global perspectives.

Pereira was wrong that Weathermen would now change their approach. Dohrn's charge that the Cubans were counterrevolutionaries was a declaration of independence; Weatherman would not be folded into the Cuban camp—or any camp.[84]

Pereira was correct about one thing, though: because of their "'Third World' global perspectives," the Weatherman leaders felt no need to establish a mass base in the United States; they saw themselves as part of the planetwide revolution. The Weatherman Manifesto of June 1969 had set out this "global" perspective, and Ayers repeated it in "A Strategy to Win" in September—saying it explained why Weatherman could not be accused of "adventurism" in its tactics.

Thus the Weatherman cadre was told that the Vietnamese and Cubans supported militant tactics and revolutionary action. *New Left Notes* editor Jonathan Lerner was under that impression: "That is what our own leaders said." FBI informant Larry Grathwohl testified in 1980 that he had been told that the Vietnamese and Cubans wanted street-fighting and guerrilla war. Thomas Power, in his biography of Diana Oughton, asserted this too.[85] In 1997 Ron Jacobs—in the first book-length history of Weatherman—still believed it. It was only in 2001 that Bill Ayers revealed the reversal of position which had been forced upon the returnees from Havana. And later he pulled back.[86]

It was not only the Cubans and Vietnamese who objected to the planned Days of Rage; so did the local Black Panthers. To be sure, Eldridge Cleaver from his exile in Algeria supported the plan—and so did Huey Newton in California. But Fred Hampton, the Panther leader in Chicago itself, opposed the intensification of violence:

> We believe [it's] anarchistic, opportunistic, individualistic, chauvinistic, Custeristic. . . . It's Custeristic, in that its leaders take people into situations where the people can be massacred, and they call it revolution. . . . We think these people may be sincere but they're misguided, they're muddleheads and they're scatterbrains.

Hampton advised Weatherman to adopt aboveground organizing and large demonstrations as the best way to go forward.[87]

Hampton's position led Weatherman leaders to condemn the Panthers themselves as "revisionists," a traditional term of Marxist abuse. Earlier, in July 1969, Weatherman had already rejected as insufficiently revolutionary the Panther plan, proposed at the United Front against Fascism conference in Oakland, that white radicals peacefully organize the white community as the best way to combat racism and protect the Panthers from police attack. Tensions led to a fistfight when Weatherman leaders came to Panther headquarters in Chicago to explain their position. Black-led guerrilla war was one of Weatherman's cardinal hopes, but after the Days of Rage, an informant told the FBI in November 1969 that Bill Ayers and Jeff Jones were criticizing the Panthers for being too close to the Communist Party U.S.A. and its belief that the "objective conditions" for a revolution simply did not yet exist in the United States. It was a basic theoretical issue. Weatherman called the Panthers "revisionists." Panther resentments at Weatherman's attitude led to another fistfight in November.[88]

White radicals, too, opposed the Days of Rage plans. The result was a clash in *New Left Notes* over revolutionary theory. Mike Klonsky, despite having been among the first to advocate reaching out to alienated proletarian youth, and despite having initially supported the "national action," now claimed that such a strategy was ill-conceived, that its politics were too narrow: he now insisted that without the support of the working class, which had to be gained through radicals pressing for higher wages and better working conditions, the white Left in America could go nowhere. It might take years to win over the workers, but the work had to be done. As for the Days of Rage, Klonsky pointed out that it had no support from "proletarian organizations."[89]

In their own *New Left Notes* article, Robbins and Rudd disagreed with Klonsky: his new politics, they wrote, was a dead end; improved worker conditions would only *strengthen* workers' support of capitalism and imperialism, which was the basic problem. The only way to make the revolution was to make the revolution— to force the historical process as Lenin and Fidel had done. Moreover, they insisted, such revolutionary violence, while lacking support from the American working class (though perhaps not from working-class youth), had the backing of the peasant revolution against U.S. imperialism all over the world. The fighters in Chicago would not be alone.[90]

Others, too, joined the debate. The *Guardian*, the most widely read radical independent weekly, published a series of articles sharply critical of the Days of Rage plan: it was, they said, lunacy based on hot air (that is, a deeply flawed theory). The Weather leaders felt otherwise and insisted that their theory would be tested by practice and "practice will prove what's what." They expected fifteen thousand to twenty thousand people to show up in Chicago, and some even thought that twenty-five thousand would appear—a real Red Army.[91]

In the event, only about four hundred people showed up. The disappointment in Chicago's Lincoln Park on the chilly evening of October 8 was crushing. But the leaders made the best of it, assured the four hundred or so militants in Lincoln Park that they were "the revolutionary vanguard of America"—and led them to the attack.[92]

Over the next three days the Weathermen battled the Chicago police. On the first night they stormed out of the park through thin police lines into wealthy neighborhoods, breaking hundreds of windows in cars and buildings. The police did not expect such audacity—they were the ones who usually did the attacking. The police quickly recovered and soon overwhelmed the small number of Weathermen.[93] After an hour, one-third of the Weathermen were under arrest, many had been injured, several had been shot. The "Women's Militia" action the next morning was a fiasco. The return to attack in the Loop on October 11 was courageous (Mellen, Jacobs, Ayers, and Robbins were in the front line), but it was close to suicidal: the police replied with overpowering numbers and counterattacks. The Weathermen did more than $100,000 worth of damage to the city, and several dozen police were injured. But many more Weathermen were injured, and almost three hundred were arrested. The cost of bail was financially crippling, both to individuals, and—amounting to almost $2 million—to SDS as an organization.[94]

Meanwhile, on October 11 Klonsky's Revolutionary Youth Movement II put on its own demonstration in Chicago; it was peaceful, supported both by the Panthers and by radical Puerto

Rican groups, and drew five times the number of people as Weatherman's riot. At Fort Dix on October 12, the march to protest military prison conditions—from which the organizers had excluded Weatherman—drew ten times the number of people as had the Days of Rage. And three days later, on October 15, Vietnam Moratorium Day brought 100,000 peaceful marchers onto the streets of Washington. The differences in scale are striking.

Despite Weatherman's tiny showing, a few radical newspapers celebrated the Chicago action. In California, the radical monthly the *Movement*, which had sympathies with Weatherman, dedicated its November 1969 issue to "the sisters and brothers who struggled in Chicago to bring the war home." Its editors later assessed the Days of Rage as good education in necessary revolutionary violence and the eradication of fear: "The weather people have taught us an important lesson." And the judgment of Bay Area Yippie leader Stew Albert was eloquent:

> What if you picked up a history book and read that in 1938 a thousand University of Berlin students ran through the streets on behalf of the Jews in the camps, breaking car windows, knocking over fat, old German ladies, and beating up the Gestapo? . . . On a moral level, they're perfect.[95]

But the majority of opinion by most radical leftists was negative. The *Guardian* took up Weatherman's challenge about "practice": the failure to bring more than four hundred people to Chicago "amounted to a movement-wide boycott of left adventurism in practice." The remnant of Wisconsin SDS was blunt: "You don't need a rectal thermometer to know who the assholes are."[96]

Further, in autumn 1969, SDS under Weatherman's control all but collapsed. Chapters all over the country announced disaffiliation. One example will stand for many. At the University of Wisconsin, three thousand students had attended the first SDS meeting of autumn 1968; a year later, at the first meeting in autumn 1969, it was down to one thousand—and Jeff Jones was ejected when he and a cadre of Weathermen tried to seize the meeting by force; Jones, in turn, called the local leaders traitors. Wisconsin SDS would not survive the events of 1970.[97] Not that the departing chapters opted to support Progressive Labor: students rejected both factions and went their own way. SDS was effectively finished as a national organization.[98]

The collapse of SDS did not bother Weatherman; after all, the revolution was not going to be made by students hostage to white skin privilege. But Weatherman's hope of recruiting a revolutionary army of young street toughs was also a failure. Some leaders were privately in despair at the massive rejection. Yet *New Left Notes* on October 21 depicted Chicago as a triumph, proclaiming:

A white fighting force was born in the streets of pig city. . . . It was war—we knew it and the pigs knew it. We came to Chicago to join the other side, to start fighting with the VC. . . . [We saw] the birth of a new brigade in the world liberation army. We came to attack. We did what we set out to do, and in the process turned a corner.

Weatherman Shin'ya Ono, writing in December, was explicit as to the corner that had been turned: the Weathermen had become an army ready to inflict violence. According to Ono, "A white fighting force" had emerged at Chicago. Even if only "a few hundred or a few thousand white revolutionaries . . . [they] understand that U.S. imperialism is really a paper tiger [that] is going to come down within our generation." Such "a disciplined fighting force," inflicting violent and damaging blows against the state, was going to be "a thousand times more effective" in creating revolutionary consciousness in the masses than any pamphlet, no matter how well written.[99]

Thus despite the Weathermen's failure to bring large numbers to Chicago, their theoretical position remained unchanged. In December 1969, a meeting took place among Bill Ayers, Jeff Jones, and the leader of a Chicago Maoist group, who unbeknownst to them was also an FBI informant. According to the informant, Jones and Ayers described Weatherman strategy at length, declaring that they were preparing to wage urban guerrilla war inside the United States, and they would not wait for "objective conditions." The informant added: "They emphasized that the task of the revolutionary was to make revolution (Debray)."[100]

This would require, as Debray had shown, the creation of a cadre of the most hardened revolutionaries. To transform themselves into ideal unsentimental warriors for the revolution, Weatherman decided to embark on a series of internal "criticism/self-criticism" sessions, designed to weed out the weak. Weatherman leaders viewed white middle-class students as too soft for revolution, but the Weathermen were themselves white middle-class students. So the weakness had to be wrung out of them. This was done by sessions in the collectives where anyone who showed deviation from the political line, or hesitation or timidity, was subjected to hours of merciless berating, often by people they had thought of as friends. The process was supposed to lead to personal transformation. Criticism/self-criticism may have come from the Chinese Communist tradition. But the Chinese idea of criticism/self-criticism was to inculcate ideological "clarity" (whatever that might mean); the Weatherman goal was different: to toughen people psychologically so that they would engage unhesitatingly in revolutionary violence. This was the "transformation" they desired—to produce true revolutionaries, hard on others, hard on themselves.[101]

Not only weakness but "individualism," too, had to be abolished because, as Bill Ayers said, individual concerns (the desire that you and yours might survive) led to weak action. This led to the "smash monogamy" campaign, in which longtime lovers and even married couples were separated—sacrificed to the collective, which would henceforth command all loyalty. "Smash monogamy" was intimately tied to Weatherman's ideal of creating psychologically hardened, ideologically inspired revolutionary soldiers.[102]

The leadership also used criticism/self-criticism to remove independent commanders from the collectives, imposing their own choices. Susan Stern describes Mark Rudd conducting a purge upon his arrival at the Seattle collective in November 1969, installing new local leaders who followed whatever the Weather Bureau said. Rudd's own memoir confirms (with regret) what Stern says he was doing in this period—and why. The leadership wanted full control over the collectives in preparation for the looming war. In late 1969, Rudd later recalled, "not to have correct politics [was] like having no soul."[103]

By this time the regimen in the Weatherman collectives was so spartan that it led to widespread physical illnesses. Yet one result of the "criticism/self-criticism" sessions was crucial to Weatherman's later survival as an underground organization. In late October, the FBI still had informants—for instance, in the New York City and Columbus, Ohio, Weatherman collectives. But Larry Grathwohl was told by his FBI handler in early February 1970 that the purges of the autumn had eliminated all informants from Weatherman except Grathwohl himself. The collectives now functioned with excellent security: when they went underground in March, with the false identities they had prepared, the government knew neither who they were nor where they were, and it never found out. The informants had been rooted out, largely through the criticism/self-criticism sessions. Nevertheless, ex-Weathermen Ron Fliegelman and Russell Neufeld strongly object today to the criticism/self-criticism sessions, on grounds that they were morally terrible.[104]

But even while Weatherman increasingly focused on and prepared itself for undertaking violent action, people in its collectives were still reading Marx and Lenin, and *New Left Notes* (now called *Fire!*) continued to be heavy with theoretical argument. The November 21, 1969, issue, for example, contained Jim Mellen's critique of Weatherman on grounds of "adventurism"—acting without the support of the masses. Howard Machtinger replied by once again reiterating Weather's familiar theory that because the revolution was happening worldwide, "it is in this light that we must look at questions of adventurism"—and reject them. Weatherman, he argued, must be regarded as part of an international anti-imperialist army. Even the FBI understood that an *ideological* struggle was still going on.[105]

It seemed obvious that war both at home and across the world was intensifying. On November 4, 1969, the Brazilian army ambushed and killed the revolutionary writer Carlos Marighella, author of the *Minimanual of the Urban Guerrilla*, a book widely read in Weatherman. On December 1, *Life* magazine published horrendous color photographs of the U.S. Army slaughter of Vietnamese civilians at My Lai in 1968. On December 4, the Panther leader Fred Hampton, asleep in his bed, was killed by Chicago police in an early-morning raid. While Weatherman had had its disagreements with Hampton, his assassination was shocking and prompted the relatively sober and cautious Ted Gold to opt for total armed struggle (and, eventually, death in the townhouse). It was in this dark mood that Weatherman held what would be the final national meeting of Students for a Democratic Society, at Flint, Michigan—the so-called Flint War Council.[106]

The walls of the dingy auditorium at Hamilton and Saginaw Streets were festooned on one side with revolutionary heroes: Castro, Ho Chi Minh, Marx, Lenin, Che, Fred Hampton. On the other side were enemies: Nixon, J. Edgar Hoover—and, astonishingly, the actress Sharon Tate, the wife of movie director Roman Polanski and pregnant murder victim of the Manson family in Los Angeles. From the ceiling hung the image of a rifle with the slogan "Give Piece a Chance." Speech after speech advocated violence. John Jacobs exclaimed, "We're against everything that's good and decent in honky America. ... We are the incubation of your mother's nightmare."[107]

Bernardine Dohrn gave a speech praising Charles Manson: "Dig it, they murdered those pigs and then ate dinner at their dining table and then stuck a fork in their bellies! Wild!" Many years later, Dohrn claimed that she was making a joke; Bill Ayers has recently taken to saying that Dohrn never praised Manson at all. But Howard Machtinger says that the Weather Bureau approved the Manson remarks beforehand, and they were meant seriously. The large image of Sharon Tate among the photos of enemies posted in the hall required Weather Bureau consent; and after Dohrn's speech the Weathermen—especially the Weather Bureau—went around saluting each other with four raised fingers: the Fork. Evidently the idea was that Manson, whatever his other proclivities, was to be admired as an outlaw who had cast terror into the hearts of the bourgeoisie. In an FBI interview in 1973, the Weatherman Nancy Ann Rudd recalled that in Ayers's Detroit collective, Manson in January 1970 was still viewed as a revolutionary hero.[108]

The crowd of four hundred or so was whipped up to a frenzy by shouting, singing, dancing, stomping, and practicing mass karate.[109] But the reporter for Liberation News Service—pro–New Left, to be sure—who covered the meeting, stressed that Flint was not some sort of countercultural freak show but rather "a serious political meeting." Larry Grathwohl—hardly a friendly observer—said: "Every few feet there was a group gathered in serious discussion." Amid the stomping and singing there was political debate on the question that had obsessed the radicals for more than a year: if it was true that the revolution could be successful only with a revolutionary mass, then where was it going to come from?[110]

No Weatherman thought of the working class. But even this was contested at Flint, by Bob Avakian, a leader of the Revolutionary Union from the San Francisco Bay Area; he urged Weatherman to earn the adherence of the working class by supporting struggles for better working conditions. This familiar position provoked a public debate between Avakian and Machtinger. Machtinger compared Weatherman to Lex Luthor, one of the villains in *Superman*, who always bounced back from defeat. This has led some commentators to believe that his speech was frivolous. But Machtinger's real argument was a traditional and serious theoretical issue: the white working class was too corrupted by the benefits of imperialist capitalism to support revolution, and corrupted as well as by "white skin privilege." Avakian, for his part, protested that this was too pessimistic a view.[111]

Some people at Flint still expressed hope in working-class youth; the LNS reporter observed serious discussions of ways of recruitment. But for most, the Days of Rage disappointment left no hope in whites at all; the only good whites left were those at Flint. The rest—all the rest—were racists. That was Machtinger's position in the debate with Avakian. Other Weatherman speakers pointed to blacks as the only required revolutionary mass. When Avakian objected that even the Panthers believed that the white masses were needed, Machtinger replied, "Well, we don't agree with the Panthers on a lot of things."[112]

Critics then and now have also argued that Weatherman, motivated almost totally by hatred of the present, had no real vision of the future. Hatred of the present there certainly was. But Flint showed that the Weatherman leaders did have a vision of the future—one, however, unlikely to appeal to many people. Just as any American revolution would be part of the planetwide revolution, so too, after the revolution, would the United States and its predatory economy fall to the supervision of "an agency of the people of the world." The Weathermen would be mere adjuncts to this international agency, which would impose a new economic structure to prevent America's evil deeds—and impose indemnities for America's planetwide looting. This vision was set out at Flint by Ted Gold. And again there was debate. Questioners from the floor accused Gold of proposing a regime of foreigners that could succeed only through harsh dictatorship—which Gold acknowledged.[113]

For Susan Stern, Flint's palpable craziness alternated with serious discussion of competing theories of revolution. Speakers explained Weatherman's insistence on violence, "the historic rationales behind our political theories." The strategy was to force the disintegration of American society via a bombing campaign to create chaos. This crisis would drive the working-class young, and perhaps eventually the working class as a whole, into revolution. Speakers cited historical examples: the success of terrorism in the Algerian Revolution, Vietcong executions of government officials, the Tupamaros in Uruguay.[114]

The bombings envisioned at Flint would be deadly—that much was clear. To Stern, this was why discussion was so serious. Mark Rudd agreed, and years later, in his memoir, he recalled, "I believed it was moral to kill people." An editorial in *Fire!* proclaimed: "During the 1960s the Amerikan government was on trial for its crimes against the people of the world. We now find the government guilty and condemn it to death."[115]

It was not just bluster. Preparations for real guerrilla war began at Flint, in meetings separate from the participants in the hall. In March 1970, a Weather Bureau member (apparently Eric Mann) reported these meetings to the *Chicago Tribune* reporter Ron Koziol—who passed the information on to the FBI. That the Weatherman leaders' plan for a campaign of lethal bombing began at secret meetings at Flint has now been confirmed by Howard Machtinger. He stresses that the leaders chose police as the primary targets, with military personnel also on the list.[116]

The Weatherman leaders set out their plan for guerrilla war in their last statement as the governing body of SDS (*Fire!* January 30, 1970): military collectives were being built across the country that would be able to strike in coordinated action, guided by a centralized command. It was how the Weather Bureau intended to jump-start the revolution.[117]

And so the war began. In January 1970 the Weatherman leadership wrecked the SDS headquarters in Chicago and New York, destroying many SDS records. Protest was dead; SDS was no more. A contemporary FBI document, previously unused in histories of Weatherman, shows how strongly the leaders were committed to revolutionary violence. The FBI at this time was wiretapping and bugging the Berkeley home of Leibel Bergman, the leader of the Revolutionary Union. Bergman himself was away in Algeria; but his children and daughter-in-law were in Weatherman and in January–February 1970 a collective was staying in the house. What the Weatherman leaders said found its way, via electronic surveillance, to the FBI.[118]

The report, by Leibel Bergman's FBI case officer, offers recent information from "a sensitive FBI source"—code for a bug or wiretap—concerning the philosophy and objectives of prominent Weatherman leaders. After listing the leadership group (Mark Rudd, Jeff Jones, Bill Ayers, and Bernardine Dohrn), the report explains that the group's goal is to build an organization "totally committed and designed to carry out guerrilla warfare in the cities":

> The SDS leadership is determined to accelerate revolutionary crises through a program of action which will be urban guerrilla warfare. It is willing and committed to the revolution, and believes it can be effective in the fashion of Fidel Castro.[119]

Thus did the FBI report within its ranks that the rhetorical hyperbole of Weatherman's public pronouncements at Flint and elsewhere—and the emphasis on Debrayist theory—was also prevailing in private discussions in the Weatherman leadership.

This ideological trajectory led to the widespread Weatherman firebombings of January and February 1970, followed by the dynamite bombs in New York City and Detroit. But after the self-inflicted debacle of the March 6, 1970, townhouse explosion, the

Weather Bureau ordered all bombing operations halted and all *focos* to go underground immediately. The collectives obeyed the bombing halt—which was evidence of the leaders' centralized control over bombing, as Larry Grathwohl, Karen Latimer, John Jacobs, and other Weather veterans have, over the years, described. And the collectives went underground so obediently, quickly, and chaotically that people were left behind—including Jonathan Lerner, the editor of *Fire!* Some of those left behind felt completely abandoned.[120]

The parents of Weathermen who suddenly disappeared were reduced to calling their children's friends to try to find out what on earth had happened to them. One must remember that the Weathermen were still young people, mostly in their early twenties, and being cut off from parents was for many a painful issue; there is plenty of eyewitness testimony on this. What is striking is that within all the virulent rhetoric of revolution, eventually plans were developed by the leadership through which at least some parents might be notified on how to make contact secretly with a son or daughter who had gone underground so that relationships could be reestablished and reassurances given. Jonah Raskin, then an aboveground Weatherman supporter, says that arranging these contacts was a task the leadership assigned to him for two full years.[121]

Both from Weatherman memoirs and from FBI documents, it is striking that the support of families for those who had gone underground tended to be strong, and especially from female family members. This support came not only from mothers but from sisters and female cousins. Howard Machtinger's mother, Yetta (who was not ordinarily political), made a name for herself in the underground newspapers as an affectionate guardian of her son; but FBI documents show that his much younger twin sisters (then students at the University of Wisconsin) also maintained an allegiance to him. Similarly, when the FBI questioned the eighty-year-old grandmother of David Barber on his whereabouts—he had gone underground after the townhouse explosion rather than testify against Weatherman—she replied that she didn't know where he was, and she was sorry she didn't, because if she did, she could what grandmas do and send him money.[122]

The leadership told some people that the townhouse dead had, like Fred Hampton, been murdered by the police. So even after March 6, devotion to lethal violence remained strong in some Weatherman groups. John Jacobs remained an advocate. Weatherman Scott Braley wavered about whether to go on with the war. Mark Rudd recalled that when he met with the remnants of the Townhouse Collective (six or seven people) on the morning after the explosion, they too were ready to go forward, attributing the tragedy merely to lack of technical expertise. Despite the deaths, Rudd remembered that "no one dared to question the basic strategy." Soon the survivors were in upstate New York, practicing with their guns. According to Ron Fliegelman, when he stated after the townhouse explosion that he might drop out, a gun was pulled on him. Larry Gray says that among the Weather people he knew, the explosion was seen not as a dreadful warning against lethal violence but as a recruiting device: the martyrs of the townhouse would be useful in enrolling new people for armed struggle. Jonah Raskin concurs.[123]

Larry Grathwohl reported to his FBI minders that on April 2, 1970, he was present when Bill Ayers met with the Buffalo, New York, Weatherman collective and stressed that the war must be continued. Ayers, he said, had just come from a meeting on the West Coast with the Weather Bureau, where the main topic was the establishment of a Red Army. Reflecting Weather Bureau opinion, Ayers negatively compared the East Coast people with the West Coast people: "East Coast people got 'hung up,' had lost three members in the Ted Gold bombing in New York City; West Coast people were more confident"; this was because they had successfully bombed a police station with no loss of Weatherman members. Ayers praised Bernardine Dohrn for her role in the operation and declared that "Weatherman had to be one-hundred percent Marxist-Leninist indoctrinated, and [he dwelled] on the ill effects of monogamy and male chauvinism to operate at the highest level of violence." By this, Grathwohl claimed, Ayers meant lethal bombs.[124]

Perhaps Grathwohl is lying. Or perhaps Ayers was boasting, or perhaps he (or Grathwohl) had confused the Berkeley antipolice dynamite bombing led by Machtinger with the Park Station bombing in San Francisco four days later. But the evidence on Detroit (see Chapter 2) suggests that Grathwohl's reports were trustworthy, and if this report on Buffalo *is* correct, then it would appear that at least in the several weeks after the townhouse explosion, the Weather Bureau—or at least some of its members—was still determined to press ahead with its lethal campaign. Grathwohl's testimony on the mood among some Weathermen dovetails with that of several other witnesses.[125]

A Weatherman bombing in Washington, D.C., on May 10 shows only slight change in method. Around 1:30 A.M., a Weatherman collective detonated a dynamite bomb at the entrance to the National Guard Association Building near Union Station. It was revenge for the killing of four students at Kent State University by Ohio National Guardsmen on May 4. No one was killed or injured, and the choice of the middle of the night suggests that the intent was primarily to damage property, not persons—a very different operation from those planned for March 6. But no warning was given, and the bomb shattered seventy plate-glass windows lining one wall of the office building, did significant damage inside, and blew out the plate-glass windows in a café across the street. Anyone who happened to be walking past the building at the time of the explosion would have been seriously injured or even killed.[126]

In May, however, the Weather Bureau changed the direction of the organization. The leaders, convening in a rented beach house near Mendocino, California, decided to reject lethal bombing as a strategy.

It is important to establish the date of the meeting in mid-May, since that provides its political context. The Mendocino meeting is often thought to have occurred in late April—that is, before the Cambodia incursion and the Kent State killings.[127] But the meeting must have been in mid-May. This is not nitpicking; it means that the Mendocino decision occurred during the great campus insurrections protesting Nixon's widening of the war in Indochina. It also occurred during the demonstrations in New Haven at the trial of Black Panther leaders, where thousands of people protested in the streets on behalf of the Panthers despite Connecticut National Guardsmen with fixed bayonets (and even right-wing bombings). It was all an apparent lesson to the underground concerning what was possible.[128]

The date of the Mendocino meeting is reliably established by Mark Rudd, whose revelatory and self-critical memoir was published in 2009. He fled underground on April 15, 1970, after the arrest of Dianne Donghi and Linda Evans in New York, engineered by the FBI via Larry Grathwohl. Rudd hid out in Philadelphia, where he spent about two weeks before he learned of the Kent State shootings. Later he sat on a bench in Rittenhouse Square, in despair that it was too dangerous for him to participate in the major demonstration going on nearby to protest the shootings. Soon thereafter he was summoned to California for the Mendocino meeting.[129]

At Mendocino, Bernardine Dohrn and Jeff Jones argued for ending lethal bombing. According to Thai Jones, relying both on his father Jeff and his mother, Eleanor Raskin (who was also there), the meeting was from the beginning carefully orchestrated by Jones and Dohrn. Thus David Gilbert suspects he was excluded "by accident" from Mendocino because he would have supported John Jacobs's hard line to keep on with lethal guerrilla war. Jacobs believed he had the morally superior position, and he had significant support at Mendocino, including at the start from Mark Rudd. But Jones and Dohrn, in private conversations, won over Bill Ayers and others. Jones and Dohrn spent several days gaining converts privately in this way, in an atmosphere engineered for comfort and relaxation—for many people, the first time in months. Only then did Jones and Dohrn allow debate on strategy. They advocated continuing bombing, but only of property; Dohrn was, as usual, eloquent. Ayers, too, now came out in favor of abandoning lethal violence. One story is that when John Jacobs protested, Dohrn simply assumed a Buddhist lotus position. A factor that may have limited Jacobs's influence was that among the female leaders he had a bad reputation for sexism. Dohrn, Jones, and Ayers eventually won the day and emerged as the new troika to run the Weatherman Underground; Jacobs, was expelled from the organization; Rudd, siding with Dohrn and Jones, was demoted. It was a coup d'état not unlike the one engineered at the SDS convention in Chicago a year before.[130]

The Mendocino decision to retreat from lethal bombings suggests that the Weather Bureau now saw a unique political opportunity. With campuses in an uproar, perhaps Weather could position itself as the vanguard of a real revolutionary mass upheaval. Hundreds of thousands of students appeared to ready to embrace a new militancy. Dozens of firebombings were occurring on campuses across the country in May, but none were apparently intended to be lethal. Weather needed to align itself with its supporters (basically, radicalized hippies and students) and not to get ahead of the "level of struggle" being pursued on campuses. And that meant giving up lethal violence. The views of their constituency influenced their thinking. What is striking is that the new mass behind the campus protests, the mass Weatherman wanted, was made up overwhelmingly of white students—the very group which Weatherman for a year had professed to despise.[131]

Weatherman claimed leadership of the student movement in a communiqué released on May 21—but its tone was still bellicose. It began: "This is Bernardine Dohrn. I am going to read A DECLARATION OF A STATE OF WAR." It continued: "Our job is to lead white kids in armed revolution. . . . Revolutionary violence is the only way." It concluded: "We will never live peaceably under this system." As Thai Jones has said, this does not read like a document created by Weatherman's "peaceful wing"—though that is what it was. The moderation of the new leading troika was only relative.[132]

The Declaration of War called on white youth to rise up and destroy the American empire. Although there were references to the plight of black people—"Never again will they fight alone"—the focus was on white students. Weatherman stated that it was starting a guerrilla war—but to be successful, guerrillas had to move like fish in the sea of the people. Weatherman declared that tens of thousands of white kids now knew the truth, and this was the sea in which Weatherman would now swim: "The alienation and contempt that young people have for this country has created the ocean for this revolution." The May events—Cambodia, the killings of demonstrators at Kent State and Jackson State—had made "thousands more revolutionaries." Thus, after the disappointment of autumn 1969, Weatherman in spring 1970 again hoped to be a Revolutionary Youth Movement: "If you want to find us, this is where we are, where kids are making love, smoking dope and loading guns." The Declaration of War also praised the town-house dead as martyrs to the revolution; their deaths were a badge of Weatherman's seriousness. The Declaration ended with a threat: Weatherman would attack a symbol or institution of "Amerikan injustice" within fourteen days.[133]

The Weatherman leaders apparently now believed that the May crisis had suddenly produced a revolutionary mass: a combination of students and hippies politicized by the deadly actions of the government. "They are the whole base of our movement," said Bernardine Dohrn's sister Jennifer the next spring. This claim of leadership of countercultural youth was underscored in the Weatherman message of September 15, 1970, following the group's spectacular success in breaking the countercultural hero Timothy Leary out of prison in California. Leary was serving ten years for possession of a small amount of marijuana. Weatherman declared that by freeing him it had fulfilled "the will of millions of kids," and went on to praise marijuana and LSD. But the communiqué ended with a stern reminder: "Now we are at war."[134]

On June 9, 1970, Weatherman carried out the threat in the Declaration of War. A group detonated a powerful bomb—fifteen sticks of dynamite, hidden in a second-floor bathroom—in the headquarters of the New York City Police Department. Penetration of headquarters was easy because in 1970, even in New York City three months after the townhouse explosion, and even after the direct threat made in the Declaration of War, no police station had metal detectors or had taken any other safety precautions; there was just the usual cop at the front desk, past whom the Weathermen walked to plant their bomb. Unlike previous Weatherman bomb attacks, however, a warning was phoned in, seventeen minutes before detonation. But the bombing also occurred at 6:43 in the evening—not in the middle of the night, when few people were around. Despite the warning, eight policemen were injured; the building was severely damaged.[135]

And the June 9 bombing in New York was intended—like March 6—to be a multicity event. At the other end of the country, another Weatherman collective placed a powerful dynamite bomb in a men's bathroom at the San Francisco Hall of Justice, which housed not only local courts but the headquarters of the city's police department. As in New York, a warning was phoned in beforehand—but the San Francisco bomb failed to explode. What happened next is unclear: David Gilbert claims that the collective itself phoned the police so that the bomb could be found and defused and no innocent person hurt (this was "our responsibility," he says); but some FBI veterans claim that the unexploded bomb was discovered only months later by a startled janitor.[136]

The day after the New York bombing came Weatherman Communiqué no. 2, which celebrated it, boasting, "We blew up the N.Y.C. Police Headquarters," shattering the myth of "pig invulnerability." Karen Latimer later said that in July, Karen Ashley—one of the authors of the Weatherman Manifesto—told her that the NYPD bombing was considered "an extremely successful action," and that Bernardine Dohrn had had a personal hand in it. The bellicosity of the second communiqué was matched by the third (July 26), which, still claiming to represent the mass protests of May ("thousands of freaks plot to build a new world"), also closed with a personal threat against Attorney General John Mitchell: "Don't look for us, Dog; we'll find you first." This was followed by Weatherman detonating two dynamite bombs at the Presidio army base in San Francisco—headquarters of the Armed Forces Police.[137]

Dohrn later said she spent much of the summer of 1970 warning Weatherman collectives and other radicals away from killing and kidnapping. If so, this suggests there was resistance among some Weathermen to the change of strategy, and that perhaps the dramatic break that Mendocino augured was slower and more hesitant. That is the view of Weatherman leader Howard Machtinger, who says that early that summer he and a small group were detailed by the Weather Bureau to kidnap a member of the Rockefeller family from its vacation home in Maine, but—being total amateurs—his group simply never figured out how to do it, and wandered around Maine uselessly. Machtinger says that the leadership back in San Francisco was furious: "You know, there's this myth that Bernardine ruled out any violent actions after Mendocino, but it's just not true. The line was much blurrier than that." Machtinger says that he himself was demoted as a result of this failure.[138]

Still, the main message of no killing was pretty clear. That summer Ron Fliegelman, an important figure in the New York group, rejected the idea of Weatherman snipers. Conversely, the late May message of nonlethality led to the dissolution of David Gilbert's collective in Denver. Meanwhile, the Weatherman leaders faced continuing public pressure from the wider radical Left to back off; the counterculture was more in sympathy with nonviolence and didn't naturally embrace acts that might risk human injuries. The *Berkeley Tribe* warned again in June—as it had in late March—that incautious bombings might lead to Weatherman's complete isolation. Similarly, Tom Hayden in July wrote in the radical magazine *Ramparts* that America was not ripe for a third-world-type violent revolution and that Weatherman should stop applauding bloodshed. These new warnings may well have helped the Weathermen to maintain the momentum to deescalate, for in the end Weather yearned for a revolutionary mass to follow it. Its leaders believed they had a constituency and wanted to keep it— and the pressure of this constituency helped push them away from lethal violence. This desire not to alienate its constituency may explain why Weatherman always had a larger aboveground support network than any other violent left group.[139]

Yet the bellicose tone of Weatherman communiqués continued in the autumn. On October 8 a communiqué praised Jonathan Jackson, who in California in August had kidnapped a judge, three jurors, and a courthouse guard in an attempt to rescue his brother George from prison—resulting in four deaths, including those of Jonathan Jackson and the judge. Weatherman called it "heroic," and now announced a "fall offensive." This had already begun on October 6, with the bombing of the Marin County Courthouse (an architectural masterpiece of Frank Lloyd Wright), site of the Jackson raid. Over the next week Weatherman detonated four more dynamite bombs, in cities from coast to coast, the last on October 14—a demonstration of its national reach. "We urge our people to prepare for war. . . . Arm yourselves and shoot to live!" The communiqué also expressed disquiet at the failure of the campuses so far this autumn to explode, and urged student leaders not to compromise with the government. Another October 8 communiqué explained the Weatherman bombing of the Marin County Courthouse. It had been set off in the middle of the night, damaging the building but causing no injuries, and Weatherman proclaimed it part of "the war against pig Amerika." Weatherman dedicated it to "the first of the new breed of freedom fighters—Jonathan Jackson and his comrades," and to Angela Davis, whom the authorities wanted for her alleged participation in the Jackson plot. An October 9 communiqué urged white youth to put up wanted posters for judges such as John Murtaugh of the Panther 21 trial (whose home the Townhouse Collective had firebombed in February): "Keep them scared."[140]

Cathy Wilkerson suggests that in autumn 1970 there was confusion about what to do—"I saw a lot more grass than guns"—yet the ideal of Weatherman as urban guerrillas continued to exercise a romantic fascination. The confusion was compounded by the inflammatory language of the leaders: "Were we renouncing armed attacks on people or not?" Nevertheless, the bombings in the Fall Offensive showed that Weatherman was capable of striking violently on a national scale.[141]

But on December 6 the Weather Underground released a new communiqué called "New Morning—Changing Weather." The tone was different from all previous messages': "This is a communication for our friends. . . . We want to express ourselves to the mass movement not as military leaders but as tribes in council." Friends? Tribes in council? It was a Weather claim to be hippies of a sort. Weatherman boasted of the nationwide underground apparatus it had created, but then reiterated that it was only part of a mass movement—which would engage in public protest rallies because mass protests "do make a difference." This was a stunning repudiation of everything Weatherman had been saying for a year and a half. The reversal was so sharp that it suggested the leaders had begun to question the assumptions that had underpinned the Debrayist theory of how best to make revolution.[142]

The communiqué condemned the idea that armed struggle was the only legitimate form of revolutionary action—a mistake, it said, that was based on the false notion that there was no revolutionary movement among white youth. The use of marijuana and LSD were again proclaimed to be revolutionary, while a sole focus on violence was now denounced as "the military error." But this error was ascribed only to the benighted comrades of the townhouse. If the communiqué was to be believed, it was only the Townhouse

Collective that had believed in ultimate armed struggle, it was only the Townhouse Collective that had been pessimistic about white youth, it was only the Townhouse that had pushed for lethal bombing. In the May Declaration of War, the townhouse dead had been the guarantors of Weatherman's seriousness; now they symbolized an antihuman mistake. Many years later, Cathy Wilkerson would claim that she had been offended at this shirking of ideological responsibility by the national leaders but was too traumatized at the time to speak up in protest.[143]

"New Morning" reiterated its positive view of the counterculture and its revolutionary potential, and Weather again claimed to be part of the counterculture. It condemned any attitude of separation and superiority ("us" vs. "them"). Where had this new confidence in white youth come from? "New Morning" was clear: the massive May protests had changed the attitude of Weatherman; thousands of new people had joined the movement for radical change, and the government was now on the defensive. The Weather conclusion: "The hearts of our people are in a good place. Freaks and hippies and a lot of people in the movement have begun to dig in for a long winter." People were more mature now, and understood it would be a protracted war: "We know how long it will take us to win." But it would be a real people's war.[144]

To fight this hoped-for people's war, Weatherman now seemed also to reject the hierarchical structure of its own organization, and its commanding attitude toward everyone else. The *focos*—the heart of the Weatherman organization—were now dismissed: "Twos and threes is not a good form for anything: it won't put out a newspaper, organize a conference on the war, or do armed actions without getting caught." Suddenly Weather was in favor of newspapers and conferences, not just armed action. And: "People . . . don't want to follow academic ideologues or authoritarians"; real leaders in touch with movements are followed "freely and with love." Was this the end of vanguard-partyism? No. Despite these statements, the Weather Underground—like any clandestine organization—needed a hierarchical command structure. And in reality the Weathermen continued to feel morally superior to everyone who did not take their difficult path: "The fugitives never found a way to get beyond browbeating, shaming, and cajoling hippies, freaks and students into the streets."[145]

Despite Weather's new regard for the revolutionary potential of disaffected white youth—"Our minds have been blown," they wrote of the widespread student upheavals of May 1970—they were once again to be disappointed. After May, the nationwide student protest had not intensified but—as Weatherman had feared in the autumn— faded. The protracted war that Weatherman now called for never occurred. If in summer 1970 there had existed a national-scale aboveground organization of leftist students to keep the radical momentum of the spring going, things might have been different in the autumn, but of course the Weather Bureau in the dark winter of 1969–1970 had decided to abolish SDS as a national organization.[146]

Nevertheless, a year later, in May 1971 in Washington, D.C., there was indeed a massive anti–Vietnam War demonstration led by "politicized hippies," most prominently by the Mayday Tribe. Organized by several groups, and inspired by ex-SDS president and former Chicago Eight defendant Rennie Davis, it had taken place under the slogan "If the government will not stop the war, we will stop the government." It resulted in the largest number of arrests in American history, more than twelve thousand. Richard Helms, then the CIA director, said of the protest, "It was obviously viewed by everybody in the administration, particularly with all the arrests and howling about civil rights and human rights and all the rest of it . . . as a very damaging kind of event. I don't think there was any doubt about that." So the post–May 1970 Weatherman hope for a social lever was not entirely fanciful.[147] But that was the high point. While Weatherman continued to engineer occasional spectacular bombings and to issue stern communiqués, the mass of youthful radicals was content to sit on the sidelines as spectators, mostly ap-provingly but mostly passively. And so Weatherman, despite having ostensibly renounced its initial lethal strategy and its theoretical spurning of the radical potential of the working class in favor of in-spiring a countercultural force comprising alienated hippies, found itself increasingly isolated, leaders again without followers.[148]

Larry Grathwohl, meanwhile, was happy to provide his FBI minders with an analysis of "New Morning." He concluded that it was an admission that Weatherman had failed to accomplish revolu-tion through armed struggle and bombings. Now it was claiming leadership of a politicized counterculture, with revolution to come slowly. This was why it declared a move away from covert *focos* (suitable for real guerrilla war) and toward larger "families and tribes."[149]

Grathwohl's assessment was accurate. Jonathan Lerner had been in Cuba when Weatherman went underground in March 1970; he lost contact for a year, and reestablished it only in mid-1971. He found the mood very different from the darkness of a year before: "The madness had become hippie mellowness. Gone were the thuggish street-fighting stance, the leather jackets, lengths of chain and steel-toed boots. In their place were moccasins, love-beads, and long hair." Lerner didn't think Weather had wholly abandoned its more militant commitment to armed struggle, but there was undeniably something real in its new attitude. People no longer carried guns on a daily basis. Jonah Raskin, who saw Jeff Jones baking bread and Bill Ayers making soufflés at this time, also believed that the counterculture impact was real and profound.[150]

Grathwohl also took "New Morning" as evidence that the leadership was tiring of underground life and wished to "return to open work such as demonstrations"—even if this meant submitting to a political trial first.[151] Here he was wrong: the leaders did not surface for seven more years—though certainly by 1975 they were thinking of it. Grathwohl also underestimated their determination to continue bombing—at first against the government, later against corporations. Weatherman followed "New Morning" with the bombing of the Capitol itself, in Washington, D.C., on March 1, 1971—a stunning act. Then, in August and September 1971, came bombings of California and New York penal system headquarters buildings—the first to protest the killing of George Jackson in a botched escape attempt from San Quentin, the second to protest the bloody and deadly suppression of the Attica Prison rebellion. In May 1972, Weatherman exploded a bomb in the Pentagon itself. Bomb attacks against corporations soon began in earnest; in the autumn of 1973 came the ITT headquarters in New York—a response, Weatherman declared, to the overthrow of Chilean President Salvador Allende. This was followed by the bombings of Gulf Oil headquarters in Pittsburgh (June 1974), and Anaconda Corporation in Boise, Idaho (September 1974). In January 1975 came the bombing of the State Department in Washington, followed by the Argentinian

Banco de Ponce in New York City, and Kennecott Corporation headquarters (September 1975)—the last bombing. In between came the bombing of an NYPD precinct headquarters (May 1973) to protest the death of a black teenager, and of a Department of Health, Education, and Welfare headquarters in San Francisco (March 1974) in protest of welfare policy.

It is an impressive list—though when the bombings are toted up, there are only twelve in the five years after the release of "New Morning." And one should not forget the bombing and violence coming from the Right in 1971–1972. In August 1971, for example, six school buses in Michigan, intended for use in integrating high schools, were dynamited. In January 1972, the Jewish Defense League firebombed the New York offices of the impresario Sol Hurok, who had arranged Soviet-American friendship tours of artists; one person was killed and thirteen injured—more casualties in one bombing than Weatherman ever inflicted. That month, too, the attempt of the mostly black Newark Boys Chorus School to move into a suburban neighborhood led to its building and its school buses being firebombed. These incidents of violence, and even dynamite bombings, have faded from public memory, whereas the Weatherman bombings have not.[152]

Over time, Weatherman developed a mode of operations that was effective in several ways but crucially ineffective in another. After June 1970, no Weatherman bombing ever inflicted any human injury. Of course, all bombing was dangerous: there was always a risk that people and institutions might not react in time to the telephoned warnings; the structural integrity of buildings damaged by dynamite bombs always constituted a danger to first responders. But the rejection of intentional lethal violence enabled Weather supporters aboveground to support the group with clear consciences—to gruffly refuse to talk to FBI agents who came to question them. Operations that were perceived as nonlethal and thus inherently moderate could be countenanced by supporters otherwise repelled by violent acts. That support was a critical factor in helping Weather to survive.[153]

After the townhouse disaster, Weathermen learned to prepare their bombings carefully. Nothing ever blew up in their faces again. By 1972 the FBI came to consider them professionals. And

Weatherman targets were carefully chosen for maximum political spectacle and publicity. Yet meanwhile, between these twelve bombings—and often these operations were separated by many months—the Weathermen hid, and (under false names) led seemingly ordinary lives.

The long periods of disappearance while spectacular bombings were being meticulously planned may explain why only one major Weatherman figure was ever caught—and even he escaped.[154] The fact was that Weatherman simply did not do enough actions, or leave enough clues—take enough risks—to get caught. Their competence and discipline both at dynamiting and at staying underground between operations was different in kind from the Red Army Faction (Baader-Meinhof Gang) in West Germany, which did many actions in 1971–1972, and whose leaders were either dead or in prison by the summer of 1972.

Yet Weather's post-Mendocino strategy was deeply flawed. Weatherman could not gain momentum, let alone ignite a revolution, if for long months it simply disappeared from public view. As a strategy for survival, it worked; as a strategy for revolution, it failed. Even as a strategy for stimulating a protracted war, it failed. The more militant among the Weathermen, such as David Gilbert, were aware of the problem.[155] Moreover, the new strategy changed the meaning of the bombings themselves: however spectacular, they could not be considered serious blows aimed at the functioning of the American state or of capitalism, as lethal attacks might have been regarded. They became protests—bombs in bathrooms.

In January 1974, Weather published a 186-page manifesto called *Prairie Fire*. Larded with Marxist-Leninist jargon, it emphasized the need to return to aboveground mass organizing, admitting "we can't make the revolution without organizing the majority." In 1975, Weather leaders began pushing for the transformation of the underground into an aboveground and legal communist party that would mostly give up armed struggle in favor of educating the working class.[156] But how could Weather leaders in 1974–1975 contemplate coming up from the underground to head such a project? The answer was that they were no longer federal

fugitives. In late 1973, prosecutors had been forced to drop all
federal charges against them because of the public discovery of
FBI lawbreaking in the Bureau's attempts to apprehend them.
Astonishingly, it would be officials of the FBI, not the fugitives of
Weatherman, who would end up in court.

CHAPTER THREE

"A Menace of National Proportions"

TEN DAYS AFTER THE townhouse explosion, on March 16, 1970, the actor Dustin Hoffman appeared on *The Dick Cavett Show*, broadcast from ABC in New York City. Hoffman's family's apartment had been in a building next to the townhouse, and it had been destroyed. He told Cavett that it was not anger that he felt against the bombers, but "fear for ourselves, our family, and our country." A few days later, on March 27, a bomb threat interrupted a concert at Carnegie Hall by folksinger Phil Ochs. The bomb threat was taken seriously; some people thought it was Weatherman, and they scrambled to clear the hall. But Ochs himself, an antiwar activist, ranted from the stage: "Dustin Hoffman was scared?—bullshit! The Weathermen call up with a bomb threat? If they bombed this concert I wouldn't object! It'd be great! Bomb my concert!" He told people to come back in for free for a second show.[1] Later that summer, in Los Angeles, the first filming of the soon-to-be-famous *Mary Tyler Moore Show* before a live audience—a crucial step in preproduction—was interrupted by a bomb threat; people cleared the studio, and again, many suspected the hand of Weatherman. In Texas that summer, a military policeman who had arrested the actress Jane Fonda at a Fort Hood demonstration in May was told by the FBI that he was on a Weatherman assassination list set up by Bill Ayers. Wherever this story came from, the military policeman was given bodyguards for months.[2] Even ten years later, in October 1980, during the trial of two high FBI officials for breaking the law in their zeal to capture Weather fugitives, fear of a Weatherman attack interrupted the proceedings. One afternoon there was a loud noise and, according to John Nields, the prosecutor of the case, "the first thought on everyone's mind was that the Weathermen had planted a bomb"; the judge fled the bench into his chambers, followed by the lawyers and their clients; spectators fled the courtroom in the other direction. The actual culprit? The janitors had turned on a central vacuuming system.[3]

The specter of a ruthless terror threat, such as Weatherman seemed to present, loomed large. The government feared that the group's deeds might well match the ferocity of its rhetoric. The media was quick to seize on the possibility and acted as a magnifier. The reality was otherwise and the actual threat Weather posed was disproportionately exaggerated both in the press and within the intelligence agencies of the government. But many officials at the time took Weatherman at its word, and its occasional spectacular bombings appeared to give credence to the group's seriousness of purpose. Former Nixon White House aide Tom Charles Huston, for one, would recall, "The fact of the matter is that the entire intelligence community, in the summer of 1970, thought we had a serious crisis."[4]

Certainly President Nixon thought so. On June 5, 1970, he met with his intelligence chiefs in the Oval Office. He was intent on increasing the efficiency of intelligence gathering against the threat he believed radicals posed to country. He began the meeting by stressing "the magnitude of the internal security problem we face." Radicals, he said, had moved in stages from civil rights activism to mass public protest against Vietnam, and finally to "the revolutionary terrorism being perpetrated today by determined professionals":

> We are now confronted with a grave and new crisis in our country—one which we know little about. Certainly hundreds, perhaps thousands, of Americans—mostly under 30—

are determined to destroy our society. . . . They are reaching out for the support—ideological and otherwise—of foreign powers and they are developing their own brand of indigenous revolutionary activism which is as dangerous as anything they could import.

Under such circumstances, Nixon said, it was vital for the government to know more about the plans and activities of the extremists, in order to curtail them:

I want each of you to know personally that this Administration is committed to the preservation of internal stability in this country. I do not intend to sit idly by while self-appointed revolutionaries commit acts of terrorism throughout the land.[5]

Nixon's solution was to increase cooperation against the far Left among the intelligence agencies—and to increase their capabilities against the target. He thought insufficient resources were being used for intelligence gathering on the revolutionaries. "We need more hard information." To ensure this, he wanted better interagency cooperation—and to ensure that "all our resources are being utilized." Nixon wanted recommendations about "additional steps which can be taken to strengthen our capabilities." He concluded that only strengthened capabilities "will enable us to halt the spread of this terrorism before it gets completely out of hand."[6]

President Nixon's chosen main weapon in what he saw as a life-and-death struggle to maintain the stability of the United States was the Federal Bureau of Investigation.

Two days after the meeting at the White House, J. Edgar Hoover addressed the heads of the U.S. intelligence services (Central Intelligence Agency, Defense Intelligence Agency, the National Security Agency, and the three branches of military intelligence). Speaking in support of Nixon's initiative, he declared:

The plain fact is that there are thousands of individuals inside this country who want to see our form of government destroyed. They have in fact pledged themselves publicly to achieving this goal. They have put their words into actions constituting revolutionary terrorism, and the total effect of their action has been disastrous.

The program of action against the far Left that Hoover was now recommending would become known as the "Huston Plan," after the White House aide who chaired the committee of intelligence officials who during the next month would draw up its details.[7]

By the late 1960s, the Federal Bureau of Investigation had a long history of combating "subversive elements" in American society. This included penetrating and neutralizing the Communist Party U.S.A. as well as the Ku Klux Klan. But it had never confronted a truly revolutionary situation, such as appeared now to exist. Its other famous target had been organized crime, the Mafia.

This reflected the two fundamental but different tasks of the Bureau. It was a primary federal instrument in amassing evidence for criminal prosecutions. But its other main function was intelligence gathering—investigating threats to domestic stability, not gathering evidence for trials. In most major countries, two separate investigative agencies deal with these separate tasks: one to deal with criminal matters, the other to deal with national-security issues: Scotland Yard and MI5 in Britain, for example. The FBI's unusual double mandate made for a huge and complex workload.[8] But at the same time the FBI was *not* trained to be (nor did it have the legal writ or powers to be) a national-scale antiterrorist agency, combating a real insurgency—the task it was asked to perform with respect to Weatherman in the spring of 1970.

The FBI was technically a unit of the Department of Justice. But under J. Edgar Hoover it was to all intents and purposes an independent agency. By long practice and custom Hoover administered the Bureau as if it were not under the purview of any of the great bureaucratic divisions of the Department of Justice overseen by assistant attorneys general. He answered only to the attorney general himself—and to the president of the United States.[9] By 1970 the Bureau had a roster of 8,500 special agents (the classic "G-men"), backed by an army of 11,500 clerks who produced an enormous amount of paperwork annually. Its budget was $290 million a year, and rising. Besides the headquarters in Washington (then in the Federal Triangle complex), it had fifty-nine field offices under special agents in charge, all in major cities. These field offices in turn controlled hundreds of smaller local resident agencies.[10] The FBI field offices had little or no contact with one another; all communication between field offices went through the central directorate in Washington.

The Bureau was headed by a legend. J. Edgar Hoover was now seventy-five years old—and in his forty-fifth year as director, having been appointed to the post in 1924. He was ill-tempered, dictatorial, increasingly eccentric, and charged with running an organization whose size was outstripping his declining administrative energy. But Hoover retained excellent political instincts; they were key to his long tenure.[11]

Though Hoover insisted on being informed of everything important and much that was trivial, and filled his time writing memo after memo to his agents, much of the real administrative work was done by subordinates. Second in command was Clyde Tolson, the FBI associate director and Hoover's great friend. Hardworking and efficient, Tolson had long been Hoover's mainstay, but he had suffered a series of strokes starting in 1964, and by 1970 he was not often able to work at the high level of energy required for his post; sometimes he was not able even to come into work at all.[12]

Below Tolson, the FBI divided into two branches, each run by an assistant to the director: one branch dealt with investigations, the other with administration. The Investigative Branch was run by Cartha DeLoach, the number-three man in the FBI bureaucracy. The administrative branch had been run for more than a decade by Gerald Mohr, the number-four man. The two branches were in turn divided into divisions, each with a different task, and each overseen by an assistant director (a post not to be confused with the more senior assistants to the director). The most important division in the Investigations Branch was Division Five, Domestic Intelligence, headed by Assistant Director William C. Sullivan from 1961 until the summer of 1970. Domestic Intelligence was larger both in number of agents and cases than the other two investigative divisions combined. This made the head of Domestic Intelligence the most powerful and prestigious of all assistant directors. Sullivan's career showed that it was the ladder to the very topmost posts.[13]

The Domestic Intelligence Division was the unit that dealt with the New Left, the division that dealt directly with Weatherman. Sullivan claimed to be the only Democrat in the FBI directorate; he was a short and energetic man with a hot temper, and a believer in operations that flouted the law if necessary. When Sullivan ran Division Five, supervisors Charles Brennan and Robert Shackelford oversaw the particular sections dealing with New Left affairs.[14] Cartha DeLoach retired in June 1970 (to join Pepsi-Cola as a high administrator), and Hoover then promoted Sullivan from head of Domestic Intelligence to assistant to the director for Investigations, number-three man below himself and Tolson. Sullivan had long been one of Hoover's favorites; he was the only person at the Bureau besides Tolson whom Hoover ever called by his first name ("Bill"); normally Hoover preferred formal address.[15]

Sullivan as assistant to the director for investigations directly oversaw all Bureau investigations and influenced all operations. He chose Charles Brennan, bespectacled and energetic, to replace him as assistant director in charge of Division Five. Brennan, only a senior special agent in 1968, had risen rapidly in the FBI as the threat from the New Left intensified: from special agent to inspector to assistant director in just two years. One reason was Brennan's closeness to Sullivan: "He was Sullivan's boy," says Brennan's successor Edward Miller. And he was resented both because of his strict administrative style and because of his elevation over men senior to him in Division Five.[16] The other reason for Brennan's promotion was his alleged New Left expertise. But this "expertise" went only so far: Both Sullivan and Brennan were frightened men in spring and summer 1970, because in reality they had no accurate idea of Weatherman's size or capabilities.

In autumn 1971, the Bureau was rocked by sudden changes in its top echelon. When the secret Vietnam War documents called "the Pentagon Papers" were stolen and portions published in the *New York Times*, President Nixon was furious and tasked the FBI with finding the culprit. Daniel Ellsberg, a former government official, was the prime suspect. Charles Brennan interrogated Leo

Marx, Ellsberg's father-in-law. But Marx was a friend of Hoover's and Hoover had forbidden that he be questioned, and Brennan originally lied about having done it. Meanwhile, Sullivan had never recovered in Hoover's estimation from a speech he had given in October 1970 downgrading the importance of the Communist Party. In mid-1971, about the time that Brennan ran afoul of Hoover, so did Sullivan—by objecting to Hoover's plans to expand FBI operations overseas. Hoover responded to this double challenge to his authority—this betrayal—by demoting Brennan from assistant director to inspector and removing him from headquarters, while forcing Sullivan into early retirement. He was still in charge of the Bureau.[17]

Hoover picked FBI veteran Alex Rosen to succeed Sullivan as assistant to the director for investigations. But he had already chosen W. Mark Felt for a brand new post, deputy associate director, above both of the assistants to the director, though below Tolson, and Felt had become the new third man in the Bureau. Felt, previously assistant director in charge of the Inspections Division, claimed to be a solver of administrative problems. According to Felt, Hoover told him he created the post of deputy associate director in summer 1971 primarily to control Sullivan, because Tolson was now too ill to exercise authority. Within the FBI, Felt was thought to be too slick and smooth, as Sullivan had been seen as too spiky; and he had naturally incurred hostility in the ranks as the man in charge of inspections. From his new position as deputy associate director, Felt got Hoover to approve Edward Miller as the new assistant director of the Domestic Intelligence Division, replacing the dismissed Brennan. Like the promotion of Brennan to run Domestic Intelligence under Sullivan, this was the victory of a faction: Ed Miller had been Felt's chief assistant in Inspections. Felt and Sullivan had detested each other, both personally and in terms of policy.[18]

Other than the director himself, these officials decided FBI national policy toward Weatherman. There were two reasons for their central role. First, they were the only high officials who had regular direct access to Hoover, and thus they could exercise some influence over the old man (a similar situation would exist under Hoover's successor, L. Patrick Gray). Second, they were the only high Bureau officials with access to all the information about Weatherman coming in daily from all fifty-nine field offices throughout the country.[19]

A sociological note: It is important to recognize, as David Cunningham has pointed out, that the FBI men involved in the battle against Weatherman were mostly graduates of second-level colleges and universities, who knew—and resented bitterly—that they were pursuing graduates of some of the best universities in the country (Columbia, Chicago, Michigan, Harvard). It is an important point. And, as noted previously, there was a profound generation gap. The FBI men were all old enough to be the Weathermen's fathers; they were also, almost all of them, combat veterans of World War II (some of them decorated)—veterans, too, of the long fight later waged against the Communist Party U.S.A. These experiences colored their entire worldview of good and evil. They were appalled by Weatherman.[20]

The FBI began collecting and analyzing the public statements of Students for a Democratic Society from the founding of SDS in 1962. This was part of the FBI's COMINFIL (communist infiltration) surveillance project; the Bureau was concerned that the young New Leftists were being infiltrated by the Communist Party.[21] Then, in 1964, the new age of student activism on campus erupted with the Free Speech Movement at the University of California at Berkeley. Since one of FSM's student leaders was Bettina Aptheker, daughter of a Communist Party U.S.A. historian and a member of the party herself, this was enough to convince J. Edgar Hoover that a serious new threat of communist infiltration and agitation was emerging.[22]

Monitoring of SDS intensified after the first big demonstrations it organized against the Vietnam War in April 1965. From this point on, the FBI began to place informants in SDS, some of whom reached positions of influence, including Bill Divale.[23] It is alleged that the Bureau also began a wiretap of the phone in SDS national headquarters in Chicago after the April 1965 demonstrations. The wiretap was certainly in place in later years.[24]

On May 28, 1968—mostly in reaction to the student takeover of Columbia University—the FBI for the first time ordered its field offices to draw up a list of New Left organizations that required monitoring; the goal was not to prosecute crimes but to know the plans of these groups. In a classified June 18, 1968, memorandum the FBI Directorate also put all elected national SDS leaders onto the Bureau's "Key Activists" List. Key activists were defined as "individuals who are the moving forces" in a targeted group—alleged extremists whose activities local field offices were to monitor on a daily basis. This memorandum also introduced Bernardine Dohrn for the first time to most special agents in charge; she received a "key activist" file because she had just been elected SDS interorganizational secretary.[25] And because the activity of New Left radicals intensified over the summer of 1968 (most noticeably at the Chicago Democratic Convention); in October the list of key activists was expanded.[26]

According to Sullivan, the FBI used the same investigative techniques against the New Left that it had used against the Communist Party: "wiretapping, informants, hidden microphones—the lot." Starting in summer 1968, the FBI also began to run counterintelligence (COINTELPRO) operations against SDS, directed by Sullivan's Domestic Intelligence Division. The purpose of COINTELPRO was to penetrate and disrupt targeted groups.[27] The justification for these operations against SDS was that SDS was thought to have been influenced by the Communist Party. The truth was considerably different: by 1968 SDS leaders saw themselves as far *more* radical than the CPUSA, which they viewed with disdain, as ineffective and old-fashioned. Besides, the New Left had from its inception been impatient with the Old Left's apologetics for Stalinism as well as its stuffy adherence to older Marxist dogma. Nevertheless, SDS was willing to make alliances with others on the Left and had refused to embrace the Cold War anticommunism that some on the liberal Left sought to make a litmus test of untainted democratic principle. SDS was firm in its anti-anticommunism. These were distinctions that were largely lost on the FBI. Still, while Sullivan knew that the link between SDS and the CPUSA was tenuous, he also knew that Hoover wanted to hear that connections existed, so he dutifully investigated them in order to keep the director happy.[28]

The FBI soon was running large informant operations against the increasingly radical SDS; by mid-1969 there were around 120

FBI informants in SDS and other New Left organizations, and they existed at almost every level. When the FBI ordered its informants attending the tumultuous June 1969 SDS convention in Chicago to vote for the faction that would become Weatherman, it did so convinced that it was the more disciplined Progressive Labor that was the more dangerous of the factions contending for control of the organization. The Bureau was mistaken.

After the Chicago convention, FBI informants maintained access even to inner levels of Weatherman planning (though perhaps not the most restricted levels). In late July 1969 an informant in the SDS National Office in Chicago, now Weatherman headquarters, told the FBI that the National Office was attempting to gain maximum publicity for Bernardine Dohrn's press conference upon her return from Cuba, worried that the press coverage would be overshadowed by the American landing on the moon. Similarly, an informant in the New York office of SDS told the FBI that Dohrn on August 18 had urged New York SDS to engage in more violence, adding that her attitude was now much harsher than at the SDS meeting in Austin back in March.[29] Besides informants, the FBI in 1969 had a wiretap on phones inside SDS headquarters in Chicago; it had existed at least since October 1968. Charles Brennan had reported to William Sullivan in December 1969 that "a sensitive and reliable source having access to the national headquarters"— FBI code for electronic surveillance—reported complaints from Weatherman Cathy Wilkerson that the group was close to going broke.[30]

After the Days of Rage riots in October 1969, the FBI also opened a file on every known Weatherman—not merely on the leaders. This put several hundred people under investigation. Charles Brennan set out the reasoning behind the decision to Sullivan on November 20: the Weatherman group might contain only a few hundred hardcore members (judging from the number who showed up for the Days of Rage), but the ideology in their June 1969 Weatherman Manifesto called for a clandestine organization of revolutionaries strong enough to defeat the U.S. government through violence. The new investigation after the Days of Rage was intended to determine whether the threat was serious enough to warrant the inclusion of all Weathermen in the FBI

Security Index; such inclusion made one a candidate for detention without trial in case of a national emergency.[31]

It is unclear how successful this anti-Weatherman project was. The Security Index contained various categories, from I (the most important personages) to III (the least important). By 1970 the total number of alleged New Leftists in all categories was approaching a shocking seven thousand people. But for the people in Categories II and III, which was most people on the list, a moratorium on continued investigation had been instituted, because the FBI was without adequate manpower to proceed. It had too much else to do.[32]

A week after the Days of Rage, the FBI also learned of what it believed was a credible Weatherman threat to assassinate the president. In the wake of the assassinations of the Reverend Martin Luther King Jr. and Senator Robert Kennedy in spring 1968, the Bureau had worried about leftist attempts to assassinate public figures at the Chicago Democratic Party Convention that summer— "not only conceivable but likely," wrote Brennan to Sullivan at the time.[33] Given that mindset, the FBI was alarmed when in mid-October 1969 it received word that one of the Weatherman leaders, Brian Flanagan, was threatening to lead his collective in an attempt to kill Richard Nixon. The information had originated from Flanagan's friend the journalist Dotson Rader (who unknowingly told an FBI informant), and Rader's predictions of Weatherman action had proven correct in the past. The threat was immediately sent to Nixon himself, and to Vice President Spiro Agnew, in a message marked "TREAT AS YELLOW," a color that denoted the second-highest security threat. Flanagan was already under indictment in Chicago for attempted murder for his attack during the Days of Rage on Richard Elrod, the counsel for the City of Chicago, who ended up paralyzed. The FBI had also heard from an informant that Flanagan had been involved in three bombings in New York City before he went to Chicago. All this made Flanagan's threat (even if it was mere boasting) appear credible.[34]

In early November 1969, the FBI gave the field offices the following appraisal of the evolution through which "the Weatherman faction of SDS" seemed to be going: it was increasingly Marxist-Leninist, and increasingly focused on violence ("including bombing and arson") in order to achieve its revolutionary objectives. This was an accurate analysis. Bureau informants inside the organization were not wrong.[35]

That month the FBI began to run another COINTELPRO operation against the group. This operation—like the "Vote Weatherman" project—has long been secret. The preliminaries began in August, when the fifty-five-year-old leader of a pro–Chinese Communist group in Chicago—who was actually an FBI informant—contacted Weatherman leaders, including Mark Rudd, and told them that the Chinese Communist government wished to be kept up to date on Weatherman plans and activities. The Weathermen sent greetings through him to the Chinese Communist Party and to Anna Louise Strong, an American left-wing journalist living in China—but provided no other information. In November, the FBI decided that the informant should offer a contribution of five hundred dollars ostensibly "from the Chinese Communist Party" as an inducement for Weatherman to start reporting regularly on their plans, with a hint of more contributions if comprehensive reports were provided. In late November the informant met in Chicago with Bill Ayers and Jeff Jones. They explained to him the reasons for Weatherman's break with the Black Panthers over the Panthers' increasing wariness of revolutionary violence. The information was duly reported to FBI higher-ups. It is uncertain how much other information about Weatherman ideology and plans the FBI obtained through this operation; it ended in March 1970 when the Weathermen suddenly disappeared underground.[36]

The FBI also knew that Weatherman had threatened violence during the huge anti-Vietnam march on Washington planned for November 15, 1969. The anxiety of the government over what might happen is clear: the November 15 marchers were forbidden to encircle the White House even at a distance, and, along with police and National Guard units, there stood ready to intervene both a regiment of Marines and a brigade of the 82nd Airborne Division.[37] Bill Ayers had told the organizers that unless they gave Weatherman twenty thousand dollars for bail and fines for the Days of Rage, he and his people would cause big trouble; the demand was refused.[38] In the event, the Weathermen—a tiny part of a crowd officially estimated at 250,000 (and perhaps much larger)—

did engage in street-fighting with police near the embassy of South Vietnam, and then led thousands of people into the courtyard of the Justice Department itself, where they threw red paint on the building, hammered at its doors, and ran up a Vietcong flag. John Mitchell, viewing the shouting mob at the Justice Department from his office, later told his wife that it looked like the Russian Revolution of 1917. More street-fighting with the police followed. The teargas released on the crowd was so powerful that when some of it wafted up to where Mitchell was standing, he himself was overcome. For Weatherman, this was a replay of the Days of Rage, but more successful.[39]

Given Weatherman's willingness to engage in violence as shown in Chicago in October and in Washington in November, the Bureau took a keen interest in the "War Council" held in Flint, Michigan, at the end of December. The Flint police photographed every person who entered the dingy ballroom where the meeting took place, and the photos were sent directly to FBI headquarters in Washington; the informant Larry Grathwohl reported in detail on the meeting, with its loose talk of bombings and attacks against the police and military. Later, the only person ever to defect from the Weatherman leadership told of a plan for lethal bombing that had been plotted by the leaders at Flint—but this information came to light only in April 1970, by which time Weatherman's plans for a lethal bombing campaign was all too clear to the Bureau.[40]

In mid-February 1970, word of another Weatherman assassination threat reached the FBI. An informant reported that he had heard Mark Rudd, speaking in a restricted but still aboveground Weatherman meeting in Cleveland on February 4–7, advocate the bombing of police and military installations as a first step toward revolution—that is, Debrayism—and heard him urge that assassination be embraced as a necessary tactic too, though Rudd did not specify any particular target. Despite Rudd's vagueness, the FBI immediately transmitted to the White House and the Secret Service what it considered a serious assassination threat, as it had done with Flanagan's reported remarks in November.[41]

Thus up to February 1970 the FBI was keeping tabs on the Weatherman group, and close tabs on the leaders, was receiving information on ideology and intentions, and had reported two assassination threats. But Weatherman was a small group, and Larry Grathwohl thought that during winter 1969–1970 his FBI handlers did not show much energy; they began to push him hard for more information only in early March 1970, after the town-house explosion and the discovery of the Detroit bombs.[42]

Meanwhile, in a preliminary investigation of Weatherman and SDS funding in November 1969, the FBI concluded that none came from foreign sources.[43] But in late February 1970, the White House, convinced that foreign powers were backing the Weathermen, pressed the FBI to produce evidence that would prove it was so. Presidential aide Egil Krogh pushed this via Robert Haynes, the FBI liaison with the White House. Krogh stressed that President Nixon himself believed the radicals were agents of a foreign communist power or powers—just like the Communist Party U.S.A. Nixon had cut his political eyeteeth fighting the CPUSA, and he had been right about the communists as foreign agents. Now he was convinced that both the FBI and the CIA had failed—through inefficiency and lack of zeal—to find the foreign link he was convinced again existed.[44] The FBI response went to the president on February 26. It stated that there was still no evidence of foreign funding of radicals, and that more intrusive investigations into funding would entail legal and political risks for the Bureau should the efforts be discovered. The dangers were set out in a twenty-two-page annex to the report.[45]

The White House replied bitterly on March 5, through a con-versation between Krogh and Haynes. The memorandum of Haynes to Sullivan, written the next day (March 6), is now fully available. It reveals that Richard Nixon in early March—*before* the townhouse explosion—was urging the FBI to use investigatory and surveillance techniques against the New Left which the FBI itself thought were dangerous:

> Krogh advised that John [*sic*] Haldeman and the President had gone over the material we furnished on February 26.
> ... Krogh stated that they understand that there are certain limitations upon what intelligence we can gather but that the President is anxious for us to do more digging ... The President wants to know who or what are the sources of

the income, the amount, and the names of contributors. He wants us to use all available means to gather this data including technical surveillances and other sophisticated techniques. If necessary, Haldeman can recommend to the President that he discuss this with the Attorney General in order to give the Bureau necessary support. The President is becoming more alarmed about New Left Activities.[46]

Richard Nixon was personally pushing this investigation. He went over the February 26 FBI report in detail with H. R. Haldeman, his chief of staff, and Nixon was impatient with any hesitation on grounds of legality regarding methods for going after the radicals. He offered to give political cover to the FBI if those methods ("technical surveillances," that is, illegal bugging) should lead to political and legal problems. The president refused again to accept this February FBI finding about lack of foreign funding—a reiteration of the November 1969 finding. In 1980, former Attorney General Mitchell—a close friend of Nixon's—testified to the president's obsessive belief that foreign communist governments were deeply involved in the antiwar movement, and not only in the large demonstrations, but in Weatherman and similar groups on the extreme Left.[47]

The FBI apparently did not take up Nixon's offer to provide political cover for intensified financial investigations. But the events of March 6 itself—the townhouse explosion and the Detroit bombing—intensified the government's concern. Then on the night of March 11–12 came bombings of the New York headquarters of Socony, Sylvania Electric Corporation, and IBM. That morning Tom Charles Huston, special aide to Nixon for internal security issues, wrote the president via Haldeman a memo titled REVOLUTIONARY VIOLENCE. Huston was blunt:

> I want to go out on a limb and warn with deadly seriousness that the threat is terribly great ... that we are not taking this problem seriously enough nor doing enough to cope with it. . . . In the past 48 hours we have had five separate incidents involving bombings. New York bombings occurred

in the offices of three large corporations—a new target of
the revolutionaries. . . .

You should be aware that the most logical target for
these people is the President and the White House. . . . I
urge you to consider a thorough review of White House
security procedures. Ask yourself how difficult it would be
for a 23 year old beauty to place her handbag with 5 sticks
of dynamite in the ladies' room in the Residence while
going through on a White House tour. . . . Those kids in
Greenwich Village had a bomb-factory set up and they
weren't manufacturing toys. Six months ago I warned that
this was where we were headed, and nothing was done. I
think a prima facie case has been made that perhaps
I haven't been whistling Dixie in the dark.[48]

Huston had indeed warned the previous August that major
violence was in the offing. He had correctly suspected that
Weatherman would become more and more violent. He had correctly predicted widespread and large demonstrations for the fall.
Now, on March 12, he predicted that "this spring [1970] may prove
the most violent on and off campus that we have yet witnessed"; he
would again be right. And, with his proven track record, he also
now predicted direct Weatherman bomb attacks on the national
government itself, including the president.[49]

Where did Huston come up with his scenario of a bomb being
planted in a women's bathroom in the White House? None of the
bombs detonated at the corporation headquarters in New York had
been placed in a women's bathroom. And the townhouse explosion
had occurred in a basement. Perhaps Huston was thinking of
the attempted Weatherman bombing of 13th Precinct in Detroit
on March 6, where a huge bomb had been placed in a women's
bathroom.[50]

Huston was a relatively junior staffperson at the White House,
and only twenty-nine years old. But he occupied a special position
with Nixon and had good access to him. A former president of the
conservative Young Americans for Freedom and a former military
intelligence officer, Huston had been personally recruited to
Nixon's side in early 1966, and had arranged a crucial meeting

between Nixon and leading Republican conservatives in Washington that August. At this meeting Nixon convinced the conservative leaders (including William Rusher, publisher of the *National Review*) of his own conservative views, and won their support—an important step on his way to the Republican nomination in 1968. Huston often signed his memos as "Cato the Younger"— the famous Roman conservative. Nixon considered him tough and smart.[51]

That same day another assassination warning was delivered to Nixon—this time from Daniel Patrick Moynihan, former assistant secretary of labor in the Johnson administration and now counselor to the president for domestic affairs, with cabinet rank. He shared the same dark vision as Huston. On March 12, he too wrote to Haldeman to express foreboding. Moynihan was aware, of course, of the recent townhouse explosion, but also of the bombings in the New York the previous night—which he attributed to Weatherman:

> For about a year now I have been keeping a file and thinking about sending you a memo on terrorism. The time has come. . . . We have simply got to assume that in the near future there will be terrorist attacks on the national government, including members of the Cabinet, the Vice President, and the President himself. . . . The war has already begun. The level of political violence has been escalating steadily for the past two or three months. For the last week or so bombs have been exploding up and down the Eastern seaboard. We have to assume, for example, that the Mad Dog faction of the Weathermen will in time learn to make anti-personnel bombs, as they evidently were trying to do in Miss Wilkerson's house. We have to assume those folks blowing up corporate headquarters in New York City will soon turn to blowing up corporation heads.

Moynihan continued:

> Political violence is not new to the nation. . . . But I do believe the present situation is different. What we are facing

is the onset of nihilism in the United States. There is an element of psychopathology in all of this. ... Consider that at the last convention of the Weathermen Charles Manson's photograph was everywhere.[52]

Moynihan then argued that the Chicago Eight trial had been a political disaster for government relations with the young. Originally, both Nixon and Hoover, in a secret meeting at the White House in April 1969, had thought the trial an excellent idea. And the trial did bring the government advantages: it kept major antiwar organizers off the street and tied up in court for a year, as they focused on the trial and raised money for their defense. In fact, this was one of purposes of the trial (and other "conspiracy" cases) as Attorney General Mitchell and the president well understood.[53]

But Moynihan declared that the trial, before the elderly and clearly biased Judge Julius Hoffman, had in itself undermined young people's faith in the entire legal system. Hoffman himself had been receiving daily death threats.[54] When the trial ended in guilty verdicts on February 25, 1970, there had been campus riots across the country; at the University of California at Santa Barbara protesters had burned down a Bank of America. After the verdict, a leader of the White Panthers—a group allied with Weatherman—issued a public statement: "I don't want to make it sound like all you got to do is kill people, kill pigs, to bring about revolution, but ... it is war, and a righteous revolutionary war." Susan Stern, in her Weatherman collective in Seattle, was certain now that a real war was coming. Even the great rock 'n' roll star Jimi Hendrix was telling his audiences that he had doubts that the country would reach the summer intact. The *Berkeley Tribe* responded to the Chicago verdict with the headline: "We Call for Total Chaos in the Capitalist Countries, Inside the United States We Will Have War." The issue included a story about an assassination threat against Richard Nixon, and an editorial, "A Call to Arms," which announced that the *Tribe* would soon start publishing instructions on the use of firearms. This issue appeared on newsstands the week before the townhouse explosion.[55]

This, of course, was not the mood of most of the country, which increasingly disdained the far-left radicals. In opposition to Hendrix,

Creedence Clearwater Revival's John Fogarty–the composer and singer of the band's hit "Bad Moon Rising," a song adopted as a kind of anthem by the Weatherman Underground—thought that the movement had gone way too far.[56] Nevertheless, Moynihan wrote, "The trial was a terrible setback to the cause of social stability. . . . Authority was made to look foolish, incompetent, impotent, corrupt." Events such as the trial were only encouraging the growth of New Left terrorism. The situation was unprecedented; in Moynihan's judgment it now required a systematic and coordinated security response, starting with protection of the White House itself:

> It simply won't do to add the extra guard detail here or there, or to pay a few more informants. . . . First, we must take a thorough look at the question of the security of the President. Times simply have changed. Second, someone really ought to look into the question of just who is in charge of our intelligence in these areas. . . . Really, dealing with the old Stalinist Communist Party was child's play compared to dealing with the Weathermen.[57]

Moynihan's concern over the low quality of intelligence available on the radical Left was widespread in the Nixon administration. That concern was especially shared by President Nixon, who was, it is fair to say, increasingly obsessed with the threat he was convinced the extreme Left posed.

In the immediate aftermath of the townhouse explosion, the view that the country might actually be on the verge of civil war was held not only by some in the White House but also by some on the moderate Left. It was what Norman Mailer thought. I. F. Stone feared the same. A critic of U.S. administrations—and uncle of townhouse survivor Kathy Boudin—Stone warned in the March 23, 1970, issue of I. F. Stone's Bi-Weekly that with the rate of bombings increasing, the country might be entering the first stage of an urban guerrilla war. Like Moynihan, Stone worried that the Chicago Eight trial had destroyed faith in the courts, and was pushing radicalized youth toward the bombers.[58]

Supreme Court Justice William O. Douglas also expressed an urgent desire to change the country's course before it was too late.

In February, he had published an extraordinary denunciation of American society, and declared that with grievances piled high and an immovable government, "those who see no escape are hopelessly embittered." He compared the establishment to George III and warned that it might suffer the same fate or be forced to suppress dissenters and rebellion by force of arms. Were that to be attempted, he predicted, "America will face, I fear, an awful ordeal."[59]

Chrissie Hynde, the future rock 'n' roll star, was then an undergraduate student at Kent State University, but her feelings of anger and foreboding were similar to those of the Supreme Court justice:

> We saw sickening images daily on television: Vietnamese families decimated, machine-gunned and napalmed—their homes burnt to the ground. Fatuous slogans like "Give Peace a Chance" further frustrated things by giving the bogus impression that we were doing something about it. But rhetoric rang hollow. . . . Talking about peace and love was airy-fairy while people were getting their limbs blown off. It was a lot of posturing in the name of protest, but like an art installation, what did it mean? How much more thought-provoking could things get? Where was the solution?[60]

March 12, 1970—the day of the Huston and Moynihan assassination warnings to Nixon—was the worst day that New York City suffered during the entire radical onslaught of the late sixties and early seventies. The explosions that rocked three skyscrapers and wrecked corporate headquarters early that morning had been preceded by warning phone calls to evacuate the buildings. During the day three hundred additional bomb threats were phoned in to the police—and after the three real explosions, no one could take any chances. Thousands of people were evacuated from one building or another—the *New York Times* estimated that fifteen thousand people were sent into the streets, from more than a dozen major office buildings. Parts of the city were totally disrupted; fears of bombing led to the cancellation of trials as far away as Long Island. The demands on the NYPD bomb squad interrupted its investigation of the ruins of the townhouse itself. "Are they blowing up that building, too?" asked one man when he saw a large crowd in the street.[61]

Many people wondered whether this was only the beginning. The president of the New York City Council, Sanford Garelick, a former police official, warned that although the terrorist groups were small, their numbers were growing and that these groups (Weatherman prominent among them), operating with ever-greater tactical sophistication, were now capable of "great destruc-tion."[62] A *New York Times* front-page story that day noted, as would I. F. Stone, that the frequency of left-wing bombings was increas-ing: Seattle had suffered thirty-two bombings in the previous year, but this included twenty in just the past four months; San Francisco had suffered sixty-two bombings in the past year, with the pace increasing in February—including the fatal bombing of a police station.[63] Many government officials were not sure what they were confronting, and their fears seemed justified by what they could see happening all around them.

Nixon himself hardly needed proof. He was prepared to act. On March 2, he had ordered Haldeman to begin a nationwide campaign to politically isolate the antiwar radicals. He was not interested in conversations or conciliation with them, as some in the administration were urging:

> From now on we are going to take a very "militant" posi-tion against these people, not simply because the public is probably with us, but because we face a national crisis in terms of this disrespect for law, etc., at all levels. . . . I con-sider this new direction as being of the highest priority. I want absolutely no deviation from it.[64]

On the evening of that March 12, the president had invited the political theorist Irving Kristol down to the White House from New York University for dinner to give him a historical perspec-tive on the intensifying terrorism. At dinner, Kristol compared Weatherman to the nineteenth-century Russian *Narodniki*—middle-class university students who had turned terrorist, identify-ing with the downtrodden peasants and workers; Kristol told the president that in 1881 they had assassinated the reformist Czar

Alexander II. That was the third warning about his personal safety that Nixon had received in a single day.[65]

Kristol's private dinner with Nixon was revealed a month later, when a story appeared in the *New York Times*. What did not became public was that immediately after Kristol's departure back to New York, Nixon convened a meeting with his closest aides and advisers, expressing worry that evidence of serious physical threats (including kidnapping and possibly outright assassination) now existed against high officials in the government, including himself. At the meeting Nixon said that he was receiving relatively little useful information about New Left terrorism, especially not from "some of the older agencies," a complaint Moynihan had also made. The FBI liaison official at the White House reported all this to his superiors; it is because of his memo that we know of the post-Kristol meeting. The next day Haldeman wrote in his diary:

> Lot of concern growing about terrorism and left-wing plans for violence. Many in staff feel it is a real and major threat and that it extends to the P[resident] and top officials, assassination or kidnapping. Feel we are not taking adequate preventive measures and that we have totally inadequate intelligence.[66]

Kristol's analogy of Weatherman to the Russian Narodniki was apt. The Weatherman, after all, had kicked off the Days of Rage by blowing up the statue in Chicago's Haymarket Square, erected to honor seven policemen allegedly killed by anarchists in the aftermath of a labor demonstration on May 4, 1886.[67] As for plots against the president, Bill Ayers later claimed that Weathermen did indeed case the White House itself for a possible attack. Nothing, however, came of this. Attorney General John Mitchell remembered at the Felt-Miller trial that he had received intelligence that Weatherman would indeed try to assassinate the president—and a document was produced to show that he did receive such information.[68] This supposed Weatherman threat to Nixon and other high officials was an exaggeration, but there clearly was a palpable sense of vulnerability in the minds of many Nixon administration officials. And if what Ayers says is true about Weatherman scouting the

White House for an attack, it is not as if the supposed threat was invented out of thin air.

Under these circumstances, Nixon didn't hesitate to increase pressure on the FBI to do something about Weatherman. The Bureau understood that the president's negative comments on March 12 about "the older agencies" had been a slap at the FBI. The FBI failure to find foreign funding of radicals no doubt played a part in Nixon's irritation. Early the next week, on March 16, Thomas Kelly, the assistant director of the U.S. Secret Service, relayed to the FBI Nixon's desire for more detailed and continuous information about New Left terrorists—and especially the president's concerns about actions that might constitute a threat to high government officials. The political problem for the FBI was clear from Kelly's assurance that he *personally* believed the information on radicals which the FBI was providing was more than adequate.[69]

Hoover responded quickly. Already on March 6, Bill Sullivan had been told, with reference to the radicals, "We are being pressured for more information and we are either going to have to produce it or say we can't." On March 12, Hoover had sent a circular to all fifty-nine special agents in charge, warning of "the growing terroristic acts of extremist groups" and ordering increased efforts to place informants in those groups. Hoover responded to Kelly's message about Nixon's demand for more information on extremists with an emphatic comment: "It is *imperative* we give this top priority, both as to *intensified coverage* as well as *dissemination* particularly to the president and others."[70]

The perpetrators of the March 12 corporation bombings called themselves Revolutionary Force 9. This was a hitherto unknown group. It is a measure of the disconnect between the FBI directorate and the youth culture that the group's name was wrongly attributed by Charles Brennan, in a memo to Sullivan, as referring to "the title of a 'Beatles' album." But it is also a measure of the growing concern about Weatherman's intentions and capabilities that presidential aides, high officials in the FBI, and J. Walter Yeagley, the assistant attorney general for the Internal Security Division at Justice, all suspected that the March 12 triple bombing was actually the work of Weatherman, and that "Revolutionary Force 9" was simply another name for Weatherman. Revolutionary

Force 9 was never caught, so no knows who they were; Weatherman itself did not give warnings of its bombings at this point in its evolution, and Weatherman targets were the government and its functionaries, not big business.[71]

Some in the FBI suspected that the New York corporation bombings might simply be the work of local perpetrators and thus outside FBI jurisdiction. (Again—nobody in government knew.) But on March 13—the day after the bombings—three assistant attorneys general pressed the FBI to investigate them. But Cartha DeLoach, the number-three man in the Bureau, demurred on grounds of FBI lack of manpower. Hoover backed DeLoach: the FBI could not investigate every bombing or bomb threat in New York City.[72] On March 16—the day that Thomas Kelly delivered the White House's demand for more information—Assistant Attorney General Yeagley again pressed DeLoach for an FBI investigation of the March 12 bombings. Again De Loach refused, this time because the FBI had "no evidence whatsoever of a violation within FBI jurisdiction." But Yeagley would not be put off, and the next day wrote to Hoover, officially requesting such an investigation on grounds that the FBI had a general mandate to collect intelligence about domestic terrorists. Hoover apparently agreed and ordered the New York field office to begin a direct investigation. But FBI headquarters in D.C. still remained intent on watching "to insure we are not indiscriminately dragged into local bombing matters."[73]

On March 17 also, FBI internal memos began to reflect a growing recognition that the townhouse bombs combined with the Detroit bomb plot suggested that Weatherman be treated as a true national threat. Assistant Director R. D. Cotter, the head of the Research Section, laid out the problem to Sullivan in a memo entitled "Nationwide Guerrilla Attacks," in which he made two crucial points: (a) the wave of bombings throughout the country, and especially those in New York City combined with the Weatherman plan to bomb police offices in Detroit, indicated rapidly growing radical violence; and (b) the president himself was expressing great concern about the national scale of these attacks.[74]

Hoover agreed that Weatherman was now a problem on a national scale, which did bring the FBI into the picture. The next day,

March 18, saw the first step in nationalizing the problem: Hoover ordered every FBI field office to prepare a survey of recent bombings and arsons by the New Left: numbers of bombings, targets, dates, types of device, extent of damages, likely perpetrators. The material would all be analyzed and then sent as a special report to the president.[75]

Then, on March 19, Hoover issued a warning to all field offices: "The Weatherman faction of Students for a Democratic Society (SDS) has implemented plans to go underground and form commando-type units to engage in bombing, arson and assassination as political weapons to bring about the revolution." The seriousness of the threat was described in four parts: (a) "On March 6, two large undetonated bombs were located in Detroit, Michigan, police facilities"—planted by Weatherman activists; (b) the townhouse explosion, also the work of "Weatherman activists"; (c) the triple corporate bombings of "Revolutionary Force 9" (assumed to be Weatherman); and (d) the purchase of large quantities of firearms and explosives by Weatherman. The special agents in charge of the field offices were given a list of thirty-three prominent Weathermen, including Bill Ayers, Bernardine Dohrn, Jeff Jones, and Mark Rudd, whom it was imperative now to locate even though they had not been charged with federal crimes. And the SACs were henceforth to append a statement to all communications about the group: Weathermen should be considered dangerous because of their acquisition of firearms and propensity for violence. This warning was reiterated on March 24 to the SACs in the sixteen cities where Weatherman had been most active.[76]

The FBI at this point was trying, in a general way, to locate the elusive Weathermen. That was the limit of their investigation. Thus when on March 25 Deputy Associate Attorney General John Dean (not yet part of Nixon's White House staff) asked on behalf of Attorney General Mitchell whether the FBI was intensively investigating the March 12 corporation bombings, he was told no, though they were going to answer Assistant Attorney General Yeagley's request for an assessment as to whether left-wing groups were responsible. As for the townhouse explosion, New York had sent an initial report to Hoover on March 13, and he had ordered a vigorous "correlative" investigation. But up until late March the

New York FBI office had done little besides report on the New York Police Department's investigation. When Dean asked on March 25 whether the FBI was itself investigating the townhouse, the answer was again negative.[77]

Things changed only on March 30, when Yeagley sent a formal, written request for FBI investigation of the townhouse explosion. As with the March 12 bombings, the request came on grounds of the FBI's duty as an intelligence agency (as opposed to an obligation for a criminal investigation). This justification was accepted by the FBI directorate, which also understood that President Nixon, Congress, and the public, concerned over the increasing frequency and power of bombings, were looking to the FBI for a solution, according to Charles Brennan, "regardless of our jurisdictional limitations."[78] Four days earlier, on March 26, these pressures had already led the FBI to establish a temporary Weatherman Squad. Its purpose was not only to investigate Weatherman on national security grounds but to investigate Weatherman for possible prosecution for criminal acts. Initially, the Weatherman Squad was woefully understaffed and had only three men, and by mid-May only five. By August, it was up to twenty. The order from Hoover to begin conducting a specific investigation of the townhouse explosion went out on April 2.[79]

The day the Weatherman Squad was created, Charles Brennan set out to his boss Sullivan a new rationale for going after the Weathermen. As with Cotter on March 16, Brennan on March 26 underlined that the combination of the townhouse and the Detroit bombs showed that Weatherman was a threat on a national scale. Brennan therefore urged that all field offices conduct an immediate study on the costs in manpower and money of an intense nation-wide investigation. Two memos on April 1 from Brennan to Sullivan are similar: Weatherman had moved from radical philoso-phizing (summer 1969), to street-fighting (the Days of Rage in October 1969), to going underground and starting a bombing cam-paign, and perhaps even to planning assassinations, all "to bring about the revolution." He too pointed to the townhouse explosion and the Detroit bombs as proof that Weatherman now was "a menace of national proportions."[80]

No one knew for sure how big Weatherman was. The FBI in-vestigation since early March had "shown how little we have seen of the iceberg. . . . The problem clearly exceeds our existing manpower." Brennan's recommendations to combat Weatherman were far-reaching: (a) every known Weatherman was to be investigated at the intensive level reserved for key activists; (b) all Weatherman collectives were to be identified and brought under police pressure; (c) microphone surveillance ("misur" work) and other technical surveillance ("tesur" work) was to be used to gain information; and (d) the penetration of Weatherman collectives by informants was to be intensified. Note that with (c), Brennan was proposing intensified use of warrantless wiretaps and bugging against suspected Weathermen or their supporters. All this would require a large reallocation of FBI manpower and money from other tasks. Field offices were ordered to conduct a survey of the manpower needed to cope.[81]

But the FBI in Hoover's last years was not a unified or smooth-running organization: an executive meeting of the assistant directors in early April rejected "the Brennan Plan." It recommended far less. They wanted a special FBI school established to deal with New Left terrorism, a memo sent to all SACs, stressing that their intelligence efforts in this area needed to be intensified, and a survey regarding the financial and manpower costs to the New York field office in establishing serious investigations of the March 12 bombings and the townhouse explosion.[82]

But more was going on. In New York City on April 10, Larry Grathwohl was told there was pressure on the Bureau to make some sort of Weatherman arrests immediately; the order was said to have come from Hoover himself. Grathwohl told his handlers that the only targets available were minor figures, namely Linda Evans and Dianne Donghi, both wanted on federal charges of crossing state lines to foment riot. Grathwohl protested that if the FBI would only wait a little longer, it might catch most of the Weather Bureau—which would have nipped the Weather revolution almost before it got started.[83] But the FBI controllers insisted the arrests had to go forward. On April 15, with Grathwohl's cooperation, Evans and Donghi were caught. Grathwohl was arrested, too—and even fought with the police in an attempt to maintain his cover; but a mistake by an NYPD official resulted in Evans and Donghi realizing he was a police agent.[84]

Perhaps Hoover wanted to assure President Nixon that the FBI at this point was at least doing *something* against Weatherman. But though the arrests made the front page of many newspapers, they actually constituted a significant setback for the Bureau. Evans and Donghi were soon out of jail on bail. As for Grathwohl, he was permanently lost as an informant, and, it would turn out, he couldn't be replaced. After April 15, the Bureau was never able to place another informant in Weatherman.[85]

The day before the New York arrests, William Sullivan told Cartha DeLoach that the FBI now faced in Weatherman "a menace of national proportions"; agents would have to be shifted from other tasks to deal with it. On April 19, Sullivan told his superiors that Brennan, as head of the Internal Security Section in Sullivan's Domestic Intelligence Division, "has the responsibility for the supervision of the area of greatest national significance facing the Bureau today." Five days later, Sullivan repeated to DeLoach that "the scope and magnitude of the threat to the nation" was clear from the New York and Detroit bombs. He estimated the cost of the Weatherman investigations as at least $14 million, and probably twice that if special agents had to be added.[86]

Sullivan's estimates about eventual costs were more than correct. When thirteen Weatherman leaders failed to appear on April 14 for trial in Chicago on felony charges stemming from the Days of Rage, this, too, expanded FBI involvement in Weatherman matters because jurisdiction was now clear: it was now a federal fugitive case. Federal jurisdiction became even more obvious in July when these same thirteen were indicted on federal bombing charges, which were even more serious. The small squad that hunted the Weatherman fugitives in April and May eventually became Squad 42 in the New York field office in June, and then expanded into the permanent Squad 47 (or the Weatherman Squad, as it was also known) in New York in August. The New York City orientation derived from the fact that many Weathermen and much of their activity (so it seemed) had originated there. By August 1970, Squad 47 had twenty agents and was headed by John J. Kearney, the most renowned "black bag operations" (burglary) agent within the FBI.[87]

The Weatherman Squad's expansion indicates the seriousness with which the FBI now took the Weatherman threat. This is confirmed by other actions the FBI took in late spring and summer of 1970 in an effort to capture the Weathermen and to hinder or stop their bombings. The list of the actions that were taken, drawn up in a secret FBI retrospective in late 1971, and made available to the public in 2011, was impressive:

- All field offices were to insure that those Weathermen arrested at the Days of Rage who could be located were to be interviewed in connection with the fugitives. There were almost three hundred individuals on this list.
- The Domestic Intelligence Division established closer connections with the Fugitive Section of the FBI Special Investigations Division (Division Nine), in order to co-ordinate and improve efforts to find the Weatherman fugitives.
- "Technical surveillances"—evidently wiretaps—were placed on key aboveground Weatherman members or supporters around the country, and lookouts placed to observe "key Weatherman support locations," that is, certain people's houses or apartments.
- A computerized "stop index" was set up, covering all known vehicles belonging to Weathermen; thus if local police stopped an automobile, they could quickly find out whether it was connected to the group.
- Local field offices were ordered "again and again" to in-tensify their efforts to put informants into Weatherman underground collectives.
- The Central Intelligence Agency was furnished in June 1970 with a list of Weatherman fugitives to be put on a CIA "stop and watch list" should they travel overseas.
- The FBI set up in September 1970 a central fingerprint file on Weatherman fugitives to help locate the fugi-tives, and other missing Weatherman members.
- A computerized index of telephone numbers was set up at FBI headquarters "to record all telephone numbers utilized by New Left individuals."
- The Laboratory Division set up a central file of hand-writing samples of all known Weatherman members,

the result of intense efforts by the FBI to obtain hand-writing samples of Weatherman leaders. It was hoped that this would help in locating fugitives even if they wrote under assumed names to friends or relatives, and would help in identifying fugitives if they were captured under assumed names.[88]

Yet all these extraordinary measures were unavailing in the hunt for the radicals—not only in 1970 but for years afterward. The field offices found they could not interview many of the 280 arrestees from the Days of Rage because many had already gone underground. The increased cooperation between the Revolutionary Groups unit in Domestic Intelligence and the Fugitives unit in General Investigations produced leads, but the leads never led anywhere. The wiretaps yielded nothing, because the aboveground Weathermen and supporters were highly security conscious when using the telephone. Physical surveillances—always labor intensive—were usually unproductive. As for the CIA, it was never able to locate any member of Weather who may have fled the country. The creation of the Weatherman automobile, handwriting, and fingerprint central lists never resulted in the capture of a single fugitive. The constant orders to the field offices to intensify efforts to place informants in the underground collectives were useless because the collectives simply could not be found.[89]

Meanwhile, high-ranking members of the Nixon administration made it clear to the press that the White House viewed the radical threat with great seriousness. According to a senior White House aide speaking to the *New York Times* on April 12, 1970, "We are facing the most severe internal security threat this country has seen since the Depression." John Mitchell recalled that White House pressure "to do something about the Weathermen" was intense and unrelenting, with "frequent discussions about the fact that the Weathermen were not apprehended."[90] The Bureau's frustration was real, the blow to its pride palpable, Hoover's humiliation growing. For the first time in its long history, the Bureau seemed to be facing not mere subversives but a potential revolution led by radicals willing to use any means necessary—radicals whom the FBI seemed helpless to apprehend or to stop.

CHAPTER FOUR

"Our Own Doors Are Being
Threatened"

I N THE SPRING AND summer of 1970, the situation in the
country seemed increasingly out of control. Within the FBI
the rising fears of revolution may have been exaggerated, but
serious concern was a reasonable reaction to real events.
Charles Brennan, the head of the Revolutionary Groups section in
the Domestic Intelligence Division at that time, wrote a stark evaluation to his boss William Sullivan on May 11: "The threat to the
Nation's ability to function in a crisis situation posed by New Left
extremists has never been more clearly drawn." Brennan estimated
that it would require at least 450 special agents and perhaps as
many as 750 to deal with the threat—a number that represented
nearly one-tenth of the total Bureau manpower available in the
field.[1]

Brennan was reacting to the titanic student uprising caused by
President Nixon's invasion of Cambodia and the killing of student
demonstrators at Kent State University (and Jackson State a few
days later) by National Guardsmen and police. Riots and demonstrations convulsed a thousand campuses across the country, and
hundreds of colleges and universities closed for the rest of the
school year. The shock to the government was enormous. On May

20, the FBI informed Vice President Spiro Agnew that the number of campus demonstrations as well as the level of student violence had doubled since the previous academic year, and was now rising sharply.[2]

"It was a time of extraordinary stress," recalled Henry Kissinger, who was then Nixon's national security adviser: "Washington took on the character of a besieged city. The very fabric of government was falling apart. The executive branch was shell-shocked." At one point, Kissinger had to move into a White House basement because his apartment house was surrounded by demonstrators. Kissinger himself was shocked when his two senior aides resigned in protest over the Cambodian invasion. Two hundred State Department employees signed an unprecedented letter of protest; Nixon's reaction was: "Fire them all!" Secretary of the Interior Walter Hickel published an open letter to Nixon in the *New York Times*, warning that the youthful protestors must be listened to or the crisis would become even worse—an act that infuriated Nixon even more.[3]

The situation seemed so fragile that when—a few days after the Kent State shootings—a massive protest demonstration occurred in Washington, the White House had readied an underground command bunker to shield the president. The White House itself was protected by a double ring of city buses, bumper to bumper. And five thousand soldiers stood ready for action against the protesters. Admiral Thomas Moorer, chairman of the Joint Chiefs of Staff, claimed that the crisis was being masterminded by a mysterious group in Berkeley; that Kent State had nothing to do with Cambodia but was part of a revolutionary plot; and that the radical "command post" in Berkeley was planning an attack on the White House. Thus spoke America's leading soldier.[4]

Just before Kent State, a high-level Democratic Party commission warned that unless young people were included more in the political process, the alternative was "the anti-politics of the street"—riots and anarchy. Two days after Kent State, on May 6, the Wisconsin National Guard reported "open warfare" in Madison. Nixon himself claimed to have been shaken by the scale of the anti-Cambodia demonstrations, and the deaths that had resulted. A reporter directly asked the president in a May 8 press conference whether he agreed with those who argued that America was heading for a revolution. That day dozens of right-wing "hard-hat" construction workers attacked and beat up antiwar demonstrators who had massed at New York's City Hall, sending them running for their lives. The scene was repeated in several other cities. Meanwhile, some on the far Left were openly calling for revolution. Brennan's May 11 memo reflected the general shock in the government and the threat that the FBI saw.[5]

In 1975, Tom Charles Huston, formerly of the Nixon White House, gave the Church Committee investigating intelligence abuses a sense of how serious the country's intelligence agencies regarded the threat they felt was posed at that time by far-left groups: "I think their concern was as great as ours because in 1970 . . . you would have been hard-pressed not to be concerned. . . . Everybody was concerned. The only question was what the results of that concern would be."[6] Huston testified:

> We were sitting in the White House getting reports day in and day out of what was happening in this country in terms of the violence, the numbers of bombings, the assassination attempts [on police]. . . . In the month of May in a two-week period we were averaging six arsons a day against ROTC facilities. . . . We convinced ourselves that this was something that was going to just continue to get worse.[7]

And in these circumstances, the FBI came to fear that Weatherman intended to attack the Bureau itself. As early as February 1970 there had been those within the Bureau who worried that if Weatherman went underground for guerrilla war, the group would specially target the police—including the FBI. The Bureau knew from an informant at the aboveground Weatherman meeting in Cleveland on February 4–7 that Mark Rudd had apparently made threats specifically about bombing military and police installations. Rudd's remarks went straight to the FBI and to the White House. Thus on February 13 Charles Brennan, then head of the Revolutionary Groups section, wrote to his boss Bill Sullivan that the Bureau's field offices had to be warned that they might be targets. Brennan further urged (successfully) that the field offices in turn warn local police agencies within their districts of the special threat of possible Weatherman attack on them, so that they, too, would be on guard.[8]

On May 21, at the height of the Kent State crisis—Bernardine Dohrn appeared to make things perfectly clear when, in the name of Weatherman, she issued a "Declaration of War." She promised a Weatherman attack on a "symbol or institution of Amerikan injustice" within fourteen days. FBI agents went to Chicago and desperately pressed four Weathermen in jail there on riot charges (Sam Karp, Joe Kelly, Russell Neufeld, and Robert Tomaschevsky) to reveal what Dohrn's target might be.[9] On May 28, J. Edgar Hoover sent a circular to all fifty-nine special agents in charge around the country, notifying them of Dohrn's threat, warning them that "bureau space may be selected as a Weatherman target," and ordering them to inform their agents of the personal danger to each of them and to increase the security of all Bureau offices.[10]

On June 9, Dohrn's threat was carried out: with seventeen minutes' warning, a bomb consisting of fifteen sticks of dynamite wrecked the second floor of the headquarters of the New York Police Department, injured eight policemen, and rendered the building useless. That Weatherman had been able to plant a large bomb within a major police headquarters caused officials the most concern. A Weatherman communiqué, issued after the bombing, gloated especially about this aspect of the action.[11]

The June 9 trauma would reverberate all summer. On August 8, Robert Shackelford, who took over as head of the FBI's Revolutionary Groups section when Brennan was promoted to assistant director in charge of the Domestic Intelligence Division, declared, "We are now faced with a large group of pro-Marxist, anarchistic, violence-prone radicals who have openly advocated arson, bombing, use of obscenity and narcotics to destroy the structure of our nation." The FBI at the time saw Weatherman as a group with no limits to their tactics, including assassination. Weatherman, in the FBI's view, was "a small, tough, paramilitary organization designed to carry out urban guerrilla warfare to bring about the revolution."[12]

Yet by August it was no longer true that there were no limits to Weatherman violence. After the townhouse explosion, Weatherman's leaders had decided in May that they were going to focus on damaging property, not people. While the June 9 New York bomb did not bear this out, it was the last Weatherman action in which there were injuries to persons. More typical of the new Weatherman policy was the July 26 bombing against military police headquarters at the Presidio in San Francisco: two small dynamite bombs in the middle of the night. Yet Weatherman's security was now so airtight that the FBI did not learn of this fundamental change in Weather's intentions and tactics until five months later, when the organization itself announced it to the public in the "New Morning" communiqué of December 6, 1970.[13]

Indeed, at the very time that the Weather leadership at its Mendocino meeting was rejecting lethal bombings, the FBI was convinced of Weather's ever-growing threat. And a particular FBI practice made the threat seem even larger than it actually was: the lumping together of Weatherman actions with Weatherman-*type* actions.

The first hint of this broadening of the term "Weatherman" can be seen in the circular Hoover sent to all special agents in charge on April 17. In setting out the new tasks that faced the Bureau, Hoover grouped together "all Weatherman individuals, *as well as those who adhere to the Weatherman ideology* of utilizing terrorist tactics in furtherance of the Revolution," as being the target of the Bureau's investigation of activities and plans. Hoover also wanted an estimate from the special agents of how much such investigations would cost in terms of men and resources.[14]

A few weeks later (May 13), Hoover ordered all field offices henceforth to classify as "Weatherman in character" *all* terrorist violence attributed to Marxist-Leninist or revolutionary groups. This decision meant that FBI headquarters would soon be receiving numerous incident reports from the field employing the description "Weatherman in character." And during the summer FBI headquarters reminded all field offices to keep using this classification: all reports on New Left terrorism or violence "must include name Weatherman in character to facilitate handling at Bureau."[15]

Hoover's FBI had always made a name for itself by publicly combating "big threats" to the nation: it started with the "kidnapping panic" and the "bank-robbing panic" of the 1930s—the Lindbergh baby kidnapping case, Bonnie and Clyde, John Dillinger—and continued into the Red Scare of the late 1940s and 1950s. In that sense, the use in 1970 of the overbroad categorization for "Weatherman" activity was traditional FBI procedure, serving to create a "big threat." But it also led to reports from the field that yielded inflated perceptions at headquarters of Weatherman's capabilities.

In other words, while Weatherman was rightly considered dangerous, especially in early 1970, the FBI's own procedures were to some extent creating a bogeyman. An example is the inflation in the number of bombs the FBI thought Weatherman was detonating around the country: Charles Brennan told *Time* magazine in late August that Weatherman was responsible for a shocking 150 bombings nationwide since the winter, and that Weatherman had perhaps one thousand underground soldiers, and five thousand aboveground direct supporters.[16] Brennan's figures for Weatherman were not simply propaganda; they originated in a top-secret report by Tom Charles Huston. Brennan's alarm was real. His immediate successor as assistant director in charge of the Domestic Intelligence Division, Edward Miller, also believed that Weatherman had set off literally hundreds of bombs.[17] The commentary of *Time* on the frightening figures Brennan disclosed aptly reflected the mood within the FBI directorate: Weatherman was probably as big in September 1970 as the Mafia, and had taken not fifty years to achieve this number, but only fourteen months.[18]

If it is a principal purpose of terrorism to sow fear, then by that measure Weatherman was a resounding success. Brennan told *Time*: "It's only going to get worse." But Brennan's estimates as well as his prediction were wildly wrong. During their *entire* six-year history of bombing (1970–1975), the Weathermen set off only about twenty-five bombs in total. To be sure, twelve of these bombs—that is, half the total of Weatherman bombings in its entire career— were detonated during 1970 itself, so there was a legitimate question in 1970 about what might be coming next. Ultimately, however, Weatherman bombings were neither devastating nor, after autumn 1970, frequent. One reason was that the actual number of Weathermen was very small. There were only about one hundred members, with perhaps two to three hundred aboveground supporters. In reality, Weatherman was never more than one-tenth the size of Brennan's public declaration.[19]

The FBI's problem was that with the loss of the informer Larry Grathwohl—outed in April 1970—it knew very little in summer 1970 about what was going on inside Weatherman, only what the Weatherman communiqués themselves said. Special Agent James Vermeersch of the Weatherman Squad in New York, assigned in the summer of 1970 to watch Bernardine Dohrn's sister Jennifer (and to lead the hunt for Bernardine herself), described the FBI's ignorance:

[We were trying] to see who in fact was the particular person that was responsible for the acts of terrorism ... because we had no idea at the time. . . . All we knew when the squad was formed was that the bombs were exploding, and no one knew, you know, who exactly was responsible, because the so-called perpetrators [the Weatherman Organization] were all underground.[20]

Vermeersch stressed that the responsibility of the FBI in this period was not only to hunt down the Weatherman fugitives but—more important—to thwart their future bombings, a serious national security issue in 1970.[21] But the stark fact was that in this task—as in the hunt for the Weather Underground itself—the FBI was not successful. The bombings, though few and far between, kept happening.

The FBI was a prestigious organization and its alarm over Weatherman quickly spread downward throughout American law enforcement, exacerbating fears about young radicals that already existed among local police.[22] As late as November 1971, the FBI was still using the category "Weatherman-type Groups"—which meant "terrorist oriented groups, related either directly or indirectly to Weatherman"—in publicity about the threat posed by revolutionary groups. The result was that actions originating in radical circles not organizationally linked to Weatherman—including the huge and lethal August 1970 bombing at the University of Wisconsin—were credited to Weatherman, intensifying public fear. And this was true within the FBI itself.[23]

Weatherman rhetoric, and other events, helped deepen this fear. On July 23, 1970, a federal grand jury in Detroit brought an indictment on bombing charges against a dozen Weatherman Underground leaders, none of whom had been caught; the plot against Detroit police installations was the centerpiece of the indictment. Three days later came a sneering Weatherman response, and along with it the first direct Weatherman threat against a high police official, namely Attorney General John Mitchell.[24]

Then, on August 7, Jonathan Jackson and three supporters stormed the Marin County Courthouse in California, seizing hostages (including a judge and an assistant district attorney) while a trial was in progress. It was a direct attack on law enforcement—and an attempt to free Jackson's brother George, who was one of the "Soledad Brothers" accused (in turn) of murdering a prison guard; this had become a cause célèbre on the Left. Jonathan Jackson, several of his comrades, and the hostage Judge Harold Haley were all killed in the ensuing gunfight with police. A picture of Jackson holding a shotgun to the judge's neck became an iconic example of the violence threatening the government.[25] Then, on August 10, Dan Mitrione—the chief public safety adviser of the U.S. embassy in Uruguay, a man thought by the Left to be an expert at torture—was found murdered by the Tupamaros urban guerrilla group. Everyone understood that the Weathermen had idolized the Tupamaros.[26]

And on August 24, a massive truck bomb packed with half a ton of explosives wrecked the building containing the Army Mathematics Research Center at the University of Wisconsin in Madison, killing postdoctoral researcher Robert Fassnacht, injuring several other people, and destroying the work of a dozen graduate students and faculty in the Department of Physics. The bomb also damaged a dozen nearby university buildings. The FBI was convinced that this huge bomb was the work of Weatherman.[27] In September, Brennan called it not only a "professionally engineered truck bomb" but a "foretaste of what might be expected this year." Ten years later he still believed that the Wisconsin bombing was a Weatherman operation.[28] In 1989, the prominent American historian Stephen Ambrose, in a work on the career of Richard Nixon, still believed this. And in 2014, Ken Hughes, another Richard Nixon expert, still did as well.[29]

In reality, the Madison attack was the work of a tiny band of local radicals, led by two Madison natives, Karl and Dwight

Armstrong, who had rarely been out of the Midwest. The bombers had not intended to kill anybody, but they were complete amateurs, and they were careless.[30] One of the group, however, was David Fine—who knew Weathermen Mark Rudd and Cathy Wilkerson. Within a week of the bombing, Fine was an FBI suspect. Shortly thereafter FBI informant Larry Grathwohl told his minders that back in mid-March, when the Weatherman leader Naomi Jaffe had come to Madison to shut down Grathwohl's operation there, she had stayed at the apartment of someone who looked remarkably like Fine. The FBI's belief that Weatherman was likely connected to the huge Madison bomb was not simply plucked out of thin air.[31]

But neither was the FBI belief correct. There was no organizational connection between Weatherman and the Army Math bombers; David Fine was a latecomer to the group, and not a leader. While both Armstrongs may have been inspired in a general way by Weatherman, as Fine would say many years later—an instance of Weatherman leading by example, as the group had hoped—the reality was that the Armstrong brothers were troubled individuals with their own local agenda.[32]

The FBI jumped to similar conclusions in the case of a Boston-area bank robbery in September 1970, in which the radical robbers shot and killed Walter Schroeder, a policeman. For months the FBI attributed this act, too, to Weatherman. Almost forty years later, Jack Kearney, the head of the New York Weatherman Squad in 1970–1972, was still making this claim. But the bank robbery was, again, the work of a group of local amateurs, in this case led by two students from Brandeis University: Katherine Ann Power and Susan Saxe.[33] It is true that Saxe and Power wrote an open letter to Bernardine Dohrn in April 1971, expressing support for the Weather Underground and its ideology. But there was no organizational tie between Weatherman and the Saxe-Power group (which included ordinary criminals, as Weatherman collectives never did). The death of Walter Schroeder during the robbery was not planned, and though the Saxe-Power group was ready to use lethal force in carrying out the robbery, the nature of their action was considerably different from what the Townhouse Collective had intended—and which, after the self-inflicted debacle of March 6, had been disavowed by the Weather leadership. Perhaps, as with the Madison bombing, Weatherman bore some moral responsibility for the Boston robbery, as the sort of thing they hoped to provoke. But for the FBI at the time, the Boston robbery deepened the Bureau's concern over Weatherman's intentions and capabilities.[34]

The day after the huge Wisconsin bombing, Robert Shackelford, the new chief of the Revolutionary Groups section of the Bureau's Domestic Intelligence Division, sent another alarming message about Weatherman to Brennan, the new assistant director for domestic intelligence. Shackelford warned of a possible Weatherman bombing attack on FBI headquarters in Washington itself, and he urged that every field office in the country be "alert[ed] to the possibility that Bureau space may be selected as a Weatherman target."[35] Brennan informed Hoover of Shackelford's warning, and on the same day, August 25, Hoover sent an urgent directive to all fifty-nine field offices. In the directive, Hoover also stressed Weatherman's Declaration of War and that Weatherman policy was "strategic sabotage against military and police installations." He warned that "the FBI, its field offices and Resident Agencies throughout the country are vulnerable to the terroristic tactics of these madmen. No office can consider itself immune to such action." Hoover also worried that the start of the university school year would be a springboard for intensified Weatherman recruiting of young people. He ordered all special agents in charge to warn local military and police officials that they, too, might be attacked by Weatherman. Hoover ended by urging: "Each Special Agent in Charge is personally responsible to insure adequate precautions and plans are taken to protect Bureau Personnel and secure Bureau space."[36]

Two days later (August 27)—with the impact of Wisconsin still reverberating—FBI officials circulated a memo urging Hoover to issue *another* warning to all special agents in charge about the threat that Weatherman now directly posed to the FBI. And the officials repeated Hoover's warning that all FBI offices were under specific Weatherman threat.[37]

It was bomb attacks that they feared most. The FBI organized an astonishing 250 conferences on precautions against bombings for local mayors and police during this period.[38] On August 28 Hoover held a special one-day meeting of representatives from all the field offices on the subject of "Bombings and Bomb Threats"; it was attended by FBI agents who were involved in training local police and the focus was on planning to handle bomb threats, specifically

> searching and evacuating buildings, the visual recognition of the more prevalent types of explosives and incendiary bombs, methods of isolating an area where a suspected explosive device has been located, and scientific aids available in bombing investigations.

Upon returning home, the FBI police trainers were immediately to discuss with their bosses, the special agents in charge, how to plan "for adequate security in our field offices, Resident Agencies, Bureau automobiles, and, where appropriate, personally owned automobiles of our personnel." Agents were to be instructed especially on the mass evacuation of FBI buildings. The memo also required that the trainer give detailed instructions on bomb security to *all* FBI personnel in his field office.[39]

Meanwhile, worry about Weatherman recruiting on campus in the fall appears as early as August 8, the day Shackelford was promoted to his new post. In a memo to Brennan, Shackelford, noting the great turmoil of the past spring, asserted that "there are indications that the coming academic year will see greater violence. . . . Non-campus groups such as Weatherman have been involved in terroristic activities and have made a 'declaration of war' against this country." On September 15, in another circular to all fifty-nine special agents in charge, Hoover himself made the same point:

> Never in our history have we been confronted with as critical a need for informant coverage. Terroristic violence surrounds us and more is threatened. Bombings, assassinations of police officers, kidnapping and murder are all part of the picture. Fanatics are at large who are at war with the Government and the American people.

And, again, Shackelford to Brennan on September 17: "The coming academic year is expected to result in additional violence and terrorism on campus and it is imperative that offices prepare for it."⁴⁰

In a September 21 memo to Sullivan (whom Hoover had now promoted to assistant to the director for investigations, number-three man in the Bureau), Brennan pointed to the allegedly "professionally-engineered" Wisconsin bombing as an indication of the size and scope of the threat the FBI faced, while again repeating Shackelford's warning about upcoming chaos on campus. That afternoon, Attorney General Mitchell met with President Nixon to discuss the lack of progress in the Wisconsin bombing case. Nixon wanted to propose a law to Congress formally expanding FBI jurisdiction to include "campus bombings and similar acts of destruction."⁴¹

Earlier, on September 2, Mark Felt, assistant director in charge of the Inspection Division and a rising figure in the Bureau, had written to Clyde Tolson, the number-two man in the FBI, warning of the Weatherman threat in similarly stark language: "Never in our history have we been confronted with as critical a need for informant coverage. Terrorist violence is all around us and more has been threatened. *Even our own doors are being threatened by Weatherman fanatics.*"⁴²

Felt urged Hoover to drop the ban in force since 1967 on the recruiting of campus informants under the age of twenty-one. The problem, he said, was pressing: "The Students for a Democratic Society have actually reserved for recruiting purposes a room in the Student Union Building at near-by University of Maryland." Felt hoped that by recruiting student-informants as freshmen, the FBI could guide them over time into positions of influence in radical organizations. But Felt argued that it was useless to wait until these students were twenty-one. By that time they were seniors, almost ready to leave the campus. And besides, Felt added—reflecting a view of the universities that was becoming increasingly common—by the time students were seniors they "have been subjected to the corrosive influence and brainwashing of ultra-liberal and radical professors."⁴³

But Felt's memo of September 2 is another example of poor FBI intelligence: it confused the existing remnants of SDS with Weatherman. If FBI agents saw recruiting for Students for a

Democratic Society going on at the student union at the University of Maryland at College Park in September 1970, it was not Weatherman. It was, in fact, Progressive Labor—the bitter enemy of Weatherman. After the split in June 1969, PL always claimed to be the real SDS. Weatherman made the same claim, of course, for several months—but when Weatherman went underground in March 1970, PL was all that was left of the stump of SDS. But Progressive Labor never succeeded in making its commitment to organizing the working class a going concern on campuses. SDS, by the time of Felt's memo, was the last gasp of a failed organization that no longer had any connection to Weatherman at all.[44]

Felt's memo gained the support of William Sullivan, who attached his own note in agreement for lowering the minimum age for informants to eighteen. He added:

> As the memorandum states, these are indeed critical times. No one can predict with accuracy the outcome of the revolutionary struggle going on in this country at this time. Those under 20 years of age are playing a predominant role in campus violence. . . . Two of the subjects in the University of Wisconsin case are under 20.[45]

Hoover was convinced. In a directive sent to all special agents in charge on September 12, he ordered that the age for campus informants be lowered to eighteen.[46]

The danger of embarrassment to the FBI if its recruitment of students so young became known was clear to all. Hoover agreed with Felt that this was "a most sensitive area." But in the perceived crisis in the country—as Brennan, Felt, Sullivan, and Hoover all declared—the chance had to be taken. And this was especially so because of the threat of attacks on the FBI itself. As Felt said, the FBI now had no choice but to employ eighteen-year-olds "in the revolutionary conflict at home."[47]

The fear of a Weatherman bomb attack on the FBI did eventually subside in the Bureau. Concern never went completely away, however. Even in January 1972, there was worry about a bomb attack on the FBI. The independent radical Ronald Kaufman had been indicted for placing nine "detonation devices with calendar clocks" in safety-deposit boxes in banks in Chicago, New York, and San Francisco; he intended to use their upcoming detonations months later to demand the release of "political prisoners" from American jails. After one of the bombs went off prematurely in a bank in 1971, Kaufman disappeared into the underground. Kaufman left behind a list of targets that he urged comrades to attack as symbolic of the U.S. government, and Shackelford was especially worried because Kaufman had on his list the new FBI Headquarters Building in Washington. Shackelford requested that Edward Miller send a memo to all field offices about the dangers of long-term bombs—because they might be a threat to FBI installations. Shackelford was concerned that people with Kaufman's point of view would follow his example. His memo ended up in an FBI Weatherman file.[48]

The FBI was also concerned about possible political kidnappings as a tactic of the extreme Left.

President Nixon, that spring and summer of 1970, was personally alarmed both about assassinations and the prospect of kidnappings. His aides told James Naughton of the *New York Times* that "these were tactics of left-wing radicals" and they would be "employed in Washington, D.C." According to Naughton's April 13, 1970, story, the administration now saw its prime domestic responsibility as "protecting the innocent from 'revolutionary terrorism.' "[49]

Five days later, on April 18, letter bombs mailed to the White House from Seattle were intercepted; the nearby Selective Service Headquarters was another target of these bombs. In talks with the FBI about the letter bombs, White House aide Jack Caulfield raised the kidnapping issue as well:

> With all the publicity given to kidnappings in other countries [by the Tupamaros], Caulfield feels that there is a distinct possibility that this tactic could be adopted by the militants in this country. He feels that a logical target could be a member of the White House staff.

In addition, Caulfield worried about radicals kidnapping foreign dignitaries visiting the United States. Caulfield and others on Nixon's staff cannot have felt reassured when the FBI failed to find the senders of the Seattle letter bombs: Seattle was a center of radicalism, and the FBI reported that there were simply too many suspects.[50]

These White House concerns were transmitted within the FBI to Charles Brennan and William Sullivan.[51] During the summer, spectacular kidnappings were carried out by leftist guerrillas in Latin America. In June a group called Vanguard of the Popular Revolution kidnapped the West German ambassador to Brazil. He was released in exchange for dozens of Brazilian political prisoners, who were flown to Algeria.[52] Then on July 31 the Tupamaros kidnapped FBI agent Dan Mitrione in Uruguay, along with a Brazilian diplomat, and then a British diplomat, and then another American diplomat. In early August came the news that the Tupamaros had killed Dan Mitrione.[53]

J. Edgar Hoover met personally with President Nixon right after Mitrione's murder to discuss the possibility that Weatherman and the Black Panthers would soon be copying the Tupamaros by kidnapping high government officials, or members of the diplomatic corps, or United Nations officials, or members of their families. This concern over the "South American model" had been laid out in great detail for Hoover before his meeting with the president by FBI Inspector George C. Moore, an official in the Internal Security Section in Brennan's Domestic Intelligence Division. Moore's conclusion: "It is reasonable to assume that extremist elements, [such] as the Panthers, the Students for a Democratic Society, including the Weatherman faction . . . may utilize this tactic with greater frequency in the future."[54] On August 17, Hoover apprised Attorney General John Mitchell of his conversation with the president about the kidnapping threat.[55]

The Tupamaros had declared that the ultimate purpose of such kidnappings was the public humiliation and the delegitimizing of a government that could be shown to protect neither its own officials nor important foreign visitors. The strategy aimed also to create a crisis within the government itself, as hardliners clashed with moderates who wished to negotiate with the kidnappers, prompting, according to the Tupamaros, "a crisis in the power-structure." The Uruguayan ambassador to the United States told the State Department in August that his government might collapse, so torn was it between hardliners and accommodationists. Ultimately, such division is what Nixon, Hoover, and their aides feared might occur within the U.S. government under similar kidnapping circumstances. A similar sharp division within the government itself had already happened over Cambodia and Kent State in May. It would soon happen in Canada over leftist kidnappings in October.[56]

Fear intensified when on September 12, 1970, Weatherman helped Timothy Leary escape from San Luis Obispo Prison in California, and spirited him out of the country. In its "Timothy Leary" communiqué of September 15, Weatherman described prisoners in American jails as "prisoners of war." And after once more declaring, "Now we are at war," the communiqué threatened: "Our organization commits itself to the task of freeing these prisoners of war." Weatherman leadership also approved of the Jonathan Jackson raid in Marin, as became clear on October 8, when two separate statements were issued praising Jackson as a revolutionary hero, and his action as heroic. And Weatherman followed up the rhetoric by bombing the Marin County Courthouse itself.[57]

The FBI, it turns out, had a right to worry; Bernardine Dohrn says that kidnappings were being discussed in collectives in the summer of 1970 (and that she spent time that summer arguing against them). Howard Machtinger, for his part, says that Dohrn herself early that summer ordered an operation to kidnap a member of the Rockefeller family—but, because of Weatherman incompetence, the plan (which Machtinger led) failed. Still, the threat was exaggerated—no kidnappings ever occurred, and despite the Weather swagger and bellicose rhetoric, the organization never attempted any prison breaks after the Leary escapade.[58]

To the FBI a special danger loomed with the opening of the autumn 1970 congressional and state political contests. Not only would there by a multitude of candidates traveling around congressional districts and states on campaign, but high government officials—in the traditional way—would be putting in appearances for one candidate or another. But 1970 was not a traditional year: now the FBI worried that officials themselves might be the targets of "kidnap, assault, assassination or intimidation by the elements of the New Left and black power." Strictly speaking, their physical protection was not the FBI's responsibility, but as part of the FBI's intelligence function, it *was* the Bureau's responsibility to warn of danger. FBI officials were particularly worried about the potential implications for the elections of thefts over the summer from armories and U.S. military posts, which suggested the stockpiling of arms and explosives by radical groups.[59]

Again, the FBI worries were not without reason. In December, the Weather Underground expressed disappointment that there had been only a few incidents of violent harassment of Republicans during the autumn election campaign; they had clearly expected it to happen on a wide scale.[60] But harassment is not kidnapping, nor does it appear that Weatherman was itself involved in the harassment (notably at Kansas State and in San Jose) that had occurred. It had done nothing involving the elections.

There were two immediate results of the FBI's worries about the election campaign. First, Robert Shackelford urged Charles Brennan on September 3 to set up a so-called SPECTAR (special targets) program focused on Weatherman. The idea was to find informants in the aboveground fringes of Weatherman and, step by step, work inward to penetrate the group. Hoover approved, and on September 4 he ordered all special agents in charge to begin local SPECTAR programs, with progress reports to be sent in to FBI headquarters every month. Hoover also warned his SACs about possible kidnappings and assaults against major political figures, noting the burglaries of weapons and explosives at military installations, and urging more effort to discover the radicals' plans: "I consider this a matter of utmost importance and I will hold you personally responsible."[61]

Also on September 4, Assistant Director Alex Rosen of General Investigations Division wrote to William Sullivan about the stream of tips that black extremists and New Leftists were considering "kidnapping or assassination of Government officials"; Rosen felt it incumbent on the FBI to inform all government agencies of the threat. The focus of the warning, Rosen said, should be on Weatherman: agencies should be informed of their statements, their advocacy of violence against military and police installations via bombing, arson, and assassination, and their public musing about kidnapping local and federal officials (as Mark Rudd had done at the Cleveland Weatherman meeting in February). Rosen then talked briefly about possible kidnappings by the Black Panthers.[62]

Similarly, Hoover on September 8 sent out a memo concerning the threat to elections; and once more, the alleged kidnapping and assassination threat from Weatherman was the focus, receiving much more space than the alleged threat from the Panthers.[63]

These FBI warnings had an impact in government circles. They alarmed Senator Hugh Scott (R-Pennsylvania)—the Senate minority leader—and many other Republican senators. On September 17 Scott requested that senior FBI officials come to the Capitol to discuss the danger that senators now faced from Weatherman, the Panthers, and Arab terrorists. William Sullivan replied that the FBI would be happy to provide information on the danger from radicals, but the Bureau itself was not a protective service. Sullivan sent Charles Brennan to brief the senators.[64]

The meeting in the Capitol took place on September 22; present were Hugh Scott, Robert Griffin (R-Michigan, Senate Republican whip), Gordon Allott (R-Colorado, Senate Republican Policy Committee), and several others. Earlier that day, Hoover met at the White House with leading senators and congressmen and had again stressed the seriousness of the far-left terrorist threat. At the Capitol, Senator Allott in particular said he was worried about kidnapping and was thinking of carrying a gun; he was prepared to "shoot to kill."[65]

A representative from the Secret Service said that his organization did not provide protection for senators—only for the president, vice president, and their families. There was discussion of a new bill to make it a federal crime to assassinate, kidnap, or assault a member of Congress or a member-elect, and providing that such a crime would come under the jurisdiction of the FBI. Allott wanted heavy penalties. The senators also wanted Attorney General Mitchell to increase protection for the Capitol and Senate Office Buildings. Mitchell himself—who had his own bodyguards—was on record as having declared that the country was on the verge of revolution.[66]

This may all seem like panic (and Senator Allott was certainly among those the most panicked). But a few months later, on March 1, 1971, the Weather Underground did explode a bomb in the Capitol Building, not far from where this meeting took place. And as we know from Bernardine Dohrn, ideas of kidnappings and assassinations were widespread in radical collectives in the summer of 1970. FBI fears about radical-left kidnapping were greatly exaggerated, but they were not completely fanciful.[67]

In mid-September, too, the Bureau learned, apparently through a wiretap, of a plot by a D.C. anarchist group—the East Coast Conspiracy to Save Lives—both to blow up the steam tunnels under the Capitol Building and to kidnap Henry Kissinger, demanding an end to U.S. bombing in Southeast Asia in exchange for his release. This threat was taken seriously by Charles Brennan, who wrote to Sullivan linking the group to the Weathermen; further, he warned Sullivan that the "likelihood of extremist terrorism is especially ominous in view of forthcoming United Nations anniversary 10/25/70 and Fall election campaign in U.S. and consequent increased vulnerability of leading officials."[68]

At a meeting in November with the House Appropriations Committee, Hoover went public with the alleged plot to kidnap Kissinger. The information was considered credible enough that the Department of Justice took its suspicions to a federal grand jury in Harrisburg, Pennsylvania, which in January 1971 issued an indictment on the kidnap accusations and the alleged plans to blow up the heating tunnels. Seven members of the East Coast Conspiracy group, including Father Philip Berrigan, its leader, went to trial in Harrisburg in February 1972; the defense team included the renowned lawyers Bill Kunstler and Leonard Boudin, father of Weatherman Kathy Boudin. On April 5, the jury found the defendants guilty on a minor charge, but could not come to a decision on the major charges—and the Justice Department dropped the case.[69]

Meanwhile, in January 1971, in connection with the Berrigan case, Hoover gave Assistant Director Mark Felt the task of improving security precautions at all local resident agencies in order to block any possible attacks on them. Felt failed. In March 1971, a band of Berrigan supporters broke into the FBI office in Media, Pennsylvania, near Philadelphia, and made off with more than a thousand documents. These were eventually leaked to newspaper and television reporters. Hoover was furious. He was made even more furious by the failure of the FBI over time—despite thousands of man-hours of investigation—to come up with any clues as to who were the culprits responsible the break-in at Media. More than forty-three years later, it was revealed that far from being the work of experienced underground guerrillas, it was the act of eight local amateur antiwar activists. Like Weatherman, they had outsmarted the FBI. The Bureau was embarrassed and humiliated.[70]

In the summer of 1971 Hoover decided to close 103 of the Bureau's 538 resident agencies in order to reduce FBI vulnerability. He also imposed stringent new rules on the number of files to be kept in the resident agencies that remained open. Such moves would hinder the FBI's ability to carry out its duties.[71]

Many of the documents stolen from the Media office were routine interoffice memos. A few were embarrassing to the Bureau. But one document was a real time bomb; it mentioned a program called COINTELPRO—New Left, which would turn out to be the name given to the long-term secret effort of the FBI to defame and disrupt various left-wing groups—including both the Black Panthers and SDS—in the name of preserving domestic tranquility. Although it is also true that the FBI launched a very effective COINTELPRO effort against the Ku Klux Klan on the far Right, the program was mostly directed against the Left. The documents raised questions about the legality of many of the Bureau's methods. Ultimately, public hearings would be held on COINTELPRO before the House and Senate Select Committees on Intelligence. The Senate published its findings in 1976—a report that denounced a pattern of reckless conduct by the FBI "that threatened our constitutional system."[72] But in the early 1970s, during Weather's rise, that reckoning was yet to come.

Meanwhile, the fear of political kidnappings prompted Hoover and his men to assign more agents to the investigation and pursuit of radical terrorists. Brennan wrote to Sullivan on September 24, 1970, that more men were needed in view of "the rising tide of terrorism on the part of New Left and black extremists," and because penetration of the far-left underground by informants was proving all but impossible. The nationwide estimate of resources needed to fight Weatherman and other radicals that had been done in April had suggested that the Bureau might need at least 450 and perhaps as many as 750 agents. But by September only 202 additional special agents had been reassigned. More effort was needed.[73]

The bureaucratic problem was plain. The careers of special agents in charge advanced through the accumulation of statistics on crimes solved and individuals arrested; but not only did investigations of political extremists require extensive manpower, they were long-term projects, often without clear results. There was thus a natural reluctance on the part of the local SACs to reassign scarce manpower resources to such a task. Yet the Weatherman threat was abundantly clear, at least to Brennan and Sullivan.

Hoover agreed, and on September 24 he sent out a circular stressing that since April there had been "a most substantial increase in new Left terrorist activity, including bombings and arsons and threats to kidnap high Government officials." Because of this, every special agent in charge was to furnish FBI headquarters with the increased number of special agents assigned to New Left terrorism since April, and to estimate how many more men would be needed. That more would be needed was assumed. Hoover gave the field offices exactly one week to report back. He was palpably impatient, both with the lack of progress against the radicals and with the sluggish local responses to orders from headquarters.[74]

On October 20, John Dean wrote to Hoover and Attorney General Mitchell that "as a result of recent acts of political terrorism," the president had personally ordered that a new interdepartmental group be set up to develop contingency plans to deal with politically inspired kidnapping. The group was to address a number of issues: (a) which federal officials deserved special protection from kidnapping, (b) what steps were needed to minimize the risk of kidnapping, (c) what intelligence resources were available to deal with the problem, (d) which groups were likely to attempt a political kidnapping and what their likely demands were, (e) what options the president should consider, and (f) what special command-and-control apparatus should be put in place to deal with a potential kidnapping. "The President," Dean announced, "has assigned a high priority to this matter."[75]

This initiative appears to have been prompted by an emergency in Canada since the kidnapping, on October 5 and 10, of two high officials by the Quebec Liberation Front (FLQ). The provincial government of Quebec had almost collapsed over whether or not to accept the kidnappers' demands for the release of dozens of imprisoned FLQ members, and the Canadian national government was in crisis.[76]

John Dean's special committee met on October 22. The attendees included Dean as chairman, Tom Charles Huston, Jack Caulfield, Fred Fielding, Egil Krogh, and Clint Hill.[77] Dean began by declaring that some five thousand people connected to the government were potential targets of kidnappers, including the president, his staff and their families, cabinet officers, elected officials, foreign official visitors, judges, military commanders, and high FBI and CIA executives.[78] The government could not provide protection for all these targets. Dean suggested that protection at least be given to cabinet-level officials and above, since if somebody of this rank were kidnapped, the entire government would be shaken. It was unclear which agency would provide this protection, or pay for it.[79]

FBI Inspector Rex Shroder assured Dean that if a kidnapping occurred, "the full resources of the FBI would be employed immediately." But how far could the Bureau's writ extend? Perhaps only if the kidnappers crossed state lines? This question was referred to William Rehnquist, then assistant attorney general in charge of the Office of Legal Counsel. The committee then wrestled with the question of whether and how far the president, when faced with a political kidnapping, should accede to the demands of the kidnappers. The possible scenarios were too varied to come up with an answer. Dean then asked Shroder how good the FBI informant system was concerning far-left terrorism; he was told that every effort was being made. Shroder didn't mention that so far the FBI had utterly failed to penetrate Weatherman. Egil Krogh found Shroder's bland assurance insufficient, especially since the administration had just added one thousand more special agents to the FBI budget. The only other help the FBI could immediately offer was a program designed to teach potential targets to reduce their vulnerability: they could be trained to be "surveillance conscious," as was done with potential kidnappees in South America.[80]

In November, Assistant Attorney General Robert Mardian took over the Internal Security Division at Justice. He, too, wanted to form a task force to determine the response of the government "should there ever be a kidnapping of a Government official such as there was in Canada recently." Mardian met with Hoover on November 25 to discuss the matter. Hoover agreed that plans had to be readied to deal with possible political kidnappings, "since it is not realistic to take the position they will not occur in this country."[81]

In hindsight, we can see that Hoover's judgment here was wrong; no political kidnappings were ever perpetrated by Weatherman—though if Howard Machtinger is correct, one was seriously attempted)—or by the Panthers. But it was unrealistic to assume that it could not happen here (ask Patty Hearst), and in summer and autumn 1970 it would have been foolhardy to underplay the possibility. To be sure, Hoover's judgment was based in part on an inflated FBI assessment both of Weather's abilities as well as its inclination to kidnap, but was also shaped by statements such as Dohrn's and Rudd's, and real events elsewhere.

On June 1, 1972, Vietnam veteran Roger Holder and his girlfriend Kathy Kirko hijacked a Western Airlines plane bound for Seattle. Holder claimed that Weatherman had kidnapped his family and forced him to hijack the plane; the organization, he said, was intent on rescuing Angela Davis, then on trial for her role in the botched Jonathan Jackson action of August 1970. Holder claimed that four Weathermen were on the Western airliner, all with bombs ("and one on LSD"). The Weatherman plan, allegedly, was to land at San Francisco International Airport, exchange the passengers (or some of them) for Angela Davis and substantial money, then fly off to North Vietnam. Another hijacking (this one out of Reno, Nevada) also occurred on June 1, and that plane was also headed for San Francisco.

Roger Holder would ultimately be judged mentally ill, and found to have acted solely with his girlfriend. The story he told about Weatherman was false, though Holder insisted that he wanted to rescue Angela Davis. Nevertheless, Holder's claim about the Weatherman kidnapping plan was *believed*: it was believed by the law enforcement people in San Francisco, believed by the city's FBI field office, which made preparations to storm the plane and battle the Weathermen, and believed by the FBI in Washington. FBI headquarters was especially alarmed by the Reno hijacking; it seemed to be evidence of a nationwide, coordinated Weatherman conspiracy to rescue Angela Davis. In reality, Reno was a coincidence—the work of a teenager acting out.[82]

CHAPTER FIVE

"The Hoover Cutoff"

THE FOURTH AMENDMENT TO the U.S. Constitution states in part that "the right of the people to be secure in their persons, houses, papers, and effects, against unreasonable searches and seizures, shall not be violated." Between 1940 and 1965, however, the FBI made regular use of "surreptitious entry" without consent or court order—that is, without legally established probable cause—to spy on those whom the Bureau suspected of being enemies of the nation. These "surreptitious entries" were known within the FBI as "black bag jobs," because black bags were originally employed to carry the bulky cameras used to take photographs of documents and papers within dwellings after entry had been made. "Black bag jobs" often led to the installation of secret microphones or wiretaps. Charles Brennan, assistant director in charge of the Domestic Intelligence Division in 1970–1971, described them to a Senate committee in 1975 as what would normally be called a burglary.[1]

The practice was so common between 1940 and 1965 that the only authorization needed for a break-in was for a street agent to make the case to his local special agent in charge, and for the SAC then to make the case to the assistant director for the appropriate the category of investigation at FBI Headquarters in Washington. In cases of suspected subversion, this meant the head of the Domestic

Intelligence Division. Special Agent John Gordon testified in 1980 that he alone ran more than fifty black bag jobs between 1956 and 1965, mostly against the Ku Klux Klan. In March 1963, however, J. Edgar Hoover tightened the protocols for such operations. Thereafter, an FBI burglary required the approval either of Hoover himself or of Clyde Tolson, his second in command.[2]

Given the strictures of the Fourth Amendment, why did Hoover and his men think the Bureau had the right to engage in trespass and burglary? Under the aegis of the executive branch, FBI break-ins had gained a veneer of legality through the mandate of the president of the United States to protect the country. This assertion of presidential power was made by President Franklin Delano Roosevelt in a classified directive on September 6, 1939, five days after the outbreak of World War II, when he put J. Edgar Hoover and the FBI in charge of all matters relating to espionage, sabotage, and "subversive activities."[3] A second secret directive from Roosevelt, on May 21, 1940, came partly in reaction to a Supreme Court decision (*Nardone v. U.S.*, 1939) that evidence from warrantless wiretaps was inadmissible in federal courts. Here, too, Roosevelt was mindful of the imminent fall of France to the Nazis and the possibility of the United States entering the war. FDR told Hoover:

> I am confident that the Supreme Court never intended any dictum [in *Nardone*] to apply to grave matters affecting the defense of the nation. You are therefore authorized and directed in such cases as you may approve after investigation ... to authorize the investigating agents that they are at liberty to secure the information by listening devices directed to the conversation or other communications of persons suspected of subversive activity.

Roosevelt added that he expected such cases to be few, and limited mostly to noncitizens. Nevertheless, in these two documents FDR by executive fiat hugely broadened the mandate of the FBI, which previously had been restricted to domestic crime fighting. Now it would do intelligence work, too.[4]

The Roosevelt authorization was followed for decades by attorneys general in subsequent administrations. Yet whenever a warrantless wiretapping case came before the Supreme Court, the Court limited its legal validity because of violation of the Fourth Amendment. Thus in May 1954 President Eisenhower's Attorney General Herbert J. Brownell felt the need to reassert Roosevelt's grant of "liberty" to FBI warrantless wiretaps and microphones in national security cases, in view of a new Supreme Court decision (*Irvine v. California*). *Irvine* disallowed the use of evidence in criminal cases obtained by local police via break-in and installation of microphones without a court order, and in general it deemed police break-ins without warrant in criminal cases as a violation of the Fourth Amendment. Nevertheless, Brownell in a secret memo told the FBI:

> It is the only possible way of uncovering the activities of espionage agents, possible saboteurs, and subversive persons. In such instances I am of the opinion that the national interest requires microphone surveillance to be utilized. This use need not be limited to the development of evidence for prosecution. The FBI has an intelligence function in connection with internal security matters equally as important.... The Department of Justice approves the use of microphone surveillance by the FBI under these circumstances and for these purposes.... It is realized that not infrequently the question of trespass arises in connection with the installation of a microphone.... It is my opinion that the Department [of Justice] should adopt that interpretation [of trespass law] that will permit microphone coverage by the FBI in a manner most conducive to our national interest. I recognize that for the FBI to fulfill its important intelligence function, considerations of internal security and the national safety are paramount, and therefore, may compel the unrestricted use of this technique in the national interest.

Brownell wrote his memo in consultation with the FBI itself, and an early draft drew this FBI response: "The Attorney General is giving us the go ahead on microphones whether or not there is a trespass"—though restricting this to important national security cases. Many years later Brownell was asked whether he agreed with this understanding. He acknowledged that he did, and added that the Constitution gave the president as commander in chief, and thus the FBI as the president's instrument, "complete power" to act in matters of national security.[5]

Yet Brownell acknowledged that there was opposition in the Justice Department even in 1954 to his position: attorneys protested in writing that the chief legal officer of the country should not be authorizing outright trespass. Nevertheless, after Roosevelt's earlier directives the Brownell Memo became another legal basis—such as it was—for FBI black bag jobs. Walter Yeagley, assistant attorney general of the Internal Security Division at Justice from 1959 to 1970, testified that in this period the Justice Department frequently allowed the FBI to use surreptitious entries. Indeed, in this period two Supreme Court justices knew about secret FBI burglaries in national security cases and said nothing to their colleagues once on the Court: Tom Clark (Harry Truman's attorney general and then Supreme Court justice, 1949–1967) and Byron White (John F. Kennedy's deputy attorney general, and then Supreme Court justice, 1962–1993).[6]

Most people in the FBI understood that even the original permission from President Roosevelt rested on shaky legal grounds; hence the FBI legend that Roosevelt had told Hoover that while he had permission to take all actions necessary against subversives, he had better not get caught. The legal predicament was made murkier by the fact that no president or attorney general had ever authorized trespass solely for the search of papers and effects, as opposed to FDR's authorizations of break-ins for bugging and wiretaps. But the search-type burglary was precisely the type of trespass the FBI would often use against Weatherman's relatives and supporters.[7]

To the FBI this distinction was meaningless: authorization of microphone surveillance was authorization for trespass, since microphones could be installed only through break-ins. In 1956 J. Edgar Hoover had presented to a meeting of the National Security Council an example of a break-in solely for the purpose of searching for papers (in this case, a burglary of Communist Party U.S.A. headquarters in New York). Both President Eisenhower and Vice President Nixon attended. Neither they nor anyone else objected. Indeed, Hoover received a complimentary letter the next day. This came close to a presidential authorization of break-in for search (as opposed to wiretap) against American citizens.[8]

Further, the fact was that a microphone surveillance installed through a break-in—the type of trespass "authorized" by presidential mandate starting with FDR—was far more invasive in Fourth Amendment terms than any break-in for a search of an individual's papers and effects. The latter type of search was over in a couple of hours, whereas a secret microphone was a continual invasive surveillance of people's activities in their homes that might go on for months, even years. The argument was that if presidential authority existed for warrantless bugging, then it also existed for break-in for search, which was a lesser act. Former Attorney General Richard Kleindienst would insist in 1980 that warrantless bugging, which had to be installed by trespass, was a worse invasion of privacy than any temporary search— yet presidents had authorized warrantless bugging.[9]

Donald E. Moore, the head of the Espionage Section of FBI Domestic Intelligence from 1956 to 1973, testified in 1980 that surreptitious entries into homes of American citizens purely for information on fugitives—precisely what the FBI engaged in against Weatherman—had been frequent in the late 1940s and 1950s. These were usually cases where the FBI was pursuing fugitive members of the CPUSA who had jumped bail: again, similar to the situation with some Weathermen. Such past break-ins were widely known in the Justice Department and no one had objected.[10] The crucial difference was that although the targets were American citizens, the government considered them agents of a hostile foreign power (the Soviet Union). Was that true of the Weathermen?

For almost twenty-five years FBI wiretapping, microphone installations, and trespass for search without court order took full advantage of the "liberty" that FDR had granted. In 1975 the FBI was compelled to reveal that during these years at least 240 trespass break-ins had occurred. These FBI actions were known to the Justice Department, especially its Internal Security Division. No one had raised any objection.[11]

The political problem with black bag jobs was brought home to the FBI in 1965, in negative public reaction to the disclosure that the

Internal Revenue Service was itself engaging in wiretaps to catch tax evaders. The revelation led to a Senate investigation, headed by Missouri Democrat Edward Long. President Lyndon Johnson's new attorney general, Nicholas Katzenbach, pressured Hoover to eliminate microphones because of trespass issues. In autumn 1965 Hoover ordered a sharp reduction in bugging. The directorate and the field offices were unhappy, but the number of wiretaps nation-wide was halved, from eighty to forty. Five years later, in 1970, about the same number of wiretaps were still in place.[12]

Hoover acted just in time: in early 1966 Senator Long de-manded discussions of possible FBI abuse of wiretapping. Hoover assured Long that the FBI engaged in only a limited number (true by that time), and only in the most serious criminal or national se-curity cases. But Long warned of great damage to the FBI should knowledge even of these reduced activities reach the public.[13]

In mid-1966, Hoover also formally banned black bag jobs. In June he instructed Special Agent Arbor Gray to write a history of FBI surreptitious entries, so he would know exactly the scope and background of these jobs. Cartha DeLoach, the Bureau's number-three man, asked William Sullivan, head of the Domestic Intelligence Division, to explain what authority the FBI had for black bag jobs. Sullivan's reply was forthright: "We do not obtain authorization for 'black bag' jobs from outside the Bureau. Such a technique involves trespass and is clearly illegal. Therefore, it would be impossible to ob-tain any legal sanction for it."[14]

Sullivan went on to justify the burglaries on the grounds that though illegal, they produced invaluable information for "combat-ing subversive activities." He gave the example of a recent warrant-less burglary that had furnished the FBI with crucial information to help the Bureau disrupt a subversive organization, in this in-stance the Ku Klux Klan. The black bag job, run by Special Agent John Gordon, not only had prevented a KKK dynamite bombing of a civil rights headquarters in Mississippi but ultimately had led to the arrest of the men responsible for the infamous murders in June 1964 of the civil rights workers James Chaney, Andrew Goodman, and Michael Schwerner.[15]

No matter. Hoover scrawled his disagreement on Sullivan's July 19, 1966, memo: "H: No more such techniques must be used."

Hoover's ban became known within the FBI as "the Hoover cutoff."[16]

There was widespread resistance. Mark Felt, for one, believed black bag jobs were legal, and that Hoover was wrong to stop them. But Felt appears to have been in the minority. Brennan had "no doubt" that black bag jobs were illegal. But like Sullivan, he believed they were so important in the fight for national security that their illegality should be ignored; "the Hoover cutoff" put unnecessary limits on FBI conduct.[17] The field offices pushed back as well. In January 1967, Hoover ordered field offices to stop sending him special requests for the use of black bag techniques: "I have previously indicated that I do not intend to approve any such request in the future."[18]

Nevertheless, the FBI continued to do black bag jobs on a limited basis. There were "certain exceptions" to Hoover's policy.[19]

For instance, Special Agent John J. Kearney ran six warrantless burglaries in New York City against the Black Panthers and other black radicals between March and June 1968; he informed his FBI superiors each time; and they sent on Kearney's information to Washington headquarters.[20] On the West Coast, the FBI ran warrantless surreptitious entries against Leibel Bergman, whom the Bureau suspected of being a Chinese agent. Bergman's Berkeley home was broken into several times between March 1968 and February 1969 to set up a hidden microphone and a wiretap, which remained in place for months. The February 1969 burglary became an entry for search: photos were made of documents and samples taken from a typewriter. In autumn 1969 the local field office actually wanted to install a hidden television camera in the San Francisco apartment to which Bergman had now moved. Mark Felt, on an inspection, refused authorization, not on the basis of legality but out of concern that the camera might be discovered. When Bergman moved back to Berkeley, the FBI followed, using surreptitious entry to install a microphone in the new house; it was still in place in early 1970. And yet the Bureau failed to produce any evidence of "subversive" ties to the Chinese Communist government; the same was true of Bergman's U.S.-China Friendship Association, whose headquarters were also burgled.[21]

A memo from Brennan to Sullivan in April 1970 shows that "technical surveillances" (wiretaps) had already been approved for locations suspected of connection to Weatherman in Detroit, Chicago, and Philadelphia; Brennan wanted more. What happened with these operations remains unknown. We do know that between February and June 1971, the FBI used warrantless electronic surveillance against Nancy Kurshan and Howard Emmer (both with Weatherman pasts) in regard to the large demonstrations in Washington, D.C., in May. Given the importance of the May Day demonstrations, it is hard to believe that Hoover did not see the memo boasting of this.[22] Julie Nichamin, an organizer of the Venceremos Brigades—formed to break the American blockade of Cuba and to show solidarity with the Cuban Revolution by cutting sugarcane—was being wiretapped in this period, as were the parents of Howard Machtinger, and the aboveground Weatherman Brian Flanagan. The table of contents in Felt-Miller Box 19 lists these wiretaps, although the material these files contain has not yet been reviewed for public release. Even the names on fourteen other wiretap files in this box have been redacted, but since this was material gathered for the Felt-Miller trial in 1980, they are linked to Weatherman in some way. None of the wiretaps or buggings or intrusions for search involving them was apparently done with the benefit of a court order.

To be sure, black bag jobs were now to be approved only by the highest level of the FBI. It appears that at a lunch with Attorney General Ramsey Clark in September 1967, Hoover got permission on a limited basis in security cases.[23]

In June 1968 Congress passed the Omnibus Crime Control and Safe Streets Act, which generally outlawed microphone and wiretap surveillance without a court order. There were two exceptions. First, nothing was to limit the president from taking actions to protect the nation from foreign subversion or internal attempts to overthrow the government by force. Second, a court order would be unnecessary in cases of national emergency. These were large loopholes—and L. Patrick Gray as acting FBI director in 1972 would attempt to drive through them in order to justify break-ins against Weatherman's supporters and relatives.[24]

Despite these exceptions, Hoover from the mid-1960s tried to rein in FBI conduct. He sensed a growing antiauthoritarian mood in the country and seemed to believe that the Bureau risked being gravely damaged if illegal activities came to light. Perhaps he also felt that having reached the mandatory federal retirement age of seventy in 1965, and having been retained as FBI director only year by year by special presidential order, he might be vulnerable to ouster in the event of an embarrassing incident. As always, maintaining the reputation of the FBI was Hoover's chief priority.[25]

Hoover continued his official stance of restraint even when American universities began to explode in protest. This is clear in a February 1969 order to all special agents in charge to avoid overly aggressive campus investigations; Hoover worried about accusations of interference with academic freedom. He also maintained the ban on campus informants under the age of twenty-one, and limited the number of campus informants in general.[26] A year later, in March 1970, even as Weatherman captured the country's headlines, Hoover told Richard Helms, the head of the CIA, that he opposed illegal operations because he knew that the public feared possible abuses—and the FBI had always relied on, and needed, popular support.[27] Of course, in reality illegal black bag jobs were going on.

The official FBI rejection of electronic surveillance was repeated at an April 13, 1970, meeting between William Sullivan and James Jesus Angleton, the head of CIA counterintelligence. Sullivan dutifully conveyed Hoover's prohibitions, even though he had made plain to Hoover his disagreement. He had found Hoover's refusal to allow the children of FBI agents to serve as informants on campus "a marked disappointment," and he was "appalled" by Hoover's limiting the use of campus informants in general. Despite his outspoken objections, Sullivan somehow remained a favorite of the director.[28]

Sullivan's men in the field, faced with a rising New Left movement, were unhappy with Hoover's new policy and protested that although methods and number of informants were being constantly restricted, Hoover still expected them to produce reliable information about this new threat. The prohibitions on method hit Sullivan's Domestic Intelligence Division especially hard. Many special agents had already been siphoned off to the South, to maintain order against white violence aimed at the civil rights struggles;

others had been transferred to deal with organized crime. Sullivan thus had fewer agents to carry out intelligence actions on other domestic security fronts; now he had also been mostly deprived of the "technical" and "sensitive" methods that had traditionally helped his agents acquire information. It was all very well for Hoover to demand that information be developed anyway. But the means to gain it were being constrained even as manpower was being reduced. And the New Left was growing ever stronger, its more extreme elements more dangerous.[29]

Helms, too, over at the CIA, thought the Hoover restrictions too stringent and said so to President Johnson in September 1968. But then Helms had his own group of agents keeping track of domestic radicals—"Operation Chaos"—a clandestine operation wholly contrary to the Agency's charter, which explicitly forbade spying within the United States.[30]

Yet Hoover, despite his misgivings and formal decrees inside the Bureau, did approve the continuation of at least some burglaries against radicals. Further, the FBI during Hoover's tenure carried out burglaries—how many is not known—against suspected aboveground supporters and relatives of Weatherman. Three such operations, to install microphones and/or wiretaps, were undertaken in Detroit, Chicago, and New York in April 1970—against whom, we do not know. And in early 1972, the FBI burgled the apartment of Murray Bookchin on February 14; the apartment of Jennifer Dohrn, the sister of Bernardine Dohrn, on March 7, March 23, and April 4; and the apartment of Leonard Machtinger, the brother of Howard Machtinger, on April 18.[31]

Did Hoover know about these particular operations? Mark Felt insisted that he did not: "Hoover jeopardized his relations with the Nixon White House by categorically barring 'black bag jobs' . . . even in national security cases."[32] But the evidence shows that Hoover knew and approved.

Consider Hoover's direct role in the evolution of the Weatherman Squad. The squad was created in late March because of the Weatherman crisis, and set up on a trial basis in New York on April 7. In May it became the main instrument in the hunt for Weatherman, centered in New York because forty-five out of the eighty-five Weatherman cases involved native New Yorkers.[33] By

June the unit (now called Squad 47) had twenty men: nineteen special agents at work under supervisor Eugene O'Neill, who had
been transferred from draft-dodger cases to hunting Weatherman.
But hunting the Weathermen proved far harder than finding draft
dodgers. The squad in spring and summer 1970 accomplished
little—though these were the months when, as an FBI memo in
May noted, fear of New Left terrorism was intensifying at the
White House, in the public, and in the Bureau. So Hoover transferred O'Neill back to chasing draft dodgers, and approved John
Kearney to succeed him, declaring that the Weatherman squad
needed someone with "a thorough knowledge of security work,"
and Kearney "has considerable security experience."[34] Kearney had
worked in the New York field office for twenty years, mostly
against the Communist Party, then, from 1968, against black radicals. He had run many black bag jobs against CPUSA people—these
arguably had some legal basis under the Roosevelt permission,
since the targets were viewed as agents of a foreign powers; and he
had run black bag jobs against the Black Panthers as well. He had
been specially trained in lock picking. Everyone inside the Bureau
knew John Kearney's reputation.[35]

Surreptitious entries, warrantless wiretaps, letter openings, installation of microphones—all began against Weatherman relatives
and supporters soon after Kearney took over the squad on August
8, 1970. Kearney would be indicted by the Justice Department
during the Carter administration for, among other things, ordering
eleven illegal wiretaps and nine illegal mail openings. Yet Kearney
retired from the FBI in early 1972—which means that all the actions for which he was indicted occurred under Hoover. How
many other black bag jobs he actually ran remains unavailable to
the public.[36]

Black bag jobs were complex operations. Each involved an initial surveillance of the targeted person, sometimes long-term, in
order to get to know his or her habits. Each job took at least a week
to prepare. The entry itself required three teams of agents, communicating via walkie-talkies, (a) to keep track of when the target left
his or her dwelling, and to warn against an early return, (b) to keep
watch outside at the target's home in case visitors unexpectedly
showed up, and (c) to make the actual break-in. For example, four-

teen men were involved in the burglary of Jennifer Dohrn's apartment on March 23, 1972.[37] Before entry a telephone call was always made into the dwelling to ensure that no one was there; the break-in team wore casual clothes to avoid being identified as FBI. If the target's home was an apartment, keys could often be secretly obtained from the apartment manager, who was either overawed by the FBI or pleased to work with the Bureau. James Vermeersch always managed to obtain keys, but he knew of cases where locks had to be picked. Everything in the residence that the agents examined and photographed had to be put back exactly in place so that the target did not know a break-in had occurred. The number of photographs taken could be large. In the second burglary of Murray Bookchin's home, for instance, FBI agents took ninety-four photographs (none of which provided any useful information).[38] Some defenders of the FBI later claimed that the Squad 47 operations were "wildcat bag jobs"—that is, unauthorized rogue actions.[39] But it strains credulity to believe that such large and complicated operations could occur without approval from higher-ups.

And in the case of Jennifer Dohrn the evidence is clear: Hoover not only knew about the burglaries—he ordered them. On March 27, 1972, Hoover wrote a secret order to New York, stressing Dohrn as a potential source of information about her sister and other Weatherman fugitives. Hoover also noted that the New York field office now had a permanent lookout post near Dohrn's residence, "as well as two highly sensitive sources reporting on her activities." He expected "determined, imaginative and aggressive" actions and urged that "every logical effort must be immediately expended to capitalize on the above-enumerated assets as it is unknown how long this opportunity will exist or if it can be repeated."[40]

"Highly sensitive sources" was the FBI phrase for a microphone or wiretap. In the case of Dohrn's apartment, it was both: FBI agents had planted a microphone in her apartment and a wiretap on her telephone.[41] But a microphone could be placed only via a surreptitious entry, and FBI procedure mandated an initial break-in to "survey" the target to determine feasibility before the *second* surreptitious break-in for the placement of the bug.[42] Hoover referred to these bugs in his March 27 memo, so he will have known about the FBI break-ins to plant the bugs in the first place. Moreover, a memo from Hoover to the special agent in charge in New York on March 31 showed that Hoover had been informed that a previous entry of Dohrn's apartment had produced copies of her handwriting, which had been forwarded to the FBI laboratory.[43]

The bugging, wiretap, and break-in for search were all done without a court order. But a conceit of legality did exist. The FBI had applied for permission not to a court but to Attorney General Mitchell for approval of the Dohrn burglaries and electronic surveillances; the application required Hoover's signature, and Mitchell, too, had agreed in writing. Because of the FDR directives and the Brownell Memo, it was generally felt at Justice that the attorney general had the authority to approve warrantless trespass and bugging in national security cases. In fact, at least two other Weatherman-related warrantless buggings (established via break-ins) were approved in writing by Attorney General Mitchell in late 1971 and early 1972. Hoover must also have been aware of these, as both applications would have required his signature.[44]

In 1977 William Sullivan claimed to then-FBI Director Clarence Kelley that Hoover in August or September 1970 had specifically given him the go-ahead to allow Jack Kearney and Squad 47 to engage in "bag jobs" in Weatherman cases. Hoover was displeased at the FBI failure to apprehend the Weather fugitives, and when Sullivan complained that the Bureau's agents were operating under procedural restraints, Hoover "told me, with some anger, that any means must be used in order to apprehend the fugitives. I gave this information to Mr. Kearney."[45]

Should Sullivan be believed? Another high FBI official told the *New York Times*, in regard to burglaries, that "it was mostly Bill who was arguing for these things, and Hoover who usually was against them"; Sullivan's letter to Director Kelley was in fact a defense against this accusation. Sullivan went on to assert, first, that he was no lone wolf but that most FBI men wanted the reinstatement of the "sensitive techniques"; and second, that Hoover had ordered him to use extralegal methods in other cases. This was true: in 1969 Hoover, at the behest of President Nixon, had ordered Sullivan to set up warrantless electronic surveillance of aides to Henry Kissinger, as well as against several journalists, in order to stop leaks from the White House to the media. Sullivan, acting under Hoover's orders, ran the illegal eavesdropping.[46]

Part of the story here was pressure from the White House for such operations. In May 1969, the FBI declared that "nothing the S.D.S. does surprises us. . . . We are ready for them if they cause trouble."[47] In October, Hoover at a dinner at his house for President Nixon, John Mitchell, and John Ehrlichman, boasted to the president that he had the Weatherman situation under complete control.[48] Six months later, the FBI's manifest failure to redeem this assurance had incurred the president's wrath. He no longer believed the Bureau could get the job done. The White House, continuously complaining about spotty and late intelligence on the far Left, leaned ever more heavily on the FBI to provide more and better information about the radicals. And from the start, President Nixon made it clear that he did not care how the FBI got this information.

The first sign of the president's discontent appeared in a June 1969 visit of White House aide Tom Huston to the FBI. He met with William Sullivan, stressed that he was visiting all the intelligence agencies as the personal representative of the president, and said that Nixon was looking particularly for evidence of "foreign influences and financing of the New Left."[49]

On June 20 Huston wrote to Hoover that the president wanted new FBI reports on foreign support of leftist revolutionaries that drew on "all the resources available." And the president wanted the term "support" to be construed broadly, to include any kind of assistance, or even mere encouragement of protests. Huston also wrote that in the president's view, "our present intelligence collecting capabilities in this area may be inadequate."[50]

But Hoover was apparently dismissive of being approached by so a junior person as Huston. The June 20 memo apparently went nowhere for months.[51]

Nevertheless, when the great antiwar marches of autumn 1969 occurred, it was through Tom Huston that the Bureau had to funnel information to Nixon about them.[52] The White House now began to pressure the FBI again about left-wing finances. On November 11, Hoover ordered all his agents to increase investigation of the sources of far-left money. He was specifically concerned with the increasing violence of Weatherman, and anxious about its revolutionary objectives. But the Weathermen's extreme Marxism-Leninism, Hoover said, was making finances difficult, so the organization's remaining sources of money must be discovered, especially tax-exempt charitable foundations or large donations from individuals. He noted that there were frequent "high-level inquiries" on this subject—that is, pressure from the White House. But nothing much resulted from Hoover's November 11 order.

Then, in February 1970, even as the radical threat was increasing, the intelligence situation worsened. First, Hoover cut most FBI ties with the CIA after he became infuriated over a CIA agent who released FBI information on an intelligence case concerning the disappearance of Professor Thomas Riha in Colorado. Hoover even disbanded the committee within the FBI that acted as liaison with the other agencies. But the White House had wanted *increased* interagency cooperation. Charles Brennan later called Hoover's action "atrocious"; James Angleton complained of its impact on the efficiency of intelligence gathering.[53]

Government intelligence capabilities were further constrained in February by a lawsuit the American Civil Liberties Union brought against the U.S. Army Intelligence Command. In mid-1968, the army had instituted a secret "Civil Disturbance Collection Plan" aimed at gathering files on civilian radicals and potential rioters. The plan was without legal sanction. The ACLU suit led to a court order that most of the army files on suspected radicals be destroyed, and any investigation of civilians by the armed forces be severely limited in scope.[54] One can well imagine the backlash from the White House if, a couple of weeks later, a Weatherman bomb attack on Fort Dix had left dozens of soldiers and their guests dead. In any case, from the White House point of view these setbacks showed a pattern of intelligence community ineffectiveness that constituted a danger to the state. Nixon's aides worried that "an intelligence system geared to monitor the communists three decades ago" was no longer adequate.

Despite the "tremendous pressure" from the White House, the FBI was unable to find foreign funding or evidence of foreign control of Weatherman, as it reported to Nixon both in November 1969 and February 1970. Its efforts, Charles Brennan would later say, were a waste of time. There was nothing. Nevertheless, President Nixon's personal alarm in the face of increasing radical-left violence was pushing the FBI toward operations he knew might violate the law.[55]

These were not only Richard Nixon's personal obsessions. In the spring of 1970 the White House and Congress were both under enormous pressure from the public. The bombings, the arsons, the disruptions on campus, and the increasing general disorder had created alarm and outrage in many sectors of the population. Nixon himself had certainly encouraged this outrage, beginning with the 1968 run for the presidency that made "law and order" a centerpiece of his campaign, and then, later, with his direct political attack on radicalism in his "Silent Majority" speech of November 1969 and his indulgence of "hard hat" violence against radicals in May 1970. But whatever the president's contribution, public pressure was a fact. And it reinforced Nixon's pressure on the FBI to do more.[56]

On May 13, at the height of the Cambodia and Kent State crises, Hoover met with Nixon, who gave the FBI two new tasks. One was to investigate the Venceremos Brigades. Nixon was convinced that the group's organizers were somehow behind the disturbances roiling the campuses. And second, the FBI was to investigate individuals who were allegedly traveling from campus to campus, stirring up trouble. Nixon seemed to be implying that the campus insurrections were at heart an enormous leftist conspiracy, originating in part with people with ties to Fidel Castro. Nixon told Hoover that he wanted specific information on this.[57]

The intelligence services' unsatisfactory performance against the revolutionaries was later underlined in a report to Bob Haldeman by Tom Huston. The full resources of the intelligence community were not being used; information coming to the White House was fragmentary and unevaluated. According to Haldeman, these ideas about intelligence inadequacy and the "conspiracy" behind the May crisis were "generated by P's [the president's] complete dissatisfaction with the results of intelligence gathering and interpretation, particularly regarding the instigation and training for the wave of violent demonstrations."[58]

Years later, Nixon would vividly recall the country's predicament as he saw it in the spring of 1970:

> We were at war.... There were reports, what I considered hard evidence, that the Weathermen had very definite foreign connections. There were, in addition, actions on their part, their own statements, indicating that they were going to engage in violent activities for the purpose of overthrowing the government.
>
> And then there was in addition the fact that from January 1969 until April 1970—and it is hard now to think this was possible—there were forty thousand bombings, bomb scares, bomb threats, twenty-three killed, hundreds were injured ....
>
> And more significantly, sixty-four percent as far as those bombings and bomb threats were concerned were by persons unknown.

These are astonishing claims.[59] But all those bombings "by persons unknown" remained unknown, Nixon was convinced, because of inefficiency in the intelligence services, especially the FBI. The president and his men were determined to correct the situation.

Nixon now ordered a complete reassessment of the methods of investigation being used against the New Left. It was imperative to know what was happening, and what was going to happen. The intelligence services had failed against Weatherman in March and April—the Weathermen had disappeared underground unmolested. They had failed in May, providing no warning of the great student uprising.

Nixon and Haldeman chose Tom Charles Huston, now promoted to associate counsel to the president, to represent the White House as head of the high-level intelligence review. The motives behind the review—and what was eventually called the Huston Plan—are clear: "The concern of the White House at the absence of hard information" about the radicals threatening the country. Further, "The President ... desired full consideration be given to any regulations, policies or procedures which tend to limit the effectiveness of domestic intelligence collections." Nixon thus formally pushed the intelligence services to drop their limitations on methods used against domestic radicalism.[60]

On May 22, 1970—still in the midst of the Cambodia crisis, and the day after Weatherman's "Declaration of War"—someone in the FBI, probably Sullivan, sent Huston the full file of material stolen in April from the Chicago apartment of Bernadine Dohrn. The file included Dohrn's notes from her summer 1969 meeting in Havana with the Vietnamese, as well as several photographs of Dohrn toasting Vietnamese officials. Weatherman, with the Vietnamese, in Cuba: one can imagine how that played in the Oval Office, intensifying the anger and the fear. A note sent to the White House with this material cautioned that "since these papers were not in the trunks specified in the search warrant [the warrant had only been for weapons—which were found], there is doubt as to whether the papers were legally detained."[61]

On June 5 the heads of the FBI (Hoover), the CIA (Helms), the Defense Intelligence Agency (General Daniel Bennett), and the National Security Agency (Admiral Noel Gayler) met in the Oval Office with Nixon, Haldeman, and Ehrlichman, who was Nixon's domestic affairs adviser. Nixon ordered them to set up an ad hoc committee to investigate the possibility of lifting of investigative restraints on the radicals. As Hoover reminded the other intelligence chiefs when they met in his office on June 8 to form the committee: "The President mentioned restrictions which were hampering our intelligence operations." Nixon wanted the group to set out both the advantages and disadvantages of lifting the restrictions, but his language showed where he wanted the balance to fall.[62]

Hoover was the chairman of the committee, but the intelligence chiefs on June 8 set up a "working subcommittee" consisting of important subordinates from each agency who would do the actual work of drafting a report. The subcommittee was overseen by Tom Huston. Hoover appointed Sullivan to represent him as chairman of the subcommittee, and since the chairman could not simultaneously be the FBI representative, the Bureau effectively got two voting representatives in the group, while the other intelligence agencies each had only one. Given his strained relations with the other intelligence services, Hoover was doubtless pleased by this bureaucratic maneuver. Sullivan in turn appointed his own chief radical hunter—Charles Brennan—to represent the FBI. Representatives from CIA, DIA, NSA and the three military intelligence services were partners in the subcommittee, which met twice a week during June. Sullivan and Brennan were apparently the main authors, along with Huston, of the plan of action that emerged, but others contributed as well.[63]

Huston's remarks when the working group met on June 9 for the first time set the tone: "The President's primary concern was to strengthen and improve American intelligence operations in every possible way. . . . The critical security needs of the day required this." Sullivan then echoed Huston's remarks about the president's wishes, and the subcommittee began work.[64]

Tom Huston was later clear on exactly who were the intended targets:

> I thought we had a serious problem. I was not concerned about people who didn't like the war. . . . I am talking about—we were talking about bombers; we were talking about assassins; we were talking about snipers. And I felt something had to be done.[65]

Charles Brennan explained the subcommittee's goal:

> What you have is the question of, are you utilizing enough wiretaps, and are you utilizing enough bag jobs, are you using enough of these sophisticated techniques that perhaps you'd used in the past, which have since been cut back, and should there be reconsideration of an intensification of the use of these techniques?[66]

The challenge was set out in the first paragraph of the Huston Plan: the New Left was an insurrection against society and government; it was growing; it was having a serious impact on society, with "a potential for serious domestic strife. . . . They intend to smash the U.S. educational system, the economic structure, and, finally, the Government itself."[67] The Black Panthers were also increasingly influential; their newspaper had a circulation of 150,000. And there was a growing and alarming unity between the black extremists and

the New Left; Black Panther speakers had been to 189 college campuses in 1969. In summer 1969 a "united front against fascism" had
even been formed among these groups. (In fact, the meeting convened by the Panthers and other groups to form such an alliance—
the United Front against Fascism conference, in Oakland,
California—had been a failure.) Thus, the document said, when the
Black Panther leader Bobby Seale was arrested in April 1970 for
having allegedly ordered the murder of a fellow Panther suspected
of being an FBI informant in Connecticut, the Justice Department
had expected not only hundreds of Panthers to show up on May 1
to protest but "possibly 1300 Weathermen and other radicals."
(Seale and the other defendants, known as the New Haven Eight,
including Panther Erika Huggins, were ultimately acquitted.)[68]

The Huston document went on to warn that the inability of the
intelligence services to give advance warning regarding antiwar
demonstrations was even more pronounced for the clandestine terrorist groups that had now emerged. The assessment was stark:
"Existing coverage of New Left extremists, the Weatherman group
in particular, is negligible." Electronic surveillance was hindered by
the nomadic lifestyle of the Weatherman commandos (that is, the
focos), and penetration by informants was impossible, for collectives
were made up solely of people who had known one another for a
long time.[69] Investigation of bombing sites produced few clues, because, as Special Agent William Dyson later said, the FBI and local
police had as yet only a little sophistication in examining the remnants of bombs for clues and in reconstructing the bombing
scenes.[70] The only hope for information was therefore "the defection of a key leader" in Weatherman, but that was considered highly
unlikely. Nor was it possible to cut off Weatherman's funds, since
they had no central source that was vulnerable to interdiction. And
though informants had penetrated the rank and file of the Black
Panthers, the Panther leaders—the ones suspected of planning dangerous actions—had not proven susceptible either to defection or
informing.[71]

The Huston planners admitted they didn't know how many
Weathermen there actually were. But they nevertheless suspected
that "at least 1,000 individuals adhere to the Weatherman ideology."
If all these people were potential guerrillas, as Brennan thought, the

threat to the country was serious.[72] The solution President Nixon sought, as Huston made clear, was removing the rules "which tend to limit the effectiveness of domestic intelligence collection." James Angleton, the committee's CIA representative, later said that Huston "knew precisely what none of us really knew, that is, the depths of the White House concern."[73]

The committee offered the president the option of removing current restrictions on (a) electronic surveillances, (b) covert mail coverage (opening of domestic mail), (c) surreptitious entries (black bag jobs), and (d) recruitment of student sources on campus, including by military intelligence. In each case the committee gave arguments in favor of retaining the restrictions as well as for removing them.[74] But the arguments in favor of removing the restrictions were almost always more extensive than the arguments for retaining them; in three crucial cases (electronic surveillance, covert mail coverage, and surreptitious entry) the arguments in favor were twice as long. Only on military intelligence recruiting on campus were the arguments pro and con equal in length, and this was the one case where Nixon kept the restriction. The president approved all other relaxations of limits on government action against radicals. And that was always the intention. As Angleton conceded: "The purpose of the recommendations that were made to the President ... was to secure the President's authorization to eliminate the restrictions that he felt were obstructing this gathering of intelligence." It was all Nixon.[75]

The report explicitly informed the president that some actions were illegal. For example, the authors noted, the proposed covert mail coverage without a court order was an "illicit act"; surreptitious entry without court order "involves illegal entry and trespass." The report included in its footnotes written objections and caveats from J. Edgar Hoover. Thus with respect to surreptitious entry, Hoover declared, "The FBI is opposed to surreptitious entry." About covert mail coverage, the report itself stated, "This coverage, not having the sanction of law, runs the risk of any illicit act, magnified by the involvement of the government itself. Hoover's footnote read: "The FBI is opposed to implementing any covert mail coverage because it is clearly illegal." In addition, Hoover made plain his concern over the risk to public relations should

news of these actions leak. With respect to the proposed intensification of campus surveillance, he wrote, "The FBI is opposed. . . .
[Such efforts] could result in charges that investigative agencies are
interfering with academic freedom."[76]

After the intelligence agency heads approved it, the Huston
Plan was submitted to Nixon on June 25, 1970. It was delivered
in an expensive black-leather binder with the title and name of
J. Edgar Hoover embossed in gold, and each intelligence chief
received his own black leather-and-gold copy.[77]

But then there was a long delay—almost three weeks.

During those weeks, Huston fought back against Hoover's protests. He argued to Haldeman that the president should overrule
Hoover, that the director's protests were "frivolous" and that
Hoover was an old man worried about his legend; "twenty years
ago," Huston, said, "he never would have raised the type of objections he has here." Huston insisted that existing constraints prevented the intelligence services from dealing effectively with the
radical crisis. Black bag jobs were necessary even though "clearly
illegal. It amounts to burglary." Huston pointed out that "this technique would be particularly helpful against the Weathermen and
Black Panthers."[78]

And beyond the fact that all the other intelligence agencies
supported the lifting of restrictions on investigative techniques,
Huston had a capping argument. Hoover, Huston said, was a mi-
nority of one within his own Bureau. His top men—Sullivan and
Brennan, the FBI members of the working group—disagreed with
Hoover's objections; "He'd fire them if he knew this."[79]

Tom Huston was correct that the plan had the approval of all
the intelligence service chiefs except the FBI—even though they
understood the illegalities. Everyone but Hoover wanted to go forward. And the legal problems certainly did not bother President
Nixon. Despite Hoover's reservations and the report's own frank
admission of illegal measures, Nixon approved it. He would later
claim on the basis of the precedent of the Roosevelt directives that
his approval of the plan in itself removed any taint or hint of illegality, especially given the crisis the country faced.[80]

Yet Sullivan, while in the Huston working group, was simultaneously telling Cartha DeLoach and Clyde Tolson that he *opposed*

lifting Hoover's limits on investigative methods. In fact, it was
Sullivan who proposed that Hoover write his objections into the
Huston document itself. Apparently Sullivan acted in order (a) to
curry favor with the director, while (b) pushing the working group
for the removal of the Hoover cutoff, which he had always opposed. Sullivan's maneuver was successful: even though the report
favored lifting the restrictions, when DeLoach retired in July,
Hoover promoted Sullivan to DeLoach's position as number-three
man in the Bureau.[81]

Haldeman told Huston on July 14 that Nixon approved most
of the provisions of the plan.[82] The intelligence chiefs were themselves informed on July 23, via letters on White House stationary:

> The President, after careful study of the Special Report . . .
> has decided that restraints on surreptitious entries should
> be removed. This technique should be used against urgent
> and high priority internal security targets. . . . Electronic
> surveillance of domestic groups and individuals who pose a
> major threat to the internal security of the United States
> . . . is to be intensified. Restraints on legal mail coverage are
> to be removed and restrictions on covert mail coverage are
> to be removed.

These were official, written presidential directives. These were, in
fact, orders to *act*.[83]

In addition, there was to be a new combined agency, called the
Intelligence Co-ordination Committee, to evaluate information
coming from all sources—and to order secret operations. It would
begin work in August, and make its first report to Nixon in
September. The president appointed Huston to have White House
responsibility for domestic intelligence and internal security affairs,
a sort of intelligence czar. He would also be the White House representative on the new committee, although as a sop to Hoover,
the FBI director would be its titular chairman.[84]

But Huston's triumph was short-lived. Hoover was furious that
the plan was to be implemented over his objections. He wrote a
sharp letter of protest to Attorney General Mitchell, then per-
suaded Mitchell in a personal conversation to protest to Nixon.

The issue in the Oval Office meeting was not illegality. Like Nixon, Mitchell greatly feared the radical left. But Mitchell told Nixon that without Hoover's wholehearted support, the plan was simply not going to work, because the new committee would be dependent on the FBI for most of its information but Hoover's opposition would doom the project. Mitchell told Nixon this was primarily because Hoover feared a public backlash if the plan leaked out. However desirable, the plan was, as a practical matter, dead on arrival. Nixon gave in. On July 27 the copies of the plan that had been sent to all the intelligence principals were ordered returned to the White House.[85]

The Senate Select Committee known as the Church Committee after its chairman, Senator Frank Church (D-Idaho) would later contend that the Huston Plan was primarily the result of Sullivan's and Huston's own ambitions. Huston wanted to become overseer of domestic intelligence operations for Nixon; Sullivan yearned to replace Hoover, and support of Huston was a way to gain Nixon's favor. Major scholars have accepted the Senate Committee's conclusion.[86]

Huston's ambitions are clear enough.[87] But Huston's authority derived ultimately from the president. The truth was that the key figure in pushing the Huston Plan was Richard Nixon. As Richard Helms later said: "The president was strongly in favor of it [the Huston Plan], was constantly stating that the FBI was not giving sufficient support in these matters, and this was something that ought to be done." Nixon was suspicious of the CIA, too—it was not being tough enough.[88]

Forty years later, Huston offered this assessment of what had happened with Hoover's scuttling of the Huston Plan:

In fairness, I will say, I didn't give Hoover credit that he deserved for his political acumen, as to the fact that the climate that existed pre-1965, during which period every one of the things that we had recommended had been ongoing for a very long time—the political climate had changed. And I think Hoover was much more sensitive to that than I was, or anyone in the West Wing was. But [at the time] I thought it was an affront to the president, but more importantly, I thought it was a disservice to the country.[89]

It was precisely because Huston's views had the support of Nixon's closest advisers and of Nixon himself that his defeat by Hoover did not end Huston's career. Nixon continued to hold him in high regard, and indeed Huston continued to receive a courier from the FBI with classified information every day in his West Wing office. A year later, during the Pentagon Papers affair of June 1971, Huston told Haldeman that the Brookings Institution had a secret file on the involvement of the Kennedy brothers in the 1963 assassination of President Ngo Dinh Diem of Vietnam. Nixon had long nurtured his resentments toward the Kennedys. When Nixon heard Huston's story about Brookings, he told Haldeman and Kissinger: "Now, if you remember Huston's plan, I want it implemented. Goddammit, get in there and get those files. Go in and get those files!" A day or so later, Nixon asked Haldeman, "Did they get Brookings raided last night? Get it done!"[90]

The "ambition" hypothesis sells short just about everyone involved. Both Sullivan and Huston were upset with the restraints on methods of surveillance that Hoover had decreed for the FBI starting in 1965; and although both men were ambitious, their desire to deal ruthlessly with the radicals was real, and it was shared, above all, by Richard Nixon. The way for both Huston and Sullivan to get ahead was to satisfy the president.

Nixon's decision not to approve the Huston Plan did not mean that its broad aims (or even many of its proposed measures) had been renounced or abandoned. By mid-September 1970 a new version of the Huston Plan emerged.

It came from John Dean, now counselor to the president, and the project had the support of John Mitchell and Bob Haldeman. The new version still included an interagency group to oversee intensified investigations of the far Left, engage in unified evaluation of information, and then run secret operations.[91] The men involved in the new project agreed that "the starting point for an effective intelligence operation should be the implementation of the recommendations in the Huston Plan," but because they feared that the public mood, not to mention Hoover himself, would disapprove of the illegal methods envisaged, it was decided that instead of blanket removal of investigative restrictions, the new interagency committee would approve "sensitive" operations on a case-by-case basis.[92]

The new project was called "the Intelligence Evaluation Committee." It first met on December 3, 1970, under John Dean and Robert Mardian, the new assistant attorney general of the Internal Security Division. Inspector George Moore, head of the Internal Security Section of the FBI Domestic Intelligence Division, attended, as did the CIA's James Angleton. Only a presidential directive could have brought together such an interagency group. The White House envisaged the Intelligence Evaluation Committee as bringing under one authority all the intelligence on revolutionaries in the country—and then deciding in which cases illegal operations needed to be undertaken. The committee would meet and act in secrecy, backed by a permanent staff directed by Morell Sharp, an associate justice of the Supreme Court of Washington State, acting as a consultant to the Justice Department. A cover story was concocted in case of a leak: the committee was merely studying ways to make the government's intelligence-gathering activities more efficient.[93]

But Hoover had sent only George Moore, a fourth-level official, to the organizing session. It was a first sign of his resistance to the new project. He did agree to provide "all relevant intelligence" to the committee, but reserved the right of the FBI to determine what intelligence was "relevant." In short, Hoover—as before—was reluctant to subordinate the FBI to an interagency committee. Most important, he said the FBI would provide no personnel for the permanent intelligence-evaluation staff whose activities were at the heart of the committee's operations. He pleaded lack of manpower. Hoover's refusal to provide personnel would kill the committee. As Mardian stressed, without a staff of FBI evaluators to vet the information that would be coming to the committee, mostly from the FBI, a joint intelligence committee was not worth the effort. Despite the White House's insistence that the committee continue without FBI staffing, it never got off the ground.[94]

Hoover's opposition to the White House plans did not mean that the FBI had discontinued its own campaign against Weatherman. Far from it. An FBI assistant directors' meeting on October 29, 1970, led by William Sullivan, proposed that the Bureau open cases on every member of SDS. This meant the 2,500 or so people that remained from the wreck of the larger organization; it was a large number of new cases. Files also were to be opened on the leaders of the 250 local student groups that made up the broader campus New Left; hundreds of people would be involved here as well. Files also were to be opened on every black campus organization across the country and on every leader of every such organization. This would affect thousands of people. Finally, the assistant directors voted to renew investigation of all persons listed as Priority II and III in the Security Index—investigations that had lapsed in February 1969 because of more pressing FBI duties.[95] The assistant directors estimated that approximately 11,000 individuals would come under FBI scrutiny—a scrutiny that they said was needed because campus youth was engaged in "violent demonstrations, bombings, arsons, and other terroristic acts." For the FBI, with its limited resources (about 8,000 special agents nationwide), the plan meant a huge new burden of campus surveillance.[96] Yet this was to be done without increased resources—and done discretely. Now Hoover agreed: "I cannot over-emphasize the importance of these cases. The violence, destruction, confrontations, and disruptions on campuses make it mandatory." Hoover feared, as he said, "Marxist-Leninist revolution." Perhaps he was amenable to this plan because it came—unlike other plans—from within the FBI itself. On November 4, Hoover directed all special agents in charge to begin the massive new campus projects. He stressed (again) discretion. The initial estimate was that 6,500 individuals would be targeted.[97] Mark Felt would later claim that the October plan was rejected by the assistant directors and that Sullivan left the October 29 meeting in fury.[98] But internal FBI memos show that the plan was approved both by the assistant directors and by Hoover. The problem was that it was beyond FBI capabilities.

Yet despite what Hoover had ordered the Bureau to do against the radicals, his foot-dragging and refusal to endorse a blank check for the use of illegal means of intelligence collection permanently soured his relationship with Nixon. Haldeman's diary for February 4, 1971, recorded a long meeting between Nixon and John Mitchell in which Nixon attacked Hoover's obstructionism and claimed that he was ready, if necessary, to remove Hoover from his

post. John Ehrlichman would later corroborate Haldeman's account in his own published memoir.[99] Weatherman's successful
bombing of the Capitol Building on March 1 spectacularly demon-
strated the FBI failure. By May, plans were apparently afoot to remove Hoover and perhaps replace him with L. Patrick Gray.
Hoover was almost removed in autumn 1971—but Nixon backed
away, apparently fearing a political firestorm, according to both
Haldeman and Ehrlichman. And he was always shy about personal
confrontation. Despite everything, Hoover stayed on.[100]

In September 1972, Hoover removed Charles Brennan as assistant
director of the Domestic Intelligence Division. He demoted
Brennan because, against Hoover's orders, Brennan had interrogated Leo Marx, a friend of Hoover's, in the Pentagon Papers affair—and then tried to cover it up. Hoover agreed to replace
Brennan with Mark Felt's choice—Edward Miller. Ed Miller's own
animus toward Weatherman was personal and long-standing. A de-
vout Catholic and a World War II combat hero, he had been assistant special agent in charge in Chicago during the Days of Rage in
October 1969. He had overseen the trial of the Chicago Eight that
autumn and winter, and had collected the daily death threats sent to
Judge Julius Hoffman. He later claimed that he gave Hoffman the
idea of chaining and gagging Bobby Seale, a notorious incident of
the trial. Miller also had been a bodyguard for the chief judge in the
chaotic arraignment of the Days of Rage rioters.[101] He was well read
in revolutionary literature, and could quote by memory from Carlos
Marighella's *Mini-manual of the Urban Guerrilla*. Further, Miller had
conducted dozens of surreptitious entries in national security cases.
And as late as 2008, he continued to claim that Weatherman bombings between 1970 and 1972 had resulted in twenty-eight deaths.[102]
The truth was otherwise: FBI reports in spring 1972 on
Weatherman bombings cite them for only one death in the previous
two years—the August 1970 Army Math bombing at the University
of Wisconsin; and that was a bombing, we now know, where
Weatherman was not in fact involved.[103]
    Miller brought with him Special Agent Hugh Mallet, another
FBI veteran of the Days of Rage, whom he placed as a senior agent
in the headquarters unit specializing in Weatherman, then headed

by Special Agent William Preusse. Mallet had previously been in charge of the bugging of the Chicago headquarters of SDS/ Weatherman when it was still aboveground.[104]

According to Robert Shackelford, the investigation of Weatherman intensified with the arrival of Miller. How Miller intended to answer the Weatherman challenge soon became clear: more black bag jobs. "I think Miller himself was obviously interested in the use of techniques from the time he walked in the door," said Shackelford: "Miller in general was much more concerned or interested in the use of techniques than Brennan had been." Mallet, too, was an advocate of such operations.[105] Within two months of Miller's taking over FBI Domestic Intelligence, a special committee produced what could be called "the Miller Plan" for a major black bag job program against the Weathermen. It was top secret. Its documents were found in 1976 in a locked file cabinet in the office of William Preusse when the investigations into FBI violations of the law had begun. These documents became available to the public only in 2013.[106]

The first push for intensified surreptitious entries came from Shackelford, the chief of "Revolutionary Groups," on October 29, 1971. In a memo to Miller, he laid out all the actions that the Domestic Intelligence Division had tried in its efforts to capture Weathermen or obstruct Weatherman activities, and admitted that these had all failed. He concluded with a plea for the restitution of black bag jobs, secret microphones, and mail openings.[107] A week and a half later, on November 8, Miller met with all Weatherman case supervisors. Miller wanted solutions. The participants stressed the failure of "conventional techniques": informants were hard to find, and in any case could not get to the hidden radicals; physical surveillances were a waste of time since agents did not know whom to watch; wiretaps had failed because of the targets' security precautions. A year and a half after Weatherman had gone underground, the FBI knew nothing about where its members had gone or their assumed identities, or even what, beyond their public pronouncements, they intended.[108]

The agents at this November 8 meeting suggested that there was only one answer to these difficulties: black bag operations. Assistant Director Miller agreed.[109] He was keen to reinstate black bag jobs as a major program. Thereafter, agents who specialized on Weatherman met every two weeks to work up such a proposal. According to Shackelford, Miller thought the Weatherman cases were so obviously in need of burglaries that they were the best way to convince Hoover to remove the ban on bag jobs altogether.[110]

On January 14, 1972, the committee authorized by Miller to explore potential targets and rationales for such operations delivered a formal five-page single-spaced draft memo to him titled "Argument for Use of Anonymous Sources—Black Bag Technique—Weatherman Investigation." This was the culmination of several earlier drafts and lists of possible individuals—suspected aboveground supporters of Weatherman—as targets for burglary. The memo stressed once more the importance of capturing Weatherman, and the difficulties involved. The purpose of the black bag jobs would be to gain intelligence on future bombings and to locate fugitives; the authors conceded that actual use of such information in court was impossible since the material would have been obtained without a search warrant. The risks of discovery and embarrassment to the Bureau were acknowledged. These would be minimized by being careful during operations.[111]

Three individuals were listed as targets in the final list of January 1972: (a) Mona Cunningham, a friend of Bernardine Dohrn's, living in San Francisco and already under physical surveillance; (b) Jennifer Dohrn, Bernardine's sister, the leading aboveground Weatherman spokesperson, living in New York; and (c) Dennis Cunningham, the estranged husband of Mona and a leader of the radical People's Law Office in Chicago. The memo noted that since Cunningham's Chicago home had already been burgled several times (!), it was unlikely to contain Weatherman information; the target of the surreptitious entries should therefore be the People's Law Office itself—where the FBI had already placed informants (though without obtaining any useful information). In fact, burglarizing the People's Law Office had already been suggested in an FBI memo the previous August; this memo had had suggested that "considerable material could be obtained related to finances of New Left groups, especially the violent Weatherman."[112]

It is not known whether Miller sent the final January 14, 1972, memo to his superior Alex Rosen, then assistant to the director for the Investigative Branch and the number-four man in the Bureau, or whether it then went to Hoover. But one fact is suggestive: several of the Miller memo proposals were in fact carried out.

On December 8, 1971, Hoover sent a signed application to Attorney General Mitchell for permission to place a bug inside the automobile of Susan Jordan, who had been named a potential target in the earlier Miller memos; Miller himself was directly involved in this application, and Mitchell agreed. On February 28, Hoover sent a signed application to Mitchell for permission to establish "a telephone surveillance" inside the home of Mona Cunningham; Miller was again directly involved, and again Mitchell agreed.[113] Jennifer Dohrn too became the victim of black bag jobs, all of which had the approval of Mitchell—which meant that Hoover had formally applied for them.[114] It is possible that other supporters of Weatherman were also targeted.[115]

Yet the case of Mona Cunningham revealed the ineptness of FBI efforts. The physical surveillance of Cunningham had been established in late 1971 by undercover Special Agent William Reagan. Posing as a hippie, and looking like the singer David Crosby, he had gotten to know Cunningham after renting an apartment in her small apartment house in San Francisco's Haight-Ashbury district. But even after the FBI in a surreptitious entry placed a bug on Cunningham's phone in early March 1972, no information was obtained about Weatherman activities or Cunningham's possible connections to them. The FBI eventually concluded that staking out her apartment had been a waste of time; Reagan was withdrawn and assigned elsewhere.[116] Somehow the FBI failed to comprehend Cunningham's usefulness to Weather. During this period, she was lending out her children, especially her eight-year-old daughter Delia, as "beards" to Weatherman couples, especially to Bill Ayers and Bernardine Dohrn, who were scouting potential bombing targets; a couple with a child would arouse less suspicion. Cunningham evidently knew how to use her telephone very carefully. The FBI never found out what was going on.[117]

On February 14, 1972, the New York apartment of Murray Bookchin, an independent radical with no ties to Weather, was burgled by the FBI Weatherman squad. The New York apartment of Leonard Machtinger, the brother of Weatherman leader Howard

Machtinger, was burgled by the FBI Weatherman squad on April 18. Neither resulted in useful information.[118] Since Hoover knew of and approved the black bag jobs carried out against Mona Cunningham, Susan Jordan, and Jennifer Dohrn, it is reasonable to assume that he also knew of, and probably approved, these other two warrantless entries. None was a "wildcat" bag job.

All these warrantless burglaries were the sort of case-by-case operation that had been envisaged as occurring in the Intelligence Evaluation Committee plan of winter 1970–1971—a plan that Hoover had blocked. The difference was that now the FBI—and Hoover personally—controlled these black bag operations. Of course, both the FBI and the White House knew that the courts had consistently forbidden warrantless electronic surveillance and burglaries as violations of the Fourth Amendment. They also knew that break-ins into the homes or offices of suspected subversives without warrant for reasons of national security had never been challenged in court—and that such break-ins had never ceased. There was a simple reason. They were top secret.

CHAPTER SIX

"Hunt Them to Exhaustion"

THE FBI PANIC OVER possible Weatherman kidnappings and attacks on the Bureau itself eventually subsided, but the Bureau remained fearful. After the Weatherman bombing of the U.S. Capitol on March 1, 1971, the FBI concluded that "one of the most pressing problems of the Administration relates to the control of activities of criminal subversives, such as the Weatherman group." The Capitol bombing led to armed guards and metal detectors being placed in all government buildings in Washington.[1] But although sporadic Weatherman bombings continued, the campus cataclysm of spring 1970 was not repeated. There was no national revolution as Weatherman had hoped to inspire. On October 1, 1970, Hoover rescinded the May 13 directive under which the FBI was to consider all bombings by leftist radicals as "Weatherman-type." It was now recognized that radical bombers might not have an organizational affiliation with Weather. Such bombings would now be categorized not as "Weatherman" but merely as "extremist."[2]

The mood of the country was changing. Nixon's rapid reduction of American forces in Vietnam during 1971 and the creation of the draft lottery—which ended the threat of the draft for young men whose birthdates fell in the bottom 150 of the lottery dates—helped to erode antiwar activism on campus. American combat deaths in Vietnam, averaging two hundred a week in May 1970, were down to thirty-five a week in May 1971—low enough to keep wavering sections of youth away from the seductions of radicals.[3] Still, the massive May Day 1971 demonstration in Washington, D.C., during which twelve thousand protesters were arrested, along with other incidents of street-fighting and civil disobedience, suggested to many Nixon officials and certainly to the FBI that radical ambitions were alive and well.

The counterculture, at least as a spectacular national movement, was beginning to fade as well. It did not disappear entirely, but, like the remnants of the New Left itself after May Day, counterculture people began to focus less on the Vietnam War than on purely local issues, such as ecology, issues that were not of interest to the FBI and could be left to the local police.[4] As for the Black Panthers and other black militants in whom Weatherman had placed such hopes, they had been severely weakened by COINTEL-PRO operations aimed at creating factionalism, and by outright violence against them by local police.[5] Weatherman, too, had developed a mode of operations that led to months-long periods of inaction, punctuated, to be sure, by the occasional spectacular bombing. Meanwhile, the gradual release to the public of the FBI papers that local radicals had stolen from the FBI office in Media, Pennsylvania, in March 1971—documents that revealed the extent of FBI investigations into the private lives and political opinions of ordinary people—left the Bureau politically vulnerable. As newspapers published exposés based on the stolen FBI files, shock at the Bureau's conduct deepened, public support for the Bureau sank, and calls for Congress to investigate the FBI grew.[6]

Still, many key government officials remained convinced that the threat posed by the radical Left remained high, and had to be fought. The men in the FBI directorate believed, and worked hard to convince law-enforcement officials, that the threat of revolution was real. In November, the FBI hosted a two-day conference in Washington, D.C., for police chiefs on the threat of "urban guerrilla warfare." Newly promoted Assistant Director Ed Miller told them that America was becoming a leftist battlefield and that "there is very good reason to believe that urban guerrilla warfare exists and is on the increase . . . a part of revolutionary efforts to destroy the U.S. Government." An FBI memo echoed his view: "Extremists, both black nationalist and New Left, are increasingly involved in urban guerrilla warfare in the U.S." FBI files show that President Nixon took a personal interest in the police chiefs conference.[7]

Five months later, in one of his last acts, Hoover sent a long memo to the field offices, explaining how to distinguish "urban guerrillas" from ordinary criminals. The list of radical behaviors was four pages long, and began with the claim that terrorist acts were increasing across the country. In September 1972, a high FBI official would write: "The nation is going through a time of terror. The concept of urban guerrilla terrorism has been adopted by extremist elements. Bombings of public buildings and national institutions ... [represent an] open declaration of war on our form of government." Even in January 1973 the FBI was still planning responses to possible kidnappings of government officials.[8] But no high U.S. official had ever been kidnapped. Fear of radical violence was disproportionate to the actual threat. The FBI's own statistics showed that the number of bombings nationwide was falling: there were sixty bombings in all of 1971 in contrast to the sixty-two bombings in San Francisco alone in the year beginning in spring 1969. The number of attacks on police in 1971 was half that of 1970; the number of police deaths was down.[9] By 1972, too, the FBI calculated that Weatherman numbered only about one hundred underground members, with about two hundred facilitators— that is, less than one tenth the numbers the FBI had feared existed in summer 1970. This did not represent a decline in Weatherman membership; rather, it was, for the first time, an accurate calculation.[10] Assertions by FBI officials that guerrilla warfare was increasing in 1971 were contradicted by the Bureau's own numbers.

It would have been reasonable for the FBI's focus on Weatherman to lessen. But this did not happen. This was so partly because of bureaucratic inertia but mostly because the Bureau was hostage to its own worst-case scenarios; it was also well practiced in fanning the most apocalyptic fears that would result in Congress increasing its budget and expanding its resources. Weather also presented a public-relations problem. Weatherman and other New Left leaders still accounted for seven slots on the FBI's "Ten Most

Wanted List" in the spring and summer of 1972, none of them—despite two years of FBI effort—having been caught. More than forty other Weathermen were sought on various charges; none of them had been caught, either.[11] Some supporters of Weatherman had thought that the group could not survive six months with the FBI after it. They were wrong. The Weather Underground not only survived but continued to detonate bombs (if infrequently), and there was fear that more was coming. Hoover repeatedly expressed his frustration in circulars to special agents in charge. According to Robert Shackelford, negative media about the FBI failure to catch Weatherman was periodically intense—especially after a successful bombing.[12]

Weatherman had excellent security. The Bureau could not find the organization, let alone penetrate it. It was not for lack of trying. For example, in November 1970 the Bureau recruited a person who traveled to Boston and New Haven, posing as a reporter for a radical newspaper; all he got were vague rumors about the Weatherman bombing in Boston the previous month. In late 1970, too, the Chicago field office found someone to pose as a revolutionary fugitive in legal trouble, in order to penetrate the People's Law Office—the firm headed by Dennis Cunningham that was suspected of having ties to Weatherman. The informant obtained contacts that had "great potential." But nothing came of it. The desperation of the Bureau to find *some* way to find the Weathermen is also apparent in a New York field office plan of November 1971 to hire Hell's Angels to ride around Vermont on their motorcycles in hopes of somehow making contact with a Weatherman collective. In Seattle, the local field office was reduced to suggesting that potential informants might be found by advertising for "footloose individuals" in ads in newspapers.[13]

In October 1971 Hoover had ordered that the field offices in Boston, Chicago, New York, and San Francisco each set up a local squad exclusively to hunt the Weatherman fugitives. He was aware of the manpower strain this would cause but demanded it nonetheless. He wanted the squads to get the best men and have complete support. But, like everything else the FBI tried, this effort produced nothing. FBI ignorance of what was occurring inside Weather was complete. For example, in autumn 1971 the Bureau still believed that Mark Rudd, a "most wanted" fugitive, was a central Weatherman leader (perhaps even *the* leader). In fact, Rudd had dropped out of Weatherman a full year earlier, and was living quietly in New Mexico under an assumed name. And the investigation into the Capitol bombing similarly went nowhere, leading to this embarrassing exchange as Hoover was grilled by Rep. Robert L. F. Sikes (D-Florida) before the House Appropriations Committee in March 1972:

> MR. SIKES: What is the status of the Capitol bombing incident?
> MR. HOOVER: It is still under active investigation.
> MR. SIKES: Almost a year ago, you thought it was ready to break.
> MR. HOOVER: Yes, we did.[14]

Yet unbeknownst to the FBI, the Bureau had struck a powerful blow against the Weathermen the year before. In March 1971 FBI agents had tailed Dennis Cunningham from the People's Law Office in Chicago to a Western Union office, and found that he had used an assumed name to dispatch a voucher for seven hundred dollars to Western Union in San Francisco. Suspecting that the money was to support the Weather Underground, the Chicago field office alerted San Francisco to the Western Union pickup. When Jeff Jones and Bernardine Dohrn drove to the Western Union office in San Francisco and Jones went inside to get the money, something aroused his suspicions. He fled and something of a car chase ensued, with Dohrn at the wheel of Jones's pickup truck. Dohrn and Jones lost the FBI pursuers when she gunned the truck through a stoplight just as it turned red. The FBI men had not arrested Jones at the Western Union office because they did not recognize him.[15]

The FBI later staked out what they thought was the abandoned pickup; when John Davis, the brother of former SDS president and former Chicago Eight defendant Rennie Davis, showed up to recover it, the FBI knew they were onto something. The truck had received parking tickets on Pine Street in San Francisco, and FBI spadework led them to suspect an apartment there was a

Weatherman safe house. Allowing a car registered under a false name to get parking tickets near one's hideout was an almost fatal error on the Weathermen's part: four major Weatherman figures were living in the apartment. But when the FBI finally raided the Pine Street address, they were gone.[16]

The FBI had come up empty: no Jeff Jones, no Bernardine Dohrn, nobody. Nor was Dennis Cunningham ever indicted for his aiding of federal fugitives, because the Justice Department hoped (in vain, as it would turn out) that, if left free, Cunningham might still lead them to the Weather Underground.[17] Yet the Pine Street raid was not a complete failure. The Weathermen had abruptly abandoned Pine Street when they learned that John Davis had been questioned as he tried to recover Jones's truck, and they realized that the truck could be linked to Pine Street. They instantly fled, leaving behind finished bombs, equipment for making them, and documents. Further, a Weatherman had used the Pine Street address to procure a driver's license under a false name, and many false identities had come from the same Pennsylvania county as the name he had used, so the FBI could find out the fugitives' false identities that way. The repercussions were enormous; the San Francisco network–the work of eight months since August 1970— collapsed.[18]

Still, there were good reasons for the FBI at the time to think it had failed. It had caught no one. Moreover, within months a Weatherman collective was back in the Bay Area and actively engaged in bombing. The Bureau's humiliation was profound.[19]

On May 2, 1972, J. Edgar Hoover died in his sleep in his modest home a few blocks from FBI headquarters. Acting Attorney General Richard Kleindienst wanted to appoint Cartha DeLoach to succeed Hoover: DeLoach had vast experience and was widely respected in the Bureau. But Kleindienst was overruled by Richard Nixon, who appointed L. Patrick Gray as acting director—a man with no experience in the FBI, or even law enforcement.[20]

Like Nixon, Gray came from an impoverished background and had made good through his intelligence and sheer hard work. A lawyer and a World War II and Korean War submarine commander with a distinguished record, Gray had in 1960 resigned from the navy, where he was headed for the admiralty, to become Vice President Nixon's adviser on military affairs and to work on Nixon's presidential campaign. After Nixon lost to Kennedy, it seemed that Gray had sacrificed his naval career for nothing; Nixon did not forget. There was no personal friendship (Nixon had few real friends), but he considered Gray "a Nixon loyalist."[21] In the 1960s Gray ran a successful legal practice in Connecticut. When Nixon was elected president in 1968, a place in the new administration was found for Gray, and by early 1971 he was the assistant attorney general in charge of the Civil Division at the Justice Department.

In that position Gray made a name for himself by spearheading a successful legal attack on demonstrators in the great May Day 1971 antiwar demonstrations in Washington. First, he won a court order preventing the Vietnam Veterans Against the War, a group Nixon especially detested, from camping on the National Mall. Gray argued the case with great emotion as a war hero. And it was Gray, too, who met with FBI men during the demonstrations—his first contact with the FBI—for advice on how the Justice Department should handle the radicals, conversations that resulted in the policy of mass arrests [22]

When John Mitchell resigned as attorney general to run Nixon's 1972 reelection campaign and Richard Kleindienst became acting attorney general, Nixon promoted Gray to acting deputy attorney general. Nixon applauded Gray's steadfast loyalty and anti-radical fervor. The post was second in command at Justice, charged with running the huge department on a day-to-day basis.

Gray, in that position, showed his loyalty once again. He was a White House point man to try to convince the FBI science laboratory that the "Dita Beard memo"—which implicated the Nixon administration in settling an antitrust case against the ITT Corporation in exchange for campaign contributions—was a forgery. When the FBI lab found the evidence inconclusive, Gray made that report available to John Dean, whom Gray had known in Justice, and who was now White House counsel. Dean turned it over to ITT experts, who declared the memo a forgery. Haldeman's notes from the White House meeting where Gray was chosen to replace Hoover succinctly named the qualities that would make Gray an ideal acting director: "Guts—ability and loyalty. Best to do today."[23]

As acting director, Gray continued to rail against the far Left. Addressing the Veterans of Foreign Wars in Minnesota, he proudly pledged his allegiance to the good old red, white, and blue, in contrast to those who "have pledged their allegiance to the red flag of communist tyranny, the black flag of anarchy, or the white flag of surrender." On another occasion, addressing Pepperdine University Law School in California, he said:

> Today we hear strident and bitter voices from a very small, though highly articulate minority that the historical institutions of America should be destroyed as completely as if the Huns or Vandals had passed through. . . . These voices, especially those of the extremist "New Left," assert that our democratic institutions are corrupt and not worth saving. We are told that our American way of life is repressive. . . . They demand that the system itself be overturned. I cannot envision what kind of rights and what kind of justice we would have if these calamity-howlers had their way.[24]

This stern warning was delivered by Gray on Saturday, June 17, 1972. It is a nice historical irony that right after the speech the special agent in charge of the Los Angeles field office informed Gray of word from Washington that a break-in had occurred at the Democratic Party's national headquarters in the Watergate Complex. This illegal act on behalf of Nixon's reelection campaign would eventually lead to the president's resignation in disgrace in August 1974. But Gray's own involvement in the Watergate scandal included his personal destruction of secret Watergate-related files given him at the White House—an act that would force Gray himself to withdraw his nomination in 1973 to be permanent FBI director. Indeed, Gray barely escaped being indicted for obstruction of justice.[25]

All this lay in the future.

Gray's appointment as acting director did not require Senate confirmation, as would have been necessary had Nixon made him permanent director; a Senate hearing was something Nixon wanted to avoid, given Gray's involvement in the ITT scandal. Further, Nixon knew full well that *acting* director was a vulnerable position; if Gray wanted Nixon's support for permanent director, he would have to please the White House. With the appointment of Gray, then, Nixon achieved a goal he had desired for three years: greater White House control over the FBI.[26]

Gray soon engineered some needed reforms: he ordered acceptance of female applicants to be special agents for the first time, much against the will of others in the Bureau's directorate; he spoke to special agents in charge in a friendly manner, and addressed them by their first names (Hoover had mandated formality); he loosened Hoover's regulations on dress and physical appearance. But the FBI directorate always viewed Gray as an outsider. Bureau veterans resented the small independent staff of lawyers (including a woman) Gray brought over with him from Justice. And they believed that one of their own should have been named director. Mark Felt—who as the de facto number-two man in Hoover's last year seemed Hoover's obvious successor—apparently especially felt that way.[27]

Gray turned out to be a lackadaisical manager. He was often absent from headquarters visiting the field offices. While these visits were good for morale (Hoover had rarely done it) and helped to familiarize Gray with FBI tasks, issues, and problems (a familiarity he did not otherwise have), it meant that the acting director was often gone from Washington. His willingness to give speeches all over the country increased his absences, as did his wish to spend his weekends at his home in Connecticut (Gray and his wife kept only a small apartment in Washington). In addition, in November and December 1972 Gray was completely out of action, hospitalized from an old war wound. He tended to delegate authority even when he was in the office, and did not keep up with the huge flow of paperwork coming to the director, as Hoover, even in his mid-seventies, had done. Hoover had worked six days a week. Some at headquarters called his successor "Three-Day Gray." Day-to-day operations were left in the hands of Mark Felt.[28]

On May 11, 1972—just a week after becoming acting director— Patrick Gray instructed each of the nine FBI assistant directors in charge of a division to prepare a position paper on the main issues before that division; these were to be presented at an inaugural two-day business meeting on May 23. Gray specified what he wanted Ed Miller's Domestic Intelligence Division to address: his memo designated the topic: "Subversion," specifically whether the FBI was legally empowered to investigate the threat posed by left-wing radicals, or whether new legislation was needed to expand its power. A report prepared within the division proposed that additional legislation might be necessary, but Ed Miller would ultimately reject the recommendation on grounds that FDR's presidential directives gave the FBI all the legal authority it needed.[29]

On May 19, the birthday of Ho Chi Minh and Malcolm X, the Weather Underground set off a large dynamite bomb in the Pentagon. A female member of Weather had simply walked into the vast building along with crowds of civilian employees to scout a suitable location for a bomb, then had returned the next day, again simply walking in. She placed the bomb in a woman's restroom opposite the Air Force Directorate of Plans and Policy. A warning call was made; the subsequent blast caused no human injuries but did result in an estimated million dollars' worth of damage, including to a computer that was vital to the bombing campaign in Vietnam, disrupting operations over Vietnam for a week. The Weather attack had indeed "brought the war home." It was also a bold affront to the FBI and its new acting director. The Pentagon was only two miles from FBI headquarters.[30]

Three days later, on May 22, Gray ordered intensification of the "sensitive coverage" on Jennifer Dohrn. Gray had wanted information about FBI operations against Dohrn even earlier than May 22, according to his reply to a memo sent to him detailing FBI operations against her. Gray's reply emphasized that Dohrn was "among the most active of the Weatherman group in New York City," and as the sister of Weather leader Bernardine Dohrn, a likely contact point between the Weather Underground and support groups. Gray acknowledged that Jennifer Dohrn had been subjected to "sensitive coverage" as well as "intensified physical surveillance." But he ordered "intensified scrutiny" in the hopes of obtaining advance knowledge of future Weatherman violent actions and bombings, as well as any information that might lead to the capture of her sister and other fugitives. Gray required that New York report to him about Dohrn on a weekly basis; Hoover had asked only for biweekly reports. And Gray expected the weekly summaries to "incorporate results of sensitive coverage." That is, Gray was requiring New York to give him continually updated information derived from the warrantless wiretap and microphone placed on Dohrn.[31]

A week later, Gray made it clear to the FBI directorate that he was also looking in general to intensify methods in the hunt for the radical bombers. On May 30 he sent a query on techniques to Miller. Gray wanted to know what major intelligence programs, if any, had been abolished, the reasons for their discontinuance, whether such programs should be reinstated, and what would be necessary to do so.[32]

Miller had William Brannigan, head of the counterintelligence section in Domestic Intelligence, draft a response which, after Miller approved it, was sent up to his boss, Mark Felt, who in turn sent it on to Gray. Brannigan urged reinstatement of several programs: the so-called C Program of surreptitious entries (targets unknown, but a program apparently connected to the CIA), which had been discontinued by Attorney General Ramsey Clark in 1967; the SAM program of opening mail destined for the Soviet Union, discontinued by Hoover in 1966; the Z coverage of opening mail coming in to selected consulates and embassies of hostile foreign governments, discontinued by Hoover in 1966; and, above all, black bag operations. The last, Brannigan informed Gray, were similar to the C program but directed against suspected domestic subversives.[33]

All these programs were "highly desirable from a counterintelligence standpoint" but carried risks of disclosure. While reinstatement was ideal, it was therefore recommended that it be deferred until after the November 1972 elections. Felt agreed. But a handwritten note from Gray was appended to the May 31 memo: "Is there a *need now?*"[34]

Meanwhile, Gray was told that the Pentagon bombing might be the beginning of a major Weatherman summer offensive. The first warning came on May 26 from the Alexandria field office, in charge of investigating the bombing: the attack revealed Weatherman's "expert knowledge of explosive devices, methodical and painstaking preparation and smooth execution"; and no clues had been left behind. Only penetration of the organization would help catch the culprits. The agent heading the investigation advised Gray to "pull out all the stops." On June 9, the Alexandria field office issued another warning: more was coming from Weatherman, perhaps bombings against military bases or defense corporations. The situation was critical. Alexandria specifically urged Gray to consider "using every investigative device and technique productive in the past."[35] These warnings helped give Gray cause for worry. What, for instance, was Weatherman planning for the Democratic National Convention and especially for the Republican National Convention in Miami, the first coming in just one month, the second in two months?[36] These fears certainly propelled Gray along the path he wished to go. But Alexandria and Washington were both mistaken: the Weathermen would do no bombing again until a full year later (May 1973); and while there were demonstrations against Nixon in Miami in July, Weather was not involved.

Gray did not wait until the election to begin reinstating the old programs. In early October 1972 he ordered Program C black bag jobs reinstituted. So, too, mail coverage against possible domestic subversives.[37] But the big goal was reinstatement of unfettered surreptitious entries. Arbor Gray (no relation to Patrick Gray), then head of the Communist Party section of the Domestic Intelligence Division, recalled that after Gray became acting director, he met with Miller and Miller's section chiefs, including Arbor Gray and Robert Shackelford. After the meeting, Miller escorted Gray out; he returned in a good mood and reported that "Mr. Gray was receptive to the use of confidential techniques against the Weathermen." Arbor Gray took this to mean wiretapping, microphones, and black bag jobs. For his part, Patrick Gray would always deny having given permission for black bag jobs against Weatherman, but the evidence suggests otherwise.[38]

The "Is there a *need now*?" memo went out on June 3. Five days later, Gray called a conference of agents from across the country to focus on techniques for hunting Weatherman: "I want to turn up the heat on our efforts to apprehend these people. To do so will require innovative tactics." The conference was held in Washington on June 22, and agents set out the usual problems in locating the

Weatherman collectives—or stopping their violence. What did Gray mean by "innovative tactics"? The written agenda gives an answer: it had as its very first topic "anonymous sources (bag jobs)."[39]

Only eight days before, on June 14, the FBI had applied to Acting Attorney General Kleindienst for a ninety-day extension on the bugging of Jennifer Dohrn. The Bureau had originally argued to Attorney General Mitchell that an extension was needed because surveillance of Dohrn was providing useful intelligence. Yet Hoover had disagreed on the value of information being obtained—which is why he had pushed so hard in March. Years later, James Vermeersch, Dohrn's case officer, admitted that the burglaries of Dohrn's apartment had helped catch no one, nor did they prevent a single Weatherman bombing.[40] Kleindienst, however, immediately approved the FBI application—which required the signature of Gray as (acting) director. Yet Gray claimed in his memoir, published in 2009, that as far as he knew the FBI had not run any black bag jobs after the "Hoover cutoff" until September 1972—and that latter operation had been directed against suspected Palestinian terrorists. Gray's June 14 application to Kleindienst suggests a different story.[41] It is hard to believe that Gray was unaware of the two bag jobs that the FBI had run on Dohrn's apartment that very week (June 6 and 13). These burglaries were reported by James Vermeersch up the FBI chain of command. They were probably undertaken in response to Gray's May 22 memo.[42]

Under Hoover, the FBI had begun holding periodic training courses to upgrade agents' capabilities; such a special training course was dubbed an "in-service." In April 1972, for example, an in-service was planned for August to deal with "general security" and the New Left. Specific terrorist organizations were mentioned in the proposed curriculum: the Jewish Defense League and the Republic of New Afrika, to name two. But one group was oddly omitted: Weatherman.[43] Patrick Gray changed all this and ordered that the August in-service be focused *exclusively* on Weatherman—and the course was scheduled to last ten days. In addition, a second Weatherman in-service was now planned for October.[44]

Gray also made preparations for new attempts at penetrating Weather collectives. On July 6 he held a special meeting of assistant directors to discuss lifting the Bureau's restrictions on hair length and clothing style so that undercover FBI agents could more easily infiltrate the countercultural sea in which the Weather fish swam. The strictures on hair and clothing were dropped. And on July 12 Gray ordered the seventeen field offices in cities where Weatherman was most active to make Weatherman their "top priority."[45]

Ed Miller later said that, under Gray, capturing the Weathermen became the main task of the Bureau's entire Domestic Intelligence Division. Gray's single-minded insistence, he thought, stemmed from the Nixon White House. FBI Inspector Donald E. Moore, who ran the Espionage section of Domestic Intelligence (1956–1973), would later testify that although some surreptitious entries went forward after the 1966 "Hoover cutoff," Hoover had set a quota on such operations; but when Pat Gray became acting director, the quota disappeared.[46]

Then, on June 19, 1972, a severe legal blow was struck against FBI methods. Title III of the 1968 Omnibus Crime and Safe Streets Act allowed warrantless wiretaps in cases of preventing the overthrow of the government, or in "any other clear and present danger to the structure or existence of the government." In a 1971 case involving the radical White Panthers (allies of Weatherman), Judge Damon Keith of the U.S. District Court for the Eastern District of Michigan ruled that the Justice Department had to turn over to the defense the transcripts of all such warrantless wiretaps. The Justice Department appealed to the Supreme Court—and the Court ruled unanimously that the entire 1968 permission for warrantless wiretaps was unconstitutional; in cases of domestic radical groups, the Fourth Amendment guaranteed their rights. The Court, however, made an exception: only in cases where there was significant *foreign* funding and influence could wiretaps without a court order by used. This ruling was known as "the Keith decision."

The ruling had its ambiguities. It condemned as unconstitutional warrantless electronic surveillance aimed at a "domestic organization composed of citizens of the United States and which has no significant connection with a foreign power, its agents, or agencies," but what constituted a "significant connection" to a foreign power went undefined. The Court conceded that it might be hard to discern a "significant" connection "where there are relationships in varying degrees between domestic groups or organizations and foreign powers or their agents." Still, after the Keith decision, FBI trespass operations were clearly out of bounds, as far as the law was concerned, as long as their targets were not "significantly" connected to a foreign power.

Nine days later, on June 28, Gray circulated new recommendations to the FBI directorate. Despite the Keith ruling, Gray pressed strongly for increased electronic surveillance, arguing—despite the evidence he had been given—that "increased electronic activity with respect to the Weathermen could be justified on grounds of possible involvement of a foreign power." This justification was to be used as much as possible: "if we do our job well, we will have a situation or two in which a Title III operation may be appropriate," he wrote in red ink to Mark Felt. That is, Gray wanted the FBI to come up with situations where bugging via surreptitious entry could be made to seem justified on grounds of alleged foreign involvement, even though this might require inventive effort. And then to ensure that no one would miss his point, he wrote in capital letters: "DO NOT LET THIS BE FORGOTTEN."[47]

But there were men in the FBI who knew that Weatherman was not covered under the Keith exception. One of them was Ed Miller. Miller wrote a memo to Mark Felt, pointing out the problem: "As to involvement of a foreign power at this time, no evidence exists of such involvement." Any requests for installation of bugs were unlikely to pass the scrutiny of any court.[48] On July 3, Assistant Director William V. Cleveland, head of the Special Investigations Division, also weighed in, as did his staff. They agreed with the FBI's own Office of Legal Counsel that any FBI push for electronic surveillances against Weatherman associates on "foreign power" grounds would not be justified. These opinions went via Felt to Gray. They were similar to the conclusions the FBI had drawn in November 1969 and February 1970 concerning the lack of foreign financing of Weatherman and other radical left groups.[49]

Yet these opinions may have been balanced by the powerful opinion of someone else; on July 6, Gray met privately with William Sullivan, the former FBI number-two man driven out by Hoover. With Hoover no longer on the scene, Attorney General

Kleindienst had invited Sullivan back into the Justice Department, this time to run the drug intelligence war. In fact, Sullivan's office was now only a few floors away from Gray's in the Federal Triangle Building. According to Gray's notes on the July 8 meeting, Sullivan—not surprisingly—urged Gray to reinstitute black bag jobs; further, he encouraged Gray by declaring that the Bureau possessed some "very good talent" for these sorts of operations.[50]

Nevertheless, in November, President Nixon's Foreign Intelligence Board also concluded in a highly classified report that there was no significant foreign involvement in Weatherman. The Bureau protested that the Keith decision now constrained FBI investigations of the Weathermen—precisely because there was no evidence of Weatherman's collaboration with foreign powers. Further, getting a court order for electronic surveillance of Weather supporters or relatives was already impossible because "probable cause of a violation of a specific statute does not exist." Yet a week before the meeting, Mark Felt had already approved yet another FBI break-in against Jennifer Dohrn.[51]

For its part the Central Intelligence Agency had already nearly two years earlier in January 1971 concluded that there was no significant foreign funding or influence in the radical left.[52]

Gray did not give up. On June 28, the same day as he emphasized the use of bugging in Weatherman cases, he urged the Justice Department to propose new legislation to legalize warrantless electronic surveillance of domestic radical groups But in late July, William Olson, the new assistant attorney general for Internal Security, assured Gray that Keith was limited to groups for which no foreign connections at all could be found—so if one simply asserted that Weatherman had *some* foreign connections, that would be enough to permit electronic surveillance without court order.[53] But in August, Olson reversed himself again, and argued that under Keith a warrantless surreptitious entry was legal only if a foreign government actually *controlled* the domestic target; any broader scope to allow for warrantless trespass would require new legislation. Gray disagreed, asserting that a "substantial" foreign connection— with *substantial* broadly defined—ought to be enough to legally authorize black bag jobs.[54]

On the evening of July 17, Gray reread both the Miller and Cleveland memos asserting there was no evidence of foreign involvement in Weatherman—and hence no Keith exception. He also reread his own replies to Mark Felt concerning those memos. In the files, these documents are all marked, in Gray's handwriting, "Read and studied again, 7/17/72., G." He was not cowed by what he read. The next day, Gray laid out with startling ferocity the policy he wished to be followed regarding Weatherman. Specifically explaining to Felt the stance to be taken at the August Weatherman in-service, Gray declared:

> I view this as . . . preparing [the agents] better to handle their assignments in the Field Divisions in order to generate the intelligence needed *to hunt Weatherman and similar groups to exhaustion.* Agents in the various Field Offices who are specializing in Weatherman: I want the full resources of the FBI to be placed behind them in the most innovative manner. I want no holds barred, and I want *to hunt Weatherman and similar groups to exhaustion. To hunt Weatherman and similar groups to exhaustion* will require a reallocation of resources. . . . Having in mind these comments, develop an overall plan of attack for prompt implementation.[55]

Copies of this memo, with "hunt them to exhaustion" repeated three times and underlined each time—accompanied by "I want no holds barred"—then went to the higher echelons of the FBI, including Miller and Shackelford. It also went to the special agents in charge in the seventeen cities where Weatherman was thought to be most active.[56]

Other FBI leaders received a typed version of this "No holds barred—hunt them to exhaustion" memo, replete with the emphases as above. But Felt, as deputy associate director, received Gray's original handwritten memo. In the handwritten version, the entire paragraph quoted above was underlined, while "I want no holds barred" was underlined twice. What Gray wanted from Felt was utterly clear: despite Keith, Gray welcomed—indeed, urged—authorizing warrantless wiretaps, microphones and surreptitious entries against supporters of Weatherman. No holds barred.[57]

Gray reinforced the "hunt them to exhaustion" policy a week later, on July 24, sending another top-secret memo with new orders to the special agents in charge in the same seventeen cities where Weatherman was presumed to be most active. He stressed the importance of disrupting Weatherman and capturing its leaders. He "specifically authorized": (a) monthly payments to be made to informants even though success was not guaranteed (a step that broke with Hoover's rule that the FBI paid informants only after receiving specific useful information); (b) field offices to seek out agents on staff who were young enough and well versed enough in youth culture to penetrate Weatherman themselves (previously this had been only a program in Los Angeles). Finally, Gray emphasized the "extreme importance" of the Weatherman cases, and that "top priority is to be given these investigations." He then commanded the field offices:

> I want your full resources to be placed behind agents handling these investigations and innovative methods devised. Where appropriate, Bureau authority should be requested to place these methods into operation. . . . I want to impress on each SAC the extreme importance of these investigations and that I expect Weatherman and similar groups to be hunted to exhaustion.[58]

In his autobiography, published posthumously in 2009, Gray wrote that when he became acting director he was appalled by the failure of Bureau to have caught even a single major member of the Weather Underground. But he denied ever having advocated the use of illegal methods:

> I immediately ordered them "hunted to exhaustion," a phrase we had used in submarine tactics. Dogged pursuit of an elusive enemy was what I had in mind. What I did not have in mind was the use of illegal means to accomplish that.

Instead, Gray wrote, "What I had in mind when I ordered them hunted to exhaustion was a greater use of shoe-leather and undercover agents." It was Mark Felt and Edward Miller who had approved illegal surreptitious entries behind his back—as, he charged, they had done previously to Hoover.[59]

Gray's denials have been accepted as fact in some quarters.[60] But it is now clear that, to start with, Hoover knew of the burglaries being carried out against supporters of Weatherman, and that in Jennifer Dohrn's case he personally ordered them (March 1972). Similarly, Gray too was aware of the burglaries against Dohrn—and he himself encouraged them soon after becoming acting director. His comment on the May 30 memo about reinstating programs of surveillance was in the same vein. Moreover, the June 14 written application to Kleindienst to continue the bugging of Dohrn could not have gone forward without his signature. Felt and Miller would later claim that Gray was aware in general of what they were doing that autumn, and that it was on his authority that they approved black bag jobs. They understood themselves to be acting under Gray's orders, and thus ultimately under the president's authority.[61] Their claim does not mean that Gray personally approved any specific Weatherman burglary, or even knew of any specific one. In this—very narrow—sense his later denial may not be false; Gray, after all, was an accomplished lawyer. But personal knowledge of specific operations was not necessary if general approval had been given to the methods used. Within the Bureau, it was the responsibility of Miller and of Felt to approve individual break-ins. As for Gray, if by "hunt them to exhaustion" he simply meant wearing out shoe leather in very traditional ways of investigation, why did he then tell the SACs in the July 24 letter that it was necessary to get approval from headquarters before instituting the "innovative methods" he was encouraging?

In 1980, on trial for abuse of his authority and charged with breaking the law in his pursuit of the Weather Underground, Felt—under cross-examination by the chief prosecutor John Nields—described the situation at FBI headquarters this way:

> Q. Mr. Felt, is it fair to say then that you were the highest official in the United States government who approved or knew of the bag jobs on Jennifer Dohrn, Frances Schreiberg, Benjamin Cohen, Murray Bookchin, and Howard Machtinger?

A. I would say that Mr. Gray was the highest official to my knowledge who gave general approval to surreptitious entries. I was the highest official who gave approval on a specific case by case basis.[62]

Gray's policy of "hunt them to exhaustion" aroused protests from the field. Special agents in charge pleaded that resources were stretched, and that other important tasks (that is, regular crime-fighting) would be neglected.[63] But it was to no avail. Top priority was to be given to the hunt for Weatherman. When Seattle claimed that it simply did not have the manpower, Gray's reply was stern: "This is unacceptable. You must allocate the necessary manpower."[64]

Street agents dealing with the Weather Underground found out what "hunt to exhaustion" meant in August at the Weatherman in-service held at the FBI training center in Quantico, Virginia. Illegal methods of information collection were discussed. Some years later, however—when the Bureau was itself under investigation for illegal actions—most of the agents who had attended the August in-service insisted that they had seen and heard nothing about illegal operations.[65]

In fact, illegal techniques *were* discussed, and discussed in some detail. There was discussion of black bag jobs by agents from New York City. There was also discussion with Bill Preusse, head of the Weatherman unit at FBI headquarters, concerning the black bag jobs being run on Jennifer Dohrn. There was discussion of the discovery of the Weatherman safe house on Pine Street in San Francisco in April 1971: agents from San Francisco complained that surreptitious entry had been denied them, and as a result the quarry had escaped before it was decided to raid the apartment. On the last day of the in-service, Gray appeared and spoke before the agents and, as one recalled, "stressed the importance of apprehending Weatherman fugitives and indicated all resources should be used to affect their apprehension."[66]

Robert Knapp, the supervising agent of Weatherman investigations in the Detroit field office, remembered that at the August in-service "there was discussion regarding surreptitious entries and it was mentioned that surreptitious entries would be approved on a limited basis." When Knapp returned home to Detroit, he informed his supervisor, Special Agent in Charge Neil J. Welch, about the discussions: "Welch exploded, and said in no way would he authorize in his office any such illegal activities."[67]

A month later, in late September 1972, Patrick Gray visited the Detroit field office. Knapp was assigned as the driver for Gray and Welch as Welch showed Gray around. Knapp overheard the following conversation:

> Gray stated that he had recently authorized a bag job in the Wadi case. Gray made the comment that the Weatherman had to be apprehended. Welch stated something to the effect, asking Gray why we were doing this, and stated it in a strong disagreeing tone of voice, indicating that he did not approve of the Bureau authorizing surreptitious entries. It was at that point that Gray made the comment that the Weatherman must be apprehended.

Knapp had no doubt that warrantless surreptitious entries in Weatherman cases were going to be approved.[68]

Knapp mentioned "the Wadi case," a secret FBI operation, as evidence that he knew what he was talking about. In early September 1972 the FBI ran a warrantless surreptitious entry into the offices of Dr. Abdul Wadi, a Palestinian living in Dallas who was suspected of being in the al-Fatah terrorist group. It was a "survey" to see whether a bug was feasible, but a list of ninety Palestinian agents was also found, as well as a plan to send lethal letter bombs to Israeli targets in the United States and Canada. Some of those involved in the plot were American citizens, but most, including Wadi himself, were not. The Munich Massacre—the slaughter of eleven Israeli athletes by Palestinian terrorists during the Olympic Games—had just occurred on September 5.[69] Gray authorized burglaries of the residences of all the people on the Wadi list. Twenty-eight cities were involved; several bag jobs were certainly carried out. Individuals on the list were intimidated by FBI visits and left the country. The Wadi operation was counted by Gray as a tremendous success that prevented a mass terror attack.[70]

The FBI break-ins during the Wadi case were legal under Keith since they involved individuals who were connected to a foreign terrorist organization, even if some were American citizens. Under these circumstances, Gray was willing to approve black bag jobs on a large scale. Yet he did not demand personal approval of each specific case.[71]

These issues came to the fore in the autumn 1980 trial in federal court of Mark Felt and Edward Miller on charges of having violated citizens' rights under the Fourth Amendment. According to J. Wallace LaPrade, the special agent in charge in Newark in 1972, Gray drew an explicit parallel between the Wadi case and Weatherman. At a meeting with other special agents in Washington on September 11–12, 1972, Gray underlined the FBI failure to capture any Weathermen. Gray stated that the FBI now had to do anything necessary to capture them, because Weatherman was such a threat to the country. When asked whether that meant using black bag jobs as in the old days, LaPrade later testified that Gray answered yes, and pointed to the recent great success in using a black bag job against Arab terrorists based in Dallas, which had prevented a serious attack. LaPrade said that Edward Miller was present when Gray made these statements.[72]

On September 13, 1972, LaPrade wrote a memo to his subordinates upon his return to Newark. The memo did not mention black bag jobs per se; LaPrade said this was because he wrote it for agents who did not need to know about them. But the memo did state that Gray had said to "do anything necessary" to catch Weatherman, and had pointed to the successful black bag job in the Wadi case as an example of what could be done.[73]

The LaPrade memo is perhaps not quite a "smoking gun" showing that Gray approved black bag jobs against relatives and supporters of Weatherman, but it comes close. Even assuming that Gray said nothing beyond what is in the LaPrade memo—and some witnesses claim he did—what other conclusion did he expect the SACs at the meeting to draw except that break-ins might be an acceptable method in targeting Weatherman?

Later, at Felt and Miller's 1980 trial, FBI Inspector Thomas Smith of Research, Assistant FBI Director Thomas Bishop of Records, and Ian McLennon, special agent in charge for Pittsburgh, all testified similarly to what LaPrade said.

There were weaknesses in the testimony of both Bishop and McLennon; as prosecutor John Nields pointed out in cross-examination, each man had a bad relationship with Gray (this was not the case with Smith), and both had only recently remembered Gray's statements at the September meeting. Both claimed in response that persistent questioning about these events had jogged their memories, and that although they disliked Gray, they were not lying.[74]

Then there was the testimony of Special Agent David Brower, who in 1972 was the FBI liaison with Congress. He testified in 1980 that early in September 1972 he met Edward Miller exiting the acting director's office. Miller, in a good mood, told Brower that Gray had just given authorization "to reinstitute all confidential techniques." Miller was going down the hall to inform Mark Felt. On cross-examination, John Nields stressed that Brower had not come forward with this information until four weeks earlier.[75]

The testimony of Robert Shackelford, head of Revolutionary Activities, was similar to Brower's: one day in early autumn 1972, Miller came up to him and said that Gray had approved surreptitious entries. Shackelford stressed that Miller's announcement was done in an open FBI hallway—and talking openly about it as Miller constantly did was bound to get back to Gray at some point. That Miller had talked openly to agents about Gray's approval of bag jobs was also noted earlier by Arbor Gray.[76]

Edward Miller's impression was that the real source for Gray's policy was probably in the White House. Two important facts support his contention. First, Patrick Gray's intensified focus on terrorism after Munich was in line with a vigorous White House response to the attack. This included a presidential order in September to form a Cabinet Committee to Combat Terrorism, including five cabinet officials, as well as representatives of the FBI, the CIA, the National Security Council, and the State Department. Second, in early October 1972 Gray ordered a renewal of surreptitious entries against individuals in Program C. Felt asserted at the trial that four other government agencies were involved in the Program C operations, and concluded that Gray "would have had to have consulted with the Attorney General and/or the President or someone on the President's staff before deciding on a policy that affected other government agencies." This was not challenged on cross-examination.[77]

Felt also testified that on the same day in October that Gray ordered the Program C break-ins, Miller told him that Gray had initiated the large program of surreptitious entries against Weatherman. Felt guessed that the White House, which had to approve the Program C plan, had approved the Weatherman policy too. John Nields argued in cross-examination that Felt had no direct knowledge of any such White House conversations. Felt admitted it—but said he was "sure" Gray consulted the White House about implementing the Weatherman black bag jobs.[78]

Should we be surprised? Richard Nixon in February 1970 had already pushed for illegal operations in financial cases concerning the Left, in July 1970 had approved a large program of illegal operations against Weatherman—including warrantless break-ins—in the Huston Plan, and after Hoover blocked the Huston Plan, had then pushed a modified version of Huston, including its illegal aspects (see Chapter 5). And we know what Nixon's attitude was toward the legalities here, from his own statements at the Felt-Miller trial: "When authority from the President of the United States is given for surreptitious entry for good cause, under those circumstances, what would otherwise be unlawful or illegal becomes legal." Nixon appears here to be basing his position on the Roosevelt Directives of 1939 and 1940 granting "liberty" to the FBI in national security cases, plus his belief that Weatherman was an agent of communist countries hostile to the United States. Pat Gray shared that belief.[79]

On October 1, 1972, Gray sent another memo to all SACs indicating the importance of the Weatherman hunt. He announced three priorities for the Bureau: drug abuse and the drug trade, which received a short paragraph in bureaucratic language; organized crime, which received a short paragraph in bureaucratic language; and domestic terrorism—which received two long paragraphs in fiery language. This section expressed disgust at the terrorist attack at the Olympic Games, and then pointed to the continuity between horrific events overseas and the actions of sinister elements in the United States: "Within our society are elements who glorify guerrilla warfare and terrorism. Weatherman

and related New Left terrorists and black extremists . . . [are] particularly dangerous." But the first draft of this memorandum, dated
September 11, was written not by Gray but by Robert Shackelford
of Revolutionary Groups, with his aide Bill Preusse. Gray was not
alone in the FBI in his linking of terrorism abroad with the terrorists at home, and concluding what had to be done about them.[80]

Not satisfied with one two-week training course on Weatherman for
selected special agents, Gray ordered a second course for October
1–6, 1972. This is consistent with the Gray's set of priorities.

We know a great deal about this second in-service from the
testimony of Robert Shackelford and William Lander at the 1980
trial. Shackelford was a reluctant witness, mostly intent on avoid-
ing a perjury charge by claiming he could remember almost nothing about the events of 1971 and 1972. But when shown a copy of
the agenda for the second in-service, he admitted that Gray personally had approved it, and that the subject listed for the last day
was "special investigative techniques."[81] The lecturer on that topic
was going to be Special Agent Courtland Jones, senior supervisor
for espionage matters at the Washington, D.C., field office.
Shackelford explained that the lecture from Jones was necessary
because most of the agents now in the Weatherman hunt were recent transfers from ordinary criminal cases (per Gray's orders in
the summer), and so knew little about "special investigative techniques." Pressed by prosecutor Nields, Shackelford admitted that
in the context of the Weatherman in-service, "special investigative
techniques" meant surreptitious entries. He also admitted that
Cortland Jones was well known in the FBI as an expert at doing
black bag jobs.[82] Shackelford then acknowledged that one of the
men attending the in-service was Special Agent James Weaver,
from the Newark field office. Three months later—under Walter
LaPrade, the SAC at Newark—Weaver ran the first of three black
bag jobs against the home of the parents of Weatherman Judy
Cohen Flatley.[83]

Called away on another mission, Courtland Jones turned the
lecture over to Special Agent William Lander, his principal assistant in burglary for the previous twenty years. Lander was forthcoming at the trial. He said he was no expert on Weatherman but a

technical expert at black bag jobs. He testified, "I was to lecture in the place of Mr. Jones on surreptitious entries"—and that is exactly what he did. Lander's testimony is startlingly frank:

> Q (NIELDS): Do you remember that you gave a lecture on black bag jobs?
> A: Oh, yes, yes.
> Q: And just so we understand each other, we're talking about, are we talking about illegal entry?
> A: Yes, trespass entries.
> Q: To do a search?
> A: Yes . . .
> Q: Without a warrant?
> A: Without a warrant.
> Q: And without consent or knowledge of the occupant?
> A: Yes.
> Q: Okay. Now, was this a lecture on how to do it?
> A: It was a how-to lecture.

Lander then went on to explain, in detail, how to run a successful surreptitious entry, from initial planning and surveillance of the target, through entry and search: the how-to lecture he gave at Quantico in 1972. This runs five full pages in the trial transcript. At Quantico the "how-to" lecture lasted two hours.[84]

Once more, the only way Pat Gray could not have known about this event would have been if he showed no interest in the agenda for the unusual second Weatherman in-service he himself had specifically ordered. And Shackelford testified that he had shown the agenda to Gray, and Gray had approved it.[85]

Gray at this point also ordered that the search for Weatherman fugitives, previously under control of the Special Investigations Division (Fugitives), be transferred to Ed Miller's Domestic Intelligence Division, which previously had simply gathered intelligence on Weatherman. Special Investigations protested—it had been working on the Weatherman fugitives for more than two years—but to no avail. The transfer was ostensibly made to end duplication of effort. But Gray's decision now concentrated all endeavors against Weatherman in the division whose chief, Edward

Miller, was the best-known FBI advocate of surreptitious entries at headquarters.[86]

Shortly after the transfer and the second Weatherman in-service, Gray sent a new memorandum to the SACs in the seven cities where Weatherman was most active: Chicago, Cleveland, Detroit, Milwaukee, New York, San Francisco, and Seattle. The October 31 circular reiterated that the cases of the Weather fugitives were "very important and high priority," and that it was "absolutely essential" that everything be done to apprehend them. The memo then listed fully forty suggestions from Gray on how to pursue the Weather fugitives. Most of the suggestions were mundane: recheck the U.S. Passport Office under the fugitive's true name and any known aliases (no. 8); forward all possible handwriting samples of a Weather fugitive to the FBI laboratory (no. 13); recheck friends, acquaintances, and associates of the fugitive, in case they have seen something (no. 17); recheck that *all* relatives of a fugitive are known, in case there is someone more cooperative than the parents have generally been (no. 36). But Gray's final suggestion, no. 40, was different. In cases where there is reasonable suspicion that a friend or relative is in contact with a fugitive directly or indirectly, "a mail cover should be considered in light of the clearly-established efficacy of this technique in the past." Gray then adds, "Bureau approval is, of course, required." Gray meant secretly opening the mail itself. In December, the SAC in New York City proudly reported just such a warrantless mail opening—addressed to the father of a person who was suspected of being (not known to be) in Weatherman.[87]

The mood that Gray was fostering in the Bureau about black bag jobs can also be shown by the following incident. On information received about a possible Weatherman bomb factory, in autumn 1972 the New York field office ran a surreptitious entry against a residence that *seemed* to be the place the informant had told them about; they were not sure, because the informant had given no address. The agents went ahead anyway with the burglary, found nothing in the apartment they invaded, and concluded either that it was the wrong apartment or that the informant was wrong. Yet this same informant was also the source who in February 1972 had led the FBI to burglarize the apartment of New York anarchist Murray Bookchin—where they had found nothing.[88]

Finally, the FBI in early 1973 ran another special conference devoted to Weatherman, called by Pat Gray personally. It assembled from around the country all FBI personnel responsible for Weatherman fugitive cases. The conference, in Chicago, February 13–14, focused on the obstacles each agent faced in trying to hunt the individual fugitives that were his responsibility. The file in which the conference announcement is found also includes handwritten notes taken by an agent who attended. This agent listed fourteen points of discussion. These included difficulties in conducting interviews with Weatherman supporters (no. 2), and special targeting of vulnerable potential informants (the SPECTAR program, no. 8). But the seventh item is "techniques of mail coverage." And the tenth item is "Bag jobs—Sophisticated techniques."[89]

A memo discussing this conference was also sent to Assistant Director Miller by Inspector Thomas Smith in Research. It demonstrates the contradictory stance of many FBI men: "The legality of wiretaps against revolutionaries where no foreign influence can be shown is highly dubious. However, we are and will continue using innovative investigative techniques to attempt to apprehend Weatherman fugitives and locate other Weatherman members."[90] Smith, like Miller, thought foreign influence on Weatherman was minimal; thus warrantless bugging in Weatherman cases did not fall under the Keith exception and was probably illegal; yet he still pressed forward with "innovative investigative techniques." No wonder that "Bag-jobs—Sophisticated techniques" appeared at the Chicago conference. And the fact that we have proof in writing that black bag jobs were discussed at Chicago, as well as the testimony of the expert who gave the actual black bag job lecture at the second Weatherman in-service at Quantico, has implications about the honesty of the agents who later testified that this was also discussed at the special Weatherman in-service in August 1972—and the honesty of those agents who denied it.

CHAPTER SEVEN

"One Lawbreaker Has Been
Pursued by Another"

THIS HAS BEEN A story about a small group of violent radicals, and opposed to them, a large and cumbersome bureaucracy.[1] It might seem strange to compare them, but they were two organized groups of confused, frightened, and very angry Americans who broke the law.[2] Their misjudgments are clear. Weatherman failed to see that mass demonstrations had worked to curb the escalation of Vietnam War, first under Johnson, then under Nixon. Instead, carried forward by a cracked Marxist-Leninist momentum, it launched a violent and clandestine revolt encumbered by strict hierarchy and ideological zealotry. For its part, the FBI panicked, seeing Weatherman as a real threat to political stability in the country and a threat to the Bureau itself. Such was the dark mood of 1969–1970. It created an FBI institutional imperative (even obsession) to capture the young would-be guerrillas—even if that meant illegal government operations, including warrantless burglaries and buggings. A late 1972 FBI memo stated that Weatherman bombings appeared to be abating, but the finding had no impact on FBI policy.[3]

Both sides willingly engaged in illegal acts. But in this clash of the nearsighted, the angry and the frightened, the FBI bears the heavier weight: in a polity where civil liberties are central, the government itself must obey the law. The FBI's exaggeration of the scale of the Weatherman threat cannot be an excuse here; it only makes their illegal actions more disturbing. Indeed, the FBI paid the higher cost. First, all federal prosecutions of Weatherman were aborted for fear of the revelation of government misconduct. Second, when the illegal operations were in the end exposed, not only was the reputation of the Bureau gravely damaged, but a federal jury in 1980 found high FBI officials guilty in court of serious violation of the rights of American citizens under the Constitution they had sworn to defend.

No one on either side really knew what they were doing. Weatherman, it turned out, was not very good at revolutionary war. Despite the intense preparations in winter 1969–1970, when the bombings planned for March 6, 1970, in Detroit and at Fort Dix did not work out, Weatherman eventually backed away from actions that were intended to kill. After June 1970 it engaged in what amounted to protest dynamite bombings against property, not serious blows against the state. The one exception is Weather's successful Pentagon bombing in May 1972, which disrupted air operations over Vietnam. As for the FBI, it had no experience dealing with self-declared revolutionary guerrillas. The steps the Bureau took were both repressive and stumbling. Faced with a new phenomenon, it used the secret and illegal tactics that had been used in the past against other groups deemed subversive. And such tactics kept being used even though they turned out to be useless for capturing the Weathermen or stopping their bombings.

Of course, the Weathermen knew they had to be careful. And they were. But Weather veterans say that they rarely felt that the FBI was hot on their heels. In autumn 1970, when Bernardine Dohrn had just appeared on the FBI's Top Ten Most Wanted Fugitives list, she and Bill Ayers, accompanied by Dennis and Mona Cunningham, were touring California campgrounds, on vacation in an old camper.[4] Three years later, in 1973, "the organization was still intact and reasonably safe from the FBI hunt; we certainly had the capacity to act."[5] The leaders experienced little problem in communicating, or in traveling between the collectives.[6] Retired FBI Special Agent William Dyson, who had personal experience hunting Weatherman, agrees: because the FBI was new to investigating true clandestine terrorist groups, "the Weathermen functioned very well," and FBI interference was almost nonexistent.[7] In fact, Weather in 1973 held its first national meeting since the Flint War Council at the end of 1970; it was not large but it went on for days; its purpose was setting out a long position paper that became the Weatherman book *Prairie Fire*. The conference involved leaders, a delegate from every collective, and selected aboveground supporters. Representatives from the conference then went out around the country to all the collectives, explaining the results. After a lot more discussions among Weather communes, *Prairie Fire* was published safely as a 186-page book by a secret Weatherman press, the Red Dragon Collective. Some forty thousand copies of the book were eventually distributed to left-wing bookstores—a massive clandestine operation. All this happened without FBI knowledge, let alone disruption, and it shows a significant Weatherman capacity to act.[8] It is true that there was a gap in Weatherman bombing between May 1972 and May 1973. But David Gilbert attributes this to growing internal ideological uncertainty (expressed soon in the debates over *Prairie Fire*), combined with the simple beguilements of the counterculture lifestyle.[9]

It was not FBI pressure that in the end wrecked the Weather Underground. It was an aspect of traditional Marxist-Leninist political life that had bedeviled the American far Left from its origins: ideological division and disagreement, combined with savage factionalism.

Division was already clear in the debates within Weather that surrounded the publication of the *Prairie Fire* manifesto in 1974.[10] Debates were ignited because Weather leaders were overtly renouncing the goal of immediate revolution via military action of small groups: that is, they were rejecting Debrayism. Weather now warned against expecting some "magical moment of insurrection"—the opposite of their position in 1969–1970. Instead, Weather urged long-term political work with the masses. Armed struggle was not abandoned, but it was deemphasized in favor of aboveground political education of the working class that would take years.[11] After all the sacrifices made by those who had gone underground since 1969–1970, and the risks they had run, this was an admission that Debrayist strategy had failed; no revolution had been ignited by Weather bombings. No wonder *Prairie Fire* was so controversial within Weather.[114]

The new debate over the role of the working class in revolution intensified in 1975. A key to the ideological formation of Weatherman had been its reliance on black national liberation movements (and young white street toughs) for revolution, as opposed to depending on the working class. But now Bernardine Dohrn, Jeff Jones, and Bill Ayers—the leadership troika—argued that the working class was diverse, composed of blacks and Hispanics, not just whites, and women as well as men. Similarly, they now saw minorities as especially exploited parts of that exploited class, not as separate revolutionary entities. The troika began to urge Weather support of issues such as better wages, in order to gain influence with the workers; the leaders argued that worker support was necessary if there was to be an actual revolution. The instrument for carrying out the new project would be Weather's new aboveground and legal organization, the Prairie Fire Organizing Committee. The troika was now advocating a position close to what Mike Klonsky and even Progressive Labor had advocated back in 1969, to Weatherman's disdain. Mark Rudd had sneered then that "*organizing* was just another word for going *slow*."[13]

In fact, the very concept of armed struggle as Weather had waged it for the previous five years came under attack in winter 1975–1976 in the new Weatherman quarterly magazine *Osawatomie*. Weatherman had actually supported the cultish and grandiosely named Symbionese Liberation Army in early 1974, including the murder of Oakland school superintendent Marcus Foster and the kidnapping of Patty Hearst.[14] Now they suddenly criticized the SLA for following the Debrayist *foco* strategy: the leaders claimed it was a mistake to believe that "guerrilla struggle itself politicizes and activates the people." This was a stunning reversal of position.[15]

And more: the leadership now floated the idea of surfacing almost the entire Weather Underground Organization to engage in legal aboveground work. Surfacing was possible because all the federal charges against the Weathermen, with their heavy penalties,

had been dropped in late 1973 in the wake of the discovery of government malfeasance; only minor charges at the local level remained. Thus, the leaders argued, there was no longer any need to
hide, and only a small rump of Weathermen should be left to carry
out some sort of underground armed struggle. The possibility
of surfacing was apparently first raised by Jeff Jones—the leading
advocate for abandoning lethal bombing back in 1970.[16] And
when in May 1975 the Weather leaders allowed themselves to be
filmed in Emile de Antonio's documentary *Underground*, Bill Ayers
for the first time declared that Weatherman had never been a
terrorist organization.[17] Meanwhile, starting in March 1975, the
central underground effort became the regular appearance of the
magazine *Osawatomie*: literary propaganda, not armed propaganda.
In de Antonio's documentary, Cathy Wilkerson said that a lot of
Weatherman time was now spent writing, and licking stamps to
distribute their literature. *Osawatomie* did not even give much play
to the three Weatherman bombings that occurred while the magazine was in print.[18]

The FBI was unable to prevent the clandestine printing and
distribution of *Prairie Fire* or of *Osawatomie*, though for a time the
magazine appeared regularly, every four months. Further, when the
FBI pressed Emile de Antonio for information about Weather, not
only did he refuse, but he offered a biting assessment of FBI incompetence: the Bureau, he said, with its vast resources, "had failed
to locate a network of fugitives that a middle-aged film director
had found with little difficulty."[19]

Within Weather, however, the dramatic change of stance provoked heated resistance. The political situation was made worse for
the leadership by the fact that the aboveground organization, the
Prairie Fire Organizing Committee (PFOC), failed to attract many
recruits. By early 1976, PFOC in Boston had only about fifteen
members, and in Philadelphia there were only about ten. Despite
the revolutionary bravado of their published declarations, nothing
much politically was going to be done with such tiny groups.[20]
Dissatisfaction broke into the open at the "Hard Times Conference"
of radicals in Chicago, January 30–February 1, 1976. The aboveground conference was primarily organized by the Prairie Fire
Organizing Committee, but Weather leaders sought to control the

conference by operating secretly through the committee. When demands by the Black Caucus and a group of women for a special hearing out of regular order were rejected, the conference collapsed amid protests, including accusations of disdain for gay rights. The collapse of the conference in the face of a wave of ferocious identity politics in turn discredited the Central Committee. Within Prairie Fire, there was resentment of secret manipulation by Weather; within the Weather Underground itself, the deference to leaders necessary in a militarized clandestine Marxist-Leninist organization now began to crack.[21]

Opposition to the ruling troika emerged via the Revolutionary Committee faction, led by Clayton van Lydegraf, an elderly, crewcut Stalinist who had been a leader in the CPUSA before any Weatherman had been born. He left the Party in the early 1960s because it was not violently revolutionary enough. He had helped found Progressive Labor but left it when it, too, came to reject immediate revolutionary violence in favor of organizing the working class. Van Lydegraf went over to Weatherman, and was a significant figure during its most violent phase in 1970; he opposed Weatherman's breaking Timothy Leary out of prison in September 1970—one of Weather's great successes—as pandering to the counterculture, which he despised.[22] Now he advocated a return to focusing on victims of racial oppression as the source and leaders of mass revolution, the old Weatherman position, rather than turning to the broader working class via bread-and-butter issues. He also advocated a return to attacking people as well as property. The Revolutionary Committee gained support among the Weather cadre and declared itself the real Weather Underground Organization; the old Central Committee people were either expelled or simply gave up. During a national campaign of "Rectification" organized by van Lydegraf's group in the spring and summer of 1976, local leaders who had agreed with the Central Committee position—for instance, Alan Berkman, Russell Neufeld, and Jennifer Dohrn—were forced to write public confessions of grave ideological wrongdoing and personal failure. Then, in November, Jeff Jones, Bernardine Dohrn, and Bill Ayers were all formally expelled from Weatherman at van Lydegraf's behest; because they had urged a focus on aboveground and legal organization, they were accused of "right deviationism," that is, moderation. Many people, such as Neufeld, soon drifted away.[23]

The new Weather Underground Organization was as hierarchal and ideologically rigid as the previous incarnation, with van Lydegraf now treated as the source of all wisdom.[24] The group's new campaign of dynamiting was to begin with the bombing of the offices of John Briggs, a California state senator who wanted to ban gays from teaching in public schools. Under Dohrn, Jones, and Ayers, Weather security had been exemplary, so good it had driven the FBI to activities that were illegal and in the end self-destructive. But when van Lydegraf took over, the new Weather Underground soon was penetrated by FBI agents. Curiously, van Lydegraf himself had never been an underground fugitive, as the original leaders had been, but had always been an aboveground figure, posing as a mere supporter. The FBI could and did penetrate aboveground groups of supporters. Of all the mistakes Weather made as a revolutionary organization, the worst was making van Lydegraf the leader of underground guerrillas. In fact, one of van Lydegraf's roommates was an FBI agent. Van Lydegraf thus unwittingly provided the FBI entrée into Weather operations for the first time since April 1970. Before the plan against Briggs could be put into effect, the five leaders of the group were arrested in November 1977. They included van Lydegraf, Mike Justesen, a Seattle leader, and Judith Bissell, who had been underground since attempting the firebombing of the ROTC at the University of Washington in January 1970. They all accepted plea bargains involving several years in prison. It was the end of Weatherman as a national organization—and the FBI's greatest Weatherman triumph.[25]

It was the only victory the Bureau had. In New York City, Squad 47 continued its work after 1973, apparently including surreptitious entries into the homes of Weather supporters and relatives, but, as usual, not coming up with any clues.[26] Because Weather was now doing few bombings, the actions of the squad seemed not merely useless but pointless. By 1976, morale was as low in Squad 47 as it was in Weatherman. And then—as with Weatherman—came catastrophe: President Gerald Ford's Justice Department discovered at FBI headquarters in Washington much evidence about the Bureau's previous illegal activities. Justice Department investigators arrived in New York; the Weatherman Squad was broken up; and special agents had to begin hiring lawyers. At one point, perhaps fifty men were threatened with indictment. Jack Kearney, the black bag man who had headed the squad from summer 1970 to summer 1972, actually was indicted (causing, ironically, the first public protest demonstration in history by FBI men), and some in the Justice Department pushed hard for the indictment of Horace Beckwith, Kearney's successor. But in 1977, Griffin Bell, President Jimmy Carter's attorney general, decided against prosecuting any of these people; after all, they were only following orders. And that is how, for Squad 47, the Weatherman war ended.[27]

Meanwhile, although the vast majority of Weather veterans decided to surface between 1977 and 1980, on the East Coast a few Weatherman bitter-enders soldiered on. They eventually formed the May 19 Communist Organization—named for the birthday of Ho Chi Minh and Malcolm X, which had been the date of the Pentagon bombing in 1972. The people in May 19 then joined with a spin-off of the Black Panthers, the Black Liberation Army, in a series of notoriously violent actions. This alliance represented a continuation of the original Weatherman belief in radical black organizations as the locus of possible revolution. Subsequent actions included breaking BLA leader Assata Shakur out of prison in 1979 and a series of bank robberies. The white radicals drove the getaway cars in these operations; the idea was that police were less likely to stop an automobile driven by a white person. Finally, at least three Weather bitter-enders participated in a Brink's armored car holdup in Nyack, New York, in October 1981, in which BLA men killed a Brink's guard, Peter Paige, and two policemen, Edward O'Grady and Waverly Brown (the latter the only black policeman on the Nyack force).[28] The white radicals, including Judy Clark, Kathy Boudin, and David Gilbert, again drove the getaway cars—but this time the police caught them, along with several BLA members. All received long sentences at trial; two, in fact, are still in prison thirty-five years later. Boudin, after serving twenty-two years, was granted parole in 2003.[29]

The Nyack killings occurred a full year after the FBI itself went on trial for its actions against Weatherman. The federal indictment—originally lodged against Gray, Felt, and Miller in District of Columbia Federal Court in 1978—charged them with violation of Title 18, U.S. Code 241, and conspiracy against rights of citizens. Specifically, these men, "together with others to the Grand Jury known and unknown," conspired

> to injure and oppress citizens of the United States who were relatives of Weatherman fugitives, in the free exercise and enjoyment of certain rights and privileges secured to them by the Constitution and laws of the United States, including the right secured to them by the Fourth Amendment to the Constitution of the United States to be secure in their homes, papers and effects against unreasonable searches and seizure.[30]

At the trial, Felt and Miller made several arguments to justify the break-ins. The first was that Acting FBI Director Patrick Gray had authorized break-ins in general (though had not ordered specific ones), and Gray was ultimately the representative of the president, who had the right under Article II, section 2 of the Constitution to protect the country from national security threats; Weatherman represented a serious national security threat. Second, the FBI had traditionally used trespass, microphones, wiretapping, and mail covers in gathering intelligence on national security. That is: what the FBI did against Weatherman had always been allowed. Thus the ban on surreptitious entry set by J. Edgar Hoover in July 1966 ("the Hoover cutoff")—which the prosecution made much of— was never actually complete; national security black bag jobs had always continued on a limited basis. Third, the Weather Underground Organization had become one organization in two parts: the underground guerrillas, and their aboveground supporters and propagandists. The aboveground supporters, friends, and relatives of Weather were thus just as subject to warrantless burglary on national security grounds as the guerrillas themselves would have been—if the FBI could have found them. Fourth, the Supreme Court in the Keith decision had ruled that a court order was required for government burglaries and bugging of members of domestic subversive groups, but groups with significant foreign connections were less protected even if they were American citizens, and the single organization called Weather, in both its underground and aboveground incarnations, had links to North Vietnam, Cuba, and China: foreign powers hostile to the United States. These links were so strong that all individuals involved in the Weather Organization, no matter in what form, fell under the foreign-power exception in Keith.[31]

Regarding the first defense argument, Patrick Gray always denied that he gave anyone permission for black bag jobs. But as we have seen, there is much evidence that he had indeed approved them. From his first weeks as acting director in May 1972, he had consistently (and sometimes ferociously) encouraged agents to mount black bag jobs against people with links to the Weather Underground. Documents assembled for the 1980 trial indicate that Gray on May 22 knew of and encouraged the electronic surveillance of Jennifer Dohrn; on June 14 he signed an application to the acting attorney general for the extending of surreptitious entry against her. And the testimony at the trial is clear that Gray authorized in a general way the surreptitious entries against Weatherman associates that were run in autumn 1972 through spring 1973, though he did not need (or wish) to be informed about each specific bag job.

This first defense argument, then, was valid—as far as it goes. The question is: how far does it go? How far do President Roosevelt's authorizations in 1939–1940 and the opinion of President Eisenhower's attorney general in 1954 absolve the FBI directorate of the charge of persistently violating the Constitution?

The executive branch had long been aware of and allowed what seem illegal operations by the FBI in the name of national security. This went back to Franklin Roosevelt's letters of permission to J. Edgar Hoover in September 1939 and May 1940, and to the memorandum to Hoover by Attorney General Brownell in 1954. Though the Supreme Court always ruled in the direction of limiting wiretaps, and though Brownell's memo raised opposition within his own Justice Department, even prosecutor John Nields admitted during his closing argument that "there were no rules in the government that told the FBI they couldn't do surreptitious entries." If so, then Felt and Miller (and Gray) had not broken any existing government regulations when they ordered the burglaries. That was a startling admission for the prosecution to make: "Mr. Miller and Mr. Felt are not in this courtroom for violating some rule of the Department of Justice or some President."[32]

But Nields went on to argue successfully to the jury that black bag jobs were nevertheless a general violation of the Fourth Amendment. Many high government officials testified for the defense on national security grounds, but in reality neither was Weatherman powerful nor was it connected to a foreign hostile power; so, said Nields, were the jury to acquit Felt and Miller, "I'm telling you right now, we don't have a Fourth Amendment. It's all gone. There's nothing left of it." Nields here was pointing to a continuing problem of governmental power—what the government, especially the executive branch, thought it was allowed to do.[33]

Ironically, the prosecution may have been helped here by Richard Nixon, eager to testify for the defense. His appearance did not go well; the disgraced former president was greeted by catcalls from courtroom spectators. But worse for the defense was what Nixon himself said in regard to the legality of the break-ins: "When the authority of the President of the United States is given for surreptitious entry for good cause, under those circumstances what would otherwise be unlawful or illegal becomes legal." This startling assertion of absolute presidential power may have acted as a powerful warning to those jurors moved by Nields's appeal to the Constitution.[34]

This was especially so because Nixon was preceded by Herbert Brownell, Eisenhower's former attorney general, who argued the same position. Thus when Nields asked whether the president could order an "unreasonable search and seizure," Brownell replied to a startled Nields that if the president ordered it, it was ipso facto not an unreasonable search and seizure. When Nields pressed him and asked whether the president could therefore order the murder of an American citizen, Brownell answered that this had not happened yet. There prompted general laughter in the courtroom.[35]

Felt similarly argued that since the FBI break-ins were not for gathering evidence for prosecution in a court—such evidence would be inadmissible because it was obtained without court order—but merely for the purposes of gleaning intelligence on a terrorist group, then traditionally a different set of rules applied to such government security activities. The gathering of intelligence information, Felt insisted, "is not limited by the Fourth Amendment prohibition against 'unreasonable searches and seizures.' ... A different set of rules has always been applied."[36]

A version of the "different set of rules" argument inspired an extraordinary scene in the trial, when Judge Bryant got into an extended argument in open court with FBI Inspector Thomas J. Smith as Smith was testifying for the defense. Bryant interrupted the questioning to argue to Smith that even if Franklin Roosevelt and his successors did authorize FBI wiretaps and microphone surveillances without warrant, presidents never authorized surreptitious entries for the purposes of search; surreptitious entries for search thus constituted simple trespass. Smith argued that since all microphone surveillances and some wiretaps required surreptitious entry in order to be placed in the target residence in the first place, and since wiretaps and microphones without warrant had been approved by presidents starting with Roosevelt, surreptitious entry by implication fell under the "different set of rules" established by FDR. Smith's point was echoed by Special Agent George Birley, testifying for the defense—and again Bryant interrupted the testimony to argue against it.[37]

Herbert Brownell himself, testifying for the defense, had the same view here—and then went further. He pointed to Hoover's March 1956 presentation of a break-in for search before the National Security Council itself, with both President Eisenhower and then Vice President Nixon in attendance: there had been no repercussions, only praise. Brownell's testimony was offered as evidence that such break-ins for search had at least the implicit approval of a former president.[38]

Smith, Birley, and Brownell had a valid point—except that it depended on the idea of unlimited presidential power. The danger this idea posed to citizens' rights was made clear in an exchange between Nields and Ian McLennon, the special agent in charge in Pittsburgh. Nields asked McLennon whether the Fourth Amendment of the Constitution was applicable in security cases; McLennon answered, simply, "No."[39] This was essentially the opinion also offered on the stand by FBI officials William Brannigan, Hunter Hegelson, Elmer

Lindberg, and Anthony Litrento, testifying for the defense. An entire Bureau culture was thus revealed. As elitist as Weatherman and
just as secretive, the FBI fought its wars—against the Communist
Party, against the Mafia, against the Klan, against the New Left,
against Weatherman—behind a wall of secrecy (as Weatherman did),
and it made its own rules, ignoring (as Weatherman did) the laws
and the Constitution in the name of a higher good.[40]

Judge Bryant, for his part, refused to accept that all surreptitious
entries were in general protected by implication because of the logistical requirements and practicalities of wiretap and microphone
installation; he asserted that without an explicit presidential or attorney general authorization on national security grounds, surreptitious entries for search were per se illegal. Such authorization was
missing in the Weatherman break-ins. But this counterargument,
too, failed to confront the more fundamental question of whether
trespass against American citizens purely for the purposes of search
on alleged national security grounds was constitutional even *with* an
explicit attorney general or presidential authorization.[41]

Third, Nixon on the stand stressed his belief that Weatherman
was the agent of a foreign power. This was what especially gave
him—and instruments of the executive branch such as the FBI more
generally—the right to commit burglaries against Weatherman supporters and relatives without obtaining a court order. But it was uncertain in the first place whether the aboveground supporters of
Weather who were victims of FBI black bag jobs could properly be
considered full members of the Weather Underground Organization. This principle hardly applied to the innocent parents of Judy
Cohen Flatley, or to Howard Machtinger's brother, or to Murray
Bookchin—each of whom the FBI burglarized.

In any case, the defense was never able to prove that
Weatherman *itself* had foreign ties so significant that it fell under
the exception in Keith as a foreign-connected subversive organization. FBI documents at the trial showed that the directorate
itself, including defendant Edward Miller, had concluded that
Weatherman's ties to foreign hostile powers were too slender to
count under Keith. FBI Assistant Director Charles Brennan also
later considered Weather's foreign connections to be slight, and
thought Nixon's constant urging of the Bureau to find a link had

been a waste of time.[42] In January 1971 the Central Intelligence Agency agreed that the foreign ties of the New Left were slender, and that even the most extreme New Leftists were self-motivated, not trained or controlled from abroad.

This conclusion could not have been comfortable for the nation's intelligence organizations to reach. The agencies were manned by veterans of the long battle with the Soviet Union and its allies abroad, or by the Soviet-funded and controlled CPUSA at home. The admission demonstrates a surprisingly high level of both integrity and intellectual flexibility in the lower and middle level of agents and analysts, and in parts of the directorates as well. Not only Miller and Brennan came to this conclusion, though that is striking enough; despite Nixon's obvious anger and the constant pressure from the White House to find what wasn't there, J. Edgar Hoover himself did not attack his men's repeated conclusion concerning the lack of foreign funding of the American far Left—though he ordered them to look closely.[43]

The CIA assessment was the result of the investigation of thousands of documents, and its conclusion was backed by 116 pages of data that were (and remain) classified. The conclusions themselves were still classified in 1980; the prosecution frequently referred to them at the trial but could not quote them. But the summary report was made available to the public in 2013. The CIA concluded:

> There is no evidence, based on available information and sources, that foreign governments, organizations, or intelligence services now control U.S. New Left movements and/or are capable at the present time of directing these movements for the purposes of instigating open insurrection or disorders; for initiating and supporting terrorist or sabotage activities; or for fomenting unrest and subversion in the United States Armed forces, among government employees, or in labor unions, colleges, and universities, and mass media . . . .
>
> In summary, foreign funding, training, propaganda, and other support does not now play a major role in the U.S. New Left. International fronts and conferences help to

promote New Left causes, but at present the U.S. New
Left is basically self-sufficient and moves under its own
impetus.[44]

The FBI itself gave a similar finding to the president's Foreign
Intelligence Advisory Board in November 1972—with specific reference to Weatherman. Nields pressed this point home repeatedly
at the Felt-Miller trial. He stressed that whatever they said in
court, the FBI leaders were aware of the problem Keith posed as
soon as the decision came down in June 1972—because the foreign
links of Weatherman were small to nonexistent. Thus as soon as
Felt and Miller heard the Keith decision, they informed Acting
Attorney General Kleindienst of the current list of Weatherman
targets of surreptitious entry, and Kleindienst then prohibited
black bag jobs because of Keith.[45] But after Keith, the FBI never
went to the attorney general to get permission for break-ins because the directorate knew it would never get such permission.

At the trial, the defense argued that there was a sound basis
for believing that a foreign and malign influence existed, citing the
fact that some radicals had visited communist countries and that
after such visits radical actions intensified. But multiple sources
suggested that far from encouraging extreme and violent behavior,
the Cubans, for example, had urged just the opposite. Information
the FBI itself obtained from its wiretap inside the Cuban mission
to the United Nations in August 1969 showed that the Cubans
had *opposed* the Days of Rage plan for Chicago that October; and
we also know that their opposition angered Bernardine Dohrn in
September. In addition, Dohrn's own handwritten notes taken in
Havana in July 1969—notes in FBI possession by April 1970—
indicated that the Vietnamese with whom she met had urged her and
her comrades to organize mass peace demonstration, like those in
1967, not to engage in battles with the police leading to guerrilla
warfare. Even in the proposed Huston Plan of June 1970, in which
the danger to the country posed by Weatherman was so strongly
emphasized, the authors had concluded that although Weatherman
identified with North Vietnam, Cuba, and North Korea, and some
Weathermen had traveled to communist countries, there was no evidence the organization was working for foreign intelligence services.

The Huston Plan writers asserted that in fact the Weathermen's fugitive situation itself acted as a deterrent to foreign powers attempting to contact the group.[46]

At bottom, Mark Felt reflected the FBI's internal culture. For decades, the Bureau had had free rein for intelligence purposes to violate people's homes. After years of subjecting the Communist Party U.S.A. to such methods—and especially in the crisis atmosphere of 1970—these attitudes were widespread in the FBI directorate. Thus Cartha DeLoach—who in his memoir depicted the Weatherman Underground as a major security threat to the United States in the summer of 1970—wrote: "No government has ever been so righteous or so foolish as to stick strictly to the letter of its laws when its very survival or the freedom of its citizens was at stake." DeLoach was never in any legal jeopardy himself; he was sincerely expressing what he saw as the government's responsibility to protect the nation. It was part of FBI culture.[47] The attitude was summed up in an exchange between Felt and John Nields. When asked whether the Bill of Rights ever limited the power of the federal government, Felt replied, "I think that's a very, very technical question.[48]

When the defense attorneys brought forward this argument as grounds for dismissing the case entirely, Judge Bryant ruled against them. His reasoning: it was obvious from the legal inadmissibility in court of material obtained without a search warrant that government agents did not have free rein on national security grounds to enter a citizen's home without such a warrant or legal probable cause. As Bryant said:

> Suppose I had three children, and suppose during a particular political situation . . . my children break away and join a radical group. Are you telling me somebody has a right to sneak into my home and go through my effects?

Mark Felt claimed to find Judge Bryant's argument incomprehensible. But Bryant was not speaking hypothetically. He was talking about the parents of Judy Cohen Flatley, who had been stunned to learn of warrantless FBI burglaries of their small apartment when they had broken no law. The FBI burglars came up with nothing useful about the Cohens' daughter—though they invaded the Cohens' small apartment three times. Bryant was deeply sympathetic especially to Benjamin Cohen, Flatley's father, who was reluctant to appear as a witness in the trial out of embarrassment and worry that his daughter's past would be exposed.[49]

Nevertheless, given Felt's beliefs, it is not surprising that he chose the following epigraph to open the first chapter of his 1979 autobiography: " 'We must not turn the Bill of Rights into a suicide pact'—Mr. Justice Robert H. Jackson, Supreme Court, 1941–1954."[50] Robert Jackson could sometimes be a civil liberties champion (most famously in *West Virginia v. Barnette,* 1943). But Jackson as FDR's attorney general had agreed with the president's 1940 declaration of "freedom" for the FBI when it came to national security, and he favored electronic surveillance of suspected subversives.[51] Felt may have sincerely believed that not resorting to illegal operations against the Weatherman threat would have been a "suicide pact" in the name of the Constitution. But given what we now know about the small size and (after May 1970) the nonlethal policies of Weatherman—and much of this the FBI itself ultimately should have known—Felt's belief, if he really held it, was absurd.

In his instructions to the jury, Judge Bryant said that since Keith, the homes of American citizens could be searched without court order under presidential authority only if the target had a significant connection to a foreign power, and—further—that specific presidential or at least attorney general authorization was necessary even for such foreign intelligence break-ins. No such presidential finding or attorney general authorization had occurred, and as far as the defense attorneys were concerned, the judge's words to the jury sealed the defendants' fate.[52] The judge then instructed the jury on what "significant connection" had to mean:

> By "significant connection," I mean acting in collaboration with or as an agent for a foreign country. Collaboration is more than casual or infrequent contact, and it is not limited to any one particular act. It occurs when an individual and foreign power work together, labor together, cooperate together, cooperate with each other or assist one another in

a meaningful manner toward an important goal or interest they might have.[53]

Judge Bryant drove home the point by noting to the jury that this case involved FBI burglarizing of homes belonging not to actual Weathermen (whom the FBI could not find) but to their supporters, friends, and relatives. Bryant concluded that the only way the jury could acquit Felt and Miller on the basis of the Keith exception was if they found that all *these* people had deep and continuing connections with a hostile foreign power. And clearly they did not.[54]

Defense attorney Thomas Kennelly, counsel for Mark Felt, was candid about the problem the defense confronted: "Let's face it, a sneak search of a person's home without his consent and without a search warrant looks like a crime, sounds like a crime, and feels like a crime." In an open courtroom it was a tough sell. Or as a contrite FBI agent told Justice Department investigator Stephen Horn, "Some of us felt that what the Bureau did constituted a far greater danger to society than what the Weathermen ever did."[55]

On November 8, 1980, the jury came back with a verdict of guilty. On December 15 came the sentencing: Judge Bryant levied a fine of five thousand dollars on Mark Felt and thirty-five hundred dollars on Edward Miller. These were mild sentences, as even the defense attorneys admitted. Further, Bryant accepted the defense attorneys' argument that since the case was going to be appealed, the defendants did not actually have to pay the government the money right away. Bryant at sentencing did not explain his leniency, nor would he do so in the future.[56] In the end, Felt and Miller would never have to pay the fine. Still, they were now convicted felons—unable, for instance, to vote. At the time of the trial, L. Patrick Gray was still under indictment on the same charges—but he was never put on trial. The Justice Department dropped the charges against him for lack of evidence. Still, neither Felt nor Miller was pleased, as the convictions for both stood.

Felt's and Miller's lawyers now began the appeals process. One of their grounds for appeal was that the government, and Judge Bryant, had denied the defense access to a thousand CIA files—which they alleged might have shown that Weathermen's foreign connections were deeper and more substantial than what had come out at the trial. Yet this was not what the CIA itself had concluded in 1971.

Miller and Felt's indictment and subsequent trial enraged the police community and the traditional supporters of law and order. The defense fund from contributions for the accused FBI men eventually totaled two million dollars. One of those incensed by these Carter administration indictments was Ronald Reagan. He told Miller that during the presidential campaign of 1980, he made himself a promise to protect men who he thought had been defending the nation from the extraordinarily serious threat posed by Weatherman. Reagan kept his promise: within nine days of his inauguration, he set in motion a presidential pardon for Felt and Miller. The original date for the pardon was March 31, 1981—but on that day Reagan was shot and almost killed by John Hinckley. Yet Reagan was so intent on granting the pardon that although he was seriously wounded, he signed the pardon just two weeks later on April 14. Reagan actually apologized to Felt and Miller for the delay caused by the assassination attempt.[57]

The language of the pardon suggested how the bitter divisions of the 1960s were still fresh in Reagan's mind:

> America was at war in 1972, and Mssrs. Felt and Miller followed procedures they believed essential to keep the Director of the FBI, the Attorney General, and the President of the United States advised of the activities of hostile foreign powers and their collaborators in this country . . . .
>
> Four years ago thousands of draft evaders and others who violated the Selective Service laws were unconditionally pardoned by my predecessor. America was generous to those who refused to serve their country in the Vietnam War. We can be no less generous to two men who acted on high principle to bring an end to the terrorism that was threatening our Nation.[58]

This comment, with which the pardon declaration ended, is filled with bitterness against the Vietnam draft resisters and their pardoning by President Jimmy Carter, combined with exaggeration of the threat—serious perhaps in 1970, but hardly by 1972—that Weatherman presented to the government. The poet Allen Ginsberg noted at the time that Reagan's eager pardon of high FBI officials who had violated the basic rights of American citizens as enshrined in the Fourth Amendment was an ironic coda to a 1980 presidential campaign whose main theme, he said, had been to "get government off our backs."[59]

Felt and Miller gratefully accepted the presidential pardon; they saw it as a vindication. Accepting the pardon required them to drop their appeal; the estimated legal costs—at least $200,000—of pursuing an appeal were daunting, and it was not clear that they would win in a higher federal court. Yet by accepting the pardon, they not only admitted their guilt but also would remain felons for the rest of their lives.[60]

Others, too, had received a kind of pardon. In late 1973, the government submitted to Judge Damon Keith a petition to drop all federal charges against the thirteen Weatherman leaders stemming from the Days of Rage riots and the much more serious charges arising from Weatherman's bombing campaign. The government now told Judge Keith that to go forward with trials against the Weatherman leaders would force it to reveal foreign sources of information—and FBI ties to "another agency"—that Washington preferred to keep secret.[61] Another issue that would have come up at trial was that the FBI informant Larry Grathwohl had been indicted on the July 1970 federal bombing charges along with the real Weathermen. This could have happened only one of two ways: either because prosecutor Guy Goodwin, the Justice Department "Weatherman prosecutor," lied to the grand jury in Detroit about Grathwohl, and presented him as a bona fide Weatherman when he was actually a paid federal employee, or—even worse—Goodwin had told the grand jury the truth, but asked it to indict Grathwohl anyway, in the hope of restoring his cover with the radicals, which had been blown in April 1970 in New York City. But federal grand juries are supposed to indict individuals for crimes, not be participants in government intelligence operations. Goodwin would have been in political and legal trouble if any of this had come out at trial.[62]

There was probably a third reason why charges were dropped. On June 5, 1973, Judge Keith had required the FBI—in view of Watergate news stories that were then emerging—to give him an affidavit that no illegal FBI operations had occurred in these Weatherman cases. On June 18, the FBI had provided such an affidavit, declaring that it had no information "which was obtained through unauthorized activities consisting of burglaries, mail searches, electronic surveillances, etc." It was a lie.[63] Given that by summer 1973 the Huston Plan was front-page news, it is likely that this lie would have been exposed in any trial proceedings in Judge Keith's court.

With the federal charges dropped, however, the Weather stalwarts faced only relatively minor local charges. With the takeover of the Weather Underground Organization by Clayton van Lydegraf in 1976, and the capture of the new van Lydegraf leadership in 1977, it had become abundantly clear that no revolution would occur. Meanwhile, the original Weather leaders faced little or no punishment. The result was that between 1977 and 1980, the vast majority of Weather people decided to abandon life on the run and to "surface," two of the last being Bill Ayers and Bernardine Dohrn in 1980.

In their Declaration of War Communiqué of May 21, 1970, the Weathermen had pledged to "never live peaceably under this system." For the vast majority of Weather radicals, that pledge would be broken. Their postunderground careers are illuminating as to the nature of American society—and about the Weathermen's capacities as people. Those who voluntarily surfaced went on to lead productive lives. They are all still very left-wing—no one has become a political conservative—but they are living in peaceably, having renounced violence in the service of radical ends.

Bill Ayers became a Distinguished Professor of Education at the University of Illinois–Chicago. In 1997 he received the Chicago Citizen of the Year Award for his work bringing a $49-million Annenberg Challenge Grant to inner-city Chicago public schools.[64] A colleague who served on a Ph.D. dissertation committee with Ayers in the 1990s commented that he was "very diligent" in his work.[65] But Ayers was denied professor emeritus status in 2010 upon his retirement from the university after twenty-five years, because during his Weatherman phrase he had dedicated *Prairie Fire* in part to Sirhan Sirhan, the assassin of Senator Robert F. Kennedy. Christopher Kennedy, the senator's son and the head of the University of Illinois Board of Trustees, led the fight against him.[66]

Bernardine Dohrn became a professor of law at Northwestern University—but she was banned from taking the bar exam and becoming a practicing lawyer because she had gone to prison for contempt of court after refusing to testify in the Nyack, New York, bank robbery case of 1981.

Jeff Jones, still in hiding in 1979, was busted for marijuana cultivation and served six months of full-time community service; he is now a political consultant on ecological causes in Albany, New York. A highly sympathetic character based on him was played by Robert Redford in the 2012 film *The Company You Keep.*

Cathy Wilkerson was for twenty-five years a teacher of mathematics in the Brooklyn, New York, school system; she jokes that she had originally had to learn math in order to build bombs. She has little to do with the Weatherman people now.

Mark Rudd became a popular professor of mathematics at Central New Mexico Community College in Albuquerque, where he taught for two decades.

Eleanor Raskin, the wife of Jeff Jones, became a lawyer and for ten years was an administrative law judge at the New York State Public Service Commission.

Howard Machtinger earned an M.A. in history from San Francisco State University and became a university administrator in North Carolina, where he still lives.

Ronald Fliegelman worked for almost thirty years as a teacher of special education students in the impoverished Bedford-Stuyvesant section of Brooklyn. His daughter with Cathy Wilkerson works in a nongovernmental organization for children in Harlem.

Russell Neufeld became a prominent defense lawyer in New York City. In the autumn of 2014 he went to Russia to work with human rights attorneys in what he called "a difficult atmosphere" under Vladimir Putin.

Brian Flanagan owns a bar in New York and won $20,000 on the television show *Jeopardy.*

Jonathan Lerner became a gay rights activist in Atlanta. His novel about Weatherman, *Alex Underground,* is well worth reading for its insights into the confusions and trauma of the underground period.

The post-1980 careers of the aboveground Weatherman supporters mentioned in this book have followed a trajectory similar to most of the Weathermen themselves:

Jennifer Dohrn gained a Ph.D. and is currently associate director of nursing at Columbia University School of Public Health.

Dana Biberman, a target of the FBI in late 1971 for her Weatherman connections, is the chief of the Tobacco Compliance Bureau at the New York State Office of the Attorney General, Manhattan.

Dennis Cunningham, who was a target of the FBI in 1970–1971 for his alleged Weatherman connections, is now a prominent lawyer in San Francisco. He successfully prosecuted the City of Chicago for the murder of Black Panther leader Fred Hampton, in a case that lasted a quarter of a century and was settled only in 2000.

Jonah Raskin, the author of many books—fiction, history, literary studies, poetry, and an excellent book on Allen Ginsberg— became a professor of English and then was chairman of the Department of Communications at Sonoma State University for twenty years.

Regis Debray became an official adviser on foreign relations to French President François Mitterrand, with a seat on the Conseil d'État.[67] He would become an apostate and scourge of the Left, renouncing his past apologetics on behalf of Fidel Castro and Che Guevara, especially in a remarkably candid and self-critical three-volume autobiography. In hindsight, he would characterize his infatuation with the radical Left as his enrollment in a "notable school of bravura and imbecility."

Cynics might argue that the Weathermen took the bridge back to middle-class life from the underground that was always open to them because of their class background, good education, and "white skin privilege"—a bridge not open, for instance, to members of the Black Panther Party. But another way of looking at it is that these were always people with promising intellectual talents. These gifts were fortified by excellent university educations: Michigan (Ayers), Chicago (Bernardine Dohrn), Columbia (Rudd, Machtinger), Harvard (Neufeld), Barnard (Eleanor Raskin), Swarthmore (Wilkerson). They had practical skills, too—as is obvious from the FBI's failure, despite hunting them for seven years, to catch them or even to significantly disrupt their activities.

But that is not the whole story of those who went into the Weather Underground Organization. There were and are bitter-enders, and their fates were often far different from those guerrillas who surfaced and took a place—often a dissenting place—within mainstream society.

Clayton van Lydegraf's Weatherman remnant did not kill anyone (though it might have), and poor security led to the arrest of five members on charges of bombing conspiracy and to sentences ranging from two to four years in California prisons. On the East Coast, Weatherman bitter-enders formed the May 19 Communist Organization, joined with the Black Liberation Army, and ended up in a lethal gun battle that followed the botched armored car robbery in Nyack in 1981.

Judy Clark of the later May 19 group was captured by the FBI in December 1970 on minor charges of riot connected to the Days of Rage, served a few months, and was then released. She joined with Jennifer Dohrn as part of the aboveground support-group for the Weather Underground Organization. David Gilbert remained underground until 1977, and supported the van Lydegraf group in the coup against Ayers, Dohrn, and Jones; he surfaced in 1977 after his lawyer arranged for all charges to be dropped against him.[68] He was now free to go, like many of his comrades, into mainstream American life, but he could not bring himself to do it. By the spring of 1979 he was underground again, eventually joining May 19. Kathy Boudin, a survivor of the townhouse explosion, had never sought to surface; Gilbert's love for her helped draw him back into the guerrilla life.[69]

Boudin, Clark, and Gilbert participated with the BLA in the Nyack holdup, in which the BLA men killed three people. The May 19 people—along with several BLA members—were caught by the police. Of the three Weather veterans, Kathy Boudin pleaded guilty at trial, on the advice of her father, the prominent lawyer Leonard Boudin; she served twenty-two years in prison and was paroled in 2003. She is now an adjunct professor at Columbia University's School of Social Work, the same university where Jennifer Dohrn now teaches.

Unlike Boudin, at trial both David Gilbert and Judy Clark refused to recognize the authority of the court and claimed to be prisoners of war, guilty of nothing but armed resistance to a fascist state. As a result, not only did a jury find them guilty of murder but the judge sentenced them each to seventy-five years in prison. In contrast to everyone else in Weatherman, Gilbert and Clark have spent most of their lives in prison. Clark has moderated her political position over time.[70] Gilbert, for his part, has said his participation in the Brink's robbery was wrong and that he regrets his role in the "tragic loss of life." No matter. It is unlikely they will ever be released.

The FBI Weather hunters are similarly irreconcilable. William Sullivan, the enemy of both Weatherman and Mark Felt, died in a hunting accident in 1979. L. Patrick Gray died in 2008, always denying that he knew anything about the illegal black bag jobs he had almost certainly approved.[71] Jack Kearney was unrepentant about the black bag jobs he had run: he remained convinced that Weathermen was a totalitarian, terrorist organization that deserved to be hounded.[72] Edward Miller died in 2011, insisting to the end that Weatherman had set off hundreds of bombings and killed dozens of people—a demonstrably inaccurate claim that Richard Nixon believed too.[73]

Mark Felt had the strangest trajectory. During the Weatherman period his daughter Joan became a hippie; he once visited her in California and found her naked in a field, breast-feeding her illegitimate son, Ludi Kohoutek. Felt had wanted to succeed J. Edgar Hoover as director of the FBI, and was embittered when Nixon chose Patrick Gray instead. He was forced into retirement from the FBI on June 23 1973, in the midst of Watergate—as part of a maneuver in which William Sullivan seems to have been involved.[74] When his wife died, Felt moved in with his daughter in Santa Rosa, north of San Francisco; she had meanwhile had two other children by different hippie men. She converted Felt to vegetarianism (his cholesterol was cut in half), and he became interested in carpentry and gardening. In 2005 it was revealed that—despite the vigorous denials in his 1979 autobiography—he was "Deep Throat," the source for the *Washington Post* stories that destroyed the careers of L. Patrick Gray and Richard Nixon, among others, in the Watergate scandal. Felt briefly became a hero to liberals and the Left; he died in 2008. To the end of his life, he hated Weatherman.[75]

Conclusion

THE WEATHER UNDERGROUND ORGANIZATION was the most notorious American radical group committed to political violence in the late 1960s and early 1970s. In retrospect, it is odd that the Federal Bureau of Investigation elevated a band of about one hundred young people, mostly college students, into a leading place on the Bureau's Most Wanted List. The FBI decision garnered Weatherman a huge amount of publicity and made some of its leaders famous. Starting in the summer of 1970, FBI wanted posters featuring images of Bill Ayers, Bernardine Dohrn, Jeff Jones, and a dozen others were hung prominently in every post office in the United States, and this continued for years. Their outlaw legend has endured to this day, surfacing, for instance, in the 2002 documentary *The Weather Underground*, which received much acclaim and was nominated for an Academy Award, or in the 2012 feature *The Company You Keep*, starring Robert Redford as a Weatherman veteran haunted by his past and Julie Christie as a Weatherman still committed to revolution.

Yet the Weather organization was minuscule. To be sure, it was almost unique among radicals in that period in using dynamite bombs to protest government policies and the practices of some corporations, as opposed to less dangerous Molotov cocktail firebombs, the use of which was more common. But Weather set off a total of only twenty-five such dynamite bombs during its seven years of existence, all of them relatively small; fully half of them were detonated early on, in 1970. After that, Weatherman on average set off only one bomb every six months, mostly in the bathrooms of government buildings and corporation headquarters. Yet for years the FBI leadership remained obsessed with capturing the Weathermen, and they remained prominent on the FBI wanted posters. Why? After all, by any rational measure, Weatherman was not an existential threat to the country, neither to the general citizenry nor to the ruling elite.

It is true that Weatherman was the only white group committed to revolutionary violence that operated on a national scale. It is true that some of its operations were spectacular: the bombing of the Capitol itself (March 1971), the bombing of the Pentagon (May 1972), the bombing of the State Department (January 1975). And the Weathermen were determined revolutionaries, not kids out on a lark. They constantly proclaimed their desire to humiliate and indeed destroy the very system the FBI stood to defend. Moreover, when in summer 1970 the original decision was made to put some Weatherman leaders onto the Most Wanted List, the FBI believed there were as many as one thousand Weatherman guerrillas at large in the United States. If that had been the case, Weatherman might have constituted a serious problem to the country—but in fact the FBI overestimated the scale of the Weatherman organization by a factor of ten, and went into a panic. A year later, by autumn 1971, it was clear to the FBI that the Weatherman threat was much more limited; yet the Bureau still committed large resources to pursue the group, diverting hundreds of agents from fighting traditional crime. This was partly because of the occasional bombings; but also because the sheer presence of all those young Weathermen faces on the wanted posters all over the country year after year constituted a humiliation of the Bureau—and the prestige of the Bureau was part of its power. Thus on the FBI side bureaucratic interests and imperatives, not only fears for national security, fostered a disproportionate effort to eradicate the group. And yet the FBI never permanently caught a single major Weatherman figure, or stopped a single bombing. In part that was because of FBI clumsiness, in part because the Weathermen were very careful—and in part because they did not do all that much.

The Weathermen remained at large until 1977–1980. At that point most of them simply gave up the revolution and surfaced, resuming their lives within society, where they have lived peacefully (if on the far Left) for the previous thirty-five years. Little punishment was ever meted out. This striking outcome to their careers as violent revolutionaries was possible because by late 1973 all federal charges against the Weathermen—and they were serious charges—had been dropped. And that was because the FBI, in its zeal to catch the Weather Underground, had itself persistently violated U.S. laws, and had been caught at it. Unable to apprehend the Weather Underground fugitives or stop the bombings—the FBI had no informers, and could not penetrate the organization—the Bureau was reduced to invading the homes of supporters and relatives of the Weathermen in search of possible leads as to where they were, and what bombings were being planned. Since the supporters and relatives had broken no laws, there was no way that a court was ever going to issue a search warrant; there was no probable cause. So the FBI in its desperation went in anyway, without search warrants. It was outright illegal burglary, and the Bureau knew it (as FBI documents prove). These operations went on during Director J. Edgar Hoover's last years, but on a greater scale once L. Patrick Gray became acting director after Hoover's death in May 1972. Gray was acting as an instrument of President Richard Nixon, who from the moment he first took office in early 1969 continually expressed his displeasure at the FBI's reluctance to increase the scale and range of illegal operations against leftist radicals. These burglaries were not only gross violations of the Fourth Amendment; they were in practical terms worthless: they produced no useful information. Fearing that the facts about the program would become known because of increased media and public scrutiny as a result of the Watergate scandal, the government withdrew all federal charges against the Weathermen in late 1973.

Moreover, after investigations of the FBI for the purpose of reform in 1975 and 1976 revealed the true scope of the program, the Department of Justice, first under President Gerald Ford and then under President Jimmy Carter, considered indicting dozens of FBI agents on federal charges of violating the Constitution. In the end Justice settled for bringing to trial Associate Director Mark Felt, the number-two man in the Bureau, and Assistant Director Edward Miller, chief of the most important of the FBI internal units, the Domestic Intelligence Division, which had carried out the burglaries. Thus the defendants in only federal trial ever held involving Weatherman were not radicals but top FBI officials. And those officials were convicted by a Washington, D.C., jury in November 1980. The following April the new president, the conservative Ronald Reagan, who had been enraged that the FBI men had even been put on trial, granted Felt and Miller a presidential pardon.

What should be emphasized is the relatively small number of violations of the Fourth Amendment involved here: the D.C. jury convicted Felt and Miller of authorizing a total of thirteen warrantless burglaries of Weatherman supporters or relatives during a nine-month period from June 1972 to March 1973. From today's post-9/11 vantage point, thirteen such intrusions without a warrant may seem paltry. Thirty-five years ago, however, it caused a furor.

But the planned scale of Nixonian repression was considerable. In the summer of 1970, Nixon backed the Huston Plan, which envisioned a vastly increased program of illegal operations against the radical Left—including burglaries on a large scale, illegal wiretaps, and mail openings by multiple intelligence agencies, all to be overseen by an intelligence "czar." What was envisioned was an early version of the Homeland Security Department. J. Edgar Hoover blocked this program. Not that Hoover was a civil libertarian: rather, he opposed any attempt to diminish the independence of the FBI by imposing a new external overseer. He also worried that a program of such magnitude would be discovered, that in the new antiauthoritarian mood of the country the public would not stand for it, and that great damage would thus be done to the existing intelligence agencies. On this latter point, and even without the Huston Plan being implemented, events would show that the old man was right.

Nevertheless, a crucial element leading to the ineffectiveness of the measures taken in the Nixonian war against Weatherman was the decision by Weather, at a meeting in Mendocino, California, in May 1970, to refrain from lethal violence. It needs to be stressed that this was a contingent event. In the early months of 1970, Weatherman planned nationwide deadly attacks, especially on the police, stretching from Berkeley, California, to New York City and New Jersey, to Detroit. In the event, none of these attacks came off: the Berkeley dynamite bombs turned out to be too small to be lethal; by contrast, the New York City bombs were deadly, but the bombers were incompetent, accidentally blowing themselves up as they were preparing to attack a U.S. Army dance at Fort Dix, New Jersey; and the powerful Detroit bombs—set to detonate in two separate police installations on the same day as the Fort Dix attack—were discovered and defused by the police through the actions of the last known FBI informer left in Weatherman. But if the New York and Detroit bombs had gone off as planned, dozens of people would have been killed on March 6, 1970, including many innocent civilians. The failed Detroit bombings, allegedly led by Bill Ayers, are little known today, but are essential for understanding Weatherman history. That is because by late 1970 the Weatherman leadership was claiming Fort Dix to have been a unique and rogue operation. It was neither.

Weatherman in the first three months of 1970 was, by any reasonable measure, a band intent on committing radical violence, not only against property but against people as well. The government was not wrong to regard the group as dangerous. But by that May the Weatherman leadership, led by Jeff Jones and Bernardine Dohrn, had disavowed lethal operations. This decision was controversial, and there were those within the leadership who argued that renouncing lethal violence might end the hope of provoking a real revolution—and if the three Weatherman leaders who blew themselves up in New York had been alive and present, it is possible that the decision would have gone the other way. The course of American history would then have been different—and much darker. The Weatherman bombers, in attempting to jump-start a revolution, would have been responsible for scores of deaths, first in March, and then over the months following the meeting in Mendocino. But even that was not the main danger. The wrath of the Nixon administration, if faced with such a chaotic situation, would have been ferocious, and any pretense of adhering to judicial or legal constraint would probably have been abandoned in favor of a no-holds-barred dragnet. Even as it was, confronting a group that did not kill but merely set off protest bombs, the FBI by October 1970 had prepared a list of eleven thousand suspected radicals who were to be rounded up and preemptively incarcerated without court order should the president declare a state of national emergency. That was the real threat—the government response. And one can imagine a Weatherman response in turn: bombings, assassinations, kidnappings of public figures.[1]

But it didn't happen. And this was because Jeff Jones and Bernardine Dohrn, eventually backed by Bill Ayers, took Weatherman down the road of deescalation. Only now can we see how close Weatherman brought the country to a political cataclysm, not so much through its own possible actions as through the government response such actions would almost certainly have provoked. What is little understood or even recognized, however, is why and how it came to pass that Weatherman stood down.

The Weathermen thought of themselves as revolutionaries—that is, not merely as aspiring urban guerrillas, but as politically minded organizers. They yearned to expand their numbers beyond a tiny revolutionary cadre. While they worried that the bulk of the white working class was hostage to relative prosperity, and ineradicable racism which they called "white skin privilege," they hoped that the counterculture, made up of disaffected young people, might be a kind of petri dish that would nurture a revolutionary constituency capable of eventually joining their revolutionary project. This constituency might not participate in revolutionary violence—at least not at first—but they might assist Weather in general, providing protection, logistical help, and aboveground political support. The meeting at Mendocino took place in the midst of the student protests in May 1970 over Nixon's Cambodia invasion and the Kent State shootings; campuses nationwide were in upheaval against the government. There seemed an opportunity now—perhaps a unique one—to gain mass support for revolution. But Weatherman bombing policy as exemplified by the townhouse disaster had not won support even on the extreme Left. Even the *Berkeley Tribe*, probably the most radical underground newspaper in the country, publicly warned that lethal bombings would discredit the movement and isolate the would-be guerrillas from potential supporters; if they killed, they would be alone.[2] Dozens of fire-bombings were occurring on campuses in May 1970, but the humane ideals of the counterculture remained powerful among the politically active young. Such firebombs were hurled against build-ings (especially campus ROTC buildings) more as a kind of violent propaganda, at targets chosen for their symbolism, rather than as a result of more lethal strategies of resistance. Thus Weatherman hoped that it might become the leader of a significant revolutionary upwelling—alienated white students—but understood that such a thing might happen only if it aligned itself with prevailing senti-ments as to the "level of struggle."[3] That is, Weatherman's putative constituency acted as a brake on the organization's wilder and more reckless ambitions, seeming to tell the revolutionaries that they needed to set a limit on their violence and explicitly to renounce any tactics that might actually kill. After the self-inflicted disaster of the townhouse explosion in early March 1970, the palpable dismay of Weatherman's natural constituency in the counterculture was a significant factor, though far from the only one, in the Mendocino decision to change course. And this pressure from the potential Weatherman constituency to reject such violence as the inner cir-cles of the organization had contemplated and planned was very different from a contingent event; rather, it had to do with the na-ture of American youth culture at the time, which overwhelmingly favored nonviolence, even while embracing ever-stronger tactics of civil disobedience and resistance to end racial injustice and to stop the carnage in Indochina.[4]

Their hippie-influenced potential supporters—even the sympa-thetic radical journalists of the *Berkeley Tribe*—rejected killing *tout court*. Further, Weatherman leaders such as Jones and Dohrn were personally influenced by the counterculture themselves; even the name of the organization—an odd name for a group of political guerrillas—derived from a line in a song by Bob Dylan.[5] One of the lessons that a study of Weatherman offers to us is how the nature of the constituency of revolutionaries can have an impact on their be-havior, encouraging some sorts of conduct, deterring others.

In this connection, we can also consider the significance of how the Weatherman war came to an end, because it was the first experience of a modern American government in fighting armed home-grown dissidents on a national scale. In this war, it is striking that the FBI never scored a tactical or operational victory against Weatherman, never caught a single leader, and never stopped a single Weatherman bombing. In that sense, Weatherman humiliated the FBI. Yet the U.S. government would ultimately triumph. The story of how the Weather Underground foiled the FBI and destroyed itself is the tale that is at the heart of this book.

In the event, the radical constituency of Weatherman would turn out to be too small to be politically effective. By 1974 the leadership realized the problem. In the 186-page book called *Prairie Fire*—clandestinely printed by Weather, and clandestinely distributed with great success—another major Weather operation that the FBI could not prevent—the leadership concluded that the only way to mount a revolution in the United States was to win over the American working class. This realization, which Weather's more orthodox Marxist-Leninist critics had long been urging, required a wholesale rethinking of the tactics and strategies that had been at the red-hot center of its origins. Such an effort with the working class, however, would take long years, and it required aboveground work, legal propagandizing. To oversimplify slightly, Weatherman the guerrilla organization had turned out to be the wrong strategy: the revolution was not going to be provoked by setting off dynamite bombs in a few bathrooms. Weatherman would need to be transformed into an aboveground mass communist party. The Prairie Fire Organizing Committee was founded to prepare the way. But the publication of *Prairie Fire* set off an ideological struggle within the Weather organization itself, one that culminated in the spring of 1976 in the triumph of the more radical wing, which insisted on focusing on the guerrilla war. From late 1976 onward, those who had proposed an aboveground mass organization—including Jones, Dohrn, and Ayers—either drifted away from Weatherman or were expelled from it on charges of having counseled moderation. Moderation, in this view, was tantamount to betrayal of first principles.

But the new leader—the elderly Stalinist Clayton van Lydegraf—was utterly incompetent, and the core of his group ended up being caught in 1977 and sent to prison. Over the next three years, the vast majority of the Weathermen, with no serious federal charges now pending against them, came up voluntarily from the underground and returned to mainstream society, where they became leftist reformers. Only a handful of people—calling themselves the May 19 Communist Organization—continued the fight. They became allies of the Black Liberation Army, a violent offshoot of the Black Panthers. As we have seen, in an armored car robbery in Nyack, New York, in 1981 the May 19 people were involved in the BLA killing of a Brinks guard and two policemen, and important May 19 Organization and BLA figures were captured. Two of those May 19 people—Judy Clark and David Gilbert—are still in prison thirty-five years later. May 19 would eventually disappear as a national organization.

It's no surprise that the most extreme, die-hard remnants of Weatherman ended up fighting alongside the Black Liberation Army. Weatherman is associated in popular consciousness primarily with opposition to the Vietnam War. And it is true that Weatherman emerged from Students for a Democratic Society (SDS), an organization that was at the very center of opposition to Vietnam on college campuses, that Weatherman itself saw Vietnam as classic instance of unfettered American imperialism, and that famous photographs show Weathermen carrying Vietcong and North Vietnamese flags in demonstrations. But this is not the whole Weatherman ideology. The people who formed Weather had always seen the plight of African Americans in American society as a key element in any revolution. Some were inspired toward violence by the ghetto insurrections of 1967 and 1968. Many believed that for the exploited and alienated black "colony" in the United States, the solution was a war of liberation. Given the prevalence of racism in American society, such a black revolution not only would be morally legitimate, and thus deserving of every help which white radicals could provide, it might even be enough in itself to overturn the system. At the very least, so some argued, such resistance in the "mother country" would encourage anti-imperialist efforts abroad by distracting the U.S. government from pursuing an unconstrained war against oppressed peoples elsewhere. Even if revolution in the United States proved to be a forlorn and doomed enterprise (and in 1969–1970 this did not seem at all certain to them), the moral obligation to make the effort struck many in Weather as reason enough to pick up the gun. For a long time Weatherman was close to the Black Panthers, and it broke with them only when the Weatherman leadership sensed that the Panthers were turning away from revolutionary violence. Indeed, the Weatherman lethal bombings planned for Detroit in March 1970 were a direct response to the acquittal of policemen in the murder of black men during the 1967 Detroit insurrection. Any understanding of Weatherman must grapple with the centrality of black issues in American society.[6]

By summer 1969 Weatherman was a revolutionary organization hell-bent on violent provocation. It is inaccurate and misleading to claim, as some have, that Weatherman was merely a more extreme wing of the broader American anti–Vietnam War movement.[7] Rather, Weatherman in late 1969 and early 1970 viewed the peace movement with contempt, as useless for changing anything fundamental in American society or the world. Conversely, the reaction of the broader peace movement and most of the Left to Weatherman's increasingly violent rhetoric and behavior was rejection.[8]

Further, if one accepts the definition of "terrorism" proposed by former Weatherman Howard Machtinger in 2009—intentional violence against innocent civilians for a political purpose—then it appears that in the opening months of 1970 Weatherman was engaged in terrorism. Both of the planned March 6 attacks, on Fort Dix and in Detroit, would have killed or injured many civilians—people in the wrong place at the wrong time—as well as police and military police.[9] Yet after May 1970, "terrorism" in this sense is a misnomer for the actions of the Weathermen; they changed from contemplating attacks on human targets to attacking only property. Yet those actions were not mere "vandalism" either, as former Weatherman leader Bill Ayers has taken to calling them.[10] Any bombing with dynamite carried an inherent risk to human life, even if preceded by a warning phone call, as were all Weather bombings after May 1970. For example, the Weather Underground bombing of the Pentagon in May 1972 missed killing a cleaning woman by only minutes.[11] In another action, the bomb malfunctioned and detonated two hours later than planned, so that only luck prevented casualties.[12] Dynamite bombs, then, are not "vandalism"; they are an instrument of (as Weatherman liked to say) "armed struggle." And these actions certainly terrorized many people in government.

Still, the original impulses behind the trend in Students for a Democratic Society that led to Weatherman were angry opposition to the Vietnam War and outrage at continuing racism in American society. In a situation where most people on the American Left believed (rightly) that thousands of Vietnamese civilians were being killed each week in Southeast Asia, and believed (rightly) that racism in the United States remained a plague, one can say that—whatever Weatherman became—the original impulses out of which it arose were antiwar and antiracist.

Further, although it can be shown that Weatherman bombing plans were more lethal than previously understood, this does not mean that everyone in Weatherman was involved in them. Especially in early 1970, knowledge of the bombing plans was limited to the Weather Bureau leaders (a central committee of ten or eleven people who set policy) and to those collectives directly engaged in the operations. All supported the idea of a clandestine organization; some people also wanted simultaneously to continue aboveground mass organizing, while others had abandoned it; all supported the bombing of property; but some people did not know about the plans for bombing human targets.[13]

Moreover, the context in which Weatherman operated—from a devastating war in Southeast Asia to daily and sometimes deadly racism at home—involved governmental violence on a far larger scale than any violence Weatherman ever perpetrated or ever thought of perpetrating. As the poet and peace activist Allen Ginsberg put it in 1971:

> The government is indulging in murderous violence on so vast a scale that nobody's mind can contain it. That's why it's easy to headline the Weatherman's bomb, lonely little bomb, lonely little antirobot bomb, that wasn't intended for humans, even.

Ginsberg was mistaken as to Weatherman intentions in 1970: sometimes they were lethal. But his general point is still valid.[14]

Nor was Weatherman the only violent group of radicals called into existence by the events of the late 1960s. In the 1969–1970 school year alone, white leftist groups set off at least 242 bombings. These were mostly on campuses, with nineteen Reserve Officers Training Corps buildings destroyed; but a number were off campus, aimed at the headquarters of major corporations.[15] Consider the serious incidents of injury and death in 1969 before Weatherman began operations: a secretary at Pomona College, Mary Ann Keatley, was blinded in one eye and lost part of a hand when a bomb exploded in a mailbox in the Department of Politics on February 26; a student at San Francisco State University, Timothy Peebles, was blinded and disfigured while trying to set off a bomb on campus (March 6); Dover Sharp, a custodian at the Faculty Club at the University of California at Santa Barbara, was burned to death when he picked up a package containing a bomb (April 11).[16] The Sam Melville radical group in New York set off a large dynamite bomb in the Marine Midland Bank building that injured twenty people, and might well have killed them all, except for the heavy file cabinets that happened to stand between the bomb and the victims (August 20).[17] By contrast, in its six years of bombing operations after June 1970, Weatherman injured no one. Yet Melville and the others are mostly forgotten now.[18]

Establishing the context for Weatherman actions would also not be complete without acknowledging violence from the Right in this period; this, too, is mostly forgotten. There is the police violence perpetrated with increasing ferocity on peaceful demonstrators after 1960: special mention should be made here of the "the Orangeburg Massacre" of February 1968, when South Carolina Highway Patrol officers opened fire on an antisegregation demonstration at black college, killing three and wounding almost thirty; and the Jackson State University killings in May 1970, which killed two black students and wounded twelve.[19] There is the lethal violence inflicted on ghetto rioters or suspected rioters during the insurrections of 1967–1968 (for instance, in Newark and Detroit in summer 1967, in Chicago after Martin Luther King's murder in spring 1968), with nearly one hundred people killed and many more wounded by police and inexperienced National Guard troops. And there is right-wing terrorist bombing: besides the

KKK firebombings of black churches and homes in the South, anti-Castro Cuban groups set off thirteen firebombs in New York City between April and August 1968 alone.[20]

But if Weatherman was not the only organization setting off bombs in the country, it is also true that most other bombs were gasoline firebombs (Molotov cocktails). These were certainly destructive, and potentially lethal. But only a few small groups ever tried more powerful explosives—and the most dangerous, the Melville group, was caught in November 1969. Weatherman did the most dynamiting, and was the most persistent (six years of it, 1970–1975). And no one in the New Left but Weatherman in 1970 or in any other year planned nationwide, multiple-city dynamite attacks.

But even allowing for Weatherman's exceptional violence, a historian has to ask how important, really, were they? Focusing on Weatherman's career risks foregrounding a dramatic but predominantly white and heterosexual narrative, as if the concurrent emergence of Hispanic, gay, Asian, and Native American radical movements—some of which had much longer-term political impact than Weatherman—was merely a background to the story of late 1960s white radicalism.[21] Further, the huge and overwhelmingly peaceful antiwar movement had a large impact, we now know, on American governmental policy, setting limits to the escalation in Vietnam that both Lyndon Johnson and Richard Nixon might have ordered, and forcing relative restraint instead.[22] Yet Weatherman, contemptuous of the antiwar movement, had no discernible impact on American foreign policy. The Weathermen's willingness to sacrifice the comforts and opportunities of their everyday American lives in the pursuit of a greater goal, a new American order, is impressive, even if one opposed their methods.[23] But the Weathermen were few in number: about one hundred guerrillas in early 1972, aided by another two hundred direct facilitators and a somewhat larger aboveground political support group.[24]

Weatherman's political impact on the New Left was in fact primarily destructive. In June 1969 its actions helped to break up the largest left-wing student organization in American history, Students for a Democratic Society. Weatherman's ideological opponents in the Progressive Labor Party helped in SDS's destruction—and it turns out that Weatherman unknowingly had the help of the FBI in this as well. And in early 1970 Weatherman jettisoned the national machinery of what remained of SDS—just three months before the existence of a working nationwide student organization might have helped to elevate the great campus protests of May 1970 into something more lasting. The story of Weatherman's rise within SDS is complicated, but its role in the collapse of the most success-ful radical left project in American history is important.[25]

Yet Weatherman alone was hardly responsible for the failure of the 1960s Left. The members were all young, and did not always understand the implications of what they were doing. And whatever the fractures and growing extremism within the movement, it was the Nixon administration, beginning in early 1969, that brought its leadership under continual federal assault, intensifying efforts that had occurred under Lyndon Johnson. There were at least seven major conspiracy indictments and trials launched by the Nixon Justice Department against the radical leadership between 1969 and 1972.[26] The Chicago Eight conspiracy trial, beginning in September 1969, against leaders of the protests at the Democratic National Convention in Chicago in August 1968, was only the most famous of the trials. None of the federal conspiracy trials resulted in major convictions, because the cases were weak. But conviction was not their only purpose: all the energy, time, and money devoted to defense by the radical leaders—even though it was successful de-fense in the end, each proclaimed as a victory—undercut the mo-mentum of protest. Even as this coordinated legal assault was going on, Nixon was withdrawing troops from the Vietnam War; the cen-tral leftist issue and recruiting device was being removed. Thus it is a distortion to focus discussion of the failure of 1960s radicalism on its internal weaknesses alone. The weakness and factionalism—to some extent natural in any student movement—certainly existed, but radicals also had to cope with powerfully destructive maneuvers against them by the government, local and state as well as federal.[27]

Yet there are two further reasons why the career of Weather-man requires study. The first has to do with whether there was continuity within the sixties Left across the devastating events of 1968, or whether there was a dramatic break after these trage-dies. Did the assassinations of Dr. Martin Luther King in April and of Senator Robert Kennedy in June, and the violence at the

Democratic National Convention in August, lead to a bitter and violent New Left that had little connection to the idealism of the early sixties and the civil rights movement?

The problematic aspects of the late sixties Left—its simplistic worldview and its revolutionary authoritarianism—in fact had their roots earlier. Several Weatherman leaders emerged from the mid-1960s SDS experience.[28] Similarly, Weatherman's fierce moralism and commitment to justice, its impulse toward going it alone and toward action, its links to the growing counterculture, its emphasis on community (the Weatherman collectives), and indeed its intellectualism, including its later drift toward a reflexive Marxism-Leninism, all represented an intensification (though not the best expression) of ideas and ideals from the earlier part of the decade. The prestige that accrued to Weathermen in many quarters of the counterculture because of their sacrifices of comfort and safety in the name of a cause echoed the civil rights movement's "hierarchy based on sacrifice." Weatherman, with its explicit embrace of violence, represented a leap into darkness, but it was also—even in its eventual rejection of lethal tactics—a continuation. In fact, considering Weatherman in contrast to the *other* Marxist-Leninist factions into which SDS had splintered by spring 1969, one can even argue with Jeffrey Herf that of those factions, "it was Weatherman's crazy blend of global Marxism-Leninism and solidarity with the Vietnamese and the Panthers, linked to the American counterculture, that was closest to the spirit of 1968 and the sixties generally."[29]

Only a few hundred people in Weatherman engaged in or facilitated its violence, but thousands of New Leftists believed in general as the Weathermen did—not in their use of dynamite but in their analysis of what had gone awry in America. The traditional sixties intellectualism of Weatherman and the dependence of its actions upon proper revolutionary theory—an aspect of conduct that has often been ignored or denied—is an important aspect of its development.

Second, Weatherman is important because recently released FBI documents show that the group's ability to frighten and anger the government was extraordinary. President Nixon worried about being assassinated by Weatherman (spring 1970); officers on military bases worried about being injured or even dying from Weatherman bombs (summer 1970); the minority leader of the United States Senate and other Republican senators worried about Weatherman kidnapping them or members of their families (autumn 1970); the FBI worried in 1970 that Weatherman would attack its agents, its local field offices, and even its Washington headquarters. Weatherman operatives did successfully bomb the Capitol building (March 1971), and the Pentagon (May 1972). Later they would bomb the State Department (January 1975). Violent Weatherman acts thus caused anger and prompted fear at the highest levels of the American government. Richard Nixon took the Weathermen seriously as a destabilizing influence within the country.

Moreover, Nixon's view of the crisis of 1969–1970 was widely shared: Max Ascoli, the editor of the Cold War liberal magazine *The Reporter*, wrote that Nixon faced a crisis similar to Lincoln's, concluding that the president "must save the Union not from a civil but a guerrilla war."[30] What the FBI knew about the actual scale of lethal Weatherman acts in 1970, even allowing for Ascoli's hyperbole, shows that this was not an unreasonable reaction. The threat also quickly diminished, but with no lessening of the FBI determination (and in some high officials, a persistent obsession) to capture the Weathermen.

The FBI was convinced for several reasons that Weatherman was dangerous. First, there was the example Weatherman set for others. In autumn 1971 Edward Miller, the new assistant director for the FBI Domestic Intelligence Division, set up a special committee to study the Weatherman problem. Its first conclusion: while Weatherman bombing activity was in itself a very serious matter, "of greater significance is the cumulative effect the successful use of terrorist tactics has upon a segment of youthful society. . . . Their rhetoric of violence and terrorist acts have encouraged many others of similar inclination to act." Weatherman had been a pacesetter and strategist in the New Left:

> From its origins in the Students for a Democratic Society (SDS) . . . it has maintained a leadership role in evolution from student disorder to its present status—a fanatic Marxist-Leninist terrorist group. Weatherman leaders were among the first to travel to Cuba (1967); call for and attempt

major street attacks on police (1968); call for the building of a small tough paramilitary organization to carryout urban guerrilla warfare in order to bring about the revolution (1969); clearly define a broad program for strategic sabotage aimed at police and Government installations (February, 1970); and actually go underground to better conduct "armed struggle" in furtherance of the program of terror (1970).

The special committee believed it was spawning bombing imitators: "the May Day Collective, Revolutionary Union, Venceremos Organization, and many others."[31]

In the FBI view, this danger was compounded by the failure of the Bureau to capture or bring to court any major Weatherman figure. That is: the radicals were getting away with it. The committee noted that every investigative technique had failed: attempted penetration of the underground collectives, telephone wiretaps of suspects, physical surveillance of suspects. A fundamental reason for the failure to catch the Weathermen was that its members did not share the weaknesses inherent in the usual FBI targets. These traditional targets were mostly ordinary criminals, who naturally associated with other ordinary criminals—people whom law enforcement could in turn pressure or bribe into becoming informers. Weatherman did engage in criminal acts, spectacular ones, but the problem was that the Weatherman milieu was not itself criminal in the ordinary way:

> Generally they are well-educated, frequently from upper-middle and wealthy backgrounds, sophisticated and intelligent. ... They do not draw upon criminal elements for support. We are dealing with dedicated communist revolutionaries committing criminal acts ... Our basic criminal techniques have not been productive against them.[32]

The FBI was continually humiliated by its failure to catch the Weathermen, and the FBI directorate feared the political consequences of failure. Yet the Weathermen made their own mistakes. They were young, after all, and only amateur guerrillas. Thus in their bombing of the U.S. Capitol they set the bomb and released a communiqué announcing the explosion (February 28, 1971)—but the bomb did not explode. Rather than accept this embarrassing failure, the collective went back into the Capitol a second time and set a second bomb right on top of the hidden first bomb. It was a huge risk, and yet—because even *after* the original Weatherman announcement, security at the Capitol remained lax—the operation was a success: both bombs detonated (early on March 1).[33]

Another example of shaky competence on both sides involved the December 1970 arrest of Judy Clark for her role in street riots a year earlier—a comparatively minor offense, given that she was currently involved in bombing. Clark had the bad luck to be seen by an FBI agent on a street in New York. Not noticing he was following her, she took the subway to the Upper East Side, where she met five other Weathermen in a movie theater; they were watching the Beatles' *Yellow Submarine*. The Weathermen were sitting two-by-two on three successive aisles. FBI men came in and arrested Clark, and took her away. Yet unaccountably they did not question, let alone arrest, Ron Fliegelman, who was sitting right next to her and was officially wanted on bombing charges, or any of the four other Weathermen who were also sitting right there. The Weathermen all promptly scooted out an exit, got away, and returned to their safe house in Brooklyn.[34]

A third example: in September 1973 Weatherman Howard Machtinger became the only Weather Bureau member ever caught by the FBI. It was partly a fluke: he was walking down East 86th Street in New York, on his way to a meeting of the Weather Bureau. But his capture was not just bad luck; the meeting was being held nearly opposite an FBI office, and two FBI agents on the street happened to see Machtinger and recognize him. Whether the choice of this site for the meeting was Weather insouciance or sheer lack of reconnaissance, it was a potentially fatal mistake.[35]

But Weatherman bumbling was matched in this case by government bumbling. First, if the FBI men had only followed Machtinger, they might have captured the entire Weather Bureau, including Bill Ayers and Bernardine Dohrn, and ended Weatherman right there. But they were too eager to make an arrest—any arrest.[36] Second, Machtinger's lawyer at arraignment was the brilliant

William Kunstler, and he told the judge that Machtinger, having made a strong political statement by going underground in 1970, was unlikely to do so again. Kunstler therefore argued for low bail—a mere $2,500—until trial on his federal charges. The judge accepted Kunstler's argument, while the assistant U.S. attorney present argued against *any* release for a defendant who had been a federal fugitive for three years, let alone a low bail. Machtinger was released into the custody of his doting mother. Three weeks later, he simply disappeared again into the underground. He explained his decision in a letter which he dated to the anniversary of John Brown's raid on Harper's Ferry—a date he got wrong. He did not resurface until 1978.[37]

A fourth example: on a mission from New York City going upstate, four Weathermen chose Mike Spiegel to drive the car, as a learning experience for Spiegel, who did not know how to drive. Not a smart move: on an upstate road, a New York state trooper eventually pulled the car over because of Spiegel's erratic driving. Spiegel was one of the Weatherman leaders on those FBI wanted posters. But the trooper simply let all them go with a warning—not even a ticket.[38]

These incidents show the complex and clumsy realities of the government's campaign against the Weatherman. It wasn't like in spy movies.[39] But the FBI did not find it amusing. The observations about the dangerous impact of Weatherman come from a January 1972 memo that was part of preparations for a formal application from Edward Miller to the FBI leadership to use FBI burglaries without search warrants in Weatherman cases. The FBI was all too aware that its efforts to catch Weatherman had failed, and that the Bureau's humiliation would intensify if the elusive underground set off another wave of bombings in the spring, thus, as one memo put it, "highlighting our inability [to catch them]."[40]

The FBI now turned to illegal conduct: burglaries perpetrated not against the underground Weatherman soldiers but against their aboveground supporters, families, and relatives. The targets would thus be American citizens, most but not all of whom were radicals, but none of whom had committed any crime and against whom no court would issue a search warrant. Internally, the FBI argued necessity: "It is imperative we succeed in apprehending these terrorists." FBI burglaries and bugging had been minimized in recent years (though never eliminated), but with Weatherman, "the absolute necessity for their use is evident." The final version of this memorandum is bluntly titled "Argument for Use of Anonymous Sources—Black Bag Technique—Weatherman Investigation."—FBI slang for burglaries and bugging.[41]

Aboveground individuals who had committed no crime would soon find their homes being secretly burgled multiple times by the FBI. The imperative was in part political in a traditional sense: in memos that favored black bag jobs, the FBI Weatherman committee stressed how the Weatherman issue might have an impact on the upcoming presidential election of 1972: "The Government's inability to cope with terrorist groups, especially the Weatherman . . . will undoubtedly be a strong point of contention by candidates of the opposition party." So the FBI misunderstand not only Weatherman; the idea that the FBI's failure to catch Weatherman could become a major issue for the Democrats seems a fantastic misunderstanding of the mood of the 1972 Democratic Party itself.[42]

As far as the actual hunt for Weatherman went, these actions, too, were futile. Nothing of intelligence value was ever discovered in the homes illegally entered, though a recipe for Indian pudding was taken from the apartment of Jennifer Dohrn, the sister of Bernardine Dohrn—and, it seems, a pair of her panties.[43] Far worse for the FBI, however, was that these burglaries were eventually discovered (1975) and publicized (1976), and when they became known, the political damage to the Bureau was severe.

The Bureau devoted enormous resources, both financial and human, to the Weatherman hunt once the radicals went underground in March 1970. Hundreds of special agents spent countless hours chasing down the most will-of-the-wisp clues: for instance, checking via the postal service all the mail that came to parents and siblings of Weather fugitives on birthdays, Mother's Day, Father's Day, parents' wedding anniversaries, Christmas, or Chanukah.[44] All for naught, with the single exception of Machtinger's arrest. Between April 15, 1970, when Dianne Donghi and Linda Evans were arrested on minor charges, ending the usefulness of the informant Larry Grathwohl, and the autumn of 1977 (with the arrest of the van Lydegraf group), only the Weather soldier Judy Clark was taken into custody (again, on minor charges, and—like Donghi and Evans, and later Machtinger, soon released). Two Weatherman dropouts, Karen Latimer and Nancy Rudd (no relationship to Weather leader Mark Rudd, who had come to national prominence as a student leader of the 1968 Columbia University building take-overs and sit-ins), were also caught, by accident, but this occurred long after they had left the organization. The information pried out of them in return for plea bargains is of significant interest to historians but was of no value for finding the Weather fugitives still at large. The FBI's frustration was repeatedly expressed within the Bureau at all levels. "We always get our man" was the FBI's famous slogan. But not in the case of Weatherman. The counterculture's refusal to betray the Weathermen aided the group's efforts to hide. And the FBI at the high point of the crisis, from 1969 to early 1972, was forbidden by Hoover to use special agents disguised as hippies to try to penetrate the organization or its fringes—because Hoover could not abide the idea of long-haired FBI agents.[45]

Ultimately, Hoover would resist the Nixon White House ef-forts to ramp up the Bureau's surveillance. His recalcitrance was largely rooted in his refusal to cede intelligence turf to elements outside his control—but he also believed these efforts ran the risk of severe criticism if the public discovered them. The White House, in turn, sought to end-run Hoover by creating its own rogue dirty-tricks and black bag operation. White House aide Tom Huston was a key figure and advocate for doing so. His plan for large-scale illegal operations was produced by a culture within the Nixon White House that was obsessed with leftist radicals. From early 1969, as soon as Nixon entered office, the president was pressing the FBI to intensify its operations against radicals; from February 1970 he was directly urging the FBI to engage in legally dubious investigative techniques against the far Left. He especially wanted the FBI to uncover links to the foreign powers that he was convinced were directing the protests against him. The FBI looked and looked but was unable to come up with any evidence of foreign meddling. It wasn't what Nixon wanted to hear. In July 1970 he approved large-scale operations that he had been explicitly advised were illegal. When Hoover blocked this plan (and a similar one later), Nixon came to view Hoover's obstructionism as a main reason to remove him as FBI director, but he did not have the courage to do it.

The war against Weatherman waged by an enraged and frightened Nixon helped lay the basis for the eventual Watergate scandal. Actions that Nixon promoted against Weatherman supporters and relatives in 1970–1971, the illegal burglaries and wiretapping—and which his minion L. Patrick Gray pushed at the FBI in 1972–1973—would in 1972 be used against the Democratic Party itself. When Hoover proved reluctant to engage in illegal operations at White House behest (though he continued to do a few such operations on his own), Nixon substituted his own White House "Plumbers" unit to do his bidding. The unit's first burglaries were aimed at just the sort of targets Nixon had wanted: antiwar activists such as Daniel Ellsberg. When the Plumbers were shifted over to Nixon's reelection campaign, the way was opened up for the Watergate burglary and the resultant scandal. In the end, and in this fashion, Weatherman did play a role in the fall of an American government—though not in the way the group had intended.

Notes

Introduction

1. One should not forget that about 85 percent of my generation were either not very active politically—a majority—or supported the war, and/or the Republicans.
2. Reverby is working on a biography of Alan Berkman, "the Weatherman doctor," who later was involved with the May 19 Communist Organization and ended up going to prison.
3. Seth Rosenfeld, *Subversives: The FBI's War on Student Radicals and Reagan's Rise to Power* (New York: Farrar, Straus and Giroux, 2013), chapter 26, "People's Park"
4. Jonah Raskin, "Looking Backward: Personal Reflections on Language, Gesture, and Mythology in the Weather Underground," *Socialism and Democracy* 20 (2006).
5. Special thanks must go here to Archivists James Mathis and Britney Crawford, who facilitated the research with grace, good humor, and hard work.
6. Personal communication with Bryan Burrough, 9/21/15.
7. Some of the FBI men (they were all men) involved centrally in the Weatherman war did give personal interviews to an FBI veterans organization, the Society of Former Special Agents of the FBI, between 2001 and 2010, before I ever became involved in this project. We are lucky to have these interviews.
8. I wish to thank James Mathis and Britney Crawford of the National Archives in College Park, Maryland (Archives II), for their crucial help in guiding me through the massive FBI files now available there.
9. Felt-Miller Box 251, File "Bu II," Fulton to Wannall, 7/29/74, p. 2. (This memo was itself marked "Confidential.")

10. Felt-Miller, Box 96, File "Sullivan and Hoover directives Re: Weatherman," Haynes to Sullivan 3/6/70, pp. 1–2 (the first example: see below and Chapter 7); Felt-Miller, Box 134, File "Weathfug-General," Miller to Felt, 6/30/72, pp. 3; Felt-Miller, Box 196: File "No Foreign Involvement," 1 of 3: Miller to Felt, 6/30/72, p. 3 (the second example).

11. For detailed discussion, see Chapter 2.

12. Raskin, "Looking Backward," 121.

13. Machtinger: Bryan Burrough, *Days of Rage: America's Radical Underground, the FBI, and the Forgotten Age of Revolutionary Violence* (New York: Penguin, 2015), 92–97 (interview). Despite Burrough, this was long suspected: see *Hearings before the Select Committee to Study Government Operations with Respect to Intelligence Activities of the United States Senate* vol. 2 (Washington, D.C., 1975), 22. Fliegelman: Burrough, *Days of Rage*, 126–131 (interview).

14. Raskin, "Looking Backward," 121.

15. Paraphrase of a personal communication from Weatherman veteran Mark Naison, 6/23/14.

Chapter One. "Angels of Destruction and Disorder"

1. See preliminary FBI report on the townhouse explosion, 3/13/70, p. 1, in Felt-Miller Box 102, "Plans to deal with WUO (Weather Underground)," File 1 of 4. This report went right to J. Edgar Hoover, whose handwritten comments on it are still visible.

2. On the discovery of Diana Oughton's corpse: ibid.; on the discovery of Terry Robbins's corpse, see "FBI Weatherfug [Weatherman Fugitive] Files," DocID 59162728, p. 75: Gale to DeLoach, 5/4/70, p. 1. On the large physical impact of the explosion on the neighborhood, see Mel Gussow, "West Eleventh Street: An End to Innocence," *New York*, 3/8/71.

3. On the escape of Cathy Wilkerson and Kathy Boudin through the front of the townhouse, see Cathy Wilkerson, *Flying Close to the Sun* (New York: Seven Stories, 2007), 345–348. There have long been rumors that several other Weathermen escaped through the back garden; see Todd Gitlin: *The Sixties: Years of Hope, Days of Rage* (1987; New York: Bantam, 1993), 400; Tom Wells, *The War Within: America's Battle over Vietnam* (Lincoln, Neb.: Authors Guild, 1994), 407. Nina Herrick, who in March 1970 lived at 19 West 10th Street, and whose small backyard thus backed on the small backyard of the Wilkerson townhouse, tells me that she and her husband heard the explosion and indeed saw three people—two women and a man, in disheveled condition—running from the back of the townhouse and west toward Sixth Avenue: interview with the author, 2/8/16. Herrick says that neither she nor any of her neighbors on West 10th Street was ever interviewed by the New York Police Department or the FBI, who apparently stuck to people on West 11th.

4. Preliminary FBI Report, 3/13/70, p. 1; Final Report, 4/14, 70: Felt-Miller Box 134, File "Not in 5/5 list [Weatherman Information]," 2 of 2.

5. The target and the horrific character of the bombs is now accepted: Ron Jacobs, *The Way the Wind Blew: A History of the Weather Underground* (New York: Verso, 1997), 95–98; Jeremy Varon, *Bringing the War Home* (Berkeley: University of California Press, 2004), 174; Dan Berger, *Outlaws of America: The Weather Underground and the Politics of Solidarity* (Oakland, Calif.: AK Press, 2006), 129 and n. 9 (source: Weatherman veteran Naomi Jaffe, 7/31/03); Wilkerson, *Flying Close to the Sun*, 343; David Barber, *A Hard Rain Fell: SDS and Why It Failed* (Jackson: University Press of Mississippi, 2008), 216; Mark Rudd, *Underground: My Life with SDS and the Weathermen* (New York: William Morrow, 2009), 194. The target and character of the townhouse bombs were first made public by Peter Collier and David Horowitz, "Doing It: The Rise and Fall of the Weather Underground," in *Destructive Generation: Second Thoughts about the Sixties*, ed. Collier and Horowitz (New York: Free Press, 1987), 100. Bryan Burrough, *Days of Rage: America's Radical Underground, the FBI, and the Forgotten Age of Revolutionary Violence* (New York: Penguin, 2015), 103 (cf. "Meet the Weather Underground's Bomb Guru," *Vanity Fair*, 3/29/15) mistakes the dance as one for officers. Following Burrough, James Lardner does the same: "The Years of Rage," *New York Review of Books*, 9/24/15, p. 62.

6. Felt-Miller Box 251, File "A.M.," SAC Chicago to Acting Director, 2/21/73, pp. 6–7 (source: a friend of Machtinger's father, Harry); ibid., Report of Special Agent L. McWilliams on Howard Norton Machtinger," 11/23/71, p. 5 (same source).

7. Robbins's father: Thomas Power, *Diana: The Making of a Terrorist* (New York: Houghton Mifflin, 1971), 188. FBI unsure even in May: "Weatherfug Files," DocID 59162728, p. 75: Gale to DeLoach, 5/4/70, p. 1.

8. "Weatherfug Files," DocID 59162728, p. 68 = Special Agent in Charge, San Francisco, to Director, 5/4/70, Thomas Ayers, Jr., Interview, 3. The interview took place on 4/30/70.

9. Communiqué No. 1: A Declaration of War, 5/21/70, in *Sing A Battle Song: The Revolutionary Poetry, Statements, and Communiqués of the Weather Underground, 1970–1974*, ed. Bernardine Dohrn, Bill Ayers, and Jeff Jones (New York: Seven Stories, 2006), 150.

10. The nomenclature can be a bit confusing. The group was originally called "Weatherman" or "the Weathermen," or later (early 1970) "the Weatherman Underground," but late in 1970 it changed its name to "the Weather Underground Organization" (WUO), dropping "-man" to avoid implications of sexism: see Jonah Raskin, "Introduction to 'The Weather Eye'" (1974), in Dohrn, Ayers, and Jones, *Sing a Battle Song*, 136. For simplicity's sake I will generally refer to the organization as "Weatherman," and members of Weatherman or WUO, of either gender,

as "Weathermen," since "Weatherpeople" is awkward English, as is "Weatherwoman." People within the group used the term "Weathermen" for both genders: see Shin'ya Ono, "You Do Need a Weatherman" (originally in *Leviathan*, December 1969), rpt. in *Weatherman*, ed. Hal Jacobs (San Francisco: Rampart, 1970), passim.

11. Jonah Raskin, "Looking Backward: Personal Reflections on Language, Gesture and Mythology in the Weather Underground," in Dohrn, Ayers, and Jones, *Sing a Battle Song*, 123–124 (a slightly different essay from the version published in *Socialism and Democracy*; see Introduction, note 4).

12. All quotations are from Weather Underground Communiqué, "New Morning—Changing Weather," in Dohrn, Ayers, and Jones, *Sing a Battle Song*, 163–164. The firebombing reference is to the attack on Judge John J. Murtaugh, presiding over "the Panther 21" trial in New York City, on February 21, 1970 (on which, see below, page oo).

13. Bill Ayers, *Fugitive Days: Memoirs of an Antiwar Activist* (Boston: Beacon, 2001), 205–206; Robbins insane: see below, p. oo and n. 14.

14. All quotations are from Varon, *Bringing the War Home*, 172–174. Ayers's depiction of John Jacobs as Charles Whitman, the man in the Texas Tower: p. 173 and note 117.

15. Ibid., 172; cf. 180 (Ayers in the countryside: *Fugitive Days*, 1–3). Varon at one point (180) does wonder whether Ayers in his own mind made Robbins into a demon.

16. Thai Jones, *A Radical Line* (New York: Free Press, 2004), 217.

17. Berger, *Outlaws of America*, 127–131.

18. Tom Hayden, *The Long Sixties: From 1960 to Barack Obama* (Boulder, Colo.: Paradigm, 2009), 115–116. Hayden adds (116) that he is not trying to demonize anybody.

19. Personal communication 5/14/13. *The Way the Wind Blew* originally gave no source for this information.

20. Marion Banhaf, "Interview with Alan Berkman, M.D., Part II," 5/5/01, p. 8. Berkman later went to prison for administering to the Nyack bank robbers. I thank Susan Reverby for access to this important document.

21. Cathy Wilkerson's review of *Fugitive Days* can be accessed from the SDS Home Page: http://www.sds-1960s.org/Wilkerson.htm.

22. One must note that Wilkerson herself had an intimate relationship with Robbins during the late 1969 and early 1970; Wilkerson, *Flying Close to the Sun*, 324–326.

23. "FBI "Weatherfug Files," DocID 59262728, p. 68: SAC San Francisco to Director, 5/4/70, Tim Ayers interview, 4/30/70, p. 3.

24. Wilkinson interview: Berger, *Outlaws of America*, 130; Jonathan Lerner, "I Was a Terrorist," *Washington Post*, 3/3/02.

25. Wilkerson, *Flying Close to the Sun*, 342.

26. This is all the more so if Ayers actually visited the Townhouse Collective in the week before the explosion—as is asserted by Burrough, *Days of Rage*, 103 (with no source named).

27. Oughton was Ayers's girlfriend: Ayers, *Fugitive Days*, 1–3, cf. 206. Oughton's collective as fanatical as the townhouse's: Wilkerson, *Flying Close to the Sun*, 342. Nancy Rudd says that Oughton in January 1970 led in the harsh weeding out of "the weak" in Detroit in preparation for going to guerrilla war: Karin Latimer FBI material (100-65559), file 309, pp. 195–196: Nancy Rudd Interview, 5/25/73, pp. 4–5. This file was released to the public on June 13, 2012.

28. Wilkerson, *Flying Close to the Sun*, Appendix: Terry Robbins, 399–404; cf., e.g., 338; Carl Oglesby, *Ravens in the Storm: A Personal History of the 1960s Anti-War Movement* (New York: Scribner, 2008), 288.

29. Wilkerson, *Flying Close to the Sun*, 334.

30. Barber, *A Hard Rain Fell*, 213–218.

31. Howard Machtinger, "You Say You Want a Revolution," *In These Times*, 2/18/09, accessed online at http://www.inthesetimes.com/article/4251/you_say_you_want_a_revolution.

32. Rudd, *Underground*, 194–195.

33. Ron Fliegelman interview with the author, 9/23/13. Fliegelman was one of the thirteen Weatherman leaders indicted for bombing by a Detroit federal grand jury on July 23, 1970; he has a child with Cathy Wilkerson.

34. Rudd, *Underground*, 214–215.

35. "JJ was a soldier": Ron Jacobs, personal communication, 3/15/13. JJ's later life: Kevin Gilles, "The Last Radical," *Vancouver Magazine*, November 1998.

36. Burrough, *Days of Rage*, 93 (Lerner interview).

37. Spiegel interview in Luca Falciola, "Pathways of an 'Early' De-Escalation: The Case of the Weather Underground Organization," ECPR General Conference, Sciences Po Bordeaux, September 2013, http://ecpr.eu/filestore/paperproposal/8bc2655b-28b2-4d8e-b6c9-5555bac1400f.pdf, 5.

38. *New York Post*, 3/29/15.

39. Felt-Miller, Box 103, "Plans to Deal w/WUO," File 3: Tolson to Director, 2/24/69.

40. Felt-Miller, Box 141, File "Bernadine Dohrn—EM Documents," Chicago Field Office memorandum on Bernardine Dohrn, 22 and 28.

41. FBI complaints about lack of informants: see, e.g., Felt-Miller, Box 103, File 4 of 4, "Plans to deal with WUO," Hoover to all SACs, 9/4/70, or 10/20/71; or Box 195, file "Trial Preps—No Foreign Involvement," W. V. Cleveland to Felt, 7/3/72. Weather leadership knowledge of success in weeding out informants: Felt-Miller, Box 251, File "A. M.," Howard Machtinger letter, 10/16/73, p. 2.

42. Felt-Miller, Box 315, Trial Transcript, Grathwohl Cross-Examination, 3625–3626.

43. Weatherman provided this account of Grathwohl's Weatherman career to the *Berkeley Tribe*, 6/12/70—with a warning that Grathwohl might now be in the Bay Area.

44. Larry Grathwohl, as told to Frank Reagan, *Bringing Down America: An FBI Informer with the Weathermen* (New Rochelle, N.Y.: Arlington House, 1976). Heavy editing and rewriting by others: Felt-Miller Box 315, Trial Transcript, Grathwohl Re-direct Testimony, 3673–3674.

45. The prosecution attempt to prevent Grathwohl from testifying: Felt-Miller Box 315, Bench Conference, 10/10/80, pp. 3511–3537.

46. Felt-Miller, Box 250, File "WUO," SAC San Francisco to Director, 10/1/17, pp. 1, 3, 5. The name of the informant is blacked out on the document, but it is clear from the description of his career (Cincinnati, Detroit, Buffalo) that it is Grathwohl who is being interviewed.

47. Karen Latimer FBI File (100-453446; docID 59161310), interview 4/14–15/77, p. 4. This file became publicly available for the first time on June 13, 2012.

48. Felt-Miller, Box 315, Grathwholh Cross-Examination, 3577.

49. Ibid. pp. 3658–3659. On the original events, see John Hersey, *The Algiers Motel Incident* (1968; Baltimore: Johns Hopkins University Press, 1998). The acquittal, 2/26/70: Thomas Sugrue, Introduction, ibid., xiv. The DPOA was indeed involved in the defense of the Algiers Motel policemen: see ibid., xviii.

50. Felt-Miller, Box 315, Grathwohl Direct Testimony, 3562–3563; this conversation is repeated on Redirect at 3695–3696. No warning to be given: 3563.

51. Ibid., 3563–3564. On Special Agent Madden and his activities in Madison, see Tom Bates, *Rads: The 1970 Bombing of the Army Math Research Center at the University of Wisconsin* (New York: Harper Collins, 1992), 209; cf. 339, 342, 349.

52. Felt-Miller, Box 315, Grathwohl Direct Testimony, 3577–3578. Ayers's accusation: *San Francisco Chronicle*, 1/25/09. Ayers has recently taken to claiming that Grathwohl wasn't even in Weatherman (*Megyn Kelly Show*, Fox News, 6/30/14), which is clearly untrue, since Weatherman leaders in June 1970 told the *Berkeley Tribe* the details of Grathwohl's Weatherman career (see n. 43).

53. Latimer File, 12–19, interview 4/14–15/77; Felt-Miller, Box 251, File "Dohrn II": "Report on Bernardine Dohrn," 1/10/75, Cover Pages HH–II. pp. 3998–3999. Machtinger: Felt-Miller Box 312, Trial Transcript, Vermeersch Re-Direct Testimony, 1919. Weather Bureau meetings: Latimer File, 17: "Report on Interview with Karen Latimer," 4/27/77, pp. 5–6. The address Latimer alleges the Weather Bureau met—331 Madrone Avenue, Larkspur (3)—is real enough: Latimer File, 181.

54. The FBI thought Bergman was a Chinese Communist agent; the phone was tapped; a hidden microphone had been installed; and the house was

under physical observation: Felt-Miler Box 316, Prosecution-Defense Stipulation, 4000, 4004–4005. Latimer's arrest on March 4: Latimer File, 213 (Department of Justice copy of Latimer arrest record). Bernardine Dohrn's doctor: Latimer File, 160.

55. Felt-Miller, Box 316, Defense-Prosecution Stipulation, 3999. Latimer said that the bomb was made not at the Berkeley house (where the FBI—unknown to her—would have overheard it) but at a Weatherman safe house in Larkspur in Marin County: Latimer file, 180, Director to SACs, 1/1/75, p. 3.

56. Felt-Miller 316, Trial Transcript, Special Agent William Regan Direct Testimony, 10/17/80, p. 4386.

57. Latimer File, 43: SAC NY to Director, 1/2/75; Latimer File, 4–5: SAC Los Angeles to SAC San Francisco, 12/11/80, p. 2 (retrospective).

58. Former FBI Special Agent William Reagan, *Megyn Kelly Show*, Fox News, 7/1/14.

59. Anthony Bottom: Latimer File, 180: Director to SACs, 1/1/75, p. 2.

60. In a 1976 history of Weatherman prepared by the FBI for Attorney General Edward H. Levi, that Weatherman did Park Station is presented simply as a fact: Felt-Miller, Box 195, File "AG Authorization for Weatherman Investigation," SAC Chicago to Director and SACs, 6/8/76: "Weather Underground Organization," pp. 4–5. Burrough, *Days of Rage*, 96–97, comes close to indicting Weatherman for Park Station—neglecting to inform his readers that a BLA soldier confessed to doing it.

61. The finding of the Detroit bombs on the morning of March 6: Felt-Miller, Box 249, File "Weatherman II (M)," Detroit SAC to Director, 6/26/70, pp. 8–9. Grathwohl then in Madison: Felt-Miller Box 315, Trial Transcript, Grathwohl Direct Testimony, 3564. Grathwohl was in touch with Madden the morning after his arrival in Madison: *Bringing Down America*, 156.

62. The second informant is referred to in Felt-Miller Box 249, File "Weatherman II (M)," Assistant Attorney General (Criminal Division) Will Wilson to Hoover, 5/21/70, p. 1; Assistant Attorney General J. Walter Yeagley (Internal Security Division) to Hoover, 5/25/70. This person then disappears.

63. Felt-Miller Trial material, Box 249, File "Weatherman II," Hoover to Special Agents in Charge, "Students for a Democratic Society (SDS)," Boston, Chicago, Cincinnati, Cleveland, Denver, Detroit, Milwaukee, New York, San Francisco, and Seattle, 3/12/70, pp. 1, 3–4.

64. Felt-Miller Box 102, File "Plans to Deal w/WUO," 3 of 4, Director to SACs, 3/19/70, pp. 1–3; also in Latimer Filer, NW 5675, DocId 59161305, pp. 95–97.

65. Felt-Miller, Box 134, File "Not on 5/5 list (Weatherman Information), 1 of 2," Director to Mitchell, 4/9/70, pp. 1–2.

66. Wilson's concern about Ayers: Felt-Miller Box 249, File "Weatherman II (M)," Wilson to Hoover, 4/10/70, pp. 3 and 4. Wilson's background: see

W. Wilson, *A Fool for a Client: Richard Nixon's Freefall towards Impeachment* (Waco, Tex.: Eakin, 2000). Wilson's hatred of antiwar protestors is discussed in John Gerassi, "Lutte armée aux États Unis (1970)," *Les Temps modernes,* May 1970.

67. Wilson's focus on Detroit: see his detailed memorandum to Hoover on witness arrangement for Department of Justice attorney Guy Goodwin's visit to Detroit, Box 249, File "Weatherman II (M)," 5/21/70. The scandal in November 1971: Wilson, *A Fool for a Client,* xi.

68. Box 103, Plans to deal with WUO," File 1 of 4, "Special Study: Bombings and Arsons in the United States," June 1970, esp. pp. 17–18. Outside the Bureau: see ibid., Rosen to Sullivan, 8/4/70 (to Joseph Ross, Office of the Deputy Attorney General).

69. Felt-Miller, Box 102, File 1 of 4 "Plans to Handle WUO," Brennan to Sullivan, "New Left Violence," 4/1/70, pp. 1, 4. Cf. also Brennan to Sullivan, 4/1/70, "Conference ... Handling of Bombing Matters," 4/1/70, p. 2. Brennan was head of the FBI Internal Security Section, and Assistant Director Sullivan, the head of the Domestic Intelligence Division, was his boss.

70. Felt-Miller Box 102, "Plans to Deal with WUO," File 3 of 4, Sullivan to DeLoach, 4/14/70, "Bombing Matters," pp. 1–2. For Detroit and New York (plus Chicago), see also ibid., Brennan to Sullivan, 4/15/70, p. 2. FBI concern over the nationwide scope of the menace: see also Box 102, Folder "Plans to Deal with WUO," File 1 of 4, J. A. Sizoo (a senior figure in the Research Section) to Sullivan, 6/11/70, p. 1.

71. Box 102, "Plans to Deal with WUO," File 1 of 4, "FBI Special Report: Nationwide Civil Disturbances, 1969–1970" (May 21, 1970), p. 13.

72. Box 103, "Plans to Deal w/WUO" (last file): "Bombings and Arsons in the United States," pp. 18–19.

73. FBI interrogations of Weathermen Sam Karp, Joe Kelly, Russell Neufeld, and Robert Tomaschevsky about Detroit: Felt-Miller Box 115, "Misc. Newsclippings," SAC Chicago to Director, 6/4/70, p. 3.

74. Box 102, "Plans to Deal with WUO," File 1 of 4, Brennan to Sullivan, 9/21/70, p. 3.

75. Box 102, File 2 of 4, "Plans to Deal with WUO": "FBI Special Report: 1970: Year of the Urban Guerrilla," p. 4; Box 102, File 3 of 4, "Plans to Deal with WUO," R. D. Cotter (of the Research Section) to Edward Miller (of Domestic Intelligence), ibid., 9/29/71.

76. Box 106, File "230 A-R ... Nixon/AG": "Profile of Urban Guerrilla Activity: Groups, Leaders, Incidents," 11/22/71, p. 4.

77. Box 102, File 3 of 4, "Plans to Deal with WUO": "FBI Special Report: The Urban Guerrilla in the United States" (2/29/72), p. 6.

78. Box 249, File "WUO III," Training Program for new Special Agents, "New Left Terrorist Groups," p. 3.

79. Interview with Jack Kearney (Society of Former Special Agents of the FBI), 1/25/06, p. 66.
80. The other two actions in the summary on the Weatherman threat are the townhouse explosion (noted to have occurred on the same day as Detroit) and the attack on New York Police Department Headquarters, which had occurred on June 9: *Senate Select Committee to Study Governmental Operations with Respect to Intelligence Activities*, vol. 2, *The Huston Plan*, 149, Committee Exhibit 1: Huston Plan, 4.
81. See *Detroit Free Press*, 3/7/70, *Chicago Tribune*, 3/17/70, 5/27/70.
82. George Lardner, Jr., "Weathermen Indicted as Terrorists," *Washington Post*, 7/24/70. Wilson was referring to overt acts 14 and 15 in the grand jury indictment. The indictment can be found in, e.g., Box 191, Felt-Miller Trial material, File "Violence by WUO #45."
83. The June 25 interview with the Michigan State trooper is found in Felt-Miller Box 249, File "Weatherman II (M)," SAC Detroit to Director, 6/16/70, pp. 13–16.
84. Ayers, *Fugitive Days*, 198–199.
85. Ibid. On the cigarette fuses, see Felt-Miller Trial material, Box 102, "Plans to Deal with WUO," file 2 of 4, "FBI Special Report: 1970: Year of the Urban Guerrilla" (April 1971), p. 4; Grathwohl, *Bringing Down America*, 144.
86. See Ayers, *Fugitive Days*, 286–304, an entire chapter called "Memory," with many examples of his failure to remember events and people that he agrees he should have.
87. See Stephen B. Oates, *To Purge This Land with Blood: A Biography of John Brown* (Boston: University of Massachusetts Press, 1970).
88. Jonah Raskin, *Outside the Whale: Growing Up in the American Left* (New York: Links, 1974), 142.
89. See Berger, *Outlaws of America*, 205–207.
90. Bernardine Dohrn, Jeff Jones, and Cellia Sojourn [pseud.], *Prairie Fire: The Politics of Revolutionary Anti-Imperialism: Political Statement of the Weather Underground* (San Francisco: Red Dragon, 1974), 4; cf. Berger, *Outlaws of America*, 122.
91. Laura Whitehorn Interview, 1/8/13, in Falciola, "Weather Underground Organization," 6. Jonathan Lerner interview, 1/15/13: ibid. Latimer statement: Latimer File, 197, SAC New York to Director, 12/16/74, p. 1.
92. Judy Cohen and ROTC: Felt-Miller Box 316, Trial Transcript, Prosecution-Defense Stipulation, 10/16/80, p. 4007. Judy Cohen had led violent demonstrators into this ROTC building in September 1969: Box 251, File "Flatley," SAC Milwaukee to Director, 3/26/70. Cohen and Armory: Felt-Miller Box 313, Trial Transcript, Special Agent James Weaver Cross-Examination, 10/2/80, pp. 2448, cf. 2452. The Milwaukee bombings appeared in a supplementary grand jury indictment of Weatherman figures in 1972: *New York Times*, 12/1/72; cf. Felt-Miller,

Box 251, File "Dohrn II (ESM)," handwritten note appended to Acting Director to SAC Milwaukee, 12/26/72. On the basis of interviews, Burrough, *Days of Rage*, 116–117, claims that this group did nothing; that is belied by the FBI files and the stipulations at the 1980 trial.

93. Susan Stern, *With the Weathermen: The Personal Story of a Revolutionary Woman* (1975; Rutgers, N.J.: Rutgers University Press, 2007), 221.

94. Burrough, *Days of Rage*, 92–97 (interviews, especially with Howie Machtinger). Burrough claims this is a previously unknown Weatherman action; not so: see Senate Hearings, 1975.

95. The most detailed account of the February 21 action is John M. Murtaugh, "Fire in the Night: The Weathermen Tried to Kill My Family," in *City Paper*, 4/30/08. Murtaugh is the son of the judge.

96. See Murray Kempton, *The Briar Patch: The People of New York v. Lumumba Shakur et al.* (New York: Dutton, 1973), 120–121.

97. "New Morning," 123–124. Kopkind's plea: "The Radical Bombers," *Hard Times*, 3/23/70, rpt. in Jacobs, *Weatherman*, 496–503 (quotation at 501). The same point was made three months later by the four ex-Weatherman authors of "It's Only People's Games You Have to Dodge," rpt. in Jacobs, *Weatherman*, 421–439. Kopkind close to the Weather people: on the evening of the townhouse explosion a friend of the survivors came to him for help, which he gave: "Which Way the Wind Blew," *Real Paper* 1/5/80, rpt. in *The Thirty Years Wars: Dispatches and Diversions of a Radical Journalist, 1965–1994*, ed. Andrew Kopkind and JoAnn Wypijewski (London: Verso, 1995), 228.

98. Burrough, *Days of Rage*, 100 (interviews). Strikingly, Bill Ayers now denies that the Murtaugh bombing *was* a Weatherman action, and when confronted with the declaration in "New Morning," says: "I didn't write it": *Megyn Kelly Show*, Fox News, 6/30/14. But it appears in the compendium of Weatherman material that Ayers himself coedited in 2006: *Sing a Battle Song*, 123–124.

99. Felt-Miller, Box 141, File "Violence by WUO #45," Daniel A. Piloseno (Special Litigations, Internal Security Div. of Dept. of Justice) to Guy L. Goodwin (Chief of Special Litigations), 10/6/72: "Summary of Statements made by Mr. and Mrs. A, Sept. 20, 1972," pp. 2–5. This material is in the Felt-Miller files because the FBI later engaged in break-ins into the home of Judy Cohen's parents—part of the federal charges against Felt and Miller. It seems that "Mr. and Mrs. A" are Lawrence D. Gondek and Mary Lou Gondek: Felt-Miller, Box 251, File "Flatley," Special Agent Raymond S. Byrne report (handwritten).

100. "Summary of Statements by Mr. and Mrs. A," 4–5.

101. Ibid., 5. The attack: see, e.g., Felt-Miller Box 251, File "Dohrn II (ESM)," handwritten note appended to Acting Director to SAC Milwaukee, 12/26/72.

102. "Summary of Statements by Mr. and Mrs. A," 7–8.

103. For Milwaukee: Box 251, File "Flatley" (i.e., Judith Cohen Flatley), Report of Special Agent Albert J. Ellis, 8/8/72, p. 9. For Fuerst see below and n. 104. On Zilzel, see Burrough, *Days of Rage*, 99; Handelsman: ibid., 373 For Emmer: see Felt–Miller, Box 250, File "Rudd," SAC Cleveland to Director, 11/12/69, p. 12.

104. The telephone numbers: Felt-Miller, Box 250, File "Fuerst/Smith," Report of Special Agent Gordon Hess, 7/21/70, interview with Mrs. Ida Smith, 4/13/70, p. 9; ibid., File "Fuerst/Smith," John Allen Fuerst File, 11/13/70, list of calls, and last page. The Chicago apartment: Felt-Miller, Box 141, Piloseno to Goodwin, 10/6/72: "Summary of Statements made by Mr. and Mrs. A, Sept. 20, 1972," 9 (comment by Piloseno). Professor Lefkowitz: Felt-Miller Box 250, File "Flatley," Report of Special Agent Albert Ellis, 8/8/72, p. 7.

105. Ahmad Evans: Power, *Diana*, 137, and Weatherman Underground communiqué no. 3, "Honk Amerika," 7/25/70, in Dohrn, Ayers, and Jones, *Sing a Battle Song*, 152–153; cf. Felt-Miller Box 141, File "Bernardine Dohrn—EM Documents," p. 52.

106. On the June 5, 1969, riot and its brutal aftermath, see Joan Crowell, *Fort Dix Stockade: Our Prison Camp Next Door* (New York: Links, 1974), 1–18.

107. Early demonstrations: ibid., 19, 26. For the racial aspect, see http://www.sirnosir.com/archives_and_resources/library/pamphlets_publications/ft_dix_38_speak_out/cover.html and the poster announcing the October 1969 demonstration: http://www.sirnosir.com/archives_and_resources/library/pamphlets_publications/flyers/free_ft_dix_38.html.

108. The Weathermen's involvement in the autumn Fort Dix demonstration is set out in great detail in Ono, "You Do Need a Weatherman," 241–249, with an ideological commentary (originally written in November 1969). Ono's account has been ignored in studies of the townhouse project the next March.

109. Ibid., 246–249; Crowell, *Fort Dix Stockade*, 37–39, discusses the Weatherman involvement in the autumn demonstration from the hostile perspective of other radical organizers.

110. Crowell, *Fort Dix Stockade*, 39—a major concession missing from Shin'ya Ono's account of these discussions.

111. Ibid., 39; cf. 41 (a few asked on the night before the demonstration).

112. The October 12 demonstration: ibid., 43. Harassment: ibid., 32–36; the final hand grenade attack: 36.

113. Eldridge Cleaver, "On Weatherman," *Berkeley Tribe*, 11/7/69; rpt. in Jacobs, *Weatherman*, 294.

Chapter Two. "We Sentence the Government to Death"

1. The list is from Jeremy Varon, *Bringing the War Home* (Berkeley: University of California Press, 2004), 5.

2. The lure of publicity: Todd Gitlin, *The Whole World Is Watching: Mass Media in the Making and Unmaking of the New Left* (Berkeley: University of California Press, 1980), 190; cf. Richard Boyd, "Representing Political Violence: The Mainstream Media and the Weatherman 'Days of Rage,' " *American Studies 41* (2000), 146. Apocalyptism: Peter Marin, "The Weathermen, Twenty Years On," *Harper's*, December 1987; cf. Varon, *Bringing the War Home*, 18, 20. The lure of personal heroism: Christopher Lasch, *The Agony of the American Left* (New York: Random House, 1969), 180, cf. 182. Toxic masculine assertion: Jane Alpert, "Mother-Right: A New Feminist Theory," *Ms.*, August 1973; Robin Morgan, *The Demon Lover: On the Sexuality of Terrorism* (New York: Norton, 1990), esp. chap. 2 and chap. 5 (whose title—"Wargasm"—is taken from a Weatherman slogan); Cathy Wilkerson's view: in Bryan Burrough, "Meet the Weather Underground's Bomb Guru," *Vanity Fair*, 3/29/15 (Wilkerson interview). The (disputed) disturbed personal psychology of Terry Robbins and/or John Jacobs: see Chapter 1.

3. James K. Glassman, "SDS in Chicago," *Atlantic*, December 1969, pp. 38–40; "Chicago: Poor Climate for Weathermen," *Time*, 10/17/69, p. 24; with the commentary of Boyd, "Representing Political Violence," 149–150; Stanley Rothman and S. Robert Lichter, *Roots of Radicalism: Jews, Christians, and the New Left* (Oxford University Press, 1982), 139.

4. Mel Gussow, "West Eleventh Street: The End of Innocence," *New York*, 3/8/71; Thomas Power, *Diana: The Making of a Terrorist* (New York: Houghton Mifflin, 1971), 169–170, complete with psychological analysis, and 180–182, with another psychological analysis.

5. Milton Viorst, *Fire in the Streets: America in the 1960s* (New York: Simon and Schuster, 1979), 481; Matthew Carr, *The Infernal Machine: A History of Terrorism from the Assassination of Tsar Alexander II to Al-Qaeda* (New York: New Press, 2006), 160. Luca Falciola, "Pathways of an 'Early' De-Escalation: The Case of the Weather Underground Organization," ECPR General Conference, Sciences Po Bordeaux, September 2013, http://ecpr.eu/filestore/paperproposal/8bc2655b-28b2-4d8e-b6c9-5555bac1400f.pdf, 7, 14; Harvey Klehr, "The Old Terrorists" (review of Bryan Burrough, *Days of Rage: America's Radical Underground, the FBI, and the Forgotten Age of Revolutionary Violence* [New York: Penguin, 2015]), *Commentary*, September 2015, p. 62.

6. *Seattle Times*, 6/11/74; cf. Susan Stern, *With the Weathermen: The Personal Story of a Revolutionary Woman* (1975; Rutgers, N.J.: Rutgers University Press, 2007), 374.

7. Many FBI agents told themselves that Weatherman was the product of "privilege run amok—'spoiled kids' ": David Cunningham, *There's Something Happening Here: The New Left, the Klan, and FBI Counter-intelligence* (Berkeley: University of California Press, 2004), 169–170. Senator Russell Long of Louisiana said the same thing on the Senate

floor: J. Kirkpatrick Sale, *SDS* (New York: Random House, 1974), 375. But Weatherman is also dismissed on these grounds as inconsequential by a left-wing academic who was close to them in 1969–1970: personal communication, 7/18/13.

8. Jacobs: interview with Toni Hart (Wellman), close friend of Jacobs, 8/5/14.

9. On how the collective got to use the townhouse, see Cathy Wilkerson, *Flying Close to the Sun* (New York: Seven Stories, 2007), 332–333. James Wilkerson was reluctant to let his daughter use it; ibid., 332. Robbins: ibid., 399; Ted Gold's father was a physician, but the family had experienced economic hardship because of the father's left-wing political beliefs: *Time*, 3/23/70.

10. On Mellen, see Varon, *Bringing the War Home*, 35; Jones: see Thai Jones, *A Radical Line* (New York: Free Press, 2004), 133–134; Jaffe's social origins: Dan Berger, *Outlaws of America: The Weather Underground and the Politics of Solidarity* (Oakland, Calif.: AK Press, 2006), 312.

11. On Machtinger's family, see Felt-Miller, Box 251, File "A. M.," SAC Chicago to Acting Director, 2/21/73, pp. 6–7. On Justesen's family, see Felt-Miller, Box 106, File "IS-2 Documents to be Destroyed (5) [Weathfug]," Acting Director to SACs Baltimore and Seattle, 1/24/73, p. 2. Clark: Judy Clark Affidavit (http://judithclark.org/docs/legal/affidavit.pdf), 12/11/02, p. 2.

12. Cohen: Felt-Miller Box 313, Cohen Motion to Quash, 10, and John Nields, interview with the author, 5/14/14; Russell Neufeld: interview with the author, 11/16/13; Dohrn's father: Carr, *Infernal Machine*, 160 (not noticing that he is contradicting his previous statement about privilege).

13. Mark Rudd and David Gilbert were in various ways upper middle class, but they did not have access to the kind of wealth that Nicholas von Hoffman, Thomas Power, or Matthew Carr are talking about. Gilbert could remember that when he was a child the family had a hard time making ends meet: *Love and Struggle: My Life in SDS, the Weather Underground, and Beyond* (Oakland, Calif.: PM, 2012), 14. Jonathan Lerner's father was a foreign service officer, but with four children, money was tight, "so we had Chevrolets … no glamorous vacations" (personal communication, 10/1/13). Linda Evans's father was a building contractor in tiny Fort Dodge, Iowa; she went to college on a scholarship (Susan Reverby, interview with the author, 3/13/16). Of the two Weathermen interviewed in Rothman and Lichter, *Roots of Radicalism*, one was lower middle class in origin (304, 305), the other blue-collar (308).

14. Stephen Spender defines radicalization as the situation where—whatever your political position is—you discover that the position to your left is far more correct: *The Year of the Young Rebels* (New York: Vintage, 1968), 18.

15. Oglesby's worries: Carl Oglesby, "1969," in *Weatherman*, ed. Hal Jacobs (San Francisco: Rampart, 1970), 126–131. "We lived on ideas": Rudd, "Che and Me," http://www.markrudd.com (2008), p. 4; Wilkerson and Spiegel in 1968–1969: Larry Gray, personal communication, 8/5/13. The Marxism-Leninism of Weatherman is also emphasized, e.g., by Naomi Jaffe, in her reaction to the 2003 documentary *The Weather Underground*: http://www.upstatefilms.org/weather/jaffe.html.

16. On the founding of SDS, see Maurice Isserman, *If I Had a Hammer: The Death of the Old Left and the Birth of the New* (New York: Basic, 1987). On the complex relationship between the unions, the LID, and SDS, see Paul Berman, *A Tale of Two Utopias: The Political Journey of the 1968 Generation* (New York: Norton, 1996), 65–75.

17. On the clash over admitting communists, see Berman, *A Tale of Two Utopias*, 66–69; Sale, *SDS*, 236–240.

18. Student groups often reach out from campus: Lewis Feuer, *The Conflict of Generations: The Character and Significance of Student Movements* (New York: Basic, 1969), 8–9. On the ERAP experience, see Sale, *SDS*, chapters 7 and 9; Wini Breines, *Community and Organization in the New Left, 1962–1968: The Great Refusal* (Rutgers, N.J.: Rutgers University Press, 1982), chapter 7. Focus on working-class youth: Richard Rothstein, "Chicago: JOIN Project," *Studies on the Left*, Summer 1965, pp. 113–115.

19. On the impact of Vietnam on SDS ideology and the spectacular growth of the organization, see Sale, *SDS*, chapters 12–19, esp. 151–161. Exact membership numbers are unknown because SDS could not keep track of all the data that flooded in: personal communication with Larry Gray, 4/1/13, 6/4/13; Gray worked in the SDS National Office in this period.

20. Max Elbaum, *Revolution in the Air: Sixties Radicals Turn to Lenin, Mao, and Che (London: Verso, 2002)*, 43. See the insightful comments of Roberta T. Ash, "Review of Feuer, *The Conflict of Generations*," *School Review* 79 (1970): 143, 145.

21. Paul Sweezy and Paul Baran, *Monopoly Capital: An Essay on the American Economic Order* (New York: Monthly Review Press, 1966); quotation: Power, *Diana*, x. On Marxism's power to explain confusing and disparate phenomena, see, e.g., Jeffrey Herf, "The New Left: Reflections and Reconsiderations," in *Political Passages: Journeys of Change Through Two Decades, 1968–1988*, ed. John H. Bunzel (New York: Macmillan, 1988), writing of his personal experience in the mid-sixties SDS.

22. See Tom Hayden, *Rebellion in Newark* (New York: Vintage, 1967), 68–70; David Barber, *A Hard Rain Fell: SDS and Why It Failed* (Jackson: University Press of Mississippi, 2008), 33–35; cf. Varon, *Bringing the War Home*, 23–25.

23. Vietnam: Carl Oglesby, *Ravens in the Storm: A Personal History of the 1960s Anti-War Movement* (New York: Scribner, 2008), 108–109. Ghetto insurrections: Greg Calvert, in the monthly the *Movement*, December 1967;

quoted in Sale, *SDS*, 261; cf. Barber, *A Hard Rain Fell*, 36–38. See also Todd Gitlin, *The Sixties: Years of Hope, Days of Rage* (1987; New York: Bantam, 1993), 244–245. The fear of an unchanging system: Ash, "Review of *Conflict of Generations*," p. 145.

24. See Sale, *SDS*, 248–254. Commemoration: *Fire!* November 7, 1969, lead editorial. Government response: Sale, *SDS*, 274.

25. On the succession of sociological "generations" in student movements, see Feuer, *Conflict of Generations*, 25–26.

26. On the growth of vanguard-partyism, see Elinor Langer, "Notes for Next Time: A Memoir of the Sixties," in *Towards a History of the New Left: Essays from Within the Movement*, ed. R. David Myers (Brooklyn, N.Y.: Carlson, 1989); Elbaum, *Revolution in the Air*, 55; cf. Gitlin, *The Sixties*, 383. Impact of PL: see especially Berman, *A Tale of Two Utopias*, 84–89. Impact here of PL combined with, Debray and Fanon, combined with the ghetto insurrections: Greg Calvert, *Democracy from the Heart: Spiritual Values, Decentralism and Democratic Idealism in the Movement of the 1960s* (Manchester, Conn.: Communitas, 1991), 75. First quotation from Lenin in *New Left Notes*: see Sale, *SDS*, 323.

27. PL's traditional Marxism: Sale, *SDS*, 243, On Mills's influence, see Kevin Mattson, *Intellectuals in Action: The Origins of the New Left and Radical Liberalism, 1945–1970* (University Park: Penn State University Press, 2001), chapter 2. On Marcuse, see, e.g., Gitlin, *The Sixties*, 244; Herf, interview, 6/6/15. PL's well-known failure with industrial workers: Sale, *SDS*, 320.

28. See, e.g., Elbaum, *Revolution in the Air*, 23–25.

29. "We were thrilled": Jonathan Lerner, personal communication, 9/30/13.

30. On the Democratic Convention events, see John Schultz, *No One Was Killed: The Democratic National Convention, August 1968* (1969; Chicago: University of Chicago Press, 2008); David Farber, *Chicago '68*, 2nd ed. (Chicago: Chicago University Press, 1994). SDS activists prominent in the demonstrations that week: Schultz, *No One Was Killed*, 70–71, 101, 102, 115, 138, 176; cf. 45. Terry Robbins at Chicago: Bill Ayers, *Fugitive Days: Memoirs of an Antiwar Activist* (Boston: Beacon, 2001), 130–131. Jeff Jones and Cathy Wilkerson at Chicago (Mike Spiegel also): Wilkerson, *Flying Close to the Sun: My Life and Times as a Weatherman* (New York, Seven Stories, 2007), 215–217; John Jacobs and Susan Stern at Chicago: Stern, *With the Weathermen: The Personal Journal of a Revolutionary Woman* (1975; Rutgers, N.J.: Rutgers University Press, 2007), 28–44. Speeches by Dohrn after Chicago, 10/1/68 (Chicago); 10/11/68 (Colorado): *Weather Underground* (Washington, D.C.: U.S. Government Printing Office, 1975).

31. Ex-Weatherman Mark Naison stresses to me that physical presence and attractiveness played a role in the eventual Weatherman leadership: Bernardine Dohrn, Bill Ayers, Jeff Jones, and Mark Rudd were (and remain to this day) very handsome people: Naison interview, 3/21/14.

32. Noel Ignatin interview in Barber, *A Hard Rain Fell*, 239, n. 63. Noel Ignatiev, "Learn the Lessons of U.S. History," *New Left Notes*, 3/25/68; Michael Klonsky, "Towards a Revolutionary Youth Movement," *New Left Notes*, 12/12/68. Analysis: Barber, *A Hard Rain Fell*, 40–42; Sale, *SDS*, 338–340.

33. Quoted in Rothstein, "Chicago: JOIN Project," 113–115. See also Gilbert, *Love and Struggle*, 130.

34. For Jeff Jones's opinion of John Jacobs as an intellectual, see Kevin Gillies, "The Last Radical," *Vancouver Magazine*, November 1998. On the influence of Gilbert's "Port Authority Statement," see Sale, *SDS*, 338–340.

35. Mere actionists and anarchists: see the contemporary worry of James Weinstein, "Weatherman: A Lot of Thunder and a Short Reign," *Socialist Revolution*, January–February 1970, rpt. in Jacobs, *Weatherman*, 385; so, too, Barber, *A Hard Rain Fell*, 148–149.

36. Robbins's dark intensity: interviews with Toni Hart (Wellman; 8/5/14), Larry Gray (2/13/15), and Lonnie Wolf (5/15/15); Robbins spoke with a strong New York accent (Wolf).

37. On Mellen in Tanzania and its impact, see John Gerassi, "Lutte armeé aux Etats Unis (1970)," *Les Temps modernes*, May 1970. Mellen's "third worldism": Mellen interview with Viorst, in *Fire in the Streets*, 471–472. His dissertation was published as *Foreign Activities of the AFL-CIO* (Iowa City: University of Iowa Press, 1967).

38. Feminism: Bernardine Dohrn and Naomi Jaffe (herself soon to be a significant Weatherman figure), "The Look Is You," *New Left Notes*, 3/28/68—the first feminist essay in *NLN*. The paper on the "intellectual working class" was also influential: Sale, *SDS*, 305, 313.

39. See, e.g., Peter Collier and David Horowitz, "Doing It: The Rise and Fall of the Weather Underground," in *Destructive Generation: Second Thoughts about the Sixties*, ed. Collier and Horowitz (New York: Free Press, 1987), 73–76.

40. See Oglesby, *Ravens in the Storm*, 122–127.

41. On the elections, see Sale, *SDS*, 318–319.

42. Klonsky's victory: "Toward a Revolutionary Youth Movement," in *Debate within SDS: RYM II vs. Weatherman*, accessed at http://www.marxists.org/history/erol/ncm-1/debate-sds/rym.htm. Wilkerson's view that "participatory democracy" was now dying: *Flying Close to the Sun*, 257.

43. On growing pessimism about *any* kind of politics, see Oglesby, "1969." On the abandonment of politics for the rural life, see, e.g., Raymond Mungo, *Famous Long Ago: My Life and Hard Times with Liberation News Service, at Total Loss Farm, and on the Dharma Trail* (Boston: Beacon, 1970). Cf. also Timothy Miller, *The 60s Communes: Hippies and Beyond* (Syracuse, N.Y.: Syracuse University Press, 1999), chapters 3 and 4.

44. Listed were Karen Ashley, Bill Ayers, Bernardine Dohrn, John Jacobs, Jeff Jones, Gerry Long, Howie Machtinger, Jim Mellen, Terry Robbins,

Mark Rudd, and Steve Tappis. Length of the document: Berger, *Outlaws of America*, 80.

45. On the conflict in SDS between Progressive Labor and the counterculture, see e.g., Doug Rossinow, " 'The Revolution Is about Our Lives': The New Left's Counterculture," in *Imagine Nation: The American Counterculture of the 1960s and 1970s*, ed. Peter Braunstein and Michael W. Doyle (New York: Routledge, 2002), 100–101.

46. "Weatherman" manifesto, in Jacobs, *Weatherman*, 51–90.

47. On Revolutionary Youth Movement II as allies of Weatherman at this time, see Sale, *SDS*, 591–592. The FBI well understood this alliance: see Felt-Miller Box 133, "Not in 5/5 list [Weatherman]," 1 of 2, Director to SACs, 12/9/69.

48. Stern, *With the Weathermen*, 65 and 67. Stern herself was not yet well schooled in Marxist-Leninist theory and found the Weatherman statement incomprehensibly difficult (65). Machtinger's theorizing on black revolution on the floor of the convention: Felt-Miller Box 251, File "A. M.," SAC Chicago to Acting Director, 2/21/73 (a retrospective report on Machtinger's career), p. 2.

49. For the struggle between Progressive Labor and Weatherman at Chicago, see the excellent contemporary analysis by Andrew Kopkind, "The Real SDS Stands Up," in Jacobs, *Weatherman*, 15–28. Jonathan Lerner, "I Was a Terrorist," *Washington Post*, 3/3/02, claims that he threw out many pro-PL ballots on various motions to make sure that RYM won.

50. On this COINTELPRO tactic see, above all, Cunningham, *Something Happening Here*, chapter 1 and appendix A; cf. also Barber, *A Hard Rain Fell*, 39 (black militant groups). In general: Nelson Blackstock, *Cointelpro: The FBI's Secret War on Political Freedom* (New York: Pathfinder, 1988). The claims of penetration of the 1968 demonstrations: Schultz, *No One Was Killed*, 204n.

51. Electronic surveillance: Felt-Miller Box 319, Trial Transcript, Mitchell Redirect, October 28, 1980, p. 5773. Informants: Felt-Miller Box 103, File "Plans to Deal with WUO," 3 of 4, Sullivan to DeLoach, 2/20/69; Tolson to Director, 2/24/69.

52. Cleveland SAC to Director, 8/1/69, p. 4. This long FBI document was first shown to me by Aaron Leonard, and historians owe him a debt for discovering it; Aaron was interested in aspects of the document other than the secret FBI support for the National Office faction, which I pointed out to him.

53. The Chicago Field Office had good sources at the convention, and its report is five large-format single-spaced pages long, testifying to the wide extent of infiltration: Felt-Miller, Box 103, File "Weatherman Underground Summary," 8/20/76, pp. 58–62. Mark Rudd, *Underground: My Life with SDS and the Weathermen* (New York: William Morrow, 2009), 152, estimates the famous walkout at six hundred people; Gitlin, *The Sixties*, 388, places it at seven hundred.

54. Cleveland SAC to Director, 8/1/69, p. 4.
55. The Bay Area radical leader Leibel Bergman was close to Weatherman leader Mark Rudd, while Bergman's daughter Randy was living at this point with Weatherman leader Jeff Jones, and the Revolutionary Union leader Bob Avakian was close to Mike Klonsky of RYM II: Felt-Miller, Box 316, Trial Transcript, Special Agent David Ryan Direct Testimony, 3990–3992.
56. See Aaron Leonard, "The FBI and the Shattering of Students for a Democratic Society," in *Truthout*, October 2014.
57. Power, *Diana*, 118. But on continuing Marxism see, for instance, "Stop the Festival of Thieves" (an international financial meeting), *New Left Notes*, 9/12/69 (complete with a nineteenth-century capitalist in top hat, smoking a cigar).
58. See Kathy Boudin, Bernardine Dohrn, and Terry Robbins, "Bringing the War Home: Less Talk, More National Action," *New Left Notes* 8/23/69.
59. Imperial system is crumbling: Bill Ayers at American University, 9/24/69, reported in Felt-Miller, Box 248, FBI Report "Students for a Democratic Society (SDS)," 11/7/69, p. 97; Shin'ya Ono, "You Do Need a Weatherman," in Jacobs, *Weatherman*, 229, 238, 246. Rudd, "Che and Me," 2. No need for defeatism on the Left: Bill Ayers, "A Strategy to Win," *New Left Notes*, 9/12/69, rpt. in Jacobs, *Weatherman*, 185; Ono, "You Do Need a Weatherman," 234, 235; Weather leader Eric Mann in Felt-Miller, Box 249, File "Weatherman IV": "Inflammatory Statements: Eric Michael Mann" (5/11/69); "The Time Is Right for Violent Revolution," *New Left Notes*, 9/20/69.
60. Pessimism and suicide: Power, *Diana*, 126; or Weinstein, "Weatherman," 386. By contrast, Dohrn's triumphalism in August 1969: Roxanne Dunbar-Ortiz, *Outlaw Woman: A Memoir of the War Years, 1960–1975*, rev. ed. (Norman: University of Oklahoma Press, 2014), 102; similar: Rudd, "Che and Me," 2.
61. Felt-Miller box 248, File "Weatherman I": "FBI Special Report: Students for a Democratic Society (SDS)," p. 115 (depiction of the Cleveland Weatherman national meeting based on informant CG T-1). Similar: Power, *Diana*, 118; Barber, *A Hard Rain Fell*, chapter 5.
62. Regis Debray, *Revolution in the Revolution? Armed Struggle and Political Struggle in Latin America* (New York: Grove, 1967) The powerful impact of Debray's book on the Weathermen is emphasized by Ron Jacobs, *The Way the Wind Blew: A History of the Weather Underground* (New York: Verso, 1997), 34–37; and by Jonah Raskin, "Introduction to 'The Weather Eye'" (1974), in *Sing a Battle Song: The Revolutionary Poetry, Statements, and Communiqués of the Weather Underground, 1970–1974*, ed. Bernardine Dohrn, Bill Ayers, and Jeff Jones (New York: Seven Stories, 2006), 136–137; see also Gitlin, *The Sixties*, 244–245.

63. "Everyone Talks about the Weather ...," pamphlet handed out in December 1969 to cadre at the Flint "War Council," rpt. in Jacobs, *Weatherman*, 446 (emphasis in the original).

64. Oughton: Power, *Diana*, 100, from a letter in which Oughton expressed her irritation with always having to explain herself. Mellen: interview in Varon, *Bringing the War Home*, 51 and n. 103. Fort Dix planning in September 1969: Joan Crowell, *Fort Dix Stockade: Our Prison Camp Next Door* (New York: Links, 1974), 41. Chicago in October 1969: Barber, *A Hard Rain Fell*, 183, n. 71. "We had a theory: Rudd, "Che and Me," 3.

65. "Everyone Talks about the Weather ...," 444.

66. On Columbia, see Rudd, *Underground*, chapters 3–5. Red flags: Toni Hart (Wellman) interview, 8/5/14.

67. On the importance of "revolution by theater," see Schultz, *No One Was Killed*, 79. Practical Debrayism: Rudd, "Che and Me," 3; cf. Jacobs, *The Way the Wind Blew*, 36.

68. Informants have consistently stressed to me the impact of the Columbia events on their lives, and that radicalized "Columbia alums" kept in touch, in aboveground networks as well as in Weatherman.

69. Prestige as oppression: Debray *Revolution in the Revolution?* 51; value of public executions: ibid., 53–54, quoted in *New Left Notes*, 10/2/69. "Strike one—educate a hundred": Debray, *Revolution in the Revolution?* 51, cf. 53. The theory is well summarized in Rudd, "Che and Me," 3–4.

70. On the impact of the Debrayist version of the Cuban revolution, see Wilkerson and Gilbert interviews in Varon, *Bringing the War Home*, 102, n. 98; also: Wilkerson, *Flying Close to the Sun*, 317; Rudd: "Che and Me." Jonah Raskin, *Outside the Whale: Growing Up in the American Left* (New York: Links, 1974), 142–143. Grathwohl: Felt-Miller, Box 315, Trial Transcript, Grathwohl Cross-Examination, 10/14/80, p. 3636.

71. The Columbia model: SAC Newark to Director, 5/26/70, in Cunningham, *Something Happening Here*, 98. Edward Miller: Felt-Miller, Box 106, File "Nixon/AG," Miller Introduction to Urban Guerilla conference, 11/29/71, pp. 1–2. Tom Charles Huston: see "Tom Charles Huston and the White House Secret Police," *Rolling Stone*, 10/25/73. Huston was influenced here by Assistant FBI Director William Sullivan.

72. On the Tupamaros, see Robert Moss, *Urban Guerrillas: The New Face of Political Violence* (London: Temple Smith, 1972), chapter 10, "The Tupamaros: Masters of the Game." Their worldwide impact: in autumn 1969 there was already a terrorist group operating in West Germany calling itself "Tupamaros—West Berlin."

73. Richard Elrod, an attorney for the City of Chicago at the time, still thinks Days of Rage was meant as a protest demonstration: see his interview in the documentary *Days of Rage 1969*, available online at http://www.youtube.com/watch?v=Y8AnF2RkMV8, at 5:16.

74. War, not complaints: Kathy Boudin, Bernardine Dohrn, and Terry Robbins, "Bringing the War Back Home," *New Left Notes*, 8/23/69. A fighting force that's out: Ono, "You Do Need a Weatherman," 237, 240. So, too, Diana Oughton to an SDS meeting on October 3: Oughton FBI File, Detroit SAC to Director and Chicago Field Office, 10/7/69 (from an informant). Toughness, to attract street youth: Mark Rudd and Terry Robbins, "Goodbye, Mike," *New Left Notes*, 8/29/69. See also Varon, *Bringing the War Home*, 74.

75. See discussion in Spender, *Year of the Young Rebels*, 111–113.

76. "Jailbreaks": The Motor City 9, "Power to the People! Bring the War Home!" *New Left Notes*, 8/23/69, rpt. in Jacobs, *Weatherman*, 161–162; cf. Stern, *With the Weatherman*, 112–113. National publicity: See Felt-Miller, Box 249, File "WUO III," SAC Chicago to Director, 7/2/71. For the tireless recruiting efforts of the collectives in summer and autumn 1969, see also Sale, *SDS*, 404–405; Stern, *With the Weathermen*, 110–133.

77. September 24 fighting: Felt-Miller, Box 251, File "A.M.," Report on Howard Machtinger (a leader in the fighting) by SAC Chicago, 1/14/74, pp. 1–2; cf. Felt-Miller, Box 249, File "Weatherman IV," SAC Chicago to Director, 1/28/74, pp. 7, 12, 14, 16–17, 18. Oughton in Detroit: Power, *Diana*, 146–147. Chicago cops' brutality, and the feeling that the war had begun: Neufeld interview. Personal toughness: Jeff Jones engaged in fist-fights in this period with those who disliked his aggressive proselytizing: Felt-Miller, Box 249, File "Weatherman I": FBI Report, "Students for a Democratic Society (SDS)," 11/7/69, p. 90.

78. "Operation Harry": Felt-Miller Box 316, Trial Transcript, Cartha DeLoach Direct Testimony, 10/10/80, p. 4107. This involved preliminary meetings in Budapest, and Bernardine Dohrn was supposedly commended for a job well done in making the arrangements; ibid. The Vietnamese wanted "Vietcong style" Weatherman guerrilla war even more than they wanted "half-measures" such as street-fighting: Burrough, *Days of Rage*, 73–74 (though they also worried about mass support).

79. For Dohrn's notes, see *Senate Report (Committee of the Judiciary): The Weather Underground* (Washington, D.C.: Government Printing Office: 1975), 141–146, esp. 143. Now we know that Dohrn's notes were captured by the Chicago police: Felt-Miller, Box 249, File "Weatherman II," SAC Chicago to Hoover, 5/19/70. For the 2006 testimony of Dohrn, Davidson, and Burlingame, see Barber, *A Hard Rain Fell*, 180–181. For Eleanor Raskin, see Jones, *A Radical Line*, 168–172, esp. 172. Mark Rudd: see *Underground*, 167–169. Russell Neufeld: interview.

80. The story changed: emphasized by Barber, *A Hard Rain Fell*, 179–181. Ayers blames John Jacobs: *Fugitive Days*, 167–168; Eleanor Raskin blames both Jacobs and Ayers: Jones, *A Radical Line*, p, 172. Ayers's public position in September 1969: "A Strategy to Win," esp. 183–184.

81. "Bring the War Home," *New Left Notes*, 9/12/69 (emphasis in the original). Barber, *A Hard Rain Fell*, 181, suggests that this emphasis post-Havana on violence is—among other things—a Weatherman macho-male cultural triumph.

82. H. R. Haldeman, *The Ends of Power* (New York: Times Books, 1978), 106–107. FBI opinion: Felt-Miller, Box 312, Trial Transcript, James Vermeersch Cross-Examination, 9/24/80, pp. 1349–1351 (complete with the misused quote, "When you come into a city . . ."). See also Box 317, Trial Transcript, Katherine Worthington Testimony, 10/20/80, and W. Mark Felt, *The FBI Pyramid from the Inside* (New York: Putnam's, 1979), 320–321.

83. Martin Kenner, personal communication, 7/12/13.

84. Felt-Miller, Box 248, File "Weatherman I," SAC to Director, 9/9/69, p. 4. The "sensitive source" was a bug installed in the Cuban mission: see Box 132, File "FM F(k)—Mission UN," Wannall to Sullivan, 4/28/70 and Wannall to Miller, 10/21/71, reporting the significant intelligence gained from the bug on those dates.

85. Jonathan Lerner, personal communication, 6/30/13, 12/14/15. Grathwohl: Felt-Miller, Box 315, Grathwohl, direct testimony transcript, 3555. Oughton: *Diana*, 130–131.

86. Jacobs: *The Way the Wind Blew*, 51. Ayers: *Fugitive Days*, 167–168. Recent histories of Weatherman accept that neither the Cubans nor the Vietnamese supported increased violence in the United States: Varon, *Bringing the War Home*, 137; Jones, *A Radical Line*, 178–182; Barber, *A Hard Rain Fell*, 180–182. But Berger, *Outlaws of America*, 103–104, still accepts the Weatherman leaders' line at the time, as does Burrough, *Days of Rage*. In 2003 Ayers reversed himself again and told Jeremy Varon that the Vietnamese *had* urged Weatherman to violent action (*Bringing the War Home*, 331, n. 75). This is belied by Dohrn's notes from Havana, as well as the testimony of numerous eyewitnesses. Jonathan Lerner says that when his contingent of Weathermen arrived in Cuba in February 1970 prepared for guerrilla war, the Cubans "very nicely told us we were nuts, and should calm down" (personal communication 12/14/15).

87. Eldridge Cleaver, "On Weatherman," *Berkeley Tribe*, 11/7/69; rpt. in Jacobs, *Weatherman*, 294; Newton in the *Berkeley Tribe*, 11/7/69. Hampton's speech, given on October 9, 1969 (the second of the Days of Rage), appears in the documentary film *Weather Underground* (2002); see also Jones, *A Radical Line*, 204.

88. The failure of the UFAF conference: Barber, *A Hard Rain Fell*, 170–171. Fistfight with Panthers afterward: Jones, *A Radical Line*, 204–205. Ayers's and Jones's criticism of Panthers in November: Felt-Miller, Box 249, File "Weatherman I": FBI Report, "Students for a Democratic Society (SDS)," 11/7/69, p. 90. The theory-based nature of the criticism: Jacobs,

"Introduction to Part IV," in *Weatherman*, 364. Second fistfight: Neufeld interview; he says that during this fistfight, Fred Hampton hit him in the head with a two-by-four.

89. Mike Klonsky, "Why I Quit," *New Left Notes*, 8/29/69. Similar criticism came from radical leader Michael Lerner: "The Politics of Despair," in Jacobs, *Weatherman*, 410, 413, 417–418.

90. Mark Rudd and Terry Robbins, "Goodbye, Mike" *New Left Notes*, 8/29/69; cf. Ono, "You Do Need a Weatherman," 230.

91. "Practice will prove . . .": Rudd and Robbins, "Goodbye, Mike." High expectations for the size of "the Red Army": FBI Report, 9/9/69: "Students for a Democratic Society (SDS)," p. 6 (confidential informant in the National Office). At least twenty-five thousand: Stern, *With the Weathermen*, 137. When some in Stern's collective expressed doubts at such numbers, they were brutally criticized; ibid.

92. See the moving passages in Stern, *With the Weathermen*, 139–140.

93. Such intelligence failures would lead President Nixon to pressure the FBI and other agencies to coordinate and intensify their surveillance—even if it meant illegalities.

94. Varon, *Bringing the War Home*, 81–82.

95. Ibid., 85–86 (with examples). "Dedication," *Movement*, November 1969, p. 2; "Seize the Time," *Movement*, January 1970, p. 7. Stew Albert, "We Sentence the Government to Death," *Movement*, January 1970, p. 6. The parallel with 1938: quoted in Varon, *Bringing the War Home*, 108.

96. "Left Adventurism: Hurricane or Hot Air?" *Guardian*, 10/18/69. "Rectal thermometer": Sale, *SDS*, 615. See also Falciola, "Pathways of an 'Early' De-Escalation," 7–9.

97. The collapse of the organization is discussed in detail in Sale, *SDS*. On the bitter scene between Jeff Jones and local Wisconsin SDS, see Tom Bates, *Rads: The 1970 Bombing of the Army Math Research Center at the University of Wisconsin* (New York: Harper Collins, 1992), 137. Similar was the collapse of the large SDS chapter at the University of Texas: see Doug Rossinow, "Letting Go: Revisiting the New Left's Demise," in *New Left Revisited*, ed. John McMillan and Paul Buhle (Philadelphia: Temple University Press, 2002), 242.

98. No support for PL: Felt-Miller, Box 141, File "Not in 5 of 5," 1 of 2, Director to SACs, 12/9/69. SDS finished as a national organization: cf. Rudd, *Underground*, 187–188; cf. Rossinow, "Letting Go," 242.

99. Private despair: Larry Gray, personal communication, 6/4/13. Bernardine Dohrn: it felt like "a terrible mistake," Varon, *Bringing the War Home*, 81 (Dohrn interview). Diana Oughton admitted to a friend that the Days of Rage was "at least partly a failure": Franks and Power, "Diana Takes the Revolution Path," *Washington Post*, 9/16/70). But a triumph, in public: "Chicago 69," *New Left Notes*, 8/21/69; Ono, "You Do Need a Weatherman," 237–238.

100. Felt-Miller, Box 248, File "How to deal with WUO," Report: "Summary of Radical Political Thought" by SA Herbert K. Stallings, 8/30/72, p. 43.
101. Chinese source of criticism/self-criticism: Shin'ya Ono, "You Do Need a Weatherman," 328. Horrific accounts of these sessions are collected in Varon, *Bringing the War Home*, 58–59. See also Stern, *With the Weathermen*, 169–185, where she is subjected to "criticism/self-criticism" sessions even though she has a concussion from being beaten by police the previous day; or Lerner, "I Was a Terrorist," where not even his best friend Jeff Jones tries to save him from savage criticism of his alleged lack of "manliness" in street-fighting.
102. Ayers, "A Strategy to Win," 185–186; cf. Felt-Miller Trial material, Box 141, File "Bernadine Dohrn—EM Documents," Cincinnati Field Office Report, 7/2/70, based on Grathwohl information, reporting a speech by Ayers to the Buffalo, New York, Weatherman collective on 4/2/70.
103. Stern, *With the Weathermen*, 185; cf. Rudd, *Underground*, 184–185 (a rueful and contrite self-portrait). "No soul": Shin'ya Ono, "You Do Need a Weatherman," 237 (a quotation from Mao Tse-tung). Burrough, *Days of Rage*, 88, misplaces the beginning of these purges to January, after the Flint War Council.
104. Illnesses: Rudd, *Underground*, 184–185. Rudd himself was often ill. Informants in New York City and Ohio in late October, 1969: Felt-Miller Box 248, File "Weatherman I," Martindale to Shackelford, 10/23/60. Grathwohl the only informant left in February 1970: Larry Grathwohl, as told to Frank Reagan, *Bringing Down America: An FBI Informer with the Weathermen* (New Rochelle, N.Y.: Arlington House, 1976), 129–130. Objections to criticism/self-criticism sessions moral grounds: Ron Fliegelman, interview with the author, 11/16/13; Neufeld interview.
105. Mindless action, no theorizing: so Power, *Diana*, 166–167. Debate continuing over adventurism: Howard Machtinger, *Fire!* 11/21/69; cf. Wayne C. Booth, *Modern Dogma and the Rhetoric of Dissent* (Notre Dame: University of Notre Dame Press, 1974), 152. Even the FBI understood: Rudd, *Underground*, 190 (quoting from his own FBI file from December 1969).
106. Death of Carlos Marighella: "A Manual for the Urban Terrorist," *Time*, 11/2/70. On the Chicago police murder of Hampton, see Jeffrey Haas, *The Assassination of Fred Hampton: How the FBI and the Chicago Police Murdered a Black Panther* (Chicago: Chicago Review Press, 2011). Impact on Ted Gold: Toni Hart (Wellman) interview, 8/15/14.
107. "Stormy Weather," *San Francisco Good Times*, 1/7/70, rpt. in Jacobs, *Weatherman*, 341.
108. Denials: Bill Ayers, on *Megyn Kelly Show*, Fox News, 7/1/14. Reality: Howard Machtinger, "Clearing away the Debris: New Left Radicalism in 1960s America," M.A. thesis, San Francisco State University, 1995,

p. 88; cf. Barber, *A Hard Rain Fell*, 211 and n. 45. On the prevalence of the fork salute at Flint, see Stern, *With the Weathermen*, 210 (eyewitness); Rudd, *Underground*, 189 (eyewitness). The Ayers collective in January in Detroit: Karin Latimer File DocId 59161309, p. 186, Nancy Rudd Interview, 5/24/73, p. 1.

109. For a typical depiction, see Burrough, *Days of Rage*, 85–86.

110. "Stormy Weather," 341; Grathwohl, *Bringing Down America*, 102.

111. "Stormy Weather," 344.

112. Ibid., 343–345.

113. No vision of the future: Oglesby, "1969." Gold's vision: "Stormy Weather," 343. Larry Grathwohl's understanding of the Weatherman vision of postrevolution America was the same: Felt-Miller Box 315, Grathwohl Cross-Examination, October 14, 1980, pp. 3668–3669.

114. Stern, *With the Weathermen*, 204–205, 210.

115. Ibid., 210; *Fire!* 12/6/69, p. 1.

116. *Senate Committee Report: The Weather Underground*, 21–22. By April, Koziol was essentially acting as an FBI informant: see "FBI Weatherfug Files," DocID 59162728, pp. 155–156, Chicago to Director, 4/24/70, pp. 2–3. Burrough, *Days of Rage*, 94 (Machtinger interview). Burrough assumes the main reason for targeting police is simple solidarity with the Black Panthers; ibid.

117. "Revolution in the 1970s," *Fire!* 1/30/70, rpt. in Jacobs, *Weatherman*, 450–451.

118. The FBI warrantless bugging and wiretapping of Bergman had been going on for more than a year. FBI transcript: Felt-Miller Box 315, Trial Transcript, David Ryan Direct Testimony, October 15, 1980, pp. 3968–3969.

119. Ibid., 3969–3970.

120. The other operation involving human targets: Berger, *Outlaws of America*, 129 (from Naomi Jaffe). Chaos: Lerner, "I Was a Terrorist." Sense of abandonment: Charlotte Marchant's complaint to Karen Latimer in Berkeley in the summer of 1973: Latimer File, SAC Los Angeles to Director, 1//24/75, pp. 5–6.

121. Parents upset: "FBI Weatherfug Files," DocId: 59162728, p. 113: Weatherman Jolee Chain's mother desperately called Janet Brown to find out whether she knew anything after Jolee disappeared. The years-long Weather program to reconnect parents and children: Jonah Raskin interview, 4/16/15; he sometimes acted as a go-between. The code was: "Someone near and dear wishes to see you."

122. On Yetta Machtinger, see Felt-Miller Box 251, File "A [*sic*].M" (Howard Machtinger's FBI file). On the FBI interrogation of Debbie Wiener, the grandmother of David Barber, see Box 250, File "Handelsman." Though Barber was also underground, this material appears in the Leonard Handelsman file because the FBI believed that her apartment was being

used as a letter drop for communications between the fugitive Handelsman and his parents, whom Debbie Wiener knew.

123. Some people told the police had murdered the townhouse people: Gilbert, *Love and Struggle*, 149. His collective learned the truth only several weeks later: ibid. Jacobs an isolated figure: Berger, *Outlaws of America*, 130. Braley: Varon, *Bringing the War Home*, 184 (Braley interview). Rudd's experience with the survivors of the Townhouse Collective: *Underground*, 196. Gun pulled on Fliegelman: Burrough, *Days of Rage*, 111 (Fliegelman interview). See also Carl Oglesby's encounter with the ferocious radical film director Robert Kramer, founder of the "Newsreel" movement, who supported the townhouse bombing plan and was preparing for war: Oglesby, *Ravens in the Storm*, 286–291. Larry Gray: interview, 6/4/13; Jonah Raskin, interview 4/16/15.

124. Felt-Miller Box 141, File "Bernadine Dohrn—EM Documents," Chicago Field Office Reports 12/2/70, p. 65, and 4/15/71, p. 20. The report from Grathwohl was included in this Dohrn folder because of Ayers's praise of Dohrn in Buffalo; ibid. The report is also in the Karen Latimer File, 191–194, Cincinnati Field Office to Director, 7/2/70, pp. 1–4. A shortened version of the scene with Ayers appears in Grathwohl, *Bringing Down America*, 169.

125. Gilbert, Braley, Rudd, Fliegelman, Gray, and Oglesby.

126. *Washington Post*, 5/11/70, p. 3. That the National Guard bombing was a Weatherman operation was acknowledged four years later: see Berger, *Outlaws of America*, 329.

127. Varon, *Bringing the War Home*, 181; Berger, *Outlaws of America*, 130.

128. On the New Haven protests, see Paul Bass, *Murder in the Model City: The Black Panthers, Yale, and the Redemption of a Killer* (New York: Basic, 2006). Impression made on Weatherman: Jonah Raskin, personal communication, 4/18/15.

129. Arrests of Donghi and Evans: Grathwohl, *Taking Down America*, 176–181. Rudd's flight: *Underground*, 210–211.

130. On the careful preparations made at Mendocino by Jones and Dohrn, see Jones, *A Radical Line*, 218. Gilbert excluded: Gilbert, *Love and Struggle*, 151. Jacobs's sense of moral superiority: Jones, *A Radical Line*, 219 (his mother, Eleanor Raskin, rode all the way from New York with Jacobs—and Bill Ayers). Rudd, like Ayers, was won over by Dohrn: Rudd, *Underground*, 213–214. Jones's and Dohrn's private propagandizing of Ayers: Jones, *A Radical Line*, 219. Lotus position: Jonah Raskin, personal communication, 6/20/14, interview 4/16/15. Jacobs's misogyny a factor: ibid. Demotion of Rudd: he was expelled from the Weather Bureau central committee and became an ordinary Weather soldier (Rudd, *Underground*, 219–220).

131. "By God, What We Need is a Little Responsible Terrorism," *Berkeley Tribe*, 3/27–4/3/70; cf. Falciola, "Pathways of an 'Early' De-Escalation,"

8; Berger, *Outlaws of America*, 130. The *Movement* in its December 1969 edition even published a Progressive Labor–inspired essay, "Who Are the Bombers?" implying that the Weathermen might be agents provocateurs. The perceived political opportunity: Berger, *Outlaws of America*, 130.

132. Jones, *A Radical Line*, 220.

133. Weatherman Communiqué #1, 149–151.

134. The new potential revolutionary mass: Gilbert, *Love and Struggle*, 197. Full text of Jennifer Dohrn's speech (originally in the *Chicago Seed*, April 1971): Felt-Miller, Box 134, File "Not in 5/5 list [Weatherman Information]," 2 of 2, SAC Chicago to Director, 4/12/71, p. 2. Implications: see Jacobs, *The Way the Wind Blew*, 124. On Timothy Leary, see Robert Greenfield, *Timothy Leary: A Biography* (New York: Harcourt, 2006). "The will of millions of kids": Weatherman communiqué "Dr. Timothy Leary," 9/15/70, in Dohrn, Ayers, and Jones, *Sing a Battle Song*, 154–155.

135. On the bombing, see *Senate Judiciary Committee Report: The Weather Underground*, 31. They just walked right in: Fliegelman interview in Burrough, *Days of Rage*, 129.

136. The failed San Francisco Hall of Justice bomb: Gilbert, *Love and Struggle*, 161; claim of FBI veterans: Burrough, *Days of Rage*, 127 n. The failure of Machtinger's bomb in June might be another argument against the idea that the all-too-successful Park Street Station bomb in February was a Weatherman job. Machtinger had now had four months more practice, yet (as with the February dynamite bombs in Berkeley) he did something wrong.

137. Weatherman Communiqué "Headquarters," 6/10/70, in Dohrn, Ayers, and Jones, *Sing a Battle Song*, 151–152. Latimer and Ashley: Latimer File, 108, SAC Los Angeles to Director, 1/17/75, p. 4 (Latimer 1975 FBI interview). Ashley was on her way to Seattle to organized "armed struggle" (pp. 4–5). Weatherman Communiqué #3, 7/26/70, in Dohrn, Ayres, and Jones, *Sing a Battle Song*, 152–153. Presidio bombings: *New York Times*, 7/28/70.

138. We owe this important information to Bryan Burrough's interview with Howard Machtinger in 2011: *Days of Rage*, 127.

139. Dohrn's efforts in imposing restraint in summer 1970: Varon, *Bringing the War Home*, 184. Fliegelman rejects snipers: Jonah Raskin, personal communication, 4/17/15. Dissolution of the Denver Collective after Mendocino: Gilbert, *Love and Struggle*, 151–152; Burrough, *Days of Rage*, 88, misdates the dissolution of the Denver collective to January, and alleges it was on orders from the Weather Bureau. New demands not to commit murder: "Notes to the Underground," *Berkeley Tribe*, 6/12–19/70; Tom Hayden, "The Trial," *Ramparts*, July 1970. See also "Life against Death," *Berkeley Tribe*, 9/23–10/2/70. Impact of constitu-

ency on maintaining deescalation: see Falciola, "Pathways of an 'Early' De-Escalation," 8. More popular support than any other radical group: see Burrough, *Days of Rage*, 89.

140. Praise of Jonathan Jackson: Communiqué "Message to Daniel Berrigan," 10/8/70, in Dohrn, Ayers, and Jones, *Sing a Battle Song*, 155–156. Announcement of "a fall offensive," and concern over quiescence on campus: Communiqué "Fall Offensive," 10/8/70, ibid., 157. Participation of Cathy Wilkerson, the townhouse veteran, in the Marin County Courthouse bombing: Wilkerson, *Flying Close to the Sun*, 363. Marin bombing dedicated to Jonathan Jackson: Communiqué "Hall of Injustice," 10/8/70, in Dohrn, Ayers, and Jones, *Sing a Battle Song*, 159. Wanted posters for repressive judges such as John Murtaugh: "Criminal Courthouse," 10/9/70, ibid., 160.

141. Wilkerson, *Flying Close to the Sun*, 358–359, 364.

142. "New Morning," 161–162. The first half of the title of the communiqué is taken from another Bob Dylan song.

143. The "military error" (ascribed only to the Townhouse Collective): "New Morning," 162–164. Jonah Raskin says he contributed part of the argument for rejecting militarized underground cells, and the general emphasis on the positive aspects of the counterculture: personal communication, 4/10/15. Marijuana and LSD revolutionary: "New Morning," 167. Cathy Wilkerson offended by scapegoating of the Townhouse but doesn't protest: Wilkerson, *Flying Close to the Sun*, 363–364.

144. "New Morning," 164, 166–168.

145. Ibid., 167–168. Need for hierarchy: Raskin, "Looking Back," 122, 128, 132. Sense of superiority never went away: ibid., 134.

146. Campus radical action fading away: Weatherman communiqué "Fall Offensive," 10/8/70), in Dohrn, Ayers, and Jones, *Sing a Battle Song*, 157. If there had been an SDS national organization to tide the student movement over the summer vacation of 1970: see the comments of Gitlin, *The Sixties*, 411.

147. On the May Day demonstrations, see L. A. Kaufman, "Ending a War, Inventing a Movement: Mayday, 1971," https://libcom.org/library/ending-war-inventing-movement-mayday-1971.

148. The hippie mass only of spectators: Raskin, "Looking Back," 127, 133.

149. Grathwohl's analysis of "New Morning": Felt-Miller, Box 249, File "WUO II (M)," SAC Chicago to Director, 12/24/70, p. 2.

150. On Weathermen masquerading (or partly masquerading) as hippies, see Lerner, "I Was a Terrorist," and personal communication, 9/30/13; Jeff Jones and Bill Ayers absorbed in cooking: Jonah Raskin, personal communication, 4/10/15.

151. Grathwohl: Box 249, File "WUO II (M)," SAC Chicago to Director, 12/24/70, p. 2.

152. Michigan: Rick Perlstein, *Nixonland* (New York: Scribner, 2009), 587–588. JDL bombing of Hurok: *New York Times*, 1/27/72. Newark: *New York Times*, 1/5/72.

153. See the comments of Jonah Raskin on Weatherman longevity already in 1974: "Looking Backward," 126; and "Introduction to 'The Weather Eye,'" 135.

154. This was the Howard Machtinger fiasco, autumn 1973.

155. Gilbert, *Love and Struggle*, 151.

156. This is implied in *Prairie Fire* and clear from statements especially by Bill Ayers in Emile de Antonio's documentary film *Underground* (filmed in summer 1975), and in interviews with de Antonio in November 1975 in *Rolling Stone*.

Chapter Three. "A Menace of National Proportions"

1. Hoffman: Mel Gussow, "West Eleventh Street: An End to Innocence," *New York*, 3/8/71; Ochs: the concert, the bomb threat that ended it, and Ochs's approval and sneer at Hoffman, can be found on the CD *Gunfight at Carnegie Hall*. Ochs was supporting Weatherman's right to deliver bomb threats, given the condition of the country. The source of the bomb threat remains unknown. Ochs himself was subjected to constant FBI pressure: see Marc Eliot, *Death of a Rebel: A Biography of Phil Ochs* (New York: Citadel, 1994).

2. Mary Tyler Moore show: Jennifer K. Armstrong, *Mary and Lou and Rhoda and Ted: All the Brilliant Minds Who Made the Mary Tyler Moore Show a Classic* (New York: Simon and Schuster, 2013), 77. Military policeman on an alleged Weatherman assassination list: Col. John Hoffman, email communication, 3/18/13. There is no evidence of such an assassination list in any available FBI files.

3. Thomas Kennelly, *One More Story and I'm Out the Door* (New York: Universe, 2009), 339. Kennelly was Edward Miller's defense attorney.

4. *Senate Select Committee to Study Governmental Operations with Respect to Intelligence Activities*, vol. 2, *The Huston Plan*, Huston testimony, 9/23/75, 17. Huston was defending his 1970 proposal that the intelligence agencies use illegal methods of surveillance against violent groups on the New Left. David Cunningham, There's *Something Happening Here: The New Left, the Klan, and FBI Counterintelligence* (Berkeley: University of California Press, 2004), thinks Huston and others were sincere (though perhaps paranoid) in 1970 in their fears of revolution: 34, 98–99, 300, n. 93.

5. *Senate Select Committee*, vol. 2, *The Huston Plan*, 396, Exhibit 63, "Presidential Talking Points," p. 1. These talking points were found in a file of Nixon's chief of staff H. R. ("Bob") Haldeman; ibid.

6. Ibid., 398; "Presidential Talking Points," 3–4.

7. Hoover's speech to the intelligence chiefs was written for him by William Sullivan, the assistant director in charge of the FBI Domestic Security Division: Felt-Miller Box 107, File "Huston Report (Supplemental)," Sullivan to DeLoach, 6/6/70, pp. 2–3. But Hoover obviously agreed with these sentiments. The reference to the declarations of revolutionary intent, followed by terrorist actions, is a clearly to Weatherman.

8. See William C. Sullivan, *The Bureau: My Thirty Years in Hoover's FBI* (New York: Norton, 1979), 162–163. On the double mandate, see also, e.g., Felt-Miller Box 103, File "Plans to Deal w/WUO" 1, Brennan to Sullivan, 7/18/68, pp. 1–2.

9. See W. Mark Felt, *The FBI Pyramid from the Inside* (New York: Putnam, 1979), 61. Originally simply the Bureau of Investigation of the Department of Justice, the Bureau added "Federal" to its name in 1935, by which time its prestige had greatly increased because of Hoover's rigid stewardship and mastery of public relations; ibid.

10. Statistics: see Felt-Miller, Box 207, File "Capbom": Appropriations 1972 (Hoover's testimony on June 24, 1971, before the Senate Committee on Appropriations, 9). On the field offices and resident agencies, see Cunningham, *Something Happening Here*, 85–86.

11. The literature on Hoover and the FBI is, of course, vast. See, e.g., Felt, *The FBI Pyramid*; Curt Gentry, *J. Edgar Hoover: The Man and his Secrets* (New York: Norton, 2001).

12. Tolson and Hoover were rumored to be lovers, but there is no substantive evidence: see the balanced assessment of Cunningham, *Something Happening Here*, 303, n. 7.

13. Interview with Edward S. Miller (Society of Former Special Agents of the FBI), 5/28/08, p. 94.

14. On the bureaucratic structure of FBI Headquarters (often called formally and pompously the Seat of Government in FBI memos), see Cunningham, *Something Happening Here*, 81–83.

15. See, e.g. W. Mark Felt, *A G-Man's Life: The FBI, Being Deep Throat, and the Struggle for Honor in Washington* (Washington, D.C.: Public Affairs, 2007), 101; Max Holland, *Leak: Why Mark Felt Became Deep Throat* (Lawrence: University of Kansas Press, 2012), 16 (very hostile to Felt).

16. Miller interview, 108 (a hostile assessment). Others outside the Bureau found Brennan a quite charming person.

17. For Sullivan's bitter account of these events, see *The Bureau*, chapters 14–16; a contrary version, hostile to Sullivan: Miller interview, 108–114.

18. Claim to administrative expertise: Felt, *The FBI Pyramid*, 76–85; promotion to deputy associate director: ibid., 133–134; hostility toward Felt within the Bureau: Holland, *Leak*, 18. John Nields, the prosecutor in the 1980 trial, saw Felt as a smooth and accomplished liar: interview with the author, 5/14/14. Miller's close relationship to Felt: Felt, *A G-Man's Life*, 90. Felt's ferocious hostility to Sullivan: ibid., pp. 110–111 (an extraordinary

passage). Meanwhile, Felt appears in exactly one short sentence in Sullivan's own memoir: *The Bureau*, 226.

19. See Cunningham, *Something Happening Here*, 81–87, 105 with n. 57.

20. Cf. ibid., 92–101 (concerned with both educational envy and generational hostility).

21. Sullivan misleadingly claims in his memoir that the New Left was unknown to the FBI until the Columbia University riots of spring 1968: *The Bureau*, 147–148. On FBI surveillance of SDS before 1968, see also W. Churchill and J. Vander Wall, *The COINTELPRO Papers: Documents from the FBI's Secret War against Dissent in the United States* (Boston: South End), 165–175.

22. Sanford J. Ungar, *FBI* (Boston: Little, Brown, 1975), 461–462; Seth Rosenfeld, *Subversives: The FBI's War on Student Radicals, and Reagan's Rise to Power* (New York: Farrar, Straus and Giroux, 2013), 204–205.

23. Wiliam T. Divale, *I Lived Inside the Campus Revolution* (Spokane, Wash.: Cowles, 1970). Divale, who was an important SDS figure at UCLA, revealed himself as an informer in 1969.

24. By 1965: Maurice Isserman and Michael Kazin, *America Divided: The Civil War of the 1960s*, 4th ed. (New York: Oxford University Press, 2012), 164 Certainly by 1968: see n. 30 below.

25. The New Left list: Cunningham, *Something Happening Here*, 92 and n. 31 (Hoover to SACs, 5/28/68). SDS leaders onto the key activist list: Felt-Miller, Box 141, "Plans to Deal with WUO," File 1, Director to SACs, 6/18/68. Dohrn: the June memo indicates that Dohrn was someone who "has not previously been the subject of an investigation"; ibid., 2.

26. Felt-Miller, Box 103, "Plans to Deal w/WUO," File 3, Director to 29 SACs, 10/21/68.

27. The full spectrum: Sullivan, *The Bureau*, 149.

28. The official FBI position on SDS and the cpusa: Cunningham, *Something Happening Here*, 95–97. Sullivan's opinion: *The Bureau*, 179. On Sullivan's troubles with Hoover after he revealed in his real opinion in public, ibid., 203–204, and above.

29. Miller's complaint: Felt-Miller Box 276, File "Microphone Exhibits," Miller to Rosen, 11/12/71, pp. 4–5. Dohrn and the moon landing: Box 141, File "Bernadine Dohrn—EM Documents," Chicago Field Office confidential memorandum on Dohrn, 22. New York SDS headquarters informant: ibid., 28. The FBI informant in Chicago may have been one of the white street thugs whom Weatherman/SDS was attempting to convert: interview with Special Agent William Dyson (Society of Former Special Agents of the FBI), January 2008, pp. 30–32; Dyson ran this informant.

30. Wiretap and bugs in NO headquarters in Chicago: Felt-Miller Box 251, File "Bu II," Assistant Attorney General Wilson (Criminal Division) to Director, 3/28/69, p. 2. In existence since October 1968: Felt-Miller Box

248, File "WM I," Chicago SAC to Director, 10/8/69. William Dyson was the special agent in Chicago who ran the bug from 1968, and he claims he got plenty of information about how SDS developed into Weatherman: Dyson interview, 28. Dyson was later involved in the hunt for Weatherman itself; ibid., 32 ff. Wiretap still going in December 1969: Felt-Miller Box 108, File "Miller Specific 267 A-B.

31. Every known Weatherman: Felt-Miller Box 141, File "Violence by WUO #45," 250, Brennan to Sullivan 11/20/69, p. 1; Felt-Miller Box 320, File "Government Trial Exhibits," Shackelford to Miller, 10/27/71 (a retrospective on FBI actions up to that date). Security Index and possible incarceration: Felt-Miller, Box 102, "Plans to Handle WUO," File 3 of 4: Brennan to Sullivan, 4/1/70 ("Handling Bombing Matters"), referring back to autumn 1969. *Senate Select Committee*, vol. 2, *The Huston Plan*, Brennan testimony, 9/25/75, pp. 117, 119. Intense FBI surveillance was still possible in late 1969 because Weatherman had not yet gone underground.

32. *Senate Select Committee*, vol. 2, *The Huston Plan*, Brennan testimony, 9/25/75, p. 118.

33. Felt-Miller, Box 103, "Plans to Deal w/WUO," File 2, Brennan to Sullivan, 6/6/68, p. 1; cf. Sullivan, *The Bureau*, 157–158. This memo was written in the immediate aftermath of the assassination of Senator Robert F. Kennedy by the Palestinian activist Sirhan Sirhan.

34. Flanagan's threat and CODE YELLOW: Felt-Miller, Box 48, File "W I," Director to the President, Vice President, Attorney General, Secretary of State, Director CIA, Director DIA, and Secret Service, 10/19/69. Flanagan and Richard Elrod: see the detailed account in Bryan Smith, "Sudden Impact," *Chicago*, December 2006. Flanagan's alleged bombings in New York City: Felt Miller Box 134, File "Not on 5/5 list, 1 of 2," Director to SAC New York, 10/19/69.

35. Felt-Miller, Box 111, File "Felt Specific Documents (2)," Director to SACs, 11/10/69, p. 1.

36. Felt-Miller, Box 134, File "Weathfug—General," Cotter to Sullivan 11/6/69, with Felt-Miller Box 133, File F(o) "Weathfug—General," SAC Chicago to Acting Director, 8/30/72, with "FBI Special Report: Summary of Radical Political Thought" (August 1972) by SA Herbert K. Stallings, 43 (Ayers and Jones), and in Box 102, "Plans to Deal with the WUO," File 2 of 4. All information on the informant is blacked out.

37. Paul Scheips, *The Role of Federal Military Forces in Domestic Disorders, 1945–1992* (Washington, D.C.: Center for Military History, 2005), 385.

38. Ayers on November 15: Jeremy Larner, "The Moratorium: A View from Inside," *Life*, 11/28/69. His threats to the Mobe, reported to the FBI: Felt-Miller, Box 141, "Violence by WUO, #45," Brennan to Sullivan, 11/20/69. This story apparently came from informants in the National Moratorium Committee. The story is confirmed by Cathy Wilkerson, *Flying Close to the Sun* (New York: Seven Stories, 2007), 310.

39. Official estimate of the crowd on November 15: James Rosen, *The Strong Man: John Mitchell and the Secrets of Watergate* (New York: Doubleday, 2008), 92; the private estimate of Nixon's chief of staff H. R. Haldeman, based on a photo count, was 350,000: ibid. Mitchell's remark to his wife: *New York Times*, 11/22/69. Mitchell overcome by the tear gas: Rosen, *The Strong Man*, 94–95.
40. *Lethal bombing plans by the Weather Bureau at Flint: Senate Committee Report: The Weather Underground*, 21–22 (source: the reporter Ron Koziol, to whom a disillusioned Weather Bureau member spoke in spring 1970); Bryan Burrough, *Days of Rage: America's Radical Underground, the FBI and the Forgotten Age of Revolutionary Violence* (New York: Penguin, 2015), 94 (interview with Howard Machtinger).
41. Felt-Miller Box 250, File "Rudd," Brennan to Sullivan 2/13/70. Rudd's assassination threat ended up as "overt act" no. 6 in his federal indictment in July 1970: Felt-Miller, Box 141, File "Bernadine Dohrn—EM Documents," Chicago Field Office Report, 3/31/71.
42. Larry Grathwohl, as told to Frank Reagan, *Bringing Down America: An FBI Informer with the Weathermen* (New Rochelle, N.Y.: Arlington House, 1976), chapter 13.
43. Felt-Miller, Box 246, File "Weatherman I," "FBI Special Report: Students for a Democratic Society," 11/7/69, cover page E.
44. Krogh Request: Felt-Miller, Box 250, File "WUO," Krogh, to Haynes, 2/23/70; cf., Box 102, "Plans to Deal with WUO," File 3 of 4, Brennan to Sullivan, 2/26/70, p. 1. Nixon was right about the CPUSA: see Harvey Klehr and John Earl Haynes, *The Soviet World of American Communism* (New Haven: Yale University Press, 1998), based on Soviet archives. Nixon's certainty that the New Left represented the same phenomenon: Richard Reeves, *President Nixon: Alone in the White House* (New York: Simon and Schuster, 2001), 230.
45. Felt-Miller, Box 102, "Plans to Deal with WUO, File 3 of 4: Haynes to Sullivan, 3/6/70, with long legal presentation of the issues.
46. Felt-Miller, Box 96, File "Sullivan and Hoover directives Re: Weatherman," Haynes to Sullivan 3/6/70 = Box 102, "Plans to Deal with WUO," File 3 of 4, Haynes to Sullivan, 3/6/70. Partially quoted: Felt-Miller Box 118, Trial Transcript, Felt Cross-Examination, 10/24/80, pp. 5227–5228.
47. Felt-Miller Box 319, Trial Transcript, Mitchell Redirect Testimony, October 28, 1980, pp. 5764–5765.
48. White House Special Files, Haldeman Box 152 NP, Huston to Haldeman, 3/12/70; cf. Tom Wells, *The War Within: America's Battle over Vietnam* (Lincoln, Neb.: Authors Guild 2005), 413; cf. Reeves, *President Nixon*, 175.
49. Tom Huston's correct predictions in summer 1969: White House Special Files, Haldeman Box 51, Huston to Haldeman, 8/22/69; cf. Reeves, *President Nixon*, 120. Huston's knowledge of SDS politics probably

derived from William Sullivan, who was in contact with Huston from June 1969. The new prediction on March 12, 1970: Huston to Haldeman, 3/12/70; cf. Wells, *The War Within*, 413.

50. Details of the placing of the corporation bombs: Homer Bigart, "Many Buildings Evacuated Here in Bomb Scares," *New York Times*, 3/13/70. In early 1970 getting such bombs into buildings—including the White House—was possible because there were as yet no metal detectors. That was true for airline travel as well, and the airlines bitterly resisted putting them in (beginning in 1972). It was another world from today.

51. On Huston's close relationship with Nixon, and the great favor he had done him in 1966, see Rick Perlstein, *Nixonland* (New York: Scribner, 2009), 130–132. "Tough and smart": Nixon memo from spring 1970, cited ibid., 462.

52. White House Special Files, Haldeman Box 152, Moynihan to Haldeman, March 12, 1970; cf. Wells, *The War Within*, 413–414. J. Walter Yeagley, the assistant attorney general for internal security, also attributed the New York corporation bombings to Weatherman. Moynihan was also aware of events at the Weatherman Flint "War Council" in December, but he has details wrong: there were no photographs of Manson, though Bernardine Dohrn praised Manson in a speech, and meant it. There *was* a large gleeful photograph of Manson's victim Sharon Tate.

53. Hoover and Nixon encouraged the Chicago conspiracy trial: Felt-Miller Box 109, File "Felt Documents (2)," Hoover to Tolson, DeLoach, Sullivan et al., 4/23/70, p. 6. The real purpose of the trial and other trials like it: see Rosen, *The Strong Man*, 80–83.

54. Death threats to Hoffman: interview with Edward S. Miller (Society of Former Special Agents of the FBI), 5/28/08, p. 78; Miller, as assistant special agent in charge in Chicago, collected the death threats daily from Hoffman. In late 1971 he would become the chief Weatherman hunter.

55. Pun Plamondon's threats, quoted in Jeff A. Hale, "The White Panthers," in *Imagine Nation: The American Counterculture of the 1960s and 1970s*, ed. Peter Braunstein and Michael W. Doyle (New York: Routledge, 2001), 143. Susan Stern certain that war was coming: Susan Stern, *With the Weathermen: The Personal Story of a Revolutionary Woman* (1975; Rutgers, N.J.: Rutgers University Press, 2007), 65. Jimi Hendrix's similar view: see the introduction to Hendrix, "Machine Gun" (early 1970), http://coldwar-hms09b.wikispaces.com/Machine+Gun+by+Jimi+Hendrix. The *Berkeley Tribe's* call for war: *Berkeley Tribe*, 2/27–3/6/70.

56. This is clear in the lyrics of Fogarty's "Who'll Stop the Rain?" The "five-year plan" denounced in that song was written by Tom Hayden in his radical collective in Berkeley: Jonah Raskin, interview with the author, 4/20/15. "Bad Moon Rising" a theme song in Weather: ibid., 9/15/15.

57. White House Special Files, Haldeman Box 152, Moynihan to Haldeman, 3/12/70; cf. Wells, *The War Within*, 414.

58. Norman Mailer, *Miami and the Siege of Chicago* (New York: World, 1968), 197–198; cf. Isserman and Kazin, *America Divided*, 4 and n. 9. I. F. Stone: "Where the Fuse on That Dynamite Leads," *I. F. Stone's Bi-Weekly*, 3/23/70; rpt. in *Weatherman*, ed. Hal Jacobs (San Francisco: Rampart, 1970), 491–495. That civil war was imminent was also the view of the social theorists Daniel Foss and Ralph Larkin: see Jeremy Varon, *Bringing the War Home* (Berkeley: University of California Press, 2004), 96. At the Chicago trial there had originally been eight defendants, but one of them, Bobby Seale, had had his case severed from the others, following a grotesque scene in which he was chained and gagged at the defendants' table.

59. W. O. Douglas, *Points of Rebellion* (New York: Random House, 1970), 88, 94–95, 97 (the last gloomy sentence in the quotation above is the final sentence of the book).

60. Chrissie Hynde, *Reckless: My Life as a Pretender* (New York: Doubleday, 2015), 77.

61. Bigart, "Many Buildings Evacuated." The *Times* carried two other page-one stories on the bombings and the bomb scare, and a large photograph of damage done to the IBM Building on Park Avenue. The quotation is from Bigart's story. Cf. Wells, *The War Within*, 407.

62. "Garelik Says Terrorists Are a Growing Threat Here," *New York Times*, 3/13/70.

63. Steven Roberts, "Bombings on Rise over the Nation," *New York Times*, 3/13/70.

64. Bruce Oudes, ed., *From: The President: Richard Nixon's Secret Files* (New York: Harper and Row, 1989), 103–104; cf. Wells, *The War Within*, 412.

65. James Naughton, "U.S. to Tighten Surveillance of Radicals," *New York Times*, 4/13/70; cf. briefly Wells, *The War Within*, 414–415. The parallel with the Narodniki was also seen by I. F. Stone: "Where the Fuse on That Dynamite Leads," 492–493. Irving Kristol was a former radical socialist and a future cofounder of neoconservatism, along with his son William. On the Narodniki, see Lewis Feuer, *The Conflict of Generations: The Character and Significance of Student Movements* (New York: Basic, 1969), chapters 1 and 4.

66. A month later: Naughton, "U.S. to Tighten Surveillance." The secret meeting after Kristol's departure: Felt-Miller, Box 102, "Plans to Deal with WUO" File 1 of 4: Al Rosen to Cartha DeLoach, 3/17/70, p. 1. Haldeman's diary entry the next day: H. R. Haldeman, *The Haldeman Diaries: Inside the Nixon White House* (New York: Putnam, 1994), 138 (3/13/70). By contrast, Haldeman himself was relatively phlegmatic; ibid., 136.

67. Jonah Raskin, *Outside the Whale: Growing Up in the American Left* (New York: Links, 1974), 147. Bill Ayers says Terry Robbins, well aware of the history, led the dynamiters: *Fugitive Days: Memoirs of an Antiwar Activist* (Boston: Beacon, 2001), 170–171.

68. Ayers's claim: *Fugitive Days*, 266. Mitchell's claim: Felt-Miller Box 319, Trial Transcript, John Mitchell Cross-Examination, 10/28/80, pp. 5761–5762, referring to a heavily redacted document put into evidence.

69. Irritation of Nixon at the FBI: Felt-Miller Box 316, Trial Transcript, Cartha DeLoach cross-examination, 10/16/80, p. 4133. Thomas Kelly's own attitude: Felt-Miller, Box 102, "Plans to Deal with WUO" File 1 of 4: Al Rosen to Cartha DeLoach, 3/17/70, p. 1.

70. Quick Hoover response to presidential demands is a theme of Sullivan's memoir *The Bureau*. The warning about Nixon on March 6, 1970: Felt-Miller Box 96, File "Sullivan and Hoover directives Re: Weatherman," Haynes to Sullivan, 3/6/70 (the issue was Nixon's belief in foreign funding of the far Left). Hoover's March 12 memo: Felt-Miller Box 103, "Plans to Deal with WUO," Final File of 4, Shackelford to Brennan, 9/30/70 (a retrospective). "It is imperative": Felt-Miller Box 102, "Plans to Deal with WUO" File 1 of 4: Rosen to DeLoach, 3/17/70, p. 3. Hoover's underlinings in the original.

71. "Revolutionary Force 9": Felt-Miller Box 102, File 1 of 4 "Plans to Handle WUO," Brennan to Sullivan, 4/1/70 ("New Left Movement—Violence"), p. 1. The title of the group actually refers to a song, "Revolution 9," on the album *The Beatles*, popularly known as the *White Album*. "Revolutionary Force 9" actually another name for Weatherman: Felt-Miller, Box 102, "Plans to Deal with WUO," File 3 of 4, Yeagley to Hoover, 3/13/70; and Brennan to Sullivan, 3/17/70. Yeagley was a holdover from the Johnson administration.

72. The March 13 meeting: Felt-Miller Box 102, File "Plans to Deal with WUO," 1 of 4: DeLoach to Tolson, 3/13/70, pp. 1–2. The three assistant attorneys general: Yeagley of the Internal Security Division, Jerris Leonard of the Civil Rights Division, Will Wilson of the Criminal Division. Hoover backs DeLoach: Felt-Miller Box 102, File "Plans to Deal with WUO," File 1 of 4: DeLoach to Tolson, 3/13/70, p. 3—with a handwritten note by Hoover criticizing the assistant AGs for not pursuing criminal prosecutions of the New Left vigorously themselves.

73. March 16 meeting and Yeagley's written request: Felt-Miller, Box 102, "Plans to Deal with WUO," File 1 of 4: DeLoach to Tolson, 3/16/70 (quotation); Brennan to Sullivan, 3/17/70, p. 1. Hoover finally grants the request: ibid., Hoover to Yeagley, 3/17/70. Charles Brennan's warnings that the Bureau resources were being strained by involvement in what might turn out to be merely local bombings: ibid., Brennan to Sullivan, 3/17/70, p. 1; Brennan File, Part 4, p. 49–50, Brennan to Hoover, 4/27/70.

74. Felt-Miller, Box 102, "Plans to Deal with WUO," File 1 of 4: Cotter to Sullivan, 3/17/70.

75. Ibid., Director to Special Agents in Charge, 3/18/70.

76. The March 19 circular: ibid., File "Plans to Deal w/WUO," 3 of 4, Director to SACs, 3/19/70, pp. 1–3; also in Latimer File, NW 5675,

DocId 59161305, pp. 95–97. The March 24 circular: Box 102, File "Plans to Deal w/WUO," 3 of 4, Director to 16 SACs, 3/24/70.

77. No intensive investigation of the corporate bombings: Felt-Miller Box 102, File 3 or 4, "Plans to Deal with WUO," Rosen to DeLoach, 3/25/70, p. 1. Hoover's order on the townhouse, March 13: ibid., "Plans to Deal with WUO," File 1 of 4, Brennan to Sullivan, 3/13/70, p. 3; "correlative investigation": ibid., Brennan to Sullivan, 4/1/70, p. 1; no intensive investigation: Box 102, "Plans to Deal with WUO," File 3 of 4: Rosen to DeLoach, 3/25/70.

78. Yeagley written request: Felt-Miller, Box 102, "Plans to Deal with WUO," File 3 of 4: Yeagley to Hoover, 3/30/70. Accepted on grounds of FBI intelligence function, and because of public pressure: ibid. Brennan to Sullivan, 4/1/70, pp. 1–2.

79. Weatherman Squad established: Box 102, File "Plans to Deal with WUO," Sullivan to DeLoach, 4/21/70. From three to five to twenty agents by August: ibid., Brennan to Sullivan, 4/15/70; cf. Box 249, File "WUO II," Brennan to Sullivan, 5/18/70, and Box 311, Special Agent James Vermeesch Direct Testimony, October 24, 1980, p. 1167. Hoover orders specific investigation of townhouse: Box 249, File "WUO II," Hoover to SAC New York, 4/2/70.

80. Felt-Miller Box 102, File 1 of 4 "Plans to Handle WUO," Brannan to Sullivan, "New Left Movement—Violence," 4/1/70 (quotation on pp. 2–3). The connection between the townhouse and Detroit was recognized by Judge William Bryant himself at the Felt-Miller trial ten years later: see Felt-Miller Box 315, Larry Grathwohl Direct Testimony, October 10, 1980, p. 3571 (Judge Bryant's comment), pp. 2–3.

81. Felt-Miller Box 102, File 1 of 4 "Plans to Handle WUO," Brennan to Sullivan, "Handling Bombing Matters," 4/1/70, pp. 5–6.

82. Ibid., p. 1.

83. Grathwohl, *Bringing Down America*, 175–176. The charges against Evans and Donghi had to do with the Days of Rage. The Bureau could have caught the entire Weather Bureau if it had waited: Mark Rudd, *Underground: My Life with SDS and the Weathermen* (New York: William Morrow, 2009), 202–203.

84. Grathwohl, *Bringing Down America*, 178–181. See also Linda Evans, "Letter to the Movement," *Berkeley Tribe*, 7/10/70, rpt. in Jacobs, *Weatherman*, 462–463.

85. Varon, *Bringing the War Home*, 176 and n. 138. Weatherman soon put out a warning on Grathwohl, appearing, for instance, in the *Berkeley Tribe* on August 21: Grathwohl, *Bringing Down America*, 180.

86. Felt-Miller, Box 102, "Plans to Deal with WUO," File 3 of 4: Sullivan to DeLoach, 4/14/70, pp. 1–2. For concern over the nationwide scope of the menace, see also Box 102, Folder "Plans to Deal with WUO," File 1 of 4, J. A. Sizoo (a senior figure in the Research Section) to Sullivan,

6/11/70, p. 1. Sullivan supports Brennan's similar conclusion: Brennan File 4, p. 27, Sullivan to Felt and Tolson, 4/19/70. His estimate of investigative costs to DeLoach: Box 102, "Plans to Deal with WUO," File 3 of 4, Sullivan to DeLoach, 4/24/70, p. 1.

87. Felt-Miller, Box 311, Special Agent James Vermeersch Direct Testimony, 1167. Twenty special agents: ibid.

88. Felt-Miller Box 320 "Government Trial Exhibits," Shackelford to Miller, 10/27/71, p. 2 (a retrospective on FBI efforts against Weatherman in 1970 and 1971).

89. Ibid., p. 2. The difficulties are laid out in detail in Felt-Miller Box 276, File "Microphone Exhibits," Miller to Rosen 11/12/71, pp. 2–4. Numerous examples of total dead ends can be found in the FBI material collected for the 1980 trial.

90. *New York Times*, 4/12/70; cf. Wells, *The War Within*, 412–413. Felt-Miller Box 319, Trial Transcript, John Mitchell Direct Testimony, October 28, 1980, pp. 5762–5763.

Chapter Four. "Our Own Doors Are Being Threatened"

1. Felt-Miller, Box 102, "Plans to Deal with the WUO," File 3 of 4, Brennan to Sullivan, 5/11/70, pp. 1–2.

2. Ibid., File 1 of 4, Cotter to Sullivan, 5/20/70, with suggested appended "FBI Special Report: Nationwide Civil Disturbances, 1969–1970."

3. Henry Kissinger, *The White House Years* (Boston: Little, Brown, 1979), 509–514, a passage whose importance is stressed in Tom Wells, *The War Within: America's Battle over Vietnam* (Lincoln, Neb.: Authors Guild, 2005), 430–431. "Fire them all!" and Nixon's fury at Warren Hickel: Richard Reeves, *President Nixon: Alone in the White House* (New York: Simon and Schuster, 2001), 215–216.

4. The underground bunker: John Dean, *Blind Ambition: The White House Years* (New York: Simon and Schuster, 1976), 21; the troops: Jeremy Varon, *Bringing the War Home* (Berkeley: University of California Press, 2004), 131. Buses around the White House, and Admiral Moorer's warning: Wells, *The War Within*, 431–432.

5. The commission report, starting with the warning, was the lead story in the *New York Times*, 4/28/70. Nixon shaken by the student response to Cambodia, and Kent State: *RN: The Memoirs of Richard Nixon* (New York: Grosset and Dunlap, 1978), 457, confirmed by H. R. The *Haldeman Diaries: Inside the Nixon White House* (New York: Putnam, 1994), 162 (5/7/70). Reporter's question to Nixon about possible revolution: Rick Perlstein, *Nixonland* (New York: Scribner, 2009), 492. The hard-hat riots begin: "After 'Bloody Friday,' New York Wonders if Wall Street Is Becoming a Battleground," *Wall Street Journal*, 5/11/70; cf. Perlstein, *Nixonland*, 497.

6. *Senate Select Committee to Study Governmental Operations with Respect to Intelligence Activities*, vol. 2, *The Huston Plan*, Huston testimony, 9/23/75, 35–36. Huston's accuracy on the concerns: see the actions taken above, n. 4.
7. Ibid., 32.
8. Felt-Miller, Box 250, File "Rudd," Brennan to Sullivan, 2/13/70. On the February Weatherman meeting and the threat of "strategic sabotage," see also Box 102, "Plans to Deal with WUO," File 1 of 4, Shackelford to Brennan 10/12/70 (a survey of extremist groups), p. 49.
9. The four were also asked about the Townhouse, the Chicago dynamite cache, and the bombs in Detroit: Felt-Miller Box 115, "Misc. Newsclippings," SAC Chicago to Director, 6/4/70, p. 3). Russell Neufeld now only remembers being questioned about Dohrn's Declaration of War (interview with the author, 11/16/13).
10. Felt-Miller Box 115, File "Misc. Newsclippings": Director to SACS, 5/28/70. The memo appears in this odd place evidently because of its connection to the Weatherman "Declaration of War" news clippings in the larger file.
11. Weatherman gloating about ability to penetrate police headquarters: Weatherman communiqué no. 2, "Headquarters," 6/10/70, in *Sing a Battle Song: The Revolutionary Poetry, Statements, and Communiqués of the Weather Underground, 1970–1974*, ed. Bernardine Dohrn, Bill Ayers, and Jeff Jones (New York: Seven Stories, 2006), 151–152.
12. Felt-Miller, Box 103, File "Plans to Deal w/WUO," Shackelford to Brennan, 8/7/70, p. 2. How the use of "obscenity" was going to destroy the structure of the country is mysterious. Still, Shackelford's rhetoric demonstrates the depth of FBI concern.
13. Weather Underground Communiqué, "New Morning—Changing Weather," 12/6/70, in Dohrn, Ayers, and Jones, *Sing a Battle Song*, 161–169.
14. Felt-Miller Box 276, File "Pressure from FBI," Director to SACs, 4/17/70, pp. 1, 3–4 (my emphasis)
15. Felt-Miller, Box 102, "Plans to Deal with WUO" File 1 of 4, Hoover to SACs, 5/13/70; Felt-Miller, Box 103, "Plans to Deal w/WUO" (final file), Hoover to SACs, 7/16/70.
16. Brennan in "Rise of the Dynamite Bombers," *Time*, 9/9/70.
17. Interview with Edward S. Miller (Society of Former Special Agents of the FBI), 5/28/08, pp. 128–129. Deep concern about the scale of Weatherman capabilities in this period (including possible murders of government figures) was also felt by ordinary field agents: interview with Special Agent William Dyson (Society of Former Special Agents of the FBI), January 2008, p. 42.
18. "Rise of the Dynamite Bombers." Origin of Brennan's numbers: the secret Huston Plan Report to President Nixon (June 1970) declared, "While Weatherman membership is not clearly defined, it is estimated

that at least 1,000 individuals adhere to Weatherman ideology. In addition, groups such as the White Panther Party, Running Dog, Mad Dog, and the Youth International Party (Yippies) are supporters of Weatherman terrorism." Felt-Miller Box 118, Trail Transcript Felt Recross, 10/23/80, p. 5168, quoting from the Huston Plan.

19. List of Weatherman bombings: see Appendix. The list in Dohrn, Ayers and Jones, *Sing a Battle Song*, 61–64, is misleadingly incomplete. Actual Weatherman numbers: see Felt-Miller Box 251, File "Bu II": "Argument for Use of Anonymous Sources-Black Bag Technique—Weatherman Investigation), 1/14/72, p. 2 ("less than 100" guerrillas), p. 3 (a total of three hundred people aboveground and below).

20. Felt-Miller Box 311, Trial Transcript, Vermeersch Direct Testimony, 9/23/ 80, pp. 1241.

21. Felt-Miller Box 312, Vermeersch Cross-Examination, 9/24/80, p. 1335.

22. Sanford J. Ungar, *FBI* (Boston: Little, Brown, 1975), 463.

23. Felt-Miller Box 106, File "230 A-R . . . Nixon/AG": "Profile of Urban Guerrilla Activity: Groups, Leaders, Incidents," 11/22/71, pp. 3–4, 5.

24. Communiqué no. 3, "Honk Amerika," 6/25/70, in Dohrn, Ayers, and Jones, *Sing a Battle Song*, 153: "And to General Mitchell we say, 'Don't look for us, Dog; we'll find you first.'"

25. On the Jonathan Jackson raid on the Marin County Courthouse, see "A Bad Week for the Good Guys," *Time*, 8/17/70.

26. On Mitrione's career, see David Ronfeldt, *The Mitrione Kidnapping in Uruguay* (Santa Monica, Calif.: Rand Corporation, 1987). The Mitrione kidnapping was later made into a pro-Tupamaros movie by the director Costa-Gavras: *State of Siege* (1973).

27. Tom Bates, *Rads: The 1970 Bombing of the Army Math Research Center at the University of Wisconsin* (New York: Harper Collins, 1992), covers the bombing in great detail; the FBI's opinion in August 1970 that Army Math was the work of Weatherman: ibid., 251–252.

28. Brennan's view of the Wisconsin bombing in 1970: Felt-Miller Box 102, "Plans to Deal with WUO," File 1 of 4, Brennan to Sullivan, 9/21/70, p. 2; for 1980: Felt-Miller Box 291, File "Brennan, Charles D.," p. 1.

29. Stephen E. Ambrose, *Nixon: The Triumph of a Politician, 1962–1972* (New York: Simon and Schuster, 1989), 369; Richard Hughes, *Chasing Shadows: The Nixon Tapes, the Chenault Affair, and the Origins of Watergate* (Charlottesville: University of Virginia Press, 2014), 74.

30. Bates, *Rads*, 264.

31. David Fine's connection to New York Weathermen: ibid. Grathwohl's information: Felt-Miller Box 315, Grathwohl Direct Testimony, 10/14/80, pp. 3578–3579. David Fine was certainly in Madison in March: see Bates, *Rads*, 264. He was a suspect in the bombing by September 1: ibid., 30–31, 34. Note that when Bates wrote *Rads*, he did not know of Grathwohl's information.

32. Bates, *Rads*, 264.
33. Kearney's opinion: interview with Jack Kearney (Society of Former Special Agents of the FBI), 1/25/06, p. 5. The reality: see Janet Landman, *Crime and Conscience: Former Fugitive Katherine Ann Power* (London: Rowan and Littlefield, 2012).
34. Another example of what happened when the FBI adopted the "Weatherman in character" category: the May 5, 1970, destruction of a dozen U.S. Army trucks in Idaho—a startling attack—ended up in an FBI file on Weatherman: Felt-Miller, Box 134, "Not in 5/5 list [Weatherman Information]," File 2 of 2.
35. Shackelford's warning, and urging of preparations for attack: Felt-Miller, Box 102, "Plans to Deal with WUO," File 1 of 4, Shackelford to Brennan, 8/25/70. The multiple FBI targets in Washington: Felt-Miller, Box 107, File "Capbomb," Hoover testimony before the House Subcommittee on Appropriations, 3/17/71, p. 107.
36. Felt-Miller, Box 102, "Plans to Deal with WUO," File 1 of 4, Hoover to SACS 8/25/70.
37. Felt-Miller, Box 103, "Plans to Deal w/WUO," Final File (of 4), Casper to Mohr, 8/27/70, p. 1.
38. Jerome Cahill, "Mitchell Moving to Nip Bombings," *Capital Times* (Madison, Wis.), 9/17/70.
39. Felt-Miller, Box 103, "Plans to Deal w/WUO," Final File (of 4), Casper to Mohr, 8/27/70. More than one conference: ibid., Shackelford to Brennan, 10/3/70, p. 2; ibid., Director to SACs, 8/28/70; Felt-Miller, Box 107, File "Capbomb," Hoover before the House Subcommittee on Appropriations, 3/17/71, p. 107.
40. Fear of Weatherman recruiting in the fall: Felt-Miller, Box 103, File "Plans to Deal with WUO," Shackelford to Brennan, 8/7/70. One can see again how seriously the FBI took Bernadine Dohrn's "Declaration of War" on May 21. Hoover repeats to all SACs Shackelford's warning of upcoming violence: ibid., File "Plans to Deal with WUO," Final File, Director to SACs, 9/12/70 (first version); Director to SACs, 9/15/70, p. 4 (final version). September 17 warning: Felt-Miller, Box 102, "Plans to Deal with WUO," File 3 of 4, Shackelford to Brennan, 9/17/70.
41. Brennan's new warning: Felt-Miller Box 102, "Plans to Deal with WUO," File 1 of 4, Brennan to Sullivan (to be passed on to Hoover) 9/21/70, pp. 1–2. Hoover meets with Nixon: Box 102, File "JEH/AG," Director for the Record, Attorney General meeting with the President, 9/21/70.
42. Felt-Miller, Box 103, "Plans to Deal w/WUO," Final File (of 4), Felt to Tolson, 9/2/70, p. 1 (my emphasis).
43. Ibid.
44. Failure of the rump SDS organization under PL leadership: see J. Kirkpatrick Sale, *SDS* (New York: Random House, 1974), 614–615, 619–620.

45. Felt-Miller, Box 103, "Plans to Deal w/WUO," Final File (of 4), Felt to Tolson, 9/2/70, addendum by Sullivan (p. 2). Also in *Senate Select Committee*, vol. 2, *The Huston Plan*, 328–329, Committee Exhibit 44.
46. Felt-Miller, Box 103, "Plans to Deal w/WUO," Final File (of 4), Director to SACs, 9/15/70, p. 4. Also in *Senate Select Committee*, vol. 2, *The Huston Plan*, 332, Exhibit 44, Director to SACs, 9/15/70, pp. 3–4.
47. Felt, to Tolson 9/2/70, p. 2; Hoover to SACs, 9/12/70. This argument for lowering the lowered voting age because of the crisis of 1970 would be reiterated by Tom Charles Huston in his testimony before the Church Committee in 1975 as a reason for developing informants who were, under then U.S. law, still minors: *Senate Select Committee*, vol. 2, *The Huston Plan*, Huston testimony, 9/23/75, p. 24.
48. Felt-Miller, Bos 102, "Plans to Deal with WUO," File 4 of 4, Shackelford to Miller, 1/18/72. Ronald Kaufman was caught only in 1986: *Chicago Tribune*, 7/17/86.
49. James Naughton, "U.S. to Tighten Surveillance of Radicals," *New York Times*, 4/13/70 (this story carried the account of Irving Kristol's dinner with Nixon on March 12, 1970); Felt-Miller Box 102, "Plans to Deal with the WUO," File 1 of 4, Sullivan to DeLoach, 4/14/70.
50. Felt-Miller, Box 102, "Plans to Deal with the WUO," File 3 of 4, Brennan to Sullivan, 4/22/70, p. 2.
51. Ibid.
52. On this incident—famous at the time, forgotten now—see Ronfeldt, *The Mitrione Kidnapping*, 27. Von Holleben's Brazilian police guards were killed during the kidnapping; ibid.
53. The FBI understood that Weatherman idealized the Tupamaros, who had killed Mitrione: see, e.g., Felt-Miller, Box 102, "Plans to Deal with the WUO," File 3 of 4, Brennan to Sullivan, 4/22/70, p. 2.
54. Hoover-Nixon meeting (ca. August 11): Felt-Miller, Box 102, "Plans to Deal with WUO," File 1 of 4, Hoover to Mitchell, 8/17/70; Box 103, "Plans to Deal with WUO," Final File of 4, Hoover to Nixon, 8/17/70. Moore's warning: Felt-Miller, Box 103, "Plans to Deal w/WUO," Final File (of 4), Moore to Brennan, 8/13/70 (and thence to Hoover).
55. Felt-Miller, Box 102, "Plans to Deal with WUO," File 1 of 4, Hoover to Mitchell, 8/17/70.
56. The quotation is from the Tupamaros' "Letter to Mariano," 8/5/70, describing the crisis within the Uruguayan government caused by the kidnapping: see Ronfeldt, *Mitrione Kidnapping*, 22–23. The fears of Uruguayan Ambassador Luisi to Undersecretary of State Crimmins on 8/4/70: ibid., 36–37. The crisis in the Canadian government caused in October by kidnappings by the Quebec Liberation Front: William Tetley, *The October Crisis: An Insider's View* (Montreal: McGill-Queen's University Press, 2010), especially chapter 14.

57. The Leary jailbreak: Weatherman communiqué "Timothy Leary," 9/15/70, in Dohrn, Ayers, and Jones, *Sing a Battle Song*, 155. FBI knowledge of the communiqué, with its threat to gain release of prisoners: it is included in the FBI collection of Weatherman communiqués in Box "Misc. Press Clippings," and in the declassified FBI CD "The Weatherman File." Weatherman praise of Jonathan Jackson: Weatherman communiqué "Message to Daniel Berrigan," 10/8/70), in Dohrn, Ayers, and Jones, *Sing a Battle Song*, 155; "Hall of Injustice," 10/8/70, ibid., 158–159.

58. Dohrn interview in Varon, *Bringing the War Home*, 184; Machtinger interview in Bryan Burrough, *Days of Rage: America's Radical Underground, the FBI and the Forgotten Age of Revolutionary Violence* (New York: Penguin, 2015), 127.

59. The FBI fear about stockpiling of weapons by radicals was based on reality: see Roxanne Dunbar-Ortiz, *Outlaw Woman: A Memoir of the War Years, 1960–1975*, rev. ed. (Norman: Oklahoma University Press, 2014), 240, on her experiences in Oregon in the summer of 1970.

60. "New Morning," 166.

61. SPECTAR: Felt-Miller, Box 103, "Plans to Deal w/WUO," Final File (of 4), Shackelford to Brennan, 9/3/70, and Director to SACs, "Informant Coverage," 9/4/70 (oversight from the center). "Utmost importance": ibid. Director to SACs, "Violence in Connection with 1970 Fall Elections," 9/4/70, pp. 1–2.

62. Felt-Miller, Box 103, "Plans to Deal w/WUO," Final File (of 4), Rosen to Sullivan, 9/4/70.

63. Ibid., Final File (of 4), Hoover to government agencies: "Threats Against United States Government Officials," 9/8/70.

64. Felt-Miller, Box 102, "Plans to Deal with WUO," File 1 of 4, Sullivan to Tolson, 9/17/70, pp. 1–2 (reporting on Senator Scott's request, and Sullivan's reply).

65. Ibid., "Plans to Deal with WUO," File 1 of 4, Sullivan to Tolson, 9/22/70, pp. 1–2.

66. Secret Service warning: ibid., p. 2. Mitchell warning at press conference (10/16/70): James Rosen, *The Strong Man: John Mitchell and the Secrets of Watergate* (New York: Doubleday, 2008), 77 and n. 1.

67. Varon, *Bringing the War Home*, 184 (Dohrn interview, 2003).

68. Felt-Miller, Box 102, "Plans to Deal with WUO," File 1 of 4, Brennan to Sullivan, 9/21/70, p. 3. William C. Sullivan, *The Bureau: My Thirty Years in Hoover's FBI* (New York: Norton, 1979), 154, implies that the information was gotten via an illegal wiretap.

69. Hoover before Congress in November 1970: Sullivan, *The Bureau*, 154–155; W. Mark Felt, *The FBI Pyramid from the Inside* (New York: Putnam's, 1979), 88; the indictment and eventual trial in early 1971: ibid., 89–90.

70. See Betty Medsger, *The Burglary: The Discovery of J. Edgar Hoover's Secret FBI* (New York: Knopf, 2014).

71. See Ungar, *FBI*, 488.

72. On this subject, the most balanced study is David Cunningham, *There's Something Happening Here: The New Left, the Klan, and FBI Counterintelligence* (Berkeley: University of California Press, 2004).

73. Felt-Miller, Box 102, "Plans to Deal with WUO," File 1 of 4, Brennan to Sullivan, 9/24/70, p. 1.

74. Ibid., "Plans to Deal with the WUO," File 1 of 4, Director to SACs, 9/24/70, p. 2.

75. Ibid., Dean to Mitchell and Hoover, 10/20/70, pp. 1–2.

76. On the Canadian crisis, see Tetley, *The October Crisis*, especially chapters 5–8. Its relationship to the new "Kidnap Committee": Felt-Miller, Box 102, "Plans to Deal with the WUO, File 1 of 4, Jones to Bishop, 11/25/70, p. 5, on the views about Canada of Robert Mardian, the new assistant attorney general of the Internal Security Division.

77. Felt-Miller Box 102, "Plans to Deal with the WUO,' File 1 of 4: "Interdepartmental Study Group Concerning Political Kidnappings," Rosen to Sullivan, 10/22/70, p. 1.

78. Ibid. Note the reference to FBI executives as potential targets: we once more see the concern that the FBI itself might come under attack from Weatherman or Weatherman-like groups.

79. Ibid.

80. Account of the October meeting: ibid., 2–3. Rehnquist, to whom the matter of legal jurisdiction was referred, would, of course, later be an associate justice and then chief justice of the Supreme Court.

81. Felt-Miller Box 102, "Plans to Deal with WUO," File 1 of 4, Jones to Bishop, 11/25/70, p. 5. Increased severity of prosecutions of far-left terrorists: ibid., 1–2.

82. On the Holder hijacking, and Holder's use of Weatherman, see Brendan I. Koerner, *The Skies Belong to Us: Love and Terror in the Golden Age of Hijacking* (New York: Crown, 2013), chapters 8 and 9.

Chapter Five. "The Hoover Cutoff"

1. *Senate Select Committee to Study Governmental Operations with Respect to Intelligence Activities*, vol. 2, *The Huston Plan*, 9/24/75, p. 98. Brennan emphasized "normally" because he felt that national security issues made the situation more complex. On the origin of the term "black bag jobs," see, e.g., Felt-Miller Box 312, Trial Transcript: Special Agent James Vermeersch Cross-Examination, 9/24/80, p. 1307.

2. "Normal" procedure: Felt-Miller Box 107, File "Policy Stmnts," Baumgartner to Sullivan, 10/20/62, p. 5; Felt-Miller Box 318, Trial Transcript, Felt Redirect Testimony, 10/23/80, pp. 5123–5126. John Gordon's experience: Felt-Miller Box 313, Gordon Direct Testimony, October 13, 1980, p. 3321. The change in 1963: Box 318, Felt Redirect Testimony, 5126.

3. Felt-Miller Box 96, "Sullivan and Hoover directives Re: Weatherman," addendum to FBI report to the White House on foreign funding of the New Left, 2/26/70, p. 19. FDR may have already given a similar oral directive to Hoover in August: Box 107, File "Bu.jurid. Intelligence Field," Memo to the Attorney General, 9/13/72, p. 2.

4. FDR's order of May, 1940: quoted in Sanford J. Ungar, *FBI* (Boston: Little, Brown, 1975), 444. The broadening of FBI power and responsibility: Felt-Miller Box 315, Trial Transcript, Herbert Brownell Direct Testimony, 10/15/80, p. 3799.

5. FBI understanding of the Brownell Memo: Felt-Miller Box 315, Trial Transcript, Herbert Brownell Direct Testimony, 10/15/80, p. 3774. "Complete Power": pp. 3775, 3777, 3785, 3789. Brownell emphasized that he himself acted as an overseer to prevent potential FBI abuses, and gave examples (p. 3792).

6. Opposition from lawyers within Justice: Brownell Cross-Examination, 3814 (quotation), and 3816. Yeagley: Felt-Miller Box 316, Trial Transcript, Yeagley Cross-Examination, 10/17/80, p. 4283. Yeagley had once been an FBI man himself. Supreme Court justices Tom Clark and Byron White knew: Felt-Miller Box 320, Trial Transcript, File "Closing Arguments," Thomas Kennelly Closing Argument (for Felt), p. 6428.

7. Opinion only: Felt-Miller Box 315, Brownell Cross-Examination, 10/15/80, p. 3816. "Don't get caught": interview with Jack Kearney (Society of Former Special Agents of the FBI), 1/25/06, p. 14.

8. Microphones *were* trespass because of installation procedure: Felt-Miller Box 313, Trial Transcript, T. J. Smith Cross-Examination, 10/3/80, pp. 2667–2673. The 1956 Hoover presentation of a break-in for search to the National Security Council, Nixon and Eisenhower: Felt-Miller Box 314, Trial Transcript, Arbor Gray Cross-Examination, 10/8/80, pp. 3098–3107 (with the contemporary documents).

9. Wiretaps and bugging more invasive: New York City SAC Arbor Gray, ibid., pp. 3110–3111; Kleindienst: Felt-Miller Box 319, Trial Transcript, Richard Kleindienst Cross-Examination, 10/23/80, pp. 5801–5802.

10. Felt-Miller Box 313, Trial Transcript, Donald E. Moore Direct Testimony, 10/6/80, p. 3051.

11. At least 240: *Senate Select Committee*, vol. 2, *The Huston Plan*, 113. No protests: Felt-Miller Box 316, Trial Transcript, Yeagley Cross-Examination, 10/17/80, p. 4250.

12. The impact of the Long Hearings, W. Mark Felt, *The FBI Pyramid from the Inside* (New York: Putnam's, 1979), 105. Hoover's conflict with Katzenbach: Felt-Miller Box 320, File "Closing Arguments," Nields Rebuttal Closing, 11/4/80, pp. 6527–6528. From eighty wiretaps to forty: *Senate Select Committee*, vol. 2, *The Huston Plan*, Brennan testimony, 9/25/75, p. 105. Unhappiness in the field: Felt, *The FBI Pyramid*, 105–106.

13. See Felt-Miller Box 276, "Microphone Exhibits," DeLoach to Tolson, 1/10/66, 1/12/66, and 1/17/66 (reporting on three detailed meetings); Director to Sen. Long, 1/20/66 (the reassuring letter): ibid. Senator Long's response: ibid., DeLoach to Tolson, 1/21/66.

14. *Senate Select Committee*, vol. 2, *The Huston Plan*, 273. Exhibit 32, Sullivan to DeLoach, 7/18/66, p. 1.

15. Illegal but necessary (Sullivan): ibid., p. 2. KKK and the Chaney-Goodman-Schwerner killings: ibid., Brennan testimony, 9/25/75, pp. 119–120; Felt-Miller Box 314, Trial Transcript, John Gordon Direct Testimony, 10/8/80, pp. 3326–3333.

16. Illegal but necessary (DeLoach): Cartha DeLoach, *Hoover's FBI: The Inside Story by Hoover's Trusted Lieutenant* (Washington, D.C.: Regnery, 1995), 296. "The Hoover cutoff": *Senate Select Committee*, vol. 2, *The Huston Plan*, 273. Exhibit 32, Sullivan to DeLoach, 7/18/66, p. 3, addendum. Cf. also Felt-Miller, Box 107, File "G 91—JEH reint. Bag jobs 241 A-L," Brannigan to Sullivan, 10/19/68 (referring to Hoover's decision).

17. Felt's opinion: Felt-Miller Box 118, Trial Transcript, Felt Cross-Examination, 10/23/80, p. 5085, repeated at p. 5098; cf. Felt, *The FBI Pyramid*, 111–112. Brennan's opinion: *Senate Select Committee*, vol. 2, *The Huston Plan*, Brennan testimony, 9/25/75, p. 106 (quotation), cf. p. 100.

18. *Senate Select Committee*, vol. 2, *The Huston Plan*, 276, Committee Exhibit 33, Director to Tolson and DeLoach, 1/5/67.

19. The FBI admitted to burglaries from 1968, but without details: *Senate Select Committee*, vol. 2, *The Huston Plan*, 113. Smith in 1980: Felt-Miller Box 313, Trial Transcript, T. J. Smith Direct Testimony, 9/30/80, p. 2064. Shackelford in 1980: ibid., Direct Testimony, 9/30/80, pp. 2248–2249.

20. Felt-Miller, Box 107, File "G91—JE reinst. Bag jobs 241 A-L." The break-ins were on March 26, March 28, April 2, May 16, May 28, and June 12 (all in the file). See also Kearney interview, 5. In Washington the Kearney material (which remains redacted) reached at least as high as Tolson: ibid., G. C. Moore to Sullivan, with copy to Tolson, 5/31/68 and 6/17/68.

21. Bergman: Felt-Miller Box 315, Special Agent David Ryan Direct Testimony, 10/15/80, pp. 3950–3952, cf. p. 3965 (with supporting contemporary documents, referred to only indirectly because they were—and are—still classified). No charges ever proven: Felt-Miller Box 316, Trial Transcript, Prosecution-Defense Stipulation, 4061; Special Agent David Ryan Cross-Examination, 10/16/80, pp. 4054–4055 (Ryan was reluctant to admit this). Felt vetoes television: ibid., p. 3965. Wiretaps and bugs in place in Bergman's Berkeley house in early 1970: ibid., p. 3969. See also Aaron J. Leonard, with Conor A. Gallagher, *Heavy Radicals: The FBI's Secret War on Maoists: The Revolutionary Union/Revolutionary Communist Party, 1968–1980* (Zero, 2015).

22. Other (unknown) wiretaps of radicals: Felt-Miller Box 102, "Plans to Deal with WUO," File 1 of 4, Brennan to Sullivan, Preparations for

Special Conference, 4/1/70, pp. 2, 4. Kurshan and Emmer: Felt-Miller Box 251, File "Bu II": "Surveys, Projects and Intensification Programs," Domestic Intelligence Division Inspection, 8/18/71. Nancy Kurshan was the girlfriend of the radical Jerry Rubin.

23. At the 1980 trial, Cartha DeLoach submitted a written "memorandum for the record" about the agreement he witnessed between Hoover and Ramsey Clark, dictated on September 8, 1967: Felt-Miller Box 316, Cartha DeLoach Direct Testimony, 10/16/80, pp. 4117, 4124–4125.

24. Section 2511 (3) of the Omnibus Crime Control Act of 1968.

25. Hoover's view of changing times: William C. Sullivan, *The Bureau: My Thirty Years in Hoover's FBI* (New York: Norton, 1979), 205; Felt, *The FBI Pyramid*, 105; *Senate Select Committee*, vol. 2, *The Huston Plan*, Brennan testimony, 9/25/75, p. 115. His concern about retaining the directorship since he was past normal retirement age: ibid., 97. Concern for the reputation of the FBI: ibid., 115.

26. The February 1969 orders: Felt-Miller, Box 103, "Plans to deal w/ WUO," File 3, Director to SACs, 2/24/69, p. 1; ibid., Director to SACs, 2/19/69: ibid., Director to SACs, 3/3/69; Director to SACs, 7/30/70, p. 1. Age limit: Felt-Miller, Box 102, File "Plans to Deal with WUO, Hoover to Yeagley, 2/18/69; Hoover to SACs, 2/19/69; Hoover to Tolson 2/24/69; Hoover to SACs, 3/5/69. Numerical limit: Box 103, "Plans to deal w/WUO," File 3, Sullivan to DeLoach, 2/25/69, p. 1.

27. *Senate Select Committee*, vol. 2, *The Huston Plan*, 354, Exhibit 51, Director to Helms, 3/31/70, p. 1.

28. Sullivan and Angleton: Exhibit 52, Sullivan to DeLoach, 4/14/70. By contrast, Sullivan's protests to Hoover: Felt-Miller, Box 102, File "Plans to Deal with WUO," Sullivan to DeLoach, 6/6/68, p. 1 (first quotation); Box 103, "Plans to deal w/WUO," File 3, Sullivan to DeLoach, 2/25/69, p. 1 (second quotation). The judgment of one special agent in charge: "Sullivan raised hell about the bag job cut-off": Felt-Miller Box 195, "My Notes" (John Nields), interview with SAC Bishop. Yet Sullivan remained a favorite of Hoover: Felt, *The FBI Pyramid*, 110–111; repeated in W. Mark Felt, *A G-Man's Life: The FBI, Being Deep Throat, and the Struggle for Honor in Washington* (Washington, D.C.: Public Affairs, 2007), 101.

29. Complaints: Felt-Miller Box 102, File "Plans to Deal with WUO," Brennan to Sullivan, 3/4/69, p. 2. Hoover's demands, despite his restrictions: Box 103, File "Plans to deal w/WUO, File 3, Director to SACs, 3/5/69. A similar message went from Hoover to all SACs in 1967, forbidding contacts on campuses for fear of embarrassment if these contacts came to light; yet this restriction did not relieve the field offices of the responsibility to provide useful information on the New Left: Box 103, "Plans to Deal w/WUO," File 2: Director to SACs, 4/27/67.

30. Helm's complaint to LBJ: *Senate Select Committee*, vol. 2, *The Huston Plan*, 403, Exhibit 65, Helms to President Johnson, 9/3/68, p. 2. "Operation

Chaos": ibid., 401, Helms to Kissinger, 2/18/69, offering the information he possessed but warning that it would be embarrassing to the CIA if such information gathering was known. See in general Frank Rafalko, *MH/CHAOS: The CIA's Campaign against the Radical New Left and the Black Panthers* (Annapolis, Md.: Naval Institute Press, 2011).

31. Felt-Miller Box 274, file "Huston Plan," Vermeersch to SAC New York, 2/14/72 (Bookchin); 3/8, 3/23/ 4/7 (Dohrn); 4/18 (Machtinger). April 1970 bugging and/or wiretap operations: Felt-Miller Box 102, "Plans to Deal with WUO," File 1 of 4, Brennan to Sullivan, "Conference of Ass't Directors," 4/1/70, p. 2.

32. Felt, *The FBI Pyramid*, 192.

33. Weatherman Squad in April: Felt-Miller, Box 96, File "Squad 47," SAC New York to Director, 4/7/70; in May: SAC New York to Director, 5/6/70 with approving addendum by Felt, 5/12/70.

34. Intensifying pressure: SAC New York to Director, 5/6/70, pp. 1–2, and Felt addendum (5/12/70). The number of special agents assigned to Squad 47 at one point reached fifty: Felt-Miller Box 311, Trial Transcript, Vermeersch Direct Testimony, 9/24/80, p. 1167. Hoover on Kearney: Box 96, File "Squad 47," Director to SAC New York, 8/5/70.

35. Kearney's career, and reputation as a "black bag job" expert: File "Squad 47": "Introduction: Squad 47"; cf. Felt-Miller Box 312, Trial Transcript, James Vermeersch Cross-Examination, 9/24/80, p. 1512. Trained in lock picking: Felt-Miller, Box 48, File "Agent Training Re: Lock-Picking," Tab 2.

36. Kearney interview, 13–14, quoting the statistics of the Department of Justice indictment against him. The indictment was later dropped because of political pressure from FBI men and conservatives.

37. Felt-Miller Box 274, File "Huston Plan," Vermeersch to SAC New York, 3/23/72 (with names).

38. Dohrn: Felt-Miller Box 311, Trial Transcript, Vermeersch Direct Testimony, 9/24/80, pp. 1173–1174, 1189–90. Bookchin: Felt-Miller Box 320, "Government Trial Exhibits," SAC New York to Acting Director, 4/9/73, p. 1.

39. "Wildcat bag jobs": Felt-Miller Box 195, "Gov't's Opposition to Gray's Motion to Dismiss," John W. Nields and Daniel S. Friedman memo, 8/8/80, p. 6.

40. Dohrn burglaries: Felt-Miller Box 274, File "Huston Plan," Vermeersch to SAC New York, 3/7/72, 3/23/72, 4/7/72. Hoover's orders on March 27, 1972: Felt-Miller, Box 276, File "30. Pressure from FBI": Hoover to SAC New York, 3/27/72, p. 1.

41. "Highly sensitive sources": Felt-Miller Box 312, Vermeersch Cross-Examination, 9/24/80, pp. 1316–1317. Vermeersch, Jennifer Dohrn's case officer, was explaining why the phrase "highly sensitive source" appears in so many documents related to Dohrn. Wiretaps and microphones: See the list of FBI wiretaps and the list of microphone surveillances as of

June 1972 in Felt-Miller Box 96, File "Gray 21—Keith," Acting Director to Attorney General, 6/19/72, p. 1.

42. "Survey" break-ins to establish feasibility always preceded the actual formal application to the attorney general for a surreptitious entry: Felt-Miller Box 316, Trial Transcript, Special Agent Francis X. O'Neill Direct Testimony, 10/17/80, pp. 4329–4331.

43. Felt-Miller Box 251, File "Dohrn II (ESM)," Director to SAC New York, 3/31/72.

44. The application to Mitchell: Felt-Miller Box 117, Trial Transcript, Felt Cross-Examination, 10/22/80, p. 5004. The other applications to Mitchell involved Susan Jordan and Mona Cunningham: on these cases, see Felt-Miller Box 117, pp. 5006–5007.

45. Felt-Miller, Box 96, File "Sullivan and Hoover directives Re: Weatherman," Sullivan to Kelly, 9/30/77.

46. For discussion of this episode see Felt (who was no friend of Sullivan), *The FBI Pyramid*, 142–146.

47. *New York Times*, May 5, 1969.

48. John Ehrlichman, *Witness to Power* (New York: Simon and Schuster, 1982), 161–162.

49. *Senate Select Committee*, vol. 2, *The Huston Plan*, Exhibit 5 (p. 203), Sullivan to DeLoach, 6/20/69.

50. Ibid., Exhibit 6 (p. 204), Huston to Director, 6/20/69.

51. Hoover dismissive of Huston: Felt-Miller Box 248, "Weatherman I," Sullivan to DeLoach 6/18/69, Hoover's handwritten addendum. John Mitchell noted this too: Felt-Miller Box 319, Trial Transcript, Mitchell Redirect Testimony, 10/23/80, p. 5789–5790.

52. Felt-Miller Box 96, File "Sullivan and Hoover Directives Re: Weatherman," Haynes to Sullivan, 3/6/70, p. 1.

53. On the Riha case and the liaison committee disbanded, see David Cunningham, *There's Something Happening Here: The New Left, the Klan, and FBI Counterintelligence* (Berkeley: University of California Press, 2004), 292 and n. 83. "Atrocious": Charles Brennan: *Senate Select Committee*, vol. 2, *The Huston Plan*, 121 (quotation); Angleton's complaint: ibid., 68.

54. On the lawsuit and its impact, see John Finnegan and Romana Danysh, *Military Intelligence* (Washington, D.C.: Government Printing Office, 1998).

55. *Senate Select Committee*, vol. 2, *The Huston Plan*, Brennan testimony, 9/25/75, pp. 105–106. This was also Brennan's opinion—little or no foreign influence on the Left, including on Weatherman—when he was deposed in March 1980 for the Felt-Miller trial: Felt-Miller Box 291, File "Brennan, Charles D.," p. 3.

56. Public mood: *Senate Select Committee*, vol. 2, *The Huston Plan*, Brennan testimony, 9/25/75, p. 108. Nixon, in turn, encouraged it: see the bitter account in Rick Perlstein, *Nixonland* (New York: Scribner, 2009), chapters 20–23.

57. Felt-Miller Box 112, File "Misc. Discovery," DeLoach to Sullivan, 5/13/70, pp. 1–2. This document is marked "Strictly Personal and Confidential," Nixon also wanted enhanced FBI security surrounding Bureau wiretapping and bugging of officials and newsmen the president believed were leaking secret information to the media: ibid., p. 1.

58. *Senate Select Committee*, vol. 2, *The Huston Plan*, 191, Huston to Haldeman (dated only to July 1970), p. 3; H. R. Haldeman, *The Haldeman Diaries: Inside the Nixon White House* (New York: Putnam, 1994), 172 (6/5/72).

59. Felt-Miller Box 320, Trial Transcript, Nixon Cross-Examination, 10/29/80, pp. 5931–5932. And these claims would later repeated by Assistant FBI Director Edward Miller: interview with Edward S. Miller (Society of Former Special Agents of the FBI), 5/28/08, pp. 28–29.

60. "The Concern of the White House": *Senate Select Committee*, vol. 2, *The Huston Plan*, 179, Committee Exhibit 1 (Huston Plan), p. 34. "The President desired": ibid., 168, Committee Exhibit 1 (Huston Plan), p. 23. Limitations to be dropped: ibid., 179, Committee Exhibit 1 (Huston Plan), p. 34.

61. Felt-Miller Box 115, File "Misc Newsclippings," [unknown] to Tom Charles Huston at the White House, 5/22/70, p. 1.

62. *Senate Select Committee*, vol. 2, *The Huston Plan*, 213; Committee Exhibit 10: Sullivan to DeLoach, 6/8/70.

63. The working committee consisted of representatives from the FBI, the CIA, the DIA, the NSA, and the three military intelligence services: ibid., p. 224, Committee Exhibit 12, "USIB Sub-Committee on Domestic Intelligence," p. 1.

64. Ibid., 261, 262, Committee Exhibit 61, James Angleton Memorandum for the Record, June 1970, pp. 1–2.

65. Ibid., Huston testimony, 9/23/75, p. 18. The reference to bombers and assassins is to Weatherman and other New Left actors; the reference to snipers has to do with the Black Panthers.

66. Ibid., Brennan testimony, 9/25/75, p. 122.

67. Ibid., 146, Committee Exhibit 1 (Huston Plan), p. 1.

68. Black Panthers: ibid., p. 154: Committee Exhibit 1 (Huston Plan), p. 9. The United Front against Fascism conference in Oakland, July 1969: ibid. In reality, the conference had split the Panthers and Weatherman, with Weatherman rejecting Panther strategies aimed at peaceful organizing of the masses, not revolution. New Haven and the threat of thirteen hundred Weathermen: ibid.; cf. Paul J. Scheips, *The Role of Federal Military Forces in Domestic Disorders, 1945–1992* (Washington, D.C.: Center for Military History, 2005), 401.

69. *Senate Select Committee*, vol. 2, *The Huston Plan*, 152, Committee Exhibit 1 (Huston Plan), p. 7.

70. Interview with Special Agent William Dyson (Society of Former Special Agents of the FBI), January 2008, pp. 39–40. Dyson describes FBI agents

scraping the remains of bomb scenes into trash bags and then leaving within ten minutes: ibid., 39. Lack of police coordination was also a problem: in some cases, local police had already "cleaned up" the crime scene before the FBI even arrived: ibid., 40.

71. Forlorn hopes for defection: *Senate Select Committee*, vol. 2, *The Huston Plan*, 152, Committee Exhibit 1 (Huston Plan), p. 7. Weatherman funding diffuse: ibid. No defections from the Panther leadership: ibid., 157, Committee Exhibit 1 (Huston Plan), p. 12.

72. Ibid., 150, Committee Exhibit 1 (Huston Plan), p. 5. Cf. Brennan's one thousand guerrillas: *Time*, 9/7/70. Actual Weather Underground guerrillas probably never numbered more than one hundred.

73. Huston's claim that Nixon wanted the limitations lifted: *Senate Select Committee*, vol. 2, *The Huston Plan*, 168, Committee Exhibit 1 (Huston Plan), p. 23. Angleton believed him: ibid., James J. Angleton Testimony, 9/23/75, p. 57.

74. Ibid., 168–184, Committee Exhibit 1 (Huston Plan), pp. 23–39.

75. Ibid., Angleton Testimony, 9/23/75, pp. 57–58.

76. Covert mail coverage: ibid., 175, Committee Exhibit 1 (Huston Plan), p. 30; surreptitious entry: ibid., 177, Committee Exhibit 1 (Huston Plan), p. 32. Ban on military recruiting of informants on campus maintained: ibid. Hoover's protest footnotes, mail coverage: ibid., 175, Committee Exhibit 1 (Huston Plan), p. 31; surreptitious entry: ibid., 178, Committee Exhibit 1 (Huston Plan), p. 33; campus surveillance: ibid., 181, Committee Exhibit 1 (Huston Plan), p. 36. See also Felt-Miller Box 318, Trial Transcript, Felt Cross-Examination, 5078–5079.

77. The expensive production: Felt-Miller Box 118, Trial Transcript, Bench Conference, 10/23/80: "Government Admission no. 1," p. 5223.

78. Huston's memos in early July: *Senate Select Committee*, vol. 2, *The Huston Plan*, Committee Exhibit 2, pp. 190, 192, Huston to Haldeman, 7/3/70, pp. 2 and 4; ibid., p. 249, Committee Exhibit 22, Huston to Haldeman 8/8/70; cf. p. 190, Committee Exhibit 2, Huston to Haldeman, 7/3/70; ibid., p. 195, Committee Exhibit 2, Huston to Haldeman, 7/3/70, addendum p. 3.

79. "He'd fire them": ibid., p. 249, Committee Exhibit 22, Huston to Haldeman 8/8/70; cf. p. 190, Committee Exhibit 2, Huston to Haldeman, 7/3/70.

80. Felt-Miller Box 120, Trial Transcript, Nixon Direct Testimony, 10/29/80, p. 5911: "The Huston Plan pointed out that surreptitious entry was illegal, but of course, in approving the plan, that would remove the illegality, as I understood it."

81. Origin of Hoover's footnotes: *Senate Select Committee*, vol. 2, *The Huston Plan*, Committee Exhibit 15, Sullivan to DeLoach, 6/19/70, p. 2; and p. 237, Exhibit 16, Sullivan to Tolson, 6/20/70, pp. 1–2. On Sullivan's duplicity, see Cunningham, There's *Something Happening Here*, 34–35, 253.

82. Nixon's approval: *Senate Select Committee*, vol. 2, *The Huston Plan*, 198, Committee Exhibit 3, Haldeman to Huston, 7/14/70.
83. Ibid., "Covert mail coverage," White House stationery: Felt-Miller Box 118, Trial Transcript, Felt Redirect, 10/23/80, p. 5108. These were orders to act: John Mitchell, in Felt-Miller Box 319, Trial Transcript, Mitchell Cross-Examination, 5787–5788. Bryan Burrough incorrectly asserts that Nixon's approval was merely verbal, and hence the intelligence chiefs, especially Hoover, were being left out on a limb if things went wrong; *Days of Rage: America's Radical Underground, the FBI, and the Forgotten Age of Revolutionary Violence* (New York: Penguin, 2015), 133.
84. *Senate Select Committee*, vol. 2, *The Huston Plan*, 201, Exhibit 4, Huston to Helms, 7/23/70, p. 2.
85. Ibid., p. 248, Committee Exhibit 21, is an example of a notification of return, 7/28/70.
86. Cunningham, *Something Happening Here*, 34–35.
87. See Huston's astonishingly preemptory memo to Helms, the head of the CIA, on July 9 concerning future operations: *Senate Select Committee*, vol. 2, *The Huston Plan*, 246, Huston to Helms, 7/9/70; p. 394, Exhibit 61, Huston to Helms, 7/9/70, marked "Secret."
88. Helms's view: James Rosen, *The Strong Man: John Mitchell and the Secrets of Watergate* (New York: Doubleday, 2008), 494 (Helms interview). Nixon's suspicions of a flabby CIA: see Stansfield Turner, *Burn before Reading: Presidents, CIA Directors, and Secret Intelligence* (New York: Hyperion, 2005), 122–126; cf. Henry Kissinger, *The White House Years* (Boston: Little, Brown, 1979), 36: "Nixon considered CIA a refuge of Ivy League intellectuals opposed to him."
89. Nixon Library, Tom Charles Huston Interview Transcript, 6/27/08, p. 21 (interviewer: Tim Naftali).
90. Richard Reeves, *President Nixon: Alone in the White House* (New York: Simon and Schuster, 2001), 335, 339 (based on Nixon Library tapes). On Nixon's obsession with the Brookings Institute, see Ken Hughes, *Chasing Shadows: The Nixon Tapes, the Chennault Affair, and the Origins of Watergate* (Charlottesville: University of Virginia Press, 2014).
91. John Dean and Mitchell: Felt-Miller Box 275, File "IEC," Dean to Mitchell, 9/18/70 (memo summarizing their conversation the previous day); *Senate Select Committee*, vol. 2, *The Huston Plan*, Exhibit 24, pp. 255–257 (Dean to Mitchell, 9/18/70). Haldeman's support: Dean to Mitchell, 9/18/70, addendum.
92. The Huston Plan would be optimal: *Senate Select Committee*, vol. 2, *The Huston Plan*, 167, Committee Exhibit 29, unsigned Justice Department memo for Mitchell, Ehrlichman, and Haldeman, 1/19/71, p. 1. Case-by-case basis instead: Felt-Miller Box 275, File "IEC," Dean to Mitchell, 9/18/70, pp. 1–2 (also *Senate Select Committee*, Exhibit 24, pp. 255–256, Dean to Mitchell, 9/18/70, p. 1–2).

93. *Senate Select Committee*, Exhibit 25, pp. 258–259, Mardian to Mitchell, 12/4/70, pp. 1–3.

94. Ibid., p. 261, Hoover claims manpower problems: Committee Exhibit 26, Hoover to Mardian, 2/3/71. Mardian: Hoover killed the project: ibid., p. 265, Committee Exhibit 27, Mardian to Mitchell, 2/12/71. White House insistence that IEC continue: ibid., p. 266, Committee Exhibit 28, Peterson to Michel, 6/11/73.

95. Ibid., pp. 317–321, Committee Exhibit 41, Executive Committee to Tolson, 10/29/70.

96. Numbers: about 6,500 white New Leftists, plus 4,000 members of black campus organizations: ibid. p. 136; cf. Committee Exhibit 41, Executive Committee to Tolson, 10/29/70, pp. 317–321. Reasons: Senate Select Committee Exhibit 41, Executive Committee to Tolson, 10/29/70, pp. 317, 319. Only 8,000 field agents: of the 8,500 special agents in 1970, five hundred were assigned to Washington headquarters: Felt-Miller Box 318, Felt Cross-Examination, 10/23/80, p. 5044.

97. Hoover agrees: *Senate Select Committee*, vol. 2, *The Huston Plan*, 321, Committee Exhibit 41, and pp. 323–326. Committee Exhibit 43, Director to SACs (2nd memo), 11/4/70). Mark Felt, who disliked Sullivan, claimed that the October plan was rejected by the assistant directors and that Sullivan left the meeting in fury: *The FBI Pyramid*, 117. But these FBI memos show that Felt is not telling the truth: the plan was approved by the assistant directors and then by Hoover.

98. Felt, *The FBI Pyramid*, 117.

99. Haldeman, *The Haldeman Diaries*, 243 (2/4/71); cf. Reeves, *President Nixon*, 310–312; John Ehrlichman, *Witness to Power*, 165–167.

100. L. Patrick Gray, *In Nixon's Web: A Year in the Crosshairs of Watergate* (New York: Times Books, 2008), 8–12; Robert Mardian: quoted in ibid., 8. Mardian had been a major supporter of the autumn 1970 version of the Huston Plan, which Hoover had scuttled. Ehrlichman: *Witness to Power*, 165–167; Haldeman, *The Haldeman Diaries*, 357 (9/20/71); cf. Max Holland, *Leak: Why Mark Felt Became Deep Throat* (Lawrence: University of Kansas Press, 2012), 14.

101. Miller's hatred of radicals, especially Weatherman: Felt-Miller Box 313, Trial Transcript, Robert Shackelford Direct Testimony, 9/30/80, pp. 2258–2260; his bitter experience in Chicago in 1969–1970 (including chaining Bobby Seale): interview with Edward S. Miller (Society of Former Special Agents of the FBI), 5/28/08, pp. 78, 80.

102. Well read: Felt-Miller Box 202, "Plans to Deal with the WUO," File 4 of 4, Assistant Directors to Tolson, 10/22/71, p. 1. At this meeting he also showed his colleagues Abby Hoffman's *Steal This Book* (ibid.). A burglary expert: Miller interview, 32. His exaggerated estimate of the damage done by Weatherman: ibid., 129–130 (his source for this figure is Richard Nixon).

103. Only one fatality (and that wrongly attributed to Weatherman): Felt-Miller Box 102, "Plans to Deal with the WUO," 4 of 4: "FBI Special Report: The Urban Guerrilla," 2/29/72, pp. 6–8; "1971: Year of the Urban Guerrilla?" 4/17/72, pp. 10–12.

104. Mallet and Preusse: Felt-Miller Box 313, Trial Transcript, Robert Shackelford Direct Testimony, 9/30/80, pp. 2259–2260. On Mallet's close relationship with Miller, see also ibid., Bench Conference, 2184. Mallett in charge of bugging SDS headquarters in Chicago: Dyson interview, 31–32.

105. Felt-Miller, Box 313, Trial Transcript, Shackelford Cross-Examination, 2313 (first quotation); Direct Testimony, 2257 (second quotation). Mallet: ibid., 2312.

106. On the provenance of these documents, see ibid., Bench Conference, 9/30/80, pp. 2178–2189.

107. Felt-Miller Box 320, "Government Trail Exhibits," Shackelford to Miller, 10/29/71, p. 4; Shackelford to Sizoo, Thompson, Preusse and Kiff, 11/4/71, p. 1.

108. November 8 meeting: Felt-Miller Box 276, File "Microphone Exhibits," Miller to Rosen 11/12/71, pp. 2–4 (this document was actually written by Hugh Mallet: Box 313, Trial Transcript, Bench Conference, 9/30/80, p. 2179).

109. Felt-Miller Box 276, File "Microphone Exhibits," Miller to Rosen 11/12/71, pp. 1, 4, 5.

110. Felt-Miller Box 313, Trial Transcript, Shackelford Cross-Examination, 9/30/80, p. 2340.

111. Ibid., "Argument for Use of Anonymous Sources—Black Bag Jobs," 1/14/72, p. 1.

112. Ibid., 4. Previous memo on burglarizing the law office: Felt-Miller, Box 48, File "Weatherman In-Service": "For Research" (anonymous), 8/12/71, p. 1.

113. Jordan: Felt-Miller Box 196: "No Foreign Involvement—Keith," File 1 of 3, Director to Attorney-General, 12/8/71, p. 1; Miller directly involved: ibid., 2. Mona Cunningham: ibid., Director to Attorney-General, 2/28/72, p. 1. Miller again directly involved: ibid., 2.

114. Felt-Miller Box 274, file "Huston Plan," Vermeersch to SAC New York, 3/7/72 and 3/23/72; two listening devices: Director to SAC New York, 3/27/72, pp. 1–2.

115. Horace Beckwith, who came into Squad 47 in very late 1971, says that a black bag job was also run against Dana Biberman: Felt-Miller Box 291, File "Horace Beckwith Pre-Trial Interview," p. 5. Biberman was nominated as a black bag target in the Weatherman committee's first two drafts to Miller, November 12 and November 19, 1971.

116. Burrough, *Days of Rage*, 228–230 (interview with Reagan). Burrough is unaware of the discussion of the Cunningham case at FBI headquarters in Washington, and hence of the bugging of Cunningham's telephone.

117. Ibid., 226–228 (interviews with Dennis Cunningham and Delia [Cunningham] Mellis).

118. Felt-Miller Box 274, file "Huston Plan," Vermeersch to SAC New York, 2/14/72 (Bookchin); 4/18/72 (Machtinger). Hoover died on May 2.

Chapter Six. "Hunt Them to Exhaustion"

1. "One of the most pressing problems": *Senate Select Committee to Study Governmental Operations with Respect to Intelligence Activities*, vol. 2, *The Huston Plan*, 268, Wannall to Brennan, 3/25/71, p. 1. Armed guards and metal detectors: Felt-Miller Box 320, File "Closing Arguments," Kennelly Closing Argument (for Miller), 6512.

2. Felt-Miller Box 102, File "Plans to deal w/WUO," 1 of 4, Shackelford to Brennan, 926/70; Hoover to SACs, 10/1/70.

3. Max Elbaum, *Revolution in the Air: Sixties Radicals Turn to Lenin, Mao, and Che*, (London: Verso, 2006) 26; David Gilbert, *Love and Struggle: My Life in SDS, the Weather Underground, and Beyond* (Oakland, Calif.: PM, 2012), 194.

4. Counterculture (and New Left) gradually becomes local: see, e.g., Doug Rossinow, "Letting Go: Revisiting the New Left's Demise," in *New Left Revisited*, ed. John McMillan and Paul Buhle (Philadelphia: Temple University Press, 2002); Tim Miller, *The 60s Communes: Hippies and Beyond* (Syracuse, N.Y.: Syracuse University Press, 1999). FBI focus on national, not local problems: David Cunningham, *There's Something Happening Here: The New Left, the Klan, and FBI Counterintelligence* (Berkeley: University of California Press, 2004), 101–103.

5. Jeffrey Haas, *The Assassination of Fred Hampton: How the FBI and the Chicago Police Murdered a Black Panther* (Chicago: Chicago Review Press, 2011). This was a Chicago police operation, but the FBI had provided information on the layout of Hampton's apartment.

6. See Sanford J. Ungar, *FBI* (Boston: Little, Brown, 1975), 487, on sudden FBI political vulnerability.

7. A leftist battlefield: Felt-Miller, Box 106, File "Nixon/AG," Assistant Directors' Conference to Tolson, 10/22/71, p. 3. Urban guerrilla warfare on the rise: Box 102, "Plans to Deal with the WUO," File 4 of 4: Cotter to Miller, 10/22/71. Nixon's interest in the police chiefs conference: ibid., File "Nixon/AG," Smith to Miller, 11/5/71.

8. Hoover's memo: Box 102, "Plans to Deal with the WUO," File 4 of 4, Hoover to SACs, 4/13/72. One helpful hint from Hoover was that ordinary criminals were unlikely to be in possession of revolutionary literature (p. 3). "A time of terror": Felt-Miller Box 107, File "Bu.jurid. Intelligence Field," Memo to Attorney General, 9/13/72, p. 6: from Assistant FBI Director Thomas Smith. Kidnapping fears: "Contingency Plans for Terrorist Attack," Felt-Miller, Box 106, File "230 A-R G54, M27 Nixon/AG," Cregar to Miller, 1/5/73 (a six-page single-spaced memo).

9. Bombings nationwide in 1971: Felt-Miller Box 102, "Plans to Deal with the WUO," File 4 of 4: "FBI Special Report: 1971: A Time of Terror?" 4/2/72, p. 2. Attacks on police numbered 223 in 1970 vs. 112 in 1971: Felt-Miller Box 102, "Plans to Deal with the WUO," File 4 of 4, "FBI Special Report: The Urban Guerrilla in the United States," 2/29/72, p. 10; ibid., "1971: A Time of Terror?" p. 2. Police deaths from guerrilla attacks fell from twelve in 1970 to seven in 1971: ibid.

10. FBI estimate of Weatherman numbers: ibid., Felt-Miller Box 251, File "Bu II": "Argument for Use of Anonymous Sources—Black Bag Technique—Weatherman Investigation)," 1/14/72, p. 2 ("less than 100" guerrillas), p. 3 (a total of three hundred people aboveground and below). Horace Beckwith, the head of Squad 47, the FBI's special Weatherman Squad from May 1972 (eighty guerrillas): Felt-Miller Box 316, Trial Transcript, Beckwith Direct Testimony, 10/17/80, p. 4410.

11. Seven of the Top Ten: Felt-Miller Box 196, File "Trial Preps: No Foreign Involvement—Keith," SAC J. F. Morley to All Agents, Division Four (HQ), 7/24/72, p. 1.

12. Could not survive six months: Gilbert, *Love and Struggle*, 170. Hoover's anger (January 1972): see, e.g., Felt-Miller Box 276, File "30. Pressure from the FBI," Hoover to fourteen SACs, 10/27/71, p. 1; Hoover to SACs, 1/21/72. Shackelford's opinion about the public-relations problem: Felt-Miller Box 313, Trial Transcript, Shackelford Cross-Examination, 10/1/80, p. 2316, a view repeated at 2317–2318. The fear of worse bombing to come: Felt-Miller Box 196, File "Trial Preps: No Foreign Involvement—Keith," SAC J. F. Morley to All Agents, Division Four (HQ), 7/24/72, p. 1.

13. Boston plan: Felt-Miller Box 112, "Counterintelligence and Special Operations," SAC New York to Director, 3/10/71, pp. 1–3. Chicago efforts: ibid., SAC Chicago, to Director, 3/10/71, pp. 1–2 (quotation from p. 2); Felt-Miller Box 48, File "WM In-Service," untitled memo "for research," 8/12/71, p. 1. Biker plan: Felt-Miller Box 102, "Plans to Deal with the WUO," File 4 of 4, Shackelford to Felt-Miller, "Students for a Democratic Society," 11/11/71, pp. 1–3. Seattle plan: Box 102, "Plans to Deal with the WUO," File 4 of 4, Shackelford to Miller, "New Left Movement—Violence," p. 1; this idea was rejected by Headquarters: p. 2.

14. Special Weatherman fugitive squads: Felt-Miller Box 102, "Plans to Deal with the WUO," File 2 of 4, Director to SAC's, 10/27/71, pp. 1–2. Misjudging Mark Rudd in late 1971 as one of the main Weather leaders and perhaps as *the* leader: Felt-Miller Box 320, Government Trial Exhibits, Shackelford to Miller 10/27/71, p. 1, vs. the reality, Rudd the Weatherman dropout: Mark Rudd, *Underground: My Life with SDS and the Weathermen* (New York: William Morrow, 2009), chapter 14. Hoover's embarrassment before Congress: Felt-Miller Box 107, File "Capbomb"; Hoover House Appropriations Committee Appearance, 3/2/72, p. 87.

15. Tail on Cunningham: Felt-Miller Box 296, File "Microphone Exhibits": "Argument for Use of Anonymous Sources—Black Bag Technique— Weatherman Investigation," 1/14/72, p. 2; cf. Box 316, Trial Transcript, William Regan Direct Testimony, 10/17/80, pp. 4380–4381. Chase through San Francisco: Thai Jones, *A Radical Line* (New York: Free Press, 2004), 225–227; Dan Berger, *Outlaws of America: The Weather Underground and the Politics of Solidarity* (Oakland, Calif.: AK Press, 2006), 157–158; Gilbert, *Love and Struggle*, 171–177 (with pseudonyms for Jones and Dohrn); Box 316, Regan Direct Testimony, 4381.

16. John Davis: Box 316, Regan Direct Testimony, 4382. The clues that led to the Pine Street raid: ibid., 4382–4384; cf. Jones, *A Radical Line*, 227; Gilbert, *Love and Struggle*, 174.

17. Felt-Miller 316, Trial Testimony, William Regan Direct Testimony, 10/17/80, p. 4387.

18. Jones, *A Radical Line*, 227; Gilbert, *Love and Struggle*, 174–175.

19. The Weatherman return to the Bay Area and the August bombs: Gilbert, *Love and Struggle*, 179–180. The Albany bomb in September: ibid., 181–182. FBI humiliation: Felt-Miller Box 276, File "30. Pressure from the FBI," Hoover to fourteen SACs, 10/27/71, p. 1; Hoover to SACs, 1/21/72.

20. Ungar, *FBI*, 507; Cartha DeLoach, *Hoover's FBI: The Inside Story by Hoover's Trusted Lieutenant* (Washington, D.C.: Regnery, 1995), 415–416.

21. Nixon himself, twice, quoted in L. Patrick Gray, *In Nixon's Web: A Year in the Crosshairs of Watergate* (New York: Times Books, 2008), 171.

22. Nixon's hatred of VVAW: Rick Perlstein, *Nixonland* (New York: Scribner, 2009), 561–564. Gray's court attack on VVAW: Ungar, *FBI*, 504–505. Gray and the May 1971 mass arrests: ibid.

23. Gray's role in the suppression of the ITT scandal: W. Mark Felt, *The FBI Pyramid from the Inside* (New York: Putnam's, 1979), 167–174; cf. Ungar, *FBI*, 507; Max Holland, *Leak: Why Mark Felt Became Deep Throat* (Lawrence: University of Kansas Press, 2012), 21–22 and n. 30. "White House fellow": Felt-Miller Box 195, File "My Notes" (Nields), SAC Kitchens. Haldeman on his loyalty and "guts": Haldeman, Handwritten Notes, Folder 1, Nixon Library, 2 May 1972; cf. Holland, *Leak*, 22. Gray, of course, presents himself as nonpartisan: *In Nixon's Web*, 24.

24. VFW speech: Ungar, *FBI*, 515. Pepperdine speech: ibid.

25. On Gray's speech at Pepperdine and his learning about Watergate burglary, see Gray, *In Nixon's Web*, 59; Felt, *The FBI Pyramid*, 247 (he is not aware of the content of Gray's speech at Pepperdine). Gray's role as FBI chief in covering up Watergate: see, e.g., Ungar, *FBI*, 515–517; Felt, *The FBI Pyramid*, 247–259; Gray (very self-justifying—though he also depicts a Nixon who is close to insane) in *In Nixon's Web*, especially chapters 7–18.

26. Holland, *Leak*, 22–23.

27. Resentment of outsiders: interview with Edward S. Miller (Society of Former Special Agents of the FBI), 5/28/08, p. 181. Jealousy: on Felt, see Holland, *Leak* (perhaps overstates the case). It is significant that Assistant to the Director Gerald Mohr, another internal candidate for director, retired within months of Gray's appointment.

28. "Three-Day Gray": see Felt-Miller Box 320, Nields Closing Argument, 6368.

29. Felt-Miller Box 107, File "Bu.jurid. Intelligence Field," Inspector T. J. Smith to Miller, 8/1/72 (a retrospective), p. 1.

30. On the Pentagon bombing, see the investigative reports in Felt-Miller Box 276, File "Pressure from the Field," Alexandria Field Office to Acting Director, 5/26/72 and 6/9/72. Details from the Weatherman side are given by Bill Ayers, *Fugitive Days: Memoirs of an Antiwar Activist* (Boston: Beacon, 2001), 264–269.

31. Felt-Miller Box 251, File "Dohrn II (ESM)," Acting Director to SAC New York, 5/22/72, pp. 1–2.

32. At the trial, this was discussed only in indirect reference: Felt-Miller Box 118, Trial Transcript, Felt Redirect, 10/23/80, pp. 5131–5132. The resulting document is now available (see next note).

33. Felt-Miller Box 320, Government Trial Exhibits, Brannigan to Miller, 5/31/72 (six pages).

34. Felt for delay: ibid.; Gray's contrary response: ibid., 6; underlining in original. Gray's handwritten responses were always written in red ink.

35. First memo from Alexandria: Felt-Miller Box 276, File "Pressure from the Field," Alexandria Field Office to Acting Director, 5/26/72, p. 11. Second memo from Alexandria: ibid., File "Pressure from the Field," Alexandria Field Office to Acting Director, 6/9/72, p. 2. Gray's worries about Weatherman action at the national party conventions: Felt-Miller Box 48, File "Weatherman In-Service, 8/72," Miller to Shackelford, 7/21/72, p. 2.

36. For fears at FBI headquarters about what Weatherman might do in Miami, see Cril Payne, *Deep Cover: An FBI Agent Infiltrates the Radical Underground* (New York: Newsweek Books, 1979), chapters 5 and 6. Payne was sent undercover into the leftist demonstrators, with an eye out for Weathermen.

37. Program C reinstated: Felt-Miller Box 314, Trial Testimony, William. Brannigan Direct Testimony, 10/8/80, pp. 3230–3232, with reference to supporting documents (still classified). Mail coverage reinstated: Felt-Miller Box 251, File "Dohrn II (ESM)," SAC New York to Assistant Director, 12/15/72, p. 3. The name of the target is still redacted.

38. Felt Miller Box 115, Trial Transcript, Arbor Gray Direct Testimony, 1983–1984.

39. June 8 memo: Box 48, File "Dir. Memo re Bureau priority in Re: Weatherman," Acting Director to SACs, 6/8/72. Description of the June 22 conference: ibid., Shackelford to Miller, 6/23/72. Bag jobs: Box

134, File "Weathfug (General)," Miller to Felt, 6/30/72, appendix to the memo: "Desired Recommendations which may Result from Weatherman Conference, June 22, 1972."

40. The June 14, 1972 application: Felt-Miller, Box 117, Trial Transcript, Felt Cross-Examination, 10/22/80, p. 5004. Vermeersch's admission: Felt-Miller, Box 311, Trial Transcript, Vermeersch Direct Testimony, 9/23/80, pp. 1200–1201.

41. Kleindienst approval: Felt-Miller Box 117, Trial Transcript, Felt Cross-Examination, 10/22/80, p. 5004. Acting director's signature required for applications to the attorney general for extension of electronic surveillances: Felt, *The FBI Pyramid*, 218. Gary's claim: *In Nixon's Web*, 114–115.

42. See Felt-Miller Box 274, File "Huston Plan," Vermeersch to SAC New York, 6/6/72 and 6/13/72. Gray's May 22 memo: above, 18–19.

43. The original Hoover in-service for August 1972: Felt-Miller, Box 133, File F(o) "Weatherfug-General," Moore to Edward Miller (now the head of Domestic Intelligence Division), 4/7/72. No mention of Weatherman in the curriculum: ibid., Box 245, File "In-Service Classes": Moore to Miller, 4/7/72 plus curriculum, 1–9.

44. The change of subject: Felt-Miller Box 48, File "Weatherman In-Service, 8/72," Shackelford to Miller, 7/21/72, p. 2, and Shackelford to Miller, 7/26/72, p. 1 (retrospective). The new curriculum (ten pages long): Felt-Miller Box 275, File "In-Service Classes": Shackelford to Miller, 7/26/70. Bryan Burrough, *Days of Rage: America's Radical Underground, the FBI, and the Forgotten Age of Revolutionary Violence* (New York: Penguin, 2015), 233–234, unaccountably places the first Weatherman in-service in June, organized by Horace Beckwith, the head of the Weatherman Squad in New York.

45. Long hair: Felt-Miller Box 107, File "Undercover Agents," Gray to staff, 6/28/72 (9:55 P.M.). Weatherman top priority: ibid., Acting Director to 17 SACs, 7/12/72, under "Surveys, Projects and/or Intensification Program" retrospective, Intelligence Division, 10/23/73, p. 1.

46. The White House at work: Miller interview, 159. End of "the Hoover cutoff" under Gray: Felt-Miller Box 313, Trial Transcript, Donald E. Moore Direct Testimony, 10/6/80, pp. 3046–3047.

47. Felt-Miller Box 196, File "No Foreign Involvement," 1 of 3, Acting Director to Felt, 6/28/72, p. 2.

48. Felt-Miller, Box 134, File "Weathfug-General," Miller to Felt, 6/30/72, pp. 3–4; = Box 196: File "No Foreign Involvement," 1 of 3: Miller to Felt, 6/30/72, pp. 3–4.

49. Felt-Miller Box 196, File "No Foreign Involvement," 1 of 3: Cleveland to Felt, 7/3/72, pp. 3–4.

50. Gray-Sullivan meeting, and Gray's notes on it: Holland, *Leak*, 67 and 223, n. 25.

51. Felt-Miller Box 117, Trial Transcript, Felt Cross-Examination, 10/22/80, pp. 5012–5013.

52. The CIA report is discussed and quoted in Chapter 8. Felt's testimony at the 1980 trial declared the opposite: Felt-Miller Box 117, Trial Transcript, Felt Cross- Examination, 10/22/80, p. 5013. See also Felt, *The FBI Pyramid*, 316–318 (emphatic).
53. Felt-Miller Box 196, File "No Foreign Involvement," 1 of 3, Gray to Wilson, 6/28/72 and 7/5/72, and Wilson's reply.
54. Felt-Miller Box 118, Trial Transcript, Felt Redirect Testimony, October 23, 1980, pp. 5133–5137. The case involved the bugging of a black radical in North Carolina, which Gray ordered to proceed.
55. Miller and Cleveland memos to Gray: Felt-Miller Box 251, File "Bu II," Miller to Felt, 6/30/72, p. 4 (initialed by Gray on 7/17/72 at 8:40 P.M.); and Cleveland to Felt, 7/3/72, p. 6 (initialed by Gray on 7/17/72 at 9:24 P.M.). Gray's initial reply to Felt, 6/28/72, reread and initialed, 9:15–9:24 P.M.: Felt-Miller Box 196: "Trial Preps: No Foreign Involvement—Keith (1 of 3). Gray's "Hunt Them to Exhaustion" memo to Felt: Felt-Miller, Box 48, File "Dir. Memos re priority in Re: Weatherman," Gray to Felt, 7/18/72; underlinings in the original.
56. Sent to Miller and Shackelford: Box 251, File "Bu II," Shackelford to Miller, 7/31/72, p. 1 (retrospective). Sent to 17 SACs: Felt-Miller Box 134, "Weathfug (General), Acting Director to 17 SACs, 7/18/72, p. 3 (quotation).
57. Felt-Miller Box 117, Trial Transcript, Felt Direct Testimony, 10/22/80, pp. 4926–4927, 4964–4966.
58. Felt-Miller, Box 133, File "F(o) Weathfug—General," Acting Director to Sacs, 7/24/72, pp. 2–3; also in Box 276, File "30. Pressure from FBI." The field offices that received this message were Albany, Boston, Chicago, Cleveland, Denver, Detroit, Los Angeles, Milwaukee, New York, Philadelphia, Portland, St. Louis, San Diego, San Francisco, Seattle, Springfield, Massachusetts, and Washington D.C.
59. Gray, *In Nixon's Web*, 120–121, 259.
60. See Holland, *Leak*, 175–176; Burrough, *Days of Rage*, 134.
61. Felt and Miller defense in 1989: see, e.g., Felt-Miller Box 117, Trial Transcript, Felt Direct Testimony, 4966–4967.
62. Felt's testimony in 1980: Felt-Miller, Box 117, Felt Cross-Examination, 10/22/80, pp. 4996–4997. See the similar debate between Felt and Nields the next day, at Box 118, Felt Re-Cross, 10/23/80, p. 5160.
63. Protests from the field: see Felt-Miller, Box 111, "Felt Specific Documents Misc," Schutz to Bates 8/25/72: the SACs concerned about less effort going to breaking up interstate car-theft rings. This memo of protest is four single-spaced pages long. On the reluctance of some SACs to divert their limited resources in pursuit of Weatherman, see also interview with Special Agent William Dyson (Society of Former Special Agents of the FBI), January 2008, pp. 40–41. But Dyson says that other local offices were enthusiastic: "there just was no consistency" (41).

64. Weatherman top priority: Felt-Miller Box 134, "Weathfug (General), Acting Director to 17 SACs, 7/18/72, p. 3. Excuses "unacceptable": Felt-Miller Box 102, File "Plans to Deal with the WUO," 4 of 4, Acting Director to SAC Seattle, 8/15/72, p. 1. Primary task of domestic intelligence in 1972–1973 was Weatherman: Miller interview, 128.

65. Felt-Miller Box 48, File "WM In-Service B" (interviews, August 1976). Refusal to answer—or even be told—questions: interview 9/9/76; cf. interview 9/14/76.

66. Dohrn break-ins: ibid., interview 8/20/76; cf. interview 9/15/76. Pine Street failure: ibid., interview 8/26/76. Complaint the previous year: Felt-Miller Box 251, File "Bu II," FBI memo on surreptitious entries (unsigned), 8/12/71, p. 2. Gray's statement at Quantico: Felt-Miller Box 48, File "WM In-Service B" (interviews August 1976, interview 8/26/76).

67. Felt-Miller Box 115, File "Knapp 302," 8/24/76, pp. 1–3.

68. Felt-Miller Box 115, File "Knapp 302," p. 3. Gray's visit to Detroit: Felt, *The FBI Pyramid*, 223 (mentioned in passing).

69. Felt-Miller Box 316, Trial Transcript, Francis X. O'Neill Direct Testimony, 10/17/80, pp. 4329–4330. Tim Weiner, *Enemies: A History of the FBI* (New York: Random House, 2013), 313–314, wrongly places the break-in in October, and wrongly implies that the targets were "Palestinian Americans."

70. The most detailed account of the Wadi events is in the trial testimony of Special Agent O'Neill: Felt-Miller Box 316, Trial Transcript, Francis X. O'Neill Direct Testimony, 10/17/80, pp. 4316–4337. Gray's personal approval of multiple bag jobs: pp. 4320–4321, 4322. Shorter accounts in Gray, *In Nixon's Web*, 114–115; W. Mark Felt, *A G-Man's Life: The FBI, Being Deep Throat, and the Struggle for Honor in Washington* (Washington, D.C.: Public Affairs, 2007), 259; Miller interview, 144.

71. Specific Wadi approval not needed: Felt-Miller Box 316, O'Neill Direct, 4320 (quotation), discussed on 4321, 4322. Felt and Miller's claims about similar procedure against Weatherman: Felt-Miller Box 318, Felt Redirect Testimony, 10/23/80, p. 5202.

72. Felt-Miller Box 117, File "Wallace J. LaPrade," 10/21/80: Trial Transcript, LaPrade direct testimony, 4667–4670.

73. Ibid., 4719–4720. LaPrade later applied for permission to run the black bag job on the home of the parents of fugitive Judith Cohen Flatley, and this was granted from Miller: ibid., 4692.

74. Ibid., McLennon Cross, 3853; Bishop Re-Direct, 3722; McLennon Cross, 3854.

75. Felt-Miller Box 316, Trial Transcript, Special Agent David Brower Direct Testimony, 10/17/80, pp. 4363–4365. Nields's counterattack: ibid., 4367–4368. Miller's judgment on the power of Brower's testimony: Miller interview, 165.

76. Felt-Miller Box 313, Trial Transcript, Robert Shackelford Cross-Examination, 9/30/80, p. 2336.
77. It was the White House: Miller interview, 159. The Cabinet Committee: Felt-Miller Box 315, Trial Transcript, Armin Meyer Direct Testimony, 10/10/80, pp. 3552, 3556–3557. The reinstitution of multiagency Program C: Felt-Miller Box 118, Trial Transcript, Felt Redirect, 10/23/80, pp. 5156–5158 (the August 30 memo, partially quoted), 5164–5165 (recross).
78. Felt-Miller Box 118, Trial Transcript, Felt Redirect, 10/23/80, pp. 5156–5158.
79. Felt-Miller Box 320, Trial Transcript, Nixon Direct Testimony, 10/29/80, p. 5911.
80. Ibid., Acting Director to SACs, 10/3/72; original draft: Shackelford to Miller, 9/11/72, pp. 1, 5.
81. On Shackelford's lack of memory see the cynical remarks of Judge Bryant: Felt-Miller Box 313, Bench Conference, 10/1/, 1980, p. 2283. The agenda for the October in-service: ibid., Shackelford Direct Testimony, 2288–2289.
82. Courtland Jones and "special investigative techniques": ibid., 2289, 2291.
83. Ibid., 2294.
84. Ibid., Lander Direct Testimony, 10/1/80, pp. 2365–2371. Two hours: ibid., Shackelford Direct Testimony, 2292.
85. Ibid., 2288–2289.
86. Gray personally made the decision: Felt-Miller Box 313, Shackelford Cross-Examination, 10/1/80, p. 2301. Special Investigations protested: ibid., Direct Testimony, 2244. The official reason: ibid., Cross-Examination, 2301–2302.
87. Felt-Miller, Box 111, File "Felt Specific Documents (2)," Acting Director to 7 SACs, 10/31/72, pp. 2–6. The boast of SAC, New York, on "mail-covers": see above.
88. Felt-Miller Box 317, Trial Transcript, Horace Beckwith Cross-Examination, 10/20/80, pp. 4490–4491.
89. The conference: Felt-Miller Box 98, File "Flyspray Document," Acting Director to 13 SACs, 1/11/73. Mail coverage and bag jobs: ibid., handwritten notes to conference.
90. Felt-Miller Box 117, File "Beckwith-Worthington-Barron," Trial Transcript, Katherine Worthington cross-examination, 10/20/80, p. 4555.

Chapter Seven. "One Lawbreaker Has Been Pursued by Another"

1. The quotation used for the chapter title is from the Supreme Court condemnation of police break-ins without warrant in *Irvine v. California* (1954).

2. As Special Agent James Vermeersch, a major FBI burglar in New York City, put it, "They were as highly organized as we were, perhaps more so": Felt-Miller Box 112, Trial Transcript, Vermeersch Cross-Examination, 9/24/80, p. 1326.

3. Felt-Miller Box 251, File "Bu II," Agenda for Inspectors' Conference, 12/17/73, p. 1.

4. See Bryan Burrough, *Days of Rage: America's Radical Underground, the FBI, and the Forgotten Age of Revolutionary Violence* (Penguin, 2015), 225 (interview with Dennis Cunningham).

5. David Gilbert, *Love and Struggle: My Life in SDS, the Weather Underground, and Beyond* (Oakland, Calif.: PM, 2012), 195 (emphatic); so, too, Ronald Fliegelman, personal communication, 7/10/14.

6. See Gilbert, *Love and Struggle*, 186, 190, 196, 199 (note that this is simply assumed to be natural); so, too, Jonah Raskin, personal communication, 4/10/15.

7. Interview with Special Agent William Dyson (Society of Former Special Agents of the FBI), January 2008, p. 37.

8. Gilbert, *Love and Struggle*, 199–202; cf. Dan Berger, *Outlaws of America: The Weather Underground and the Politics of Solidarity* (Oakland, Calif.: AK Press, 2006), 183–185. The manifesto was published on January 1, 1974, as Bernardine Dohrn, Jeff Jones, and Cellia Sojourn [pseud.], eds., *Prairie Fire: The Politics of Revolutionary Anti-Imperialism: Political Statement of the Weather Underground* (San Francisco: Red Dragon, 1974). According to Ron Jacobs, *The Way the Wind Blew: A History of the Weather Underground* (New York: Verso, 1997), the book went through four revisions among the collectives (158). That's a lot of relatively unfettered communication.

9. Gilbert, *Love and Struggle*, 192–196.

10. On the difficulties with agreeing on *Prairie Fire*, see Jacobs, *The Way the Wind Blew*, 158; Gilbert, *Love and Struggle*, 199–202.

11. See Jacobs, *The Way the Wind Blew*, 160, and Jeremy Varon, *Bringing the War Home: The Weather Underground, the Red Army Faction, and Revolutionary Violence in the Sixties and Seventies* (Berkeley: University of California Press, 2004), 294–295, for good overall views.

12. See the bitter comments of Naomi Jaffe in Berger, *Outlaws of America*, 195–196. The angry conflicts over the new *Prairie Fire* position is emphasized ibid., 204–205, 211.

13. Rudd's comment: Todd Gitlin, personal communication, 7/24/14.

14. See Berger, *Outlaws of America*, 193 with quotation from the Weatherman communiqué on this. This communiqué is missing from the Weatherman material in Bernardine Dohrn, Bill Ayers, and Jeff Jones, eds., *Sing a Battle Song: The Revolutionary Poetry, Statements, and Communiqués of the Weather Underground, 1970–1974* (New York: Seven Stories, 2006).

15. *Osawatomie*, no. 4, winter 1975–1976; cf. Berger, *Outlaws of America*, 214. *Osawatomie* was named after a victory won by outnumbered antislavery forces led by John Brown in Kansas in 1856. The magazine ran twenty-eight to thirty-two pages every issue.

16. Berger, *Outlaws of America*, 221 (interview with Jones). Note that the leader of the aboveground Prairie Fire Organizing Committee in New York was Annie Stein, a veteran nonviolent leftist who was also the mother of Jones's longtime partner Eleanor Raskin.

17. Jones's idea: ibid., 223. *Underground* was filmed in May 1975, released in 1976.

18. Ibid., 195–196, 205, 214.

19. See Randolph Lewis, *Emile de Antonio: Radical Filmmaker in Cold War America* (Madison: University of Wisconsin Press, 2000), 199.

20. Resistance: David Gilbert's criticism of these policies as "defeatist": *Love and Struggle*, 211–212. Many cadres at the time opposed the views of the leadership: Berger, *Outlaws of America*, 209–210. PFOC small numbers: PFOC internal newsletter, May 1976, p. 20 (Boston); p. 22 (Philadelphia).

21. Gilbert, *Love and Struggle*, 217–218.

22. A figure in early 1970: clear from Latimer File, NW 5675, DocID 59161310, p. 14: Report on Latimer FBI Interview, April 14/15, 1977, p. 3. Van Lydegraf's earlier career advocating immediate violence and opposition to the Leary operation and the counterculture: see Mark Rudd, *Underground: My Life with SDS and the Weathermen* (New York: William Morrow, 2009), 226–228.

23. For discussion of this coup from a figure favoring the van Lydegraf group, see Gilbert, *Love and Struggle*, 210–224. Rightly hostile to van Lydegraf: Burrough, *Days of Rage*, chapter 16. Important people drifted away: ibid., 372 (Silvia Baraldini interview). A harrowing account of how Jeff Jones was treated in this period: Thai Jones, *A Radical Line* (New York: Free Press, 2004), 251–257.

24. Gushing over "Van": PFOC internal newsletter, May 1976.

25. On the FBI breaking of van Lydegraf and the Revolutionary Committee, see Burrough, *Days of Rage*, 373. The FBI agents involved in penetrating the group were Richard Giannottti and William Reagan; Reagan is the agent who had singularly failed against Mona Cunningham in 1970–1971.

26. The number of illegal burglaries is unclear, but certainly greater than the thirteen that eventually resulted in federal indictments.

27. For a good summary of this period, see Burrough, *Days of Rage*, 373–379. In the end, of course, only Assistant Director Ed Miller, Associate Director Mark Felt, and Acting Director L. Patrick Gray were indicted—to the outrage of some Justice Department investigators. And the indictment against Gray was later withdrawn.

28. On the Nyack events, see David Castelluci, *The Big Dance: The Untold Story of Weatherman Kathy Boudin and the Terrorist Family That Committed the Brink's Robbery Murders* (New York: Dodd-Mead, 1986).

29. A second Brink's guard, Joe Trombino, was severely wounded but survived; he died on September 11, 2001, while making a money delivery to north tower of the World Trade Center in New York City when it was hit by a jihadist-piloted passenger plane.

30. Box 195, File "Gray Dismissal—Variance," Alan Baron Memorandum, 4/30/79, p. 1; Box 320, Trial Transcript, Judge Bryant, Instructions to the Jury, 6566–6567.

31. Right to defend the country from national security threats: Felt-Miller, Box, 320, "Closing Arguments," Frank Dunham Closing Argument for Felt, esp. 6437–6445. Weatherman as one organization aboveground and underground: see Felt-Miller Box 112, Trial Transcript, Vermeersch Direct Testimony, 9/23/80, pp. 1322–1324. Alleged foreign connections of Weatherman a constant defense refrain: interview with Edward S. Miller (Society of Former Special Agents of the FBI), 5/28/08, p. 167; Dyson interview, 37–38, 46.

32. Felt-Miller Box 320, Trial Transcript, Nields Closing Argument, 6367.

33. Ibid., 6367–6368, 6520–6521 (Nields Rebuttal Closing); quotation: 6521.

34. Catcalls at Nixon: Miller interview, 184. Nixon's assertion of presidential power: Felt-Miller, Box 320, Trial Transcript, Nixon Direct Testimony, 10/31/80, p. 5911.

35. Felt-Miller Box 315, Trial Transcript, Brownell Cross-Examination, 3819–3820. Some people may not be laughing now, in view of the use of drones against American citizens fighting for al-Qaeda overseas.

36. W. Mark Felt, *The FBI Pyramid from the Inside* (New York: Putnam's, 1979), 323; repeated in W. Mark Felt, *A G-Man's Life: The FBI, Being Deep Throat, and the Struggle for Honor in Washington* (Washington, D.C.: Public Affairs, 2007), 267.

37. Smith: Felt-Miller, Box 313, Trial Transcript, T. J. Smith Cross-Examination, 10/3/80, pp. 2668–2673. Birley: Box 314, Birley Direct Testimony, 10/10/80, pp. 3343–3344. Ironically, in September 1972 T. J. Smith had chaired a committee within Division Five that concluded that the Roosevelt permissions did not constitute sufficient grounds in themselves for surreptitious entry, because they were so out of date, though one could argue that there was statutory authority for investigation of specific crimes: Felt-Miller Box 107, File "Bu-jurid Intelligence Field," Smith to Miller, 8/1/72, p. 1, with "Position Paper: Domestic Intelligence Division: Scope of FBI Authority and Responsibility in Domestic Intelligence Investigations," 7/31/72, esp. "Conclusions," 40. Nothing came of this document.

38. Brownell: Box 315, Trial Transcript, Brownell Direct Testimony, 10/15/80, p. 3775.

39. Ibid., Felt-Miller, Box 315, Trial Transcript, McLennon Cross-Examination, 10/15/80, p. 3853.
40. Box 313, Trial Transcript, William A. Brannigan Direct Testimony, 10/13/80, p. 3222; Box 315, Assistant Special Agent in Charge Hunter Hegelson Cross-Examination, 10/15/80 pp. 3874–3875; Special Agent in Charge Elmer Lindberg Cross-Examination, 10/15/80, p. 3910; Special Agent Anthony P. Litrento Direct Examination, 10/15/80, p. 3482. Litrento was the head of the Soviet Section of the Domestic Intelligence Division; Brannigan was the head of Counter-Intelligence within the Division.
41. Ibid., Box 320, Trial Transcript, Judge Bryant Instruction to the Jury, 6581–6582.
42. *Senate Select Committee*, vol. 2, *The Huston Report*, Brennan testimony, 9/25/75, pp. 106–107.
43. John Nields suspects that Ed Miller never took the stand in his own defense in 1980 because he knew he would have to lie about the "foreign ties" issue: Nields interview with the author, 5/15/14.
44. Felt-Miller Box 196, File "CIA Summary Assessment: Foreign Influence (or lack of)": "Definition and Assessment of Existing Internal Security Threat—Foreign," 1/5/71, pp. 1, 3. The 116 pages of classified data: see Box 116, Trial Transcript: John Barron Testimony, 10/20/80, pp. 4853–4856.
45. Kleindienst later testified for the defense that he now thought otherwise; but Nields believes this was one of his strongest points at trial: interview, 5/14/14.
46. *Senate Committee on Intelligence Operations*, vol. 2, *The Huston Report*, 149, Committee Exhibit 1 (the Huston Report), p. 4.
47. Cartha DeLoach, *Hoover's FBI: The Inside Story by Hoover's Trusted Lieutenant* (Washington, D.C.: Regnery, 1995), 296; DeLoach was writing specifically about the Felt-Miller trial.
48. Felt-Miller Box 117, Trial Transcript, Felt Cross-Examination, 10/22/80, p. 5042.
49. Bryant's argument incomprehensible: Felt, *A G-Man's Life*, 276. The Cohens: Judge Bryant listed the Cohen break-ins and the dates of their occurrence in his instructions to the jury; it was part of the list of particulars against Felt and Miller: Felt-Miller Box 320, Trial Transcript, Judge Bryant Instructions to the jury, 10/28/80, pp. 6570–6573. Benjamin Cohen said that if the FBI had only *asked* to search, he would have gladly allowed it, because he was patriotic: ibid., Cohen Direct Testimony, 10/2/80, p. 2397.
50. Felt, *The FBI Pyramid*, 11. Felt misquotes from Jackson's dissent in *Terminiello v. City of Chicago* (1949). Jackson as attorney general supported the Hobbs Bill (1941), which would have legalized FBI wiretapping; it failed to pass Congress.

51. Felt-Miller Box 117, Trial Transcript, Felt Direct Testimony, 10/22/80, p. 4867.

52. Felt-Miller Box 320, Trial Transcript, Judge Bryant Jury Instructions, 10/28/80, pp. 6580–6581; cf. Thomas Kennelly, *One More Story and I'm Out the Door* (New York: Universe, 2009), 341.

53. Felt-Miller Box 320, Trial Transcript, Judge Bryant Instructions to the Jury, 6581.

54. Ibid.

55. Kennelly, *One More Story*, 340–341; Burrough, *Days of Rage*, 376 (Stephen Horn interview).

56. Felt-Miller Box 320, File "Sentencing, 12/15/80), esp. p. 10. Bryant's leniency: Kennelly, *One More Story*, 341. No explanation: Box 320, File "Sentencing," p. 10.

57. Reagan had promised himself: Miller interview, 174. As soon as he was president: the White House contacted Miller's lawyer Thomas Kennelly on January 30, 1981, with this information: ibid. Delay caused by the attempted assassination—a delay for which Reagan apologized: Kennelly, *One More Story*, 342; Miller interview, 175.

58. Text of the pardon: *New York Times*, 4/15/81.

59. Allen Ginsberg, Introduction to "Smoking Typewriters" (1981), collected in *Deliberate Prose: Selected Essays, 1952–1995* (New York: HarperCollins, 2000), 17. This "Smoking Typewriters," not to be confused with John McMillian's recent history of the sixties underground press, was the lead essay in a City Lights Bookstore compendium *Unamerican Activities: The Campaign against the Underground Press*, edited by Geoffrey Rips and Anne Janowitz.

60. Miller interview, 176.

61. Felt-Miller Box 276, File "Microphone Exhibits," Smith to Miller 9/27/73 (many but not all redactions have been restored on this document); "Dropping Bomb Conspiracy Case Saves U.S. Public Answers," *Washington Post*, 11/11/73.

62. The latter explanation is what makes the most sense to indictee Russell Neufeld: interview with the author, 11/16/13.

63. Felt-Miller Box 112, File "Substitute Documents for in camera 7/16/79," Director, FBI to Attorney General, 8/18/73, p. 1: "Note."

64. Dorothy Shipps, Karen Sconzert, and Holly Swyers, *The Annenberg Challenge: The First Three Years* (Chicago: Consortium of Chicago School Research, 1999).

65. Personal communication with Eric Arnesen.

66. See Bill Ayers, *Public Enemy: Confessions of an American Dissident* (Boston: Beacon, 2014).

67. See Keith Reader, *Regis Debray: A Critical Introduction* (London: Pluto, 1995).

68. See Berger, *Outlaws of America*, 243.

69. Gilbert, *Love and Struggle*, 254 (going underground again), 265–271 (Boudin). Their theme song was "Reunited," by Peaches and Herb (266).
70. Tom Robbins, "Judith Clark's Radical Transformation," *New York Times Magazine*, 1/12/12.
71. L. Patrick Gray, *In Nixon's Web: A Year in the Crosshairs of Watergate* (New York: Times Books, 2008), especially 119–122, 270–271.
72. Interview with Jack Kearney (Society of Former Special Agents of the FBI), 1/25/06, pp. 3–6.
73. Miller interview, 128–130.
74. See Max Holland, *Leak: Why Mark Felt Became Deep Throat* (Lawrence: University of Kansas Press, 2012), chapter 1, esp. p. 8.
75. Felt, *A G-Man's Life*, chapters 22–23.

Conclusion

1. On this grim "alternative history" scenario, see Jeremy Varon, *Bringing the War Home* (Berkeley: University of California Press, 2004), 174–175.
2. "By God, What We Need Is a Little Responsible Terrorism," *Berkeley Tribe*, 3/27–4/3/70; cf. Luca Falciola, "Pathways of an 'Early' De-Escalation: The Case of the Weather Underground Organization," ECPR General Conference, Sciences Po Bordeaux, September 2013, http://ecpr.eu/filestore/paperproposal/8bc2655b-28b2-4d8e-b6c9-5555bac1400f.pdf, 8.
3. Cf. Dan Berger, *Outlaws of America: The Weather Underground and the Politics of Solidarity* (Oakland, Calif.: AK Press, 2006), 130.
4. Falciola, "Pathways of an 'Early' De-Escalation," 8.
5. On the hippie influence on Jones and Dohrn, see Thai Jones, *A Radical Line* (New York: Free Press, 2004), 217–219. The organization's name: "You don't need a weatherman to know which way the wind blows," from Dylan's 1965 song "Subterranean Homesick Blues."
6. The centrality of black issues to Weatherman: Ron Fliegelman, interview with the author, 6/2/15.
7. See Howard Machtinger, "You Say You Want a Revolution?" *In These Times*, 2/18/09. In that sense, the title of Bill Ayers's book on Weather, *Fugitive Days: Memoirs of an Antiwar Activist* (Boston: Beacon, 2001), is misleading.
8. See Jonah Raskin, *Outside the Whale: Growing Up in the American Left* (New York: Links, 1974), 148; Jonah Raskin, "Looking Backward: Personal Reflections on Language, Gesture, and Mythology in the Weather Underground," *Socialism and Democracy* 20 (2006), 124, 126; cf. Machtinger, "You Say You Want a Revolution?" Also: Falciola, "Pathways of an 'Early' De-Escalation."
9. On the definition—a reasonable one—see Machtinger, "You Say You Want a Revolution?"; similar is the definition of terrorism offered by

Marge Piercy—who denies that Weatherman ever engaged in such behavior: *Vida*, Introduction to the New Edition (New York: PM Press, 2006), v–vi.

10. For instance, Bill Ayers, interview with *Daily Beast*, 4/3/13 (with great emphasis: "What we did was a lot of *vandalism*"); or Ayers on *Megyn Kelly Show*, Fox News, 6/30/14, 7/1/14.

11. Felt-Miller Box 276, File "Pressure from the Field," Alexandria Field Office to Acting Director, 5/26/72, p. 4 (part of a report on the Pentagon bombing).

12. David Gilbert, *Love and Struggle: My Life in SDS, the Weather Underground, and Beyond* (Oakland, Calif.: PM, 2012), 184.

13. Russell Neufeld interview with the author, 8/5/14; on the differences in tactics within Weatherman in early 1970, see also Ayers, *Fugitive Days*, 205–206.

14. Alison Colbert, "A Talk with Allen Ginsburg," *Partisan Review* 38 (1971), 304; cf. Richard Boyd, "Representing Political Violence: The Mainstream Media and the Weatherman 'Days of Rage,' " *American Studies* 41 (2000), 141; Varon, *Bringing the War Home*, 195 (quoting Tom Hayden).

15. Statistics gathered in J. Kirkpatrick Sale, *SDS* (New York: Random House, 1974), 441 and n. 30.

16. Mary Ann Keatley: Pomona College Timeline, 1969, www.pomona.edu/timeline 1960s/1969.aspx. Timothy Peebles: *Sacramento Bee*, 3/6/69. Dover Sharp: *UCSB and Isla Vista Walking Tour* (Department of Recreation, UCSB), 6, no. E.

17. "Blasts Rips Bank in Financial Area," *New York Times*, 8/21/69.

18. An important exception is Bryan Burrough, *Days of Rage: The American Underground, the FBI, and the Forgotten Age of Revolutionary Violence* (New York: Penguin, 2015), chapter 1.

19. On South Carolina State University, see Jack Bass and Jack Nelson, *The Orangeburg Massacre* (Macon, Ga.: Mercer University Press, 2003); on Jackson State, see William B. Scranton, Chairman, *The Report of the President's Commission on Campus Unrest*, (Washington, D.C.: Government Printing Office, 1970), 442–444.

20. On the ghetto dead and wounded, see the excruciating discussion in Rick Perlstein, *Nixonland* (New York: Scribner, 2009), 185–199. On anti-Castro bombings in New York City: ibid., 339–340. Anti-Castro Cubans also launched bomb attacks in Chicago, Los Angeles, and Miami.

21. The criticism of Max Elbaum, *Revolution in the Air: Sixties Radicals Turn to Lenin, Mao, and Che* (London: Verso, 2006), 35–37; see Martha Biondi, *The Black Revolution on Campus* (Berkeley: University of California Press, 2014).

22. Nixon himself admits this: *RN: The Memoirs of Richard Nixon* (New York: Grosset and Dunlap, 1978), 402.

23. Leslie Woodcock Tentler, a former Students for a Democratic Society leader, personal communication, 6/29/13.

24. These are FBI estimates of Weatherman numbers as of early January 1972: Felt-Miller Box 48, file "WM In-Service," Memo on "Black Bag Technique," 1/14/72, pp. 2, 3.

25. Sale, *SDS*, 419; Todd Gitlin, *The Sixties: Years of Hope, Days of Rage*, (1987; New York: Bantam, 1993), 411. Paul Berman, *A Tale of Two Utopias: The Political Journey of the 1968 Generation* (New York: Norton, 1996), 73–74; David Barber, *A Hard Rain Fell: SDS and Why It Failed* (Jackson: University Press of Mississippi, 2008), 224. See now the regret expressed now by the Weatherman leader Mark Rudd about his role in the destruction of SDS: *Underground: My Life with SDS and the Weathermen* (New York: William Morrow, 2009), 205, 224; Mark Rudd, "The Death of SDS," at http://www.markrudd.com/?sds-and-weather/the-death-of-sds.html.

26. *Newsweek*, 4/30/73. There were numerous prosecutions on the local level as well.

27. On the federal legal assault: see James Rosen, *The Strong Man: John Mitchell and the Secrets of Watergate* (New York: Doubleday, 2008), 82–84. Natural weaknesses of student movements, and susceptibility to radicalization over time: Lewis Feuer, *The Conflict of Generations: The Character and Significance of Student Movements* (New York: Basic, 1969). A vivid example of the sense of failure and guilt among movement people by the early 1970s: Hunter S. Thompson, *Fear and Loathing in Las Vegas* (New York: Simon and Schuster, 1972).

28. For instance: Bill Ayers, Kathy Boudin, John Jacobs, Terry Robbins, and Cathy Wilkerson. Noted by Gitlin, *The Sixties*, 387.

29. Gitlin, *The Sixties*, stresses a break, but recognizes continuity too. See also, e.g., Jeffrey Herf, "Striking a Balance: Remembering 1968 and After," *Partisan Review* (1999), esp. 284–287, quotation on 286. The other major factions in SDS in spring 1969 were much more traditional in their Marxist analyses.

30. Richard Reeves, *President Nixon: Alone in the White House* (New York: Simon and Schuster, 2001), 72; cf. Perlstein, *Nixonland*, 403.

31. First quotation: Felt-Miller Box 48, File "WM In-Service": "Need for Sophisticated Investigative Techniques against Weatherman Activists," 1. Second quotation: Felt-Miller Box 276, "Microphone Exhibits," Miller to Rosen, 12/6/71, p. 1 (a secret memo marked not for ordinary filing). Third quotation: Felt-Miller Box 276, "Microphone Exhibits," Miller to Rosen, 11/19/71, p. 1 (also a secret memo not for ordinary filing). The Venceremos Organization, radicals in the Bay Area, is not to be confused with the Venceremos Brigades, which organized far-left visitors to Cuba to work on the sugarcane crop.

32. Felt-Miller Box 48, File "WM In-Service": "Need for Sophisticated Investigative Techniques against Weatherman Activists," 1 (undated, but early January 1972); see also, but more briefly, Miller to Rosen, 11/19/71 (a), p. 2 (including failure of traditional techniques of investigation).

33. See Ron Jacobs, *The Way the Wind Blew: A History of the Weather Underground* (New York: Verso, 1997), 129–130 (based on Weatherman interviews in Emile De Antonio's 1976 film *Underground*).

34. Ronald Fliegelman, personal communication, 7/10/14; Jonah Raskin, personal communication, 7/15/14 (he witnessed the escapees' breathless return to their Brooklyn collective).

35. Background to the Machtinger arrest: personal communication with Jonah Raskin, 6/20/14. The agents involved may also have feared what would happen to their careers if they followed Machtinger and then lost him. That is, institutional pressures may have led to faulty police work.

36. Jonah Raskin, personal communication, 6/20/14. The FBI reports show that they did not know that they almost captured the entire leadership.

37. Machtinger's arrest and release, September 19–20, 1973: Felt-Miller Box 251, File "A. [*sic:* should be "H"] M.," Summary report of Special Agent Parrick J. McLaughlin, 2/28/74. Machtinger's letter, explaining his jumping bail: Howard Machtinger to friends, 10/16/73. He had the Harper's Ferry Raid in 1858, instead of 1859.

38. Jonah Raskin, interview with the author, 4/20/15.

39. See the comment of Gilbert, *Love and Struggle*, 177. FBI Special Agent William E. Dyson, who was involved in the Weatherman hunt, ruefully acknowledges that the FBI never solved a single Weatherman bombing—because the Bureau simply didn't know yet how to investigate clandestine revolutionary groups: interview with Special Agent William Dyson (Society of Former Special Agents of the FBI), January 2008, p. 36.

40. Felt-Miller Box 276, File "Microphone Exhibits," Miller to Rosen, 11/12/71; quotation: Miller to Rosen, 11/19/71 (a), p. 2.

41. Felt-Miller Box 276, File "Microphone Exhibits," Miller to Rosen, 11/19/71 (a), pp. 2–3; ibid., 12/6/71, pp. 2–3 (including the specific list of targets; quotation: p. 3); Felt-Miller Box 276, File "Argument for Use of Anonymous Sources," 1/14/72, pp. 3–5.

42. Felt-Miller Box 276, File "Microphone Exhibits," Miller to Rosen, 12/6/71, p. 2. See also ibid., Miller to Rosen, 11/19/71 (a), p. 2; Miller to Rosen, 11/19/17 (b), p. 2.

43. Indian pudding: see Felt-Miller Box 251, File "Dohrn II (ESM). Panties: personal communication from Jonah Raskin, 6/20/14 (Jennifer Dohrn told him personally that this had happened). The story was widely related in Weatherman circles: Ronald Fliegelman and Russell Neufeld, interviews with the author, 11/16/13.

44. See, e.g., the astonishing collection of material in Felt-Miller Box 106.

45. On Hoover's policy, see Cril Payne, *Deep Cover: An FBI Agent Infiltrates the Radical Underground* (New York: Newsweek Books, 1979), chapter 1.

Acknowledgments

THIS BOOK IS DEDICATED to Jeffrey Herf. It's not simply that he is a wonderful professional historian and colleague, and an original thinker who has been a staunch friend for many years. But Jeffrey, who had attended the SDS convention in Chicago in June 1969 that resulted in the official emergence of Weatherman, and who had participated in the peaceful counter–Days of Rage demonstration in Chicago that October organized by Mike Klonsky's Revolutionary Youth Movement II, also urged me to transform a lecture at the Woodrow Wilson Center into a serious book-length study. He urged me to go see what information was available at the National Archives II facility, which is part of the University of Maryland campus. He was with me when we opened the first boxes of what turned out to be thousands of newly released FBI documents, brought forth by the helpful archivists. That was the start. But Jeffrey won't like some of my conclusions.

Many other people have helped in this project. Susan Reverby, who is writing her own study of "the Weatherman doctor" Alan Berkman, has been a constant intellectual companion throughout this project, as we explored the events of our youth, our feelings about them, and discussed intently how to portray people for whom we have both empathy and sympathy, while also remaining as objective as possible about what the facts show. Judy Hallett has been another source of strength; and because she knows everybody in the world, she introduced me to her high school friend Ron Fliegelman, who became a major Weatherman figure. I owe the Weather veterans who agreed to be interviewed, as well as people closely associated with Weather who agreed to be interviewed, a great debt for their time and their self-criticism: Ron Fliegelman, Toni Hart (Wellman), Ron Jacobs, Thai Jones, Martin Kenner, Jonathan Lerner, Steve Mariotti, Mark Naison, Russell Neufeld, Jonah Raskin, and others who wish to remain anonymous. My interviews with them transformed my understanding both of the times and the people. My long conversations with Larry Gray—a cofounder of SDS at Tulane in 1967, later at SDS in Washington, D.C., and then on the outskirts of Weatherman—gave me an appreciation of SDS's changing mood in 1967–1969. Kevin Coogan, a veteran of the New York City Left, with an unmatched knowledge of New York in that period, provided much useful information and perspective. Aaron Leonard, doing his own research on the FBI and American Maoists, came up independently with a crucial FBI document. I also want to thank former prosecutor John Nields for taking time from his busy legal practice to answer numerous questions about a trial in 1980 that is still of great meaning to him. Colonel John Hoffman provided me the story of how in June 1970 he was told by the FBI that he was going to be assassinated by Weatherman because he had arrested Jane Fonda.

And then there are the friends who offered support and counsel: Todd Gitlin, who gave me the benefit of his enormous experience and deep insights Erich Gruen, who predicted that the Weather people would be intensely charismatic, because that was partly how they did what they managed to do; Maurice Isserman, who provided much needed encouragement; Paul Landau, with whom I discussed parallels and nonparallels with the African National Congress; Sonya Michel, who stressed gender and race issues; Mike Ross, who gave a broader American historical perspective; Selma Rutenburg, who stressed psychological and cultural issues; and Phil Soergel, who first pointed out to me—a Bay Area person—that the heart of Weatherman was in the Midwest, in Detroit and Ann Arbor, and not just in New York. My wife, Jeannie Rutenburg, would have loved researching this book and interviewing the people.

I also owe a great debt to James Mathis, a chief archivist at the National Archives, and to his assistant Britney Crawford. They organized the dozens of boxes of FBI material for me, provided an outline of what files were in each box, and even underlined which boxes would hold the most interesting files. Moreover, James gave me his deep historical insights into the FBI in the last years of J. Edgar Hoover; and Britney provided expertise at my talk at the Woodrow Wilson Center.

Finally, Steve Wasserman at Yale University Press has been an editor of enormous skill and insight, transforming a very bulky (and, frankly, stodgy) manuscript into a book that is readable yet scholarly, and whose themes are (we hope) easily grasped. And Dan Heaton was a first-class copyeditor (especially in disentangling the complex endnotes).